MODERN JEWISH HISTORY

A Source Reader

Edited by Robert Chazan and Marc Lee Raphael

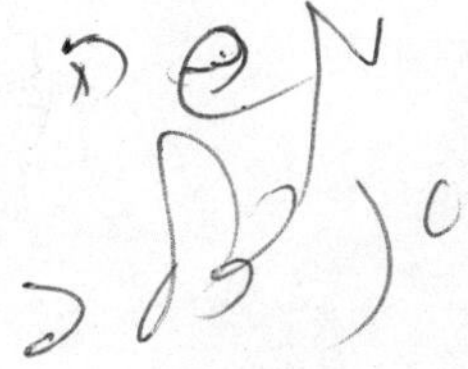

SCHOCKEN BOOKS · NEW YORK

Manufactured in the United States of America

Library of Congress Cataloging in Publication Data

Chazan, Robert, comp.
Modern Jewish history.

Includes bibliography and index.
1. Jews—History—1789—1945—Sources.
I. Raphael, Marc Lee, joint comp. II. Title.
DS125.C4 1975 909'.04'924008 74-9131

To our parents

M.L.R.

R.C.

CONTENTS

F. The Holocaust

G. Postwar Turmoil

INTRODUCTION

Modern Jewish life has been characterized by major dislocation, upheaval, and change. The Jewish world has been the scene of demographic growth and displacement, rapid economic and social shifts, hopeful innovations, and appalling catastrophes.

During the past few centuries, old centers of Jewish life have declined or disappeared. Western European Jewry, once the world's most powerful Jewish community, now struggles painfully toward rebuilding and revitalization; the ancient Jewish settlements of the Middle East are virtually nonexistent. In their stead, new Jewries have come to the fore, particularly those of the United States and the State of Israel. The distribution of world Jewish population has undergone radical transformation.

Jewish political status has been irrevocably altered. Beginning in Western Europe, liberal voices—Jewish and non-Jewish alike—called for an end to the separate and inferior Jewish status bequeathed by the Middle Ages. It was argued that Jews had irrefutable rights to equality and, moreover, that such equality would eliminate the ills of Jewish existence. It was claimed that commonly assumed Jewish shortcomings were the results of burdensome restrictions and would disappear only when Jews were accorded equal treatment and could share the hopes and aspirations of their neighbors. Since post-Revolutionary France first made the experiment, nation after nation has emancipated its Jews, offering them a new place in society and new possibilities for achievement.

In the wake of these demographic and political alterations, other aspects of Jewish life have changed as well. New economic opportunities have developed. Emancipated Jews have enjoyed newfound options for earning their livelihoods; indeed many Jews and non-Jews have contended that emancipation entailed responsibility for restructuring Jewish economic life toward greater diversification and usefulness. Social relations between Jews and their neighbors have become far more open. Jewish segregation and separateness have dissipated; Jews have associated more freely with non-

Jews, enjoying directly many of the delights of nineteenth- and twentieth-century civilization.

Yet obviously all has not been simply sweetness and light. Age-old prejudices against Jews have survived with a remarkable tenacity. Even into the twentieth century the medieval accusation that Jews utilize Christian blood for their religious ritual was still being heard, endless refutations by medieval and modern Jewish and Christian authorities notwithstanding. Unhappily, the nineteenth and twentieth centuries added their own variations to the recurrent themes of anti-Semitism. Jewishness was now defined anthropologically as a set of ineffaceable racial characteristics; supposed Jewish malevolence was transformed into a worldwide international network committed to subverting the foundations of Western society; hatred of the Jews became the underpinning of organized political movements. Out of all this emerged Adolf Hitler and the Nazis, rising to power on a tide of fear and fanaticism and perpetrating the most destructive single calamity in the entire history of the Jewish people.

The painful realities of recent Jewish suffering have spawned new gropings and innovative programs designed to break the repetitive cycle of persecution. For some, the answer was to be found in migration, particularly in the flight from Eastern Europe and its traditional animosities toward fabled America and its reputed equality for all men. For others, the solution remained emancipation and integration; suffering was to be seen not as the failure of emancipation but as the failure to achieve full emancipation. When emancipation would be fully realized, then persecution would be a thing of the past. New spokesmen pushed forward as well. Some contended that anti-Semitism was merely symptomatic of deep-seated disease in general society. Jews must throw themselves into the struggle to create a new and better socialist state; with victory, the Jewish problem would wither away and disappear. Others argued that anti-Semitism was inevitable in every society, Russian and American, capitalist and socialist, so long as the Jews remained a minority people with no homeland of their own. Only with normalization of Jewish existence through creation of a state could the specter of anti-Semitic outbursts finally be laid to rest. Each of these views has been held with great intensity; partisans of each have criticized vigorously the errors and shortcomings of the others; each has made a profound contribution to the dynamism of modern Jewish life.

Never in the millennia of Jewish history has so much been transformed in such a short period of time, and never have so many Jewish men and women found themselves so badly battered by the winds of change.

There is a wealth of useful material available, both primary sources and secondary readings, for courses in modern Jewish history. The editors of this volume, working independently, have come to the shared conclusion that primary documents consistently prove the most enlightening, the most stimulating, and the most enjoyable vehicles for conveying the drama and intensity of the modern Jewish experience. While much has been written concerning the Dreyfus Affair, nothing can capture the pathos and bewilderment of the once-self-confident Jewish officer as well as his own diary or the rage and venom of his supporters as well as Emile Zola's "J'Accuse." Despite all the literature on Jewish migration, the immediacy of the immigrant experience can still best be gleaned from Mary Antin's lively depiction of one wanderer or from the amusing but poignant Yiddish letters beseeching advice from the all-knowing newspaper editor.

Having sampled student reaction to a wide variety of readings over a number of years, we are both firmly convinced of the utility of primary materials and have both prepared extensive syllabi based on such sources. The results have been pedagogically successful but cumbersome in practice, as students are directed to thirty-five or forty volumes, many out of print, in order to do their work. From our own dissatisfaction and the encouragement of numerous colleagues has emerged the desire to edit a compact, one-volume source book which could be used as the text in a modern Jewish history course based on primary documents.

Our selections have been organized to emphasize the dimensions of disruption and change in modern Jewish history. Thus the focus at the outset is on Western European Jewry, its emancipation, its internal crises, and the development of a postemancipation anti-Semitism by the close of the nineteenth century. During the last decades of that century, the larger Jewish communities of Eastern Europe, under renewed attack, slowly rose from their torpor and began to seek solutions to their dilemma. Coverage of the twentieth century is divided into the period of 1914–1939, the World War II years and the Holocaust, and the dramatic decades from 1945 to the present. Obviously, while organizing their courses and readings, others may wish to avail themselves of the materials that we have collected in a somewhat different fashion.

We have appended at the end of the volume lists of further primary sources and of useful secondary references. We have also added a compilation of fictional works and of movies that relate to modern Jewish history. It has been our experience that such aids can often enhance substantially student understanding of modern Jewish life.

Ultimately it is, of course, our goal to fail. That is to say, we strongly hope that Alfred Dreyfus, Leo Pinsker, Isaac Babel, and Chaim Weizmann prove so engaging that our collection will serve only as a stepping stone toward fuller immersion into the riches and turbulence of recent Jewish experience.

MODERN JEWISH HISTORY

A. The Onset of Change

1. NEW VIEWS IN WESTERN EUROPE

Published attacks against the Jews of France were quite common in the eighteenth century, and few were more vehement than that of François J. A. Hell, the leader of Alsatian anti-Semitism. Urged by some French and German Jewish leaders to respond, Christian Wilhelm Dohm (1751–1820), an enlightened historian, economist, and Prussian government official, published a controversial defense of the Jews in 1781. It was titled *Über die bürgerliche Verbesserung der Juden (Concerning the Amelioration of the Civil Status of the Jews)*.

Dohm began his argument with a historical survey of Jewish suffering and an economic defense that would have appealed to enlightened French officials. He noted France's "endeavors to increase the population," and suggested this be done by reversing the current policy whereby the Jew "is everywhere entirely excluded" and by integrating him into the national state. "In our firmly established states," he argued, "any citizen must be welcome who observes the laws and adds through his industry to the wealth of the state."

To those who would respond that the Jews were "more morally corrupt than the other nations," Dohm demonstrated that the history of the repression of the Jews, not their intrinsic character, had caused their peculiar functions in the modern state. "If the oppression in which he has lived for centuries has corrupted his morals," Dohm frankly wrote in typical eighteenth-century enlightened fashion, "better treatment will improve them again." With an end to economic restrictions, cultural exclusion, and civil injustices, the Jews would "become better, more useful members of society." With an improvement in their status, therefore, their character would be enhanced.

Dohm is a spokesman for a certain kind of human justice, modeled upon enlightenment concepts of reason and natural law, to be applied to all people, including Jews; for "the Jew is even more man than a Jew." His conceptual structure is strikingly like that found in the Austrian Emperor Joseph II's Edict of Toleration issued for the Jews in the same year as Dohm's essay; this same thinking pervaded the writings of key French liberals pressing for Jewish emancipation during the tumultuous 1780s and 1790s.

Christian Wilhelm Dohm's *Concerning the Amelioration of the Civil Status of the Jews* was translated by Helen Lederer, edited by Ellis Rivkin, and published by the Hebrew Union College Press in 1957. The following condensation is reprinted by permission of the Hebrew Union College.

Christian Wilhelm Dohm, *Concerning the Amelioration of the Civil Status of the Jews*

When one considers the eager endeavors to increase the population, it is strange that in a majority of states one still makes an exception to this principle for a certain class of men. In almost all parts of Europe the laws and the entire constitution of the state aim to prevent as much as possible the increase in numbers of these unfortunate Asiatic refugees, the Jews. In some states they are not allowed to stay at all, and one permits them to enjoy the protection of the ruler for a certain price only for a short time (often only for one night). In most of the other states the Jews were received under most cumbersome conditions, not as citizens, but as inhabitants and subjects only. In most cases settlement is permitted only to a limited number of Jewish families, and this concession is usually limited to certain places and has always to be purchased with a large sum of money. In many countries the possession of a fortune already acquired before settlement is a prerequisite for the permission to settle there. If a Jewish father has several sons, he is usually allowed to bequeath the permission for settlement in the land of his birth to only one of them, and has to send forth the others with a portion of his fortune to other parts where they have to fight similar obstacles. Regarding his daughters, the great question is whether he is lucky enough to link them by marriage to one of the local families. Seldom, therefore, will a Jewish father enjoy the happiness of living among his children and grandchildren, nor establish the worldly welfare of his family on stable and durable ground. . . . If a Jew has received permission to stay in a state, he has to pay a heavy tax every year to renew the permit, and he is not allowed to marry except with a license which he can obtain only under certain conditions, and for which he has once again to pay. Every child adds to his tax load and almost every one of his actions is taxed again. In every enterprise of life the laws of the country are aimed at him with threatening severity, and the more lenient treatment accorded to the rest of the population makes this seem even harder.

And with all these various expenses the Jew is severely restricted in earning a living. From the honor to serve the state in peace as well as in war he is everywhere entirely excluded. The most important of all occupations, agriculture, is everywhere forbidden to him, and almost nowhere is he allowed to own land in his own name. Every trade guild would consider itself dishonored if it accepted a circumcized man as a member, so the Hebrew is in almost all countries excluded from artisan and mechanical arts. . . . No other way but commerce is open to acquire means for improving his lot for earning a living. But even that way is made difficult by many limitations and taxes; and only a small number of that nation have enough capital to undertake trade in a larger volume. So they are mostly forced into retail trade, where only the frequent repetition of small profits can enable them to earn a modest living; or they are forced to loan out to others the money which they themselves are not permitted to utilize. In how many ways is that single area, commerce, restricted in almost all countries! Many kinds of trade are forbidden them. With respect to other kinds of trade, they are under restrictions regarding time, place, and person; and the little that is left is taxed so heavily, and those regulations require so much official investigation and are dependent on so many petty officials, that the profit of the Jew is exceedingly small and only attractive to persons used to the extremes of poverty and who have no choice save this or starvation. . . .

What might be the reasons that induced the governments of almost all European states almost unanimously to deal so harshly with the Jewish nation? What has induced them (even the wisest) to make this one exception from the laws of an otherwise enlightened policy according to which all citizens should be incited by uniform justice, support of trade, and the greatest possible freedom of action so as to contribute to the general welfare? Should a number of industrious and law-abiding citizens be less useful to the state because they stem from Asia and differ from others by beard, circumcision, and a special way—transmitted to them from their ancient forefathers—of worshiping the Supreme Being? This latter would certainly disqualify them from full rights of citizenship, and justify all restrictive measures, if it contained principles which would keep the Jews from fulfilling their duties to the state, and from keeping faith in their actions within the community and with single members of the community; and if hatred against those who do not belong to their faith would make them feel an obligation to deal crookedly with and disregard the rights of others.

It would have to be clearly proved that the religion of the Jews contains such antisocial principles, that their divine laws are contrary to the laws of justice and charity, if one were to justify before the eyes of reason that the rights of citizenship should be withheld entirely only from the Jew, and that he should be permitted only partially to enjoy the rights of man. According to what has become known about the Jewish religion so far, it does not contain such harmful principles. . . .

The great and noble business of the government is to mitigate the mutually exclusive principles of all these varied [social and economic] groups so that they will not harm the greater union which comprises all of them, so that the separateness will incite only greater activity and competition, not antipathy and withdrawal, so that all the single notes are dissolved in the great harmony of the state. The government should allow each of the special groups its pride, and even its harmful prejudices, but should endeavor to instill in each member a greater love of the state. This great goal is achieved if the nobleman, the peasant, the scholar, the artisan, the Christian, and the Jew consider their separateness as secondary, and their role as citizen, primary. Thus the citizens of the great states of antiquity were not divided because of divergent beliefs in various gods. They were patriots first. And so today, on the other side of the ocean, Catholics, Episcopalians, and Puritans are fighting together for the new state which is to unite all of them, and for freedom and justice to be enjoyed by all of them. And so we, too, in some European countries already see the citizens united in harmony for the pursuit of happiness in this life, even though they seek the happiness of a future life on different paths. So even if actually in the faith of today's Jews there should be some principles which would restrict them too strongly to their special group and exclude them from the other groups of the great civil society, this would still not justify their persecution—which can only serve to confirm them in their opinions—so long as their laws are not contrary to the general principles of morality and do not permit antisocial vices. The only business of the government in this case would be (1) to have an exact knowledge of those principles, or indeed only the conclusions drawn from religious principles, and the actual influence of these on their actions, and (2) to endeavor to weaken the influence of these principles, by general enlightenment of the nation, by advancing its morals independently of religion, and, in general, by furthering the refinement of its sentiments.

More than anything else a life of normal civil happiness in a well-ordered state, enjoying the long-withheld freedom, would tend to do away with clannish religious opinions. The Jew is even more man than Jew, and how would it be possible for him not to love a state where he could freely acquire property and freely enjoy it, where his taxes would be not heavier than those of the other citizens, where he could reach positions of honor and enjoy general esteem? Why should he hate people who are no longer distinguished from him by offensive prerogatives, who share with him equal rights and duties? The novelty of this happiness, and unfortunately, the probability that this will not in the near future happen in all states, would make it even more precious to the Jew, and gratitude alone would make him the most patriotic citizen. He would look at his country with the eyes of a long misjudged, and finally after long banishment, reinstated son. These human emotions would talk louder in his heart than the sophistic sayings of his rabbis. . . .

One might oppose to all these reasons the general experience of our states of the political harmfulness of the Jews, intending to justify the harsh way our governments are dealing with them by the assertion that the character and spirit of this nation is so unfortunately formed that on this ground they cannot be accepted with quite equal rights in any civil society. Indeed, quite often in life one hears this assertion that the character of the Jews is so corrupt that only the most restricting and severest regimentation can render them harmless. To these unfortunates, it is said, has been transmitted from their ancestors, if not through their most ancient Law, then through their oral tradition and the later sophistic conclusions of the rabbis, such a bitter hatred of all who do not belong to their tribe that they are unable to get used to looking at them as members of a common civil society with equal rights. The fanatic hatred with which the ancestors of the Jews persecuted the founder of Christianity has been transmitted to their late posterity and they hate all followers of this faith. Outbreaks of this hatred have often shown themselves clearly unless held in check by force. Especially have the Jews always been reproached by all nations with lack of fairness and honesty in the one field in which they were allowed to make a living—commerce. Every little dishonest practice in commerce is said to be invented by Jews; the coin of any state is suspect if Jews took part in the minting, or if it went frequently through Jewish hands. One hears also in all places where they were allowed to multiply in numbers the accusation that they monopolize almost entirely the branches of trade permitted to them and that Christians are unable to compete with them in these. For this reason, it is further said, the governments of nearly all states have adopted the policy, in a unanimity from which alone it can be concluded that it is justified, to issue restrictive laws against this nation and to deviate, in its case alone, from the principle of furthering a continuous rise in population. They could not concede to these people who are harmful to the welfare of the rest of the citizens the same rights, and had to adopt the stipulation of a certain amount of property for those permitted to settle down, as guarantee for compliance with the laws and abstinence from criminal activities.

If I am not entirely mistaken there is one error in this reasoning, namely, that one states as cause what in reality is the effect, quoting the evil wrought by the past erroneous policy as an excuse for it. I may concede that the Jews may be more morally corrupt than other nations; that they are guilty of a proportionately greater number of crimes than the Christians; that their character in general inclines more toward usury and fraud in commerce; that their religious prejudice is more antisocial and clannish; but I must add that this supposed greater moral corruption of the Jews is a necessary and natural consequence of the oppressed condition in which they have been living for so many centuries. A calm and impartial consideration will prove the correctness of this assertion.

The hard and oppressive conditions under which the Jews live almost everywhere would explain, although not justify, an even worse corruption than they actually can be accused of. It is very natural that these conditions cause the spirit of the Jew to lose the habit of noble feelings, to be submerged in the base routine of earning a precarious livelihood. The varied kinds of oppression and contempt he experiences are bound to debase him in his activities, to choke every sense of honor in his heart. As there are almost no honest means of earning a living left to him, it is natural that he falls into criminal practices and fraud, especially since commerce more than other trades seduces people to such practices. Has one a right to be surprised if a Jew feels himself bound by laws which scarcely permit him to breathe, yet he cannot break them without being punished? How can we demand willing obedience and affection for the state from him, who sees that he is tolerated only to the extent that he is a means of revenue? Can one be surprised at his hatred for a nation which gives him so many and so stinging proofs of its hatred for him? How can one expect virtue from him if one does not trust him? How can one reproach him with crimes he is forced to commit because no honest means of earning a livelihood are open to him; for he is oppressed by taxes and nothing is left him to care for the education and moral training of his children?

Everything the Jews are blamed for is caused by the political conditions under which they now live, and any other group of men, under such conditions, would be guilty of identical errors. For those common traits of thought, opinions, and passions which are found in the majority of people belonging to one nation and which are called its individual character are not unchangeable and distinctive qualities stamping them as a unique modification of human nature. As it has been clearly recognized in our time, these are influenced by the climate, the food, and most of all the political conditions under which a nation lives. If, therefore, the Jew in Asia is different from the Jew in Germany, this will have to be regarded as a consequence of the different physical environment. If, however, in Cracow as well as in Cadiz he is accused of dishonesty in commerce, this must be a consequence of the oppression to which he is subjected equally in the most distant parts of Europe.

The accusation that today's Jews even now regard the Christians with the fanatic hatred which caused some of their ancestors eighteen centuries ago to crucify Jesus, hardly deserves a serious reply. Only in barbarian times could the distant descendants in France and Germany be punished for a crime committed many centuries ago on the Asiatic coast of the Mediterranean. It is a fact that the mutual antipathy of the two religious groups which have a common origin has persisted longer than the philosophic mind would guess and desire after such a long time. But just that is the fault of the governments which were unable to reduce the friction between the religious principles separating them and could not incite in the hearts of Jews and Christians alike a patriotic feeling which should long ago have abolished the prejudices of both groups. These were Christian governments, and we therefore cannot deny, if we want to be impartial, the reproach that we have contributed the greater part to the hostile feelings of the two groups. We were always the rulers, and therefore it would have been up to us to induce the Jew to feel humanly by proving that we have such feelings ourselves.

In order to heal him of his prejudices against us we first have to get rid of our own. If, therefore, those prejudices today prevent the Jew from being a good citizen, a social human being, if he feels antipathy and hatred against the Christian, if he feels himself in his dealings with him not so much bound by his moral code, then all this is our own doing. His religion does not command him to commit these dishonesties, but the prejudices which we have instilled and which are still nourished by us in him are stronger than his religion. We ourselves are guilty of the crimes we accuse him of; and the moral turpitude in which that unfortunate nation is sunk—thanks to a mistaken policy—cannot be a reason that would justify a continuation of that policy. That policy is a remnant of the barbarism of past centuries, a consequence of a fanatical religious hatred. It is unworthy of our enlightened times and should have been abolished long ago. . . .

If it is permissible to draw conclusions from the majority of a nation about its essential qualities, no one can deny that the Jews possess excellent intelligence, industry, and the capability to adjust to all kinds of situations. If Jews are made use of in public business, one is almost always very satisfied with their zeal and sagacity. Their luck in commerce and manufacture is well known, and often those who envy them ascribe to fraud what is only a consequence of their greater industry and application. Where they are allowed to be artisans and workers, they usually do excellent work. The oppression under which they have lived until now is at fault if they have not done more in the sciences and fine arts; they certainly do not lack the capability. Most of those who occupied themselves with these interests have made good progress, even if they are not known to the public like a Moses Mendelssohn and a Pinto. Among their greater merchants one finds perhaps more broad view and skill in coordination, and among their common people, more intelligence and industry than among an equal number of Christians. As regards the moral character of the Jews, it is like that of all men: capable of the most lofty development and of the most unfortunate deterioration, and as I remarked already, the influence of the external environment is quite clearly visible. . . .

A very happy influence on the moral character of the Jews has been their closeness and segregation, forced on them in part by their strange religion and in part by oppression. Their almost equal fate has linked all Jews so closely with one another that they share in the fate of their fellow Jews with much more interest than is possible in a more numerous nation. Nowhere are their poor a burden on the state; they are taken care of by the prosperous among them, and the whole community takes sympathetic interest in the affairs of the individual. The Jews seem to enjoy the bliss of domestic life with more simplicity than is at present usual, at least in big cities. Most of them are good husbands and fathers. Luxury has with them not yet reached the stage as with Christians in similar circumstances. The purity of their marriages is greater; crimes of unchastity, especially perversities, are much rarer. Almost never has a Jew committed treachery or a crime against the state. Almost everywhere they are devoted to the country in which they live, if only they are not treated too badly. In danger they have shown a zeal which one would not have expected from members of society who are so little favored.

In contrast to these fine traits of the Jewish character is the exaggerated love of the nation for every kind of profit, usury, and crooked practices, a fault which is nourished in many by their exclusive religious principles and rabbinic sophistries, and more still by Christian oppression and the antipathy against other religions which they are taught. Breaking of laws which limit trade, import or export of contraband merchandise, forgery of mint or precious metals, are natural consequences of this character trait; and in almost all modern states the Jews are accused of these. But as I remarked already, all these crimes do not stem from the national character of the Jews, but from the oppressed state in which they live, and are in part consequences of the profession to which they have been restricted exclusively.

There is no record that Jews did all these things as long as they lived in their own state and as long as their only occupation was agriculture; nor during the period when they, dispersed over the whole Roman Empire, enjoyed all human and civil rights. Only from the time on when one began to deny them those rights and forced them, so unpolitically, to live on commerce alone did crookedness and usury become more and more apparent as special traits of the Jewish character. . . .

The Jews have been forced for many centuries now to live on commerce exclusively. Is it surprising that the spirit of this occupation became entirely their spirit and by long heredity has gained strength and now determines so much more the faulty formation of their character? Love of profit must be much more vivid in the Jews because it is the sole means of survival for them; the little business tricks must be more known to them since they have been practiced so long. Usury and unfair profits must be considered more permissible by them because all branches of their trade were heavily taxed, so that regular profits would not have sufficed to pay all these fees. Logically the soul of the young Jew must be entirely conditioned to desire profit in commerce when he notices early in life that this is the only way for him to make a living, since his parents and all other Jews of his acquaintance know no more plentiful theme for conversation than their trade. One has to consider that of necessity an occupation which for more than a thousand years was the only one carried on by a nation must have had a one-sided influence on its character and must have transmitted with the most powerful intensity faulty impressions to its character.

If this reasoning is correct, then we have found in the oppression and in the restricted occupation of the Jews the true source of their corruption. Then we have discovered also at the same time the means of healing this corruption and of making the Jews better men and useful citizens. With the elimination of the unjust and unpolitical treatment of the Jews will also disappear the consequences of it; and when we cease to limit them to one kind of occupation, then the detrimental influence of that occupation will no longer be so noticeable. With the modesty that a private citizen should always show when expressing his thoughts about public affairs, and with the certain conviction that general proposals should always be tailored, if they should be useful, to the special local conditions in every state, I dare now, after these remarks, to submit my ideas as to the manner in which the Jews could become happier and better members of civil societies.

To make them such it is FIRST necessary to give them equal rights with all other subjects. Since they are able to fulfill the necessary duties, they should be allowed to claim the equal impartial love and care of the state. No humiliating discrimination should be tolerated, no way of earning a living should be closed to them, none other than the regular taxes demanded from them. They would have to pay all the usual taxes in the state, but they would not have to pay protection money for the mere right to exist, no special fee for the permission to earn a living. It is obvious that in accordance with the principle of equal rights, also special privileges favoring the Jews—which exist in some states—would have to be abolished. . . .

SECOND. Since it is primarily the limitation of the Jews to commerce which has had a detrimental influence on their moral and political character, a perfect freedom in the choice of a livelihood would serve justice, as well as represent a humanitarian policy which would make of the Jews more useful and happier members of society.

It might even be useful, in order to achieve this great purpose, if the government would first try to dissuade the Jews from the occupation of commerce, and endeavor to weaken its influence by encouraging them to prefer such kinds of livelihoods as are most apt to create a diametrically opposed spirit and character—I mean artisan occupations. . . .

THIRD. The Jews should not be excluded from agriculture. Unless the purchase of landed property is restricted in a country to certain classes of the inhabitants, the Jews should not be excluded, and they should have equal rights to lease land. . . .

From several sides the proposal has been made that the Jews should be allotted separate districts for settlement and be kept isolated there from the rest of the subjects. In my opinion it would not be advisable to make the religious difference more noticeable and probably more permanent by this step. The Jews, left entirely to themselves, would be strengthened in their prejudices against Christians, and vice versa. Frequent intercourse and sharing the burdens and advantages of the state equally is the most certain way to dull the edge of the hostile prejudices on both sides. The *Judengasse (Juiveries* in France) and restricted districts of Jewish residence in many cities are remnants of the old harsh principles. In many places (for instance, Frankfort on the Main where the *Judengasse* is locked up every night) the evil consequence is that the Jews are forced to build their houses many stories high and live under very crowded conditions resulting in uncleanliness, diseases, bad policing, and greater danger of fire.

FOURTH. No kind of commerce should be closed to the Jews, but none should be left to them exclusively, nor should they be encouraged by privileges. . . .

FIFTH. Every art, every science should be open to the Jew as to every other free man. He, too, should educate his mind as far as he is able; he, too, must be able to rise to promotion, honor, and rewards by developing his talents. The scientific institutions of the state should be for his use, too, and he should be as free as other citizens to utilize his talents in any way.

Another question is whether in our states Jews should be admitted to public office immediately. It seems, in fact, that if they are granted all civil rights, they could not be excluded from applying for the honor to serve the government and, if they are found to be capable, from being employed by the state. I think, however, that in the next generations this capability will not yet appear frequently, and the state should make no special effort to develop it. In most countries there is no lack of skilled civil servants, and without any efforts on the part of the government there are enough applicants for public office. For some of these jobs early education and scholarship, which are hard for Jews to achieve under the present circumstances, is required. Other jobs require that the applicant be far removed from any suspicion of misdemeanors due to greed, and this will probably not always be the case in the Jews of today and of the next generation. The mercantile spirit of most Jews will probably be broken more easily by heavy physical labor than by the sedentary work of the public servant; and for the state as well as for himself it will be better in most cases if the Jew works in the shops and behind the plow than in the state chancelleries. The best middle way would probably be to allow the Jews, without especially encouraging them, to acquire the education necessary for public service, even to employ them in cases where they show special capability, if only to overcome the prejudice which will no doubt endure for a long time. But just impartiality would demand that if a Jewish and a Christian applicant show equal capability, the latter deserves preference. This seems to me to be an obvious right of the majority in the nation—at least until the Jews by wiser treatment are changed into entirely equal citizens and all differences are effaced.

SIXTH. It should be a special endeavor of a wise government to care for the moral education and enlightenment of the Jews, in order to make at least the coming generations more receptive to a milder treatment and the enjoyment of all advantages of our society. . . .

SEVENTH. With the moral improvement of the Jews there should go hand in hand efforts of the Christians to get rid of their prejudices and uncharitable opinions. In early childhood they should be taught to regard the Jews as their brothers and fellowmen who seek to find favor with God in a different way—a way they think erroneously to be the right one, yet which, if they follow in sincerity of heart, God looks at with favor. . . .

EIGHTH. An important part of civil rights would be the right for Jews in all places of free worship to build synagogues and employ teachers at their own expense. . . . Government supervision of the Jewish poorhouses and hospitals would be useful, in order to assure the healthiest and best organization and the best utilization of the money appropriated for them. The Jewish community, just as any other organized religious society, should have the right to excommunicate for a period of time or permanently, and in case of resistance the judgment of the rabbis should be supported by the authorities. Regarding the execution of this ban, the state should interfere less when it does not go beyond a religious society and has no effect on the political society, for the excommunicated member of any church can be a very useful and respected citizen. This is a principle of general church jurisprudence which should no longer be doubtful in our times.

NINTH. The written laws of Moses that do not refer to Palestine and the old judicial and ritual organization, known as the oral law, are regarded by the Jews as permanently binding divine commandments. Besides, various commentaries to these laws and argumentations from them by famous Jewish scholars are held in the same respect as laws. Therefore, if they are to be granted full human rights, one has to permit them to live and be judged according to these laws. This will no more isolate them from the rest of the citizens of the state than a city or community living according to their own statutes; and the experiment made with Jewish autonomy during the first centuries in the Roman Empire as also in some modern states has shown that no inconvenient or detrimental consequences are to be feared. . . .

A constitution shaped according to these principles would, it seems to me, bring the Jews into society as useful members and at the same time would abolish the many ills that have been done to them and of which they were forced to make themselves guilty. Men of higher insight will decide if my assertions are correct, my proposals feasible. I shall be content to have been the one who called attention to such an important matter. I shall be glad when wiser men will find my ideas worthy of examination and correction, and especially when in the execution of them they will add all the modifications which the constitutions of the various states will make necessary. However varied these modifications may be, I think I am not erring in the main point and shall have the applause of all people who are free of prejudice in my assertion that the Jews have been given by nature the same capability to become better, more useful members of society, that only oppression, unworthy of our age, has corrupted them, and that it is in accordance with humanity, justice, and enlightened politics to banish that oppression and improve the lot of the Jews to their own benefit and the benefit of the state. I dare even to congratulate the state which will first put these principles in action. The government will create new loyal and grateful subjects from its own midst, it will make good citizens of its own Jews, and if it only starts treating them as such (and other states do not follow its steps soon), it will attract them from outside its frontiers, for they will certainly prefer the country which promises them human rights and the advantages of citizenship. . . .

2. *THE EMANCIPATION OF FRENCH JEWRY*

During the Napoleonic era, 80 percent of French Jewry lived in Alsace-Lorraine. When the Jews chose to foreclose on loans granted to the local peasantry for the purchase of *emigré* lands during the 1790s, deputations of destitute farmers and petty landowners beseeched Napoleon for assistance. Met by their pleas upon his return from the Austrian campaign of 1806, fearful of a popular uprising, and incensed by the persistence of usury, Napoleon and his Council of State issued the Decree of 1806—a one-year moratorium on debts owed Jews in Alsace-Lorraine and the ordering of an Assembly of Jewish Notables to convene in Paris.

This assembly was to declare France's Jews to be "Frenchmen" and "faithful subjects, determined to conform in everything to the laws . . . which ought to regulate the conduct of all Frenchmen." This meant, for Napoleon, that the Jews of France were to declare themselves no longer "a nation within a nation" and that Jewish law would yield, without exception, to French law.

Jewish "notables," handpicked by French officials, deliberated from July 30 to August 12, 1806. The entire assembly approved the answers worked out by a committee of rabbis and laymen—answers that were to signal the end of the autonomous Jewish community and the supremacy of the laws of the state over Jewish laws.

The twelve questions proved to be immensely embarrassing, for Napoleon demanded to know the position of Jewish law rather than custom, practice, or preference. Some questions thus had to be answered with lies, others received no direct answer, and still others could be answered only with serious qualifications. Question #3 seems to have proved the most difficult of all (Can a Jewess marry a Christian, or a Jew a Christian woman, or has the law ordered that the Jews should only intermarry among themselves?); the truth would insult French Christians while an accommodation would ignore fifteen hundred years of clear Jewish legislation against intermarriage. The answer, which divided Jewish law into nonexistent categories, was unique in its historical importance as well as its ingenuity.

Questions #11 and #12, dealing with usury, are handled equally adroitly by the assembly. Moving from a well-argued rejection of the Vulgate's translation of a biblical word meaning "interest of any amount" as "usury" to a less reasoned exposition of the permissibility of "commercial loans" in postbiblical times, it yields an answer neatly applicable to the early nineteenth century in France.

The final answers of the assembly were not sufficiently clear nor authoritative for Napoleon, and a more impressive conference, the "Great Sanhedrin," was convened to approve the conclusions of the assembly. The following sampling of answers of the assembly are taken from the *Transactions of the Parisian Sanhedrin or Acts of the Assembly of Israelitish Deputies of France and Italy,* collected by Diogene Tama and translated by F. D. Kirwan (London, 1807).

The Acts of the Israelitish Deputies of France and Italy

Gentlemen,
His Majesty, the Emperor and King, having named us Commissioners to transact whatever relates to you, has this day sent us to this assembly to acquaint you with his intentions. Called together from the extremities of this vast empire, no one among you is ignorant of the object for which His Majesty has convened this assembly. You know it. The conduct of many among those of your persuasion has excited complaints, which have found their way to the foot of the throne; these complaints were founded on truth. Nevertheless, His Majesty has been satisfied with stopping the progress of the evil, and he has wished to hear you on the means of providing a remedy. You will, no doubt, prove worthy of so tender, so paternal a conduct, and you will feel all the importance of the trust thus reposed in you. Far from considering the government under which you live as a power against which you should be on your guard, you will assist it with your experience and cooperate with it in all the good it intends; thus you will prove that, following the example of all Frenchmen, you do not seclude yourselves from the rest of mankind.

The laws which have been imposed on individuals of your religion have been different in the several parts of the world: often they have been dictated by the interest of the day. But as an assembly like the present has no precedent in the annals of Christianity, so will you be judged, for the first time, with justice, and you will see your fate irrevocably fixed by a Christian Prince. The wish of His Majesty is that you should be Frenchmen; it remains with you to accept of the proffered title, without forgetting that, to prove unworthy of it, would be renouncing it altogether.

You will hear the questions submitted to you; your duty is to answer the whole truth on every one of them. Attend, and never lose sight of that which we are going to tell you; that, when a monarch equally firm and just, who knows everything, and who punishes or recompenses every action, puts questions to his subjects, these would be equally guilty and blind to their true interests, if they were to disguise the truth in the least.

The intention of His Majesty is, Gentlemen, that you should enjoy the greatest freedom in your deliberations: your answers will be transmitted to us by your President, when they have been put in regular form.

As to us, our most ardent wish is to be able to report to the Emperor that, among individuals of the Jewish persuasion, he can reckon as many faithful subjects, determined to conform in everything to the laws and to the morality which ought to regulate the conduct of all Frenchmen.

One of the Secretaries read afterward the following twelve questions proposed by the Commissioners.

Questions proposed to the Assembly of the Jews by the Commissioners named by His Majesty the Emperor and King to transact whatever concerns them.

1. Is it lawful for Jews to marry more than one wife?
2. Is divorce allowed by the Jewish religion? Is divorce valid, although not pronounced by courts of justice and by virtue of laws in contradiction with the French Code?
3. Can a Jewess marry a Christian, or a Jew a Christian woman? Or has the law ordered that the Jews should only intermarry among themselves?
4. In the eyes of Jews are Frenchmen considered as brethren or as strangers?
5. In either case what conduct does their law prescribe toward Frenchmen not of their religion?
6. Do the Jews born in France, and treated by the law as French citizens, acknowledge France as their country? Are they bound to

defend it? Are they bound to obey the laws, and to follow the directions of the civil code?

7. What kind of police jurisdiction have the rabbis among the Jews? What judicial power do they exercise among them?
9. Are the forms of the elections of the rabbis and their police jurisdiction regulated by the law, or are they only sanctioned by custom?
10. Are there professions from which the Jews are excluded by their law?
11. Does the law forbid the Jews from taking usury from their brethren?
12. Does it forbid or does it allow usury toward strangers?

During the reading of these questions, the assembly manifested by unanimous and spontaneous emotions how deeply it was affected by the doubt which the questions seemed to convey, as to the attachment of Frenchmen, following the law of Moses, for their fellow citizens, and for their country, and as to their sense of the duty by which they are bound to defend it.

The assembly was not able to conceal the emotions caused by the sixth question, in which it is asked if Jews born in France and treated by the law as French citizens acknowledge France as their country and if they are bound to defend it. The whole assembly unanimously exclaimed, "Even to death." . . .

The assembly proceeded afterward to form a commission to prepare the groundwork of the discussions, which are to take place on the communications which the Commissioners of His Majesty have made to the assembly. The President names to compose it—MM. Berr-Isaac-Berr, Segre, Rabbi, David Zinzheimer, Rabbi, Abraham Andrade, Rabbi, Jacob Lazare, Jacob Gondebaux Berr, Moses Levy, Rodrigues, Samuel Jacob Guediglia, Michel Berr, Baruch-Cerf-Berr, and Lyon Marx.

Previous to the rising of the assembly, the President observed that it was unnecessary for him to observe that no answer will be sent to the Commissioners without having been previously submitted to the deliberation of the assembly. . . .

The President took the chair at twelve o'clock; one of the secretaries read the minutes of the sitting of the 29th of July last, which passed without any objection.

The President named MM. May, of Paris, Samuel Wittersheim, and Gumpel Levy as commissioners to maintain order in the assembly.

The President read a letter from His Excellency the Minister of the Interior, indicating that His Majesty the Emperor and King had consented to admit the assembly into his presence, in a body, whenever its labors shall be sufficiently forwarded to promise some results. The reading of this letter was followed by repeated acclamations of "Long live the Emperor, long live the Imperial Family."...

The President proposed afterward to name a commission to prepare the ceremonies of a festival to be celebrated in the synagogues, on the 15th of August next, in commemoration of His Majesty's birthday, and of the reestablishment of religious worship, as one of the greatest blessings of his reign.

The assembly adopted this proposition unanimously, and the President named as commissioners to prepare this festival, MM. J. Rodrigues, sen. of La Gironde; Gumpel Levy, of Nancy; May, jun. of Paris; Sabaton Constantini, of Marseilles; and Aaron Schmol, of Paris, who are to consult with the administrators of synagogues. . . .

DECLARATION ADOPTED BY THE ASSEMBLY AND THE ANSWERS TO THE QUESTIONS

DECLARATION

Resolved, by the French deputies professing the religion of Moses, that the following Declaration shall precede the answers returned to the questions proposed by the Commissioners of His Imperial and Royal Majesty.

"The assembly, impressed with a deep sense of gratitude, love, respect, and admiration for the sacred person of his Imperial and Royal Majesty, declares, in the name of all Frenchmen professing the religion of Moses, that they are fully determined to prove worthy of the favors His Majesty intends for them, by scrupulously conforming to his paternal intentions; that their religion makes it their duty to consider the law of the prince as the supreme law in civil and political matters; that, consequently, should their religious code, or its various interpretations, contain civil or political commands at variance with those of the French Code, those commands would, of course, cease to influence and govern them, since they must, above all, acknowledge and obey the laws of the prince.

"That, in consequence of this principle, the Jews have, at all times, considered it their duty to obey the laws of the state, and that, since the revolution, they, like all Frenchmen, have acknowledged no others."

FIRST QUESTION

Is it lawful for Jews to marry more than one wife?

ANSWER

It is not lawful for Jews to marry more than one wife: in all European countries they conform to the general practice of marrying only one.

Moses does not command expressly to take several; but he does not forbid it. He seems even to adopt that custom as generally prevailing, since he settles the rights of inheritance between children of different wives. Although this practice still prevails in the East, yet their ancient doctors have enjoined them to restrain from taking more than one wife, except when the man is enabled by his fortune to maintain several.

The case has been different in the West; the wish of adopting the customs of the inhabitants of this part of the world has induced the Jews to renounce polygamy. But as several individuals still indulged in that practice, a synod was convened at Worms in the eleventh century, composed of one hundred rabbis, with R. Gershom at their head. This assembly pronounced an anathema against every Israelite who should, in future, take more than one wife.

Although this prohibition was not to last forever, the influence of European manners has universally prevailed.

SECOND QUESTION

Is divorce allowed by the Jewish religion? Is divorce valid although not pronounced by courts of justice and by virtue of laws in contradiction with those of the French Code?

ANSWER

Repudiation is allowed by the law of Moses; but it is not valid if not previously pronounced by the French Code.

In the eyes of every Israelite, without exception, submission to the prince is the first of duties. It is a principle generally acknowledged among them that in everything relating to civil or political interests the law of the state is supreme. Before they were admitted in France to share the rights of all citizens, and when they lived under a particular legislation which set them at liberty to follow their religious customs, they had the facility of repudiating their wives; but it was extremely rare to see it put into practice.

Since the revolution, they have acknowledged no other laws on this head but those of the empire. At the epoch when they were admitted to the rank of citizens, the rabbis and the principal Jews appeared before the municipalities of their respective places of abode, and took an oath to conform in everything to the laws, and to acknowledge no other rules in all civil matters.

Consequently they can no longer consider as valid the repudiation pronounced by their rabbis, since, to make it valid, it must have been previously pronounced by competent tribunals; for, in like manner as by an arret of the Consular Government, the rabbis could not impart the matrimonial benediction till it appeared to them that the civil contract had been performed before the civil officer, in like manner they cannot pronounce repudiation, until it appears to them that it has already been pronounced by a sentence which gives it validity. Supposing even that the aforesaid arret had been silent on this head, still the rabbinical repudiation could not be valid; for, according to the rabbis who have written on the civil code of the Jews, such as R. Joseph Caro in the *Even ha-Ezer*, repudiation is valid only in case there should be no opposition of any kind. And as the law of the state would form an opposition in point of civil interests—since one of the parties could avail himself or herself of it against the other—it necessarily follows that, under the influence of the civil code, rabbinical repudiation cannot be valid. Consequently, since the time the Jews have begun to enter into engagements before the civil officer, no one, attached to religious practices, can repudiate his wife but by a double divorce—that pronounced by the law of the state, and that prescribed by the law of Moses; so that under this point of view, it may be justly affirmed that the Jewish religion agrees on this subject with the civil code.

THIRD QUESTION

Can a Jewess marry a Christian, and a Jew a Christian woman? Or does the law allow the Jews to intermarry only among themselves?

ANSWER

The law does not say that a Jewess cannot marry a Christian, nor a Jew a Christian woman; nor does it state that the Jews can only intermarry among themselves.

The only marriages expressly forbidden by the law are those with the seven Canaanite nations, with Amon and Moab, and with the Egyptians. The prohibition is absolute concerning the seven Canaanite nations; with regard to Amon and Moab, it is limited, according to many Talmudists, to the men of those nations, and does not extend to the women; it is even thought that these last would have embraced the Jewish religion. As to Egyptians, the prohibition is limited to the third generation. The prohibition in general applies only to nations in idolatry. The Talmud declares formally that modern nations are not to be considered as such, since they worship, like us, the God of heaven and earth. And, accordingly, there has been, at several periods, intermarriage between Jews and Christians in France, in Spain, and in Germany: these marriages were sometimes tolerated and sometimes forbidden by the laws of those sovereigns who had received Jews into their dominions.

Unions of this kind are still found in France; but we cannot dissemble that the opinion of the rabbis is against these marriages. According to their doctrine, although the religion of Moses has not forbidden the Jews from intermarrying with nations not of their religion, yet as marriage, according to the Talmud, requires religious ceremonies called *kiddushin,* with the benediction used in such cases, no marriage can be *religiously* valid unless these ceremonies have been performed. This could not be done toward persons who would not both of them consider these ceremonies as sacred; and in that case the married couple could separate without the *religious* divorce; they would then be considered as married *civilly* but not *religiously.*

Such is the opinion of the rabbis, members of this assembly. In general they would be no more inclined to bless the union of a Jewess with a Christian, or of a Jew with a Christian woman, than Catholic priests themselves would be disposed to sanction unions of this kind. The rabbis acknowledge, however, that a Jew who marries a Christian woman does not cease on that account to be considered as a Jew by his brethren, any more than if he had married a Jewess civilly and not religiously. . . .

FOURTH QUESTION

In the eyes of Jews, are Frenchmen considered as their brethren? Or are they considered as strangers?

ANSWER

In the eyes of Jews Frenchmen are their brethern, and are not strangers.

The true spirit of the law of Moses is consonant to this mode of considering Frenchmen.

When the Israelites formed a settled and independent nation, their law made it a rule for them to consider strangers as their brethren.

With the most tender care for their welfare, their lawgiver commands to love them. "Love ye therefore the strangers," says he to the Israelites, "for ye were strangers in the land of Egypt."

Respect and benevolence toward strangers are enforced by Moses, not as an exhortation to the practice of social morality only, but as an obligation imposed by God himself. "When ye reap the harvest of your land," says he to them, "thou shalt not make clean riddance of the corners of the field when thou reapst, neither shalt thou gather any gleaning of thy harvest; thou shalt leave them unto the poor and to the stranger; I am the Lord thy God." "When thou cuttest down thy harvest in the field, thou shalt not go back again to fetch it: it shall be for the stranger, for the fatherless, and the widow: that the Lord thy God may bless the work of thy hands." "Thou shalt neither vex a stranger, nor oppress him." "The Lord your God doth execute the judgment of the fatherless and widow, and loveth the stranger, in giving him food and raiment. Love ye therefore the stranger; for ye were strangers in the land of Egypt."

To these sentiments of benevolence toward the stranger, Moses has added the precept of general love for mankind: "Love thy fellow creature as thyself."

David also expresses himself in these terms: "The Lord is good to all: and his tender mercies are over all his works." This doctrine is also professed by the Talmud.

"We are bound," says a Talmudist, "to love as our brethren all those who observe the Noachide Laws, whatever their religious opinions may otherwise be. We are bound to visit their sick, to bury their dead, to assist their poor, like those of Israel. In short, there is no act of humanity which a true Israelite is not bound to perform toward those who observe the

Noachide Laws." What are these precepts? To abstain from idolatry, from blasphemy, from adultery, not to kill or hurt our neighbors, neither to rob or to deceive, to eat only the flesh of animals killed; in short, to observe the rules of justice; and therefore all the principles of our religion make it our duty to love Frenchmen as our brethren.

A pagan having consulted the Rabbi Hillel on the Jewish religion, and wishing to know in a few words in what it consisted, Hillel thus answered him: "Do not to others what thou shouldst not like to have done to thyself. This," said he, "is all our religion; the rest are only consequences of this principle."

A religion whose fundamental maxims are such—a religion which makes a duty of loving the stranger, which enforces the practice of social virtues—must surely require that its followers should consider their fellow citizens as brethren.

And how could they consider them otherwise when they inhabit the same land, when they are ruled and protected by the same government and by the same laws? when they enjoy the same rights, and have the same duties to fulfill? There exists even between the Jew and Christian a tie which abundantly compensates for religion—it is the tie of gratitude. This sentiment was at first excited in us by the mere grant of toleration. It has been increased, these eighteen years, by new favors from government, to such a degree of energy, that now our fate is irrevocably linked with the common fate of all Frenchmen. Yes, France is our country; all Frenchmen are our brethren, and this glorious title, by raising us in our own esteem, becomes a sure pledge that we shall never cease to be worthy of it.

FIFTH QUESTION

In either case, what line of conduct does their law prescribe toward Frenchmen not of their religion?

ANSWER

The line of conduct prescribed toward Frenchmen not of our religion is the same as that prescribed between Jews themselves; we admit of no difference but that of worshiping the Supreme Being, everyone in his own way.

The answer to the preceding question has explained the line of conduct which the law of Moses and the Talmud prescribe toward Frenchmen not of our religion. At the present time, when the Jews no longer form a separate people, but enjoy the advantage of being incorporated with the Great Nation (which privilege they consider as a kind of political redemption), it is impossible that a Jew should treat a Frenchman not of his religion in any other manner than he would treat one of his Israelitish brethren.

SIXTH QUESTION

Do Jews born in France, and treated by the laws as French citizens, consider France as their country? Are they bound to defend it? Are they bound to obey the laws and to conform to the dispositions of the civil code?

ANSWER

Men who have adopted a country, who have resided in it these many generations, who, even under the restraint of particular laws which abridged their civil rights, were so attached to it that they preferred being debarred from the advantages common to all other citizens, rather than leave it, cannot but consider themselves as Frenchmen in France; and they consider as equally sacred and honorable the duty of defending their country.

Jeremiah exhorts the Jews to consider Babylon as their country, although they were to remain in it only for seventy years. He exhorts them to till the ground, to build houses, to sow, and to plant. His recommendation was so much attended to that Ezra says that, when Cyrus allowed them to return to Jerusalem to rebuild the temple, 42,360 only left Babylon; and that this number was mostly composed of the poorer people, the wealthy having remained in that city.

The love of the country is in the heart of Jews a sentiment so natural, so powerful, and so consonant to their religious opinions that a French Jew considers himself, in England, as among strangers, although he may be among Jews; and the case is the same with English Jews in France.

To such a pitch is this sentiment carried among them that, during the last war, French Jews have been seen fighting desperately against other Jews, the subjects of countries then at war with France.

Many of them are covered with honorable wounds, and others have obtained, in the field of honor, the noble rewards of bravery.

SEVENTH QUESTION

Who names the rabbis?

ANSWER

Since the revolution, the majority of the chiefs of families names the rabbi, wherever there is a sufficient number of Jews to maintain one, after previous inquiries as to the morality and learning of the candidate. This mode of election is not, however, uniform; it varies according to place, and, to this day, whatever concerns the election of rabbis is still in a state of uncertainty. . . .

EIGHTH QUESTION

What police jurisdiction do rabbis exercise among the Jews? What judicial power do they enjoy among them?

ANSWER

The rabbis exercise no manner of police jurisdiction among the Jews.

The qualification of rabbi is nowhere to be found in the law of Moses, neither did it exist in the days of the first Temple; it is only mentioned toward the end of those of the second.

At these epochs the Jews were governed by Sanhedrin or tribunals. A supreme tribunal, called the Grand Sanhedrin, sat in Jerusalem, and was composed of seventy-one judges.

There were inferior courts, composed of three judges for civil causes and for police; and another composed of twenty-two judges, which sat in the capital to decide matters of less importance, and which was called the "Lesser Sanhedrin."

It is only in the Mishnah and in the Talmud that the word "rabbi" is found for the first time applied to a doctor in the law; and he was commonly indebted for this qualification to his reputation and to the opinion generally entertained of his learning.

When the Israelites were totally dispersed, they formed small communities in those places where they were allowed to settle in certain numbers.

Sometimes, in these circumstances, a rabbi and two other doctors formed a kind of tribunal, named *bet din,* that is, house of justice; the rabbi fulfilled the functions of judge, and the other two those of his assessors.

The attributes, and even the existence, of these tribunals have, to this day, always depended on the will of governments under which the Jews have lived, and on the degree of tolerance they have enjoyed. Since the revolution those rabbinical tribunals are totally suppressed in France and in Italy. The Jews, raised to the rank of citizens, have conformed in everything to the laws of the state; and, accordingly, the functions of rabbis, wherever any are established, are limited to preaching morality in the temples, blessing marriages, and pronouncing divorces.

In places where there are no rabbis, the Jew who is best instructed in his religion may, according to the law, impart the marriage benediction without the assistance of a rabbi; this is attended with an inconveniency, the consequences of which it certainly would be proper to prevent, by extending to all persons called upon to bless a marriage the restrictions which the consular arret places on functions of rabbis in this particular.

As to judicial powers, they possess absolutely none; for there is among them neither a settled ecclesiastical hierarchy nor any subordination in the exercise of their religious functions.

NINTH QUESTION

Are these forms of election and that police-judicial jurisdiction regulated by the law, or are they only sanctioned by custom?

ANSWER

The answer to the preceding questions makes it useless to say much on this, only it may be remarked that, even supposing that rabbis should have, to this day, preserved some kind of police-judicial jurisdiction among us, which is not the case, neither such jurisdiction nor the forms of the elections could be said to be sanctioned by the law; they should be attributed solely to custom.

TENTH QUESTION

Are there professions which the law of the Jews forbids them from exercising?

ANSWER

There are none: on the contrary, the Talmud expressly declares that "the father who does not teach a profession to his child rears him up to be a villain."

ELEVENTH QUESTION

Does the law forbid the Jews from taking usury from their brethren?

ANSWER

Deuteronomy says, "Thou shalt not lend upon *interest* to thy brother, interest of money, interest of victuals, interest of any thing that is lent upon interest."

The Hebrew word *neshekh* has been improperly translated by the word "usury": in the Hebrew language it means *interest* of any kind, and not *usurious* interest. It cannot then be taken in the sense now given in the word "usury."

It is even impossible that it could ever have had that connotation; for usury is an expression relative to, and compared with, another and a lawful interest; and the text contains nothing which alludes to the other term of comparison. What do we understand by usury? Is it not an interest above the legal interest, above the rate fixed by the law? If the law of Moses has not fixed this rate, can it be said that the Hebrew word means an unlawful interest? The word *neshekh* in the Hebrew language answers the Latin word *faenus:* to conclude that it means "usury," another word should be found which would mean "interest"; and as such a word does not exist, it follows that all interest is usury, and that all usury is interest.

What was the aim of the lawgiver in forbidding one Hebrew to lend upon interest to another? It was to draw closer between them the bonds of fraternity, to give them a lesson of reciprocal benevolence, and to engage them to help and assist each other with disinterestedness.

The first thought had been to establish among them the equality of property, and the mediocrity of private fortune; hence the institution of the sabbatical year, and of the year of jubilee; the first of which came every seventh year, and the other every fifty years. By the sabbatical year all debtors were released from their obligations: the year of jubilee brought with it the restitution of all estates sold or mortgaged.

It was easy to foresee that the different qualities of the ground, the greater or lesser industry, the untowardness of the seasons, which might affect both, would necessarily make a difference in the produce of land, and that the more unfortunate Israelite would claim the assistance of him whom fortune should have better favored. Moses did not intend that this last should avail himself of this situation, and that he should require from the other the price of the service he was soliciting; that he should thus aggravate the misery of his brother and enrich himself by his spoils. It is with a view to this that he says, "Thou shalt not lend upon interest to thy brother." But what want could there exist among the Jews, at a time when they had no trade of any kind, when so little money was in circulation, when the greatest equality prevailed in property? It was, at most, a few bushels of corn, some cattle, some agricultural implements; and Moses required that such services should be gratuitous; his intention was to make of his people a nation of husbandmen. For a long time after him, and though Idumaea was at no great distance from the seashores, inhabited by the Tyrians, the Sidonians, and other nations possessing shipping and commerce, we do not see the Hebrews much addicted to trade; all the regulations of their lawgiver seemed designed to divert their attention from commerce.

The prohibition of Moses must therefore be considered only as a principle of charity and not as a commercial regulation. According to the Talmud, the loan alluded to is to be considered almost as a family loan, as a loan made to a man in want; for in case of a loan made to a merchant, even a Jew, profit adequate to risk should be considered as lawful.

Formerly the word "usury" carried no invidious meaning; it simply implied any interest whatever. The word "usury" can no longer express the meaning of the Hebrew text: and accordingly the Bible of Osterwald and that of the Portuguese Jews call "interest" that which Sacy, from the Vulgate, has called "usury."

The law of Moses, therefore, forbids all manner of interest on loan, not only between Jews, but between a Jew and his countryman, without distinction of religion. The loan must be gratuitous whenever it is to oblige those who claim our assistance, and when it is not intended for commercial speculation.

We must not forget that these laws, so humane and so admirable at these early periods, were made for a people which then formed a state and held a rank among nations.

If the remnants of this people, now scattered among all nations, are attentively considered, it will be seen that, since the Jews have been driven from Palestine, they no longer have had a common country, they no longer have had to maintain among them the primeval equality of property. Although filled with the spirit of their legislation, they have been sensible that the letter of the law could no longer be obeyed when its principle was done away; and they have, therefore, without any scruple, lent money on interest to trading Jews, as well as to men of different persuasions.

TWELFTH QUESTION

Does it forbid or does it allow to take usury from strangers?

ANSWER

We have seen, in the answer to the foregoing question, that the prohibition of usury, considered as the smallest interest, was a maxim of charity and of benevolence, rather than a commercial regulation. In this point of view it is equally condemned by the law of Moses and by the Talmud; we are generally forbidden, always on the score of charity, to lend upon interest to our fellow citizens of different persuasions, as well as to our fellow Jews.

The disposition of the law, which allows to take interest from the stranger, evidently refers only to nations in commercial intercourse with us; otherwise there would be an evident contradiction between this passage and twenty others of the sacred writings.

"The Lord your God loveth the stranger, in giving him food and raiment; love ye therefore the stranger, for ye were strangers in the land of Egypt." "One law shall be to him that is home-born, and to the stranger." "Hear the causes between your brethren, and judge righteously between every man and his brother, and the stranger that is with him." "If a stranger sojourn with thee in your land you shall not vex him." "Thou shalt neither vex a stranger nor oppress him, for ye were strangers in the land of Egypt." "If thy brother be waxen poor, or fallen in decay with thee, thou shalt then relieve him; yea, though he be a stranger, or a sojourner."

Thus the prohibition extended to the stranger who dwelt in Israel; the Holy Writ places them under the safeguard of God; he is a sacred guest, and God orders us to treat him like the widow and like the orphan.

It is evident that the text of the Vulgate, *Extranei faenaberis et fratri tuo non faenaberis,* can be understood only as meaning foreign nations in commercial intercourse with us; and, even in this case, the Holy Writ, in allowing to take interest from the stranger, does not mean an extraordinary profit, oppressive and odious to the borrower. *Non licuisse Israelitis,* say the doctors, *usuras immoderatas exigere ab extraneis, etiam divitibus, res est per se nota.*

Can Moses be considered as the lawgiver of the universe, because he was the lawgiver of the Jews? Were the laws he gave to the people, which God had entrusted to his care, likely to become the general laws of mankind? "Thou shalt not lend upon interest to thy brother." What security had he, that, in the intercourse which would be naturally established between the Jews and foreign nations, these last would renounce customs generally prevailing in trade, and lend to the Jews without requiring any interest? Was he then bound to sacrifice the interest of his people, and to impoverish the Jews to enrich foreign nations? Is it not absolutely absurd to reproach him with having put a restriction on the precept contained in Deuteronomy? What lawgiver but would have considered such a restriction as a natural principle of reciprocity?

How far superior in simplicity, generosity, justice, and humanity is the law of Moses, on this head, to those of the Greeks and of the Romans! Can we find in the history of the ancient Israelites, those scandalous scenes of rebellion excited by the harshness of creditors toward their debtors; those frequent abolitions of debts to prevent the multitude, impoverished by the extortions of lenders, from being driven to despair?

The law of Moses and its interpreters have distinguished, with a praiseworthy humanity, the different uses of borrowed money. Is it to maintain a family? Interest is forbidden. Is it to undertake a commercial speculation, by which the principal is adventured? Interest is allowed, even between Jews. "Lend to the poor," says Moses. Here the tribute of gratitude is the only kind of interest allowed; the satisfaction of obliging is the sole recompense of the conferred benefit. The case is different in regard to capital employed in extensive commerce: there, Moses allows the lender to come in for a share of the profits of the borrower; and as commerce was scarcely known among the Israelites, who were exclusively addicted to agricultural pursuits, and as it was carried on only with strangers, that is with neighboring nations, it was allowed to share its profits with them.

It is in this view of the subject that M. Clermont-Tonnerre made use of these remarkable words in the first National Assembly: "It is said that usury is permitted to the Jews; this assertion is grounded only on a false interpretation of a principle of benevolence and fraternity which forbade them from lending upon interest to one another."

This opinion is also that of Pufendorf and of other writers on the law of nations.

The antagonists of the Jews have laid a great stress on a passage of Maimonides, who seems to represent as a precept the expression *la-nokhri tashikh* (make profit of the stranger). But although Maimonides has presumed to maintain this opinion, it is well known that his sentiments have been most completely refuted by the learned rabbi Abarbanel. We find, besides, in the Talmud that one of the ways to arrive at perfection is to lend without interest to the stranger, even to the idolator. Whatever besides might have been the condescension of God to the Jews, if we may be allowed the expression, it cannot be reasonably supposed that the common father of mankind could, at any time, make usury a precept.

The opinion of Maimonides, which excited all Jewish doctors against him, was principally condemned by the famous rabbis Moses of Gerona and Solomon ibn Adret, upon the grounds, first, that he had relied on the authority of a private sage, whose doctrine has not been sanctioned by the Talmud; for it is a general rule that every rabbinical opinion which is not sanctioned by that work is considered as null and void. Secondly, because, if Maimonides understood that the word *nokhri* (stranger) was applicable to the Canaanite people doomed by God to destruction, he ought not to have confounded a public right, arising from an extraordinary order of God to the Israelites, considered as a nation, with the private right of an individual toward another individual of that same nation.

It is an incontrovertible point, according to the Talmud, that interest, even among Israelites, is lawful in commercial operations, where the lender, running some of the risk of the borrower, becomes a sharer in his profits. This is the opinion of all Jewish doctors.

It is evident that opinions, teeming with absurdities, and contrary to all rules of social morality, although advanced by a rabbi, can no more be imputed to the general doctrine of the Jews than similar notions, if advanced by Catholic theologians, could be attributed to the evangelical doctrine. The same may be said of the general charge made against the Hebrews that they are naturally inclined to usury: it cannot be denied that some of them are to be found, though not so many as is generally supposed, who follow that nefarious traffic condemned by their religion.

But if there are some not overnice in this particular, is it just to accuse one hundred thousand individuals of this vice? Would it not be deemed an injustice to lay the same imputation on all Christians because some of them are guilty of usury?

B. Disequilibrium and the Jewish Response

3. *TORTURED DRIFTING*

The new status created by the French Revolution confronted European Jewry with a combination of exciting possibilities and threatening challenges. Barriers that had once isolated and insulated the Jewish community now began to tumble, leaving numerous Jews exposed to the enticing blandishments of European culture and civilization. Many of these Jews questioned the meaning and relevance of the tradition in which they had been raised. For some, this questioning was rooted in material considerations—was adherence to Judaism really worth the sacrifices that it entailed in their career opportunities? For others, the issue was a deeper one—had the Jewish faith in fact been superseded by nineteenth-century Christianity and the culture it had spawned? The popular symbol of this period of tortured drifting was the Mendelssohn family. Just as Moses Mendelssohn had once served as the paradigm of an enlightened Jew worthy of political rights, so did his children and grandchildren come to represent the headlong flight from Judaism which emancipation engendered in some circles.

A bizarre, but interesting, example of this drifting is provided by the talented and picaresque Polish Jew, Solomon Maimon. Nurtured in traditional surroundings and excelling in Talmudic studies, Maimon wandered out of Poland and into Germany in search of newer and broader knowledge. Like many of his coreligionists, Maimon was deeply impressed with the intellectual advances of the late eighteenth century and increasingly disgruntled with the older attitudes which still held sway in Jewish society. His novel interests left him, like so many others, adrift, at home neither in his former setting nor in the new world opening before him. At one point,

Maimon even considered formally breaking his ties with the Jewish community; however, his frank admission of profound religious skepticism made the Christian clergyman to whom he turned reject his overtures. By the latter years of his life, Maimon's brilliant philosophic writings began to bring him long-denied recognition and fame.

In 1792 Maimon published an amusing and revealing autobiographical portrait. The following selection is reprinted by permission of Schocken Books Inc. from chapters 21–23 of *Solomon Maimon: An Autobiography*, edited and with a Preface by Moses Hadas. Copyright © 1947 by Schocken Books Inc.

Solomon Maimon, *Autobiography*

My return journey to Hamburg was agreeable, but here I fell into circumstances of the deepest distress. I lodged in a miserable house, had nothing to eat, and did not know what to do. I had grown too enlightened to return to Poland, to spend my life in misery without rational occupation or society, and to sink back into the darkness of superstition and ignorance, from which I had hardly delivered myself with so much labor. On the other hand I could not count on success in Germany owing to my ignorance of the language, as well as of the manners and customs of the people, to which I had never yet been able to adapt myself properly. I had learned no particular profession, I had not distinguished myself in any special science, I was not even master of any language in which I could make myself perfectly intelligible. It occurred to me, therefore, that for me there was no alternative left but to embrace the Christian religion and get myself baptized in Hamburg. Accordingly, I resolved to go to the first clergyman I should come upon, and inform him of my resolution, as well as of my motives for it, without hypocrisy, in a truthful and honest fashion. But as I could not express myself well orally, I put my thoughts into writing in German with Hebrew characters, went to a schoolmaster, and got him to copy it in German characters. The purport of my letter was in brief as follows:

"I am a native of Poland, belonging to the Jewish nation, destined by my education and studies to be a rabbi; but in the thickest darkness I have perceived some light. This induced me to search further after light and truth, and to free myself completely from the darkness of superstition and ignorance. To this end, which could not be attained in my native place, I came to Berlin, where by the support of some enlightened men of our nation I studied for some years, not indeed after any plan, but merely to satisfy my thirst for knowledge. But as our nation is unable to make use not only of such planless studies but even of those conducted on the most perfect plan, it cannot be blamed for becoming tired of them, and pronouncing their encouragement to be useless. I have therefore resolved, in order to secure temporal as well as eternal happiness, which depends on the attainment of perfection, and in order to become useful to myself as well as others, to embrace the Christian religion. The Jewish religion, it is true, comes nearer to reason in its articles of faith than Christianity. But in practical use the latter has an advantage over the former; and since morality, which consists not in opinions but in actions, is the aim of all religion in general, clearly the latter comes nearer than the former to this aim. Moreover, I hold the mysteries of the Christian religion for that which they are, that is, allegorical representations of the truths that are most important for man. By this means I make my faith in them harmonize with reason, but I cannot believe them according to their common meaning. I therefore most respectfully beg an answer to the question whether after this confession I am worthy of the Christian religion or not. In the former case, I am ready to carry my proposal into effect; but in the latter, I must give up all claim to a religion which enjoins me to lie, that is, to deliver a confession of faith which contradicts my reason."

The schoolmaster to whom I dictated this was astonished at my audacity; never before had he listened to such a confession of faith. He shook his head in perplexity, interrupted the writing several times, and wondered whether the mere copying was not itself a sin. With great reluctance he copied it out, merely to get rid of the thing. I then went to a prominent clergyman, delivered my letter, and begged for a reply. He read it with great attention, likewise showed astonishment, and on finishing entered into conversation with me.

"So," he said, "I see your intention is to embrace the Christian religion, merely in order to improve your temporal circumstances."

"Excuse me, Herr Pastor," I replied, "I think I have made it clear enough in my letter that my object is the attainment of perfection. For this, it is true, the removal of all hindrances and the improvement of my external circumstances are a prerequisite condition. But this condition is not the chief end."

"But," said the pastor, "do you not feel any inclination of the soul to the Christian religion without reference to any external motives?"

"I should be telling a lie if I were to give you an affirmative answer."

"You are too much of a philosopher," replied the pastor, "to be able to become a Christian. Reason has taken the upper hand with you, and faith must accommodate itself to reason. You hold the mysteries of the Christian religion to be mere fables, and its commands to be mere laws of reason. For the present I cannot be satisfied with your confession of faith. You should therefore pray to God, that He may enlighten you with His grace, and endow you with the spirit of true Christianity; and then come to me again."

"If that is the case," I said, "then I must confess, Herr Pastor, that I am not qualified for Christianity. Whatever light I may receive, I shall always illuminate it with the light of reason. I shall never believe that I have fallen upon new truths if it is impossible to see their connection with the truths already known to me. I must therefore remain what I am, a stiff-necked Jew. My religion enjoins me to *believe* nothing, but to *think* the truth and to *practice* goodness. If I find any hindrance in this from external circumstances, it is not my fault. I do all that lies in my power."

With this I bade the pastor goodbye.

Meanwhile a young man, who had known me in Berlin, heard of my arrival. He called on me to say that Herr W———, who had seen me in Berlin, was now residing in Hamburg, and that I might very properly call upon him. I did so, and Herr W———, who was a very clever, honorable man, of a naturally benevolent disposition, asked me what I intended to do. I represented my whole circumstances to him, and begged for his advice. He said that in his opinion the unfortunate position of my affairs arose from the fact that I had devoted myself with zeal merely to the acquisition of scientific knowledge, but had neglected the study of language and was therefore unable to communicate my knowledge to others or make any use of it. Meanwhile, he thought, nothing had been lost by delay; and if I were still willing to accommodate myself to circumstances, I could attain my object in the gymnasium in Altona, where his son was studying; he himself would provide for my support.

I accepted this offer with many thanks, and went home with a joyful heart. Meanwhile Herr W——— spoke to the professors of the gymnasium, as well as to the principal, but more particularly to the syndic, Herr G———, a man who cannot be sufficiently praised. He represented to them that I was a man of uncommon talents who wanted merely some further knowledge of language to distinguish himself in the world, and who hoped to obtain that knowledge by a short residence in the gymnasium. They acceded to his request. I was matriculated, and had a lodging assigned me in the institution.

Here I lived several years in peace and contentment. But the pupils in such a gymnasium, as may be supposed, make very slow progress; and it was therefore natural that I, who had already made considerable attainments in science, should find the lessons at times somewhat tedious. During the whole period of my residence in the gymnasium the professors were unable to form any correct idea of me, because they never had an opportunity of getting to know me. By the end of the first year I thought I had attained my object of acquiring a good foundation in languages. I had also become tired of the inactive life, and therefore resolved to quit the gymnasium, But Director Dusch, who gradually grew acquainted with me, begged me to stay at least another year, and as I wanted for nothing I consented. . . .

At the end of my second year I began to reflect that it would favor my future success as well as be fair to the gymnasium if I should make myself better known to the professors. Accordingly, I went to Director Dusch, announced to him that I was soon to leave, and told him that as I wished a certificate from him, it would be well for him to examine me on the progress I had made, so that this certificate might correspond to the truth. To this end he had me translate some passages from Latin and English works in prose as well as in verse, and was very well pleased with the translation. Afterward, he entered into conversation with me on some subjects in philosophy, but found me so well versed in these, that he was obliged to retreat for his own safety. At last he asked me, "But how is it with your mathematics?" I begged him to examine me in this also. "In our mathematical lessons," he began, "we had advanced to somewhere about the subject of solids. Will you work out yourself a proposition not yet taken up in the lessons, for example, that about the relation of the cylinder, the sphere, and the cone to one another? You may take some days to do it." I replied that this was unnecessary, and offered to perform the task on the spot. I then demonstrated not only the proposition prescribed, but several others out of Segner's *Geometry*. The director was much surprised, called all the pupils in the gymnasium, and represented to them that the extraordinary progress I had made should make them ashamed of themselves. Most of them did not know what to say to this; but some replied, "Do not suppose, Herr Director, that Maimon made this progress in mathematics here. He has seldom attended the mathematical lessons, and even when he was there he paid no attention." They were going to say more, but the Director commanded silence, and gave me an honorable certificate, which became a constant spur to higher attainments.

I now bade goodbye to the teachers and officers of the gymnasium, who all complimented me by saying I had done honor to their institution. I then set out once more for Berlin.

On my arrival in Berlin I called upon Mendelssohn, as well as other old friends, and asked them, as I had now acquired some knowledge of languages, to employ me in some occupation suited to my capacity. They hit upon the suggestion that, in order to enlighten the Polish Jews still living in darkness, I should prepare in Hebrew, as the only language intelligible to them, some scientific works, which these philanthropists would then print at their own expense, and distribute among the people. This proposal I accepted with alacrity. But now the question arose, with what sort of works should a beginning be made? On this point my excellent friends were divided in their opinions. One thought that the history of the Jewish nation would be most serviceable for the purpose, inasmuch as the people would discover in it the origin of their religious doctrines and of the subsequent corruption which these had undergone. They would also come to understand that the fall of the Jewish state, as well as all the subsequent persecution and oppression which the Jews had suffered, had arisen from their own ignorance and opposition to all rational planning. Accordingly, this gentleman recommended that I translate Basnage's *History of the Jews* from the French. He provided me with the book and asked me to submit a specimen of my translation. The specimen gave satisfaction to them all, even to Mendelssohn, and I was ready to take the work in hand. But one of our friends thought that we ought to begin with something on natural religion and rational morality, inasmuch as this is the object of all enlightenment. Accordingly, he recommended that for this purpose I translate the *Natural Religion* of Reimarus. Mendelssohn withheld his opinion, because he believed that whatever was undertaken in this line, though it would do no harm, would also be of little use. I myself undertook these works, not from any conviction of my own, but at the requests of my friends.

Without fixing a definite plan for my labors, my friends resolved to send me to Dessau, where I could carry on my work at leisure.

I reached Dessau, hoping that after a few days my friends in Berlin would reach some definite decision, but in this I was deceived, for as soon as I turned my back on Berlin, nothing further was done about the plan. I waited about a fortnight, and when I still received no communication, I wrote to Berlin in the following terms: "If my friends cannot unite upon a plan, they might leave the settlement of it to my own judgment. For my part, I believe that to enlighten the Jewish people, we must begin neither with history nor with natural theology and morals. One of my reasons for thinking so is that these subjects, being easily intelligible, are not adapted to instill regard for science in general among the more learned Jews, who are accustomed to respect only those studies which involve a strain upon the highest intellectual powers. But a second reason is that the subjects would frequently conflict with religious prejudices, and so would never be admitted. Besides, properly speaking, there is no history of the Jewish people, for they have scarcely ever stood in political relation with other civilized nations. With the exception of the Old Testament, Josephus, and a few fragments on the persecutions of the Jews in the Middle Ages, nothing is to be found recorded on the subject. I believe, therefore, that it would be best to make a beginning with some science which, besides being most favorable for the development of the mind, is also self-evident, and stands in no connection with any religious opinions. Of this sort are the mathematical sciences; and therefore with this object in view I am willing to write a mathematical textbook in Hebrew."

To this I received the answer that I might follow my plan. Accordingly, I applied myself with all diligence to the preparation of this textbook, using the Latin work on mathematics by Wolff as a basis; and in two months it was finished. I then returned to Berlin to give an account of my work, but immediately received from one of the interested gentlemen the disappointing information that, as the work was very voluminous and would entail heavy expenditure, especially on account of the copperplates required, he could not undertake the publication at his own expense; I might therefore do with my manuscript whatever I chose. I complained to Mendelssohn; and he thought that it was certainly unreasonable to let my work go without remuneration, but that I could not require my friends to undertake the publication of a work which could not be expected to produce effective results in consequence of that aversion to all science which I myself knew to be prevalent among the Jewish people. His advice, therefore, was that I should get the book printed by subscription. With this I must needs content myself. Mendelssohn and the other enlightened Jews in Berlin subscribed. For my pains I received only my manuscript and the list of subscriptions. The whole plan received no further attention.

On this I again fell out with my friends in Berlin. In this dispute Mendelssohn remained neutral, because he thought that both parties had right on their side. He promised to use his influence to induce my friends to provide for my subsistence in some other way. But when even this was not done, I became impatient, and resolved to quit Berlin once more, and go to Breslau. I took with me some letters of introduction, but they were of little service; for before I reached Breslau myself, letters in the spirit of those which Uriah carried had preceded me, and left a bad impression with most of those to whom my letters of introduction were addressed. Naturally, I was coldly received; and as I knew nothing of the later letters, I found it impossible to explain my reception, and had made up my mind to quit Breslau.

Irritated by my disheartening situation, I resolved to form the acquaintance of Christian scholars, by whose recommendation I thought I might find a hearing among the wealthy men of my own people. I could not but fear, however, that my defective language might form an obstacle to the expression of my thoughts; so I prepared a written essay, in which I recorded my ideas on the most important questions of philosophy, in the form of aphorisms. With this essay I went to the celebrated Professor Garve, explained my intention briefly, and submitted my aphorisms for examination. He discussed them with me in a very friendly manner, gave me a good testimonial, and also recommended me orally in very emphatic terms to the wealthy banker, Lipmann Meier. The gentleman settled a monthly allowance on me for my support, and also spoke to some other Jews on the subject.

My situation now improved every day. Many young men of the Jewish people sought my society. Among others, the second son of Herr Aaron Zadig took so much pleasure in my humble personality that he desired to enjoy my instruction in the sciences. This he earnestly begged his father to allow; and the latter, being a well-to-do, enlightened man of great good sense, who wished to give his children the best German education and spared no expense for that object, willingly gave his consent. He sent for me, and made the proposal that I should live at his house, and for a moderate honorarium should give his second son lessons for two hours a day in physics and *belles lettres,* and also a lesson in arithmetic of an hour a day to his third and youngest son. This proposal I accepted with great willingness.

In this house I was able to carry on but little study for myself. In the first place, there was a want of books; and, in the second place, I lived in a room with the children, where they were occupied with other matters every hour of the day. Besides, the liveliness of these young people did not suit my character which had already become somewhat austere; and therefore I often had occasion to be annoyed by petty outbursts of unruliness. Consequently, as I was obliged to pass most of my time in idleness, I sought society. I often visited Herr Heimann Lisse, a plump little man of enlightened mind and cheerful disposition. With him and some other jolly companions, I spent my evenings in talk and jest and play of every sort. During the day I strolled about among the coffee houses.

I soon became acquainted in other families also, particularly in those of Herr Simon, the banker, and Herr Bortenstein, both of whom showed me much kindness. All sought to persuade me to devote myself to medicine, for which I had always entertained a great dislike. But when I saw from my circumstances that it would be difficult for me to find support in any other way, I allowed myself to be persuaded. Professor Garve introduced me to Professor Morgenbesser, and I attended his medical lectures for some time. But after all I could not overcome my dislike for the art, and accordingly gave up the lectures. By and by I became acquainted with other Christian scholars, especially with the late Herr Lieberkühn, who was so justly esteemed on account of his abilities as well as for his warm interest in the welfare of mankind. I also made the acquaintance of some teachers of merit in the Jesuits' College at Breslau.

At last my situation in Breslau also grew precarious. The children of Herr Zadig, in pursuance of the occupations to which they were destined in life, entered into commercial situations, and therefore required teachers no longer. Other means of support also gradually failed. As I was thus obliged to seek subsistence in some other way, I devoted myself to giving lessons. I taught Euler's *Algebra* to a young man, gave two children instruction in the rudiments of German and Latin, and had other pupils. But even this did not last long, and I found myself in a sorrowful plight. . . .

I remained in Breslau for some time; but as my circumstances became worse and worse, I resolved to return to Berlin.

When I came to Berlin, Mendelssohn was no longer alive, and my former friends were determined to know nothing more of me. I did not know what to do. In the greatest distress I received a visit from Herr Bendavid, who told me that he had heard of my unfortunate circumstances, and had collected a small sum of about thirty thalers, which he gave to me. Besides, he introduced me to a Herr Jojard, an enlightened and high-minded man, who received me in a very friendly manner, and made some provision for my support. A certain professor, indeed, tried to do me an ill turn with this worthy man by denouncing me as an atheist; but in spite of this I gradually got on so well, that I was able to hire a lodging in a garret from an old woman.

I had now resolved to study Kant's *Critique of Pure Reason,* of which I had often heard but which I had never yet seen. The method by which I studied this work was quite peculiar. On the first perusal I obtained a vague idea of each section. This I afterward endeavored to make distinct by my own reflection, and thus to penetrate into the author's meaning. Such is properly the process which is called *thinking oneself into a system.* But as I had already mastered the systems of Spinoza, Hume, and Leibnitz in this way, I was naturally led to think of a system that would synthesize them all. This in fact I found, and I gradually put it in writing in the form of explanatory observations on the *Critique of Pure Reason,* just as this system unfolded itself to my mind. Such was the origin of my *Transcendental Philosophy.*

When I had finished this work, I showed it to Marcus Herz. He acknowledged that he was reckoned among the most eminent disciples of Kant and had applied himself assiduously while attending Kant's philosophical lectures, as may indeed by seen from his writings, but that he was not yet in a position to pass judgment on the *Critique* itself or on any word relating to it. He advised me, however, to send my manuscript directly to Kant himself, and submit it to his judgment, and promised to accompany it with a letter to the great philosopher. Accordingly, I wrote to Kant, sending him my work and enclosing the letter from Herz. A good while passed before an answer came. At length Herz received a reply, in which, among other things, Kant said:

"But what were you thinking about, my dear friend, when you sent me a big packet containing the most subtle researches, not only to read through, but to think out thoroughly, while I am still, in my sixty-sixth year, burdened with a vast amount of labor in the completion of my plan! Part of this labor is to finish the last part of the *Critique,* namely, that on the Faculty of Judgment, which is soon to appear; part is to work out my system of the Metaphysic of Nature, as well as the Metaphysic of Ethics, in accordance with the requirements of the *Critique.* Moreover, I am kept incessantly busy with a multitude of letters requiring special explanations on particular points; and in addition to all this, my health is frail. I had already made up my mind to send back the manuscript with an excuse so well justified on all these grounds; but a glance at it soon enabled me to recognize its merits, and showed not only that none of my opponents had understood me and the main problem so well, but that very few could claim so much penetration as Herr Maimon in profound inquiries of this sort. This induced me . . ." and so on.

In another passage of the letter Kant says: "Herr Maimon's work moreover contains so many acute observations that he cannot give it to the public without its producing an impression strongly in his favor." In a letter to myself he said: "Your esteemed request I have endeavored to comply with as far as was possible for me; and if I have not gone the length of passing a judgment on the whole of your treatise, you will gather the reason from my letter to Herr Herz. Certainly it arises from no feeling of disparagement, which I entertain for no earnest effort in rational inquiries that interest mankind, and least of all for such an effort as yours, which, in point of fact, betrays no common talent for the profounder sciences."

It may easily be imagined how important and agreeable to me the approbation of this great thinker must have been, and especially his testimony that I had understood him well. For there are some arrogant Kantians who believe themselves to be sole proprietors of the Critical Philosophy, and therefore dispose of every objection, even though intended not as refutation but as fuller elaboration, by the mere baseless assertion that the author has failed to understand Kant. Now these gentlemen were no longer in a position to bring this charge against my book, inasmuch as, by the testimony of the founder of the Critical Philosophy himself, I have a better right than they to make use of this argument.

I was living in Potsdam at the time with a gentleman who was a leather manufacturer. When Kant's letters arrived, I went to Berlin, and devoted my time to the publication of my *Transcendental Philosophy*.

At this time I also began to work for the *Journal für Aufklärung*. My first article was on *Truth*, and was in the form of a letter to a friend in Berlin. The article was occasioned by a letter which I had received from this friend during my stay in Potsdam. He had written me in a humorous vein that philosophy was no longer a marketable commodity, and that I ought therefore to take advantage of the opportunity which I was enjoying to learn tanning. I replied that philosophy is not a coinage subject to the vicissitudes of the exchange; and this proposition I afterward developed in my article. I also wrote an article on *Bacon and Kant*, in which I instituted a comparison between these two reformers of philosophy.

A number of young Jews from all parts of Germany had united, during Mendelssohn's lifetime, to form a society under the designation, *Society for Research into the Hebrew Language*. They correctly observed that the evil condition of our people, morally as well as politically, has its source in their religious prejudices, in their want of a rational exposition of the Holy Scriptures, and in the arbitrary exposition to which the rabbis are led by their ignorance of the Hebrew language. Accordingly, the object of their society was to remove these deficiencies, to study the Hebrew language at its sources, and by that means to introduce a rational exegesis. For this purpose they resolved to publish a monthly periodical in Hebrew under the title of *Hameassef* ("The Collector"), which was to present expositions of difficult passages in Scripture, Hebrew poems, prose essays, translations from useful works, and the like.

The intention of all this was certainly good; but that the end would scarcely be reached by any such means, I saw from the very beginning. I was too familiar with the principles of the rabbis and their style of thought to believe that such means would bring about any change. The Jewish people is, aside from accidental modifications, a perpetual aristocracy under the appearance of a theocracy. The learned men, who form the nobility, have for many centuries been able to maintain their position as the legislative body with so much authority among the common people that they can do with them whatever they please.

I was therefore neither for nor against this monthly periodical; at times I even contributed Hebrew articles to it. Among these I will mention only one, an exposition of an obscure passage in the commentary of Maimonides on the Mishnah, which I interpreted by the Kantian philosophy. The article was afterward translated into German, and printed in the *Berlinische Monatsschrift.*

Some time afterward I received from this society, which now styles itself the *Society for the Promotion of the Noble and Good,* a commission to write a Hebrew commentary on Maimonides' celebrated work, *Moreh Nebukhim.* This commission I undertook with pleasure, and the work was soon done. So far, however, only a part of the commentary has appeared. The preface to the work may be considered as a brief history of philosophy.

I had been an adherent of all philosophical systems in succession, Peripatetic, Spinozist, Leibnitzian, Kantian, and finally Skeptic; and I was always devoted to that system which for the time I regarded as alone true. At last I observed that all these systems contain something true, and are in certain respects equally useful. But as the differences of philosophical systems depend on the ideas which lie at their foundation in regard to the objects of nature, their properties and modifications, which cannot, like the ideas of mathematics, be defined in the same way by all men and presented *a priori,* I determined to publish for my own use, as well as for the advantage of others, a philosophical dictionary, in which all philosophical ideas should be defined according to a somewhat free method, that is, without attachment to any particular system, but either by an explanation common to all, or by several explanations from the point of view of each. Of this work also only the first part has as yet appeared.

In the popular German monthly already mentioned, the *Berlinische Monatsschrift,* various articles of mine have appeared, on Deceit, on the Power of Foreseeing, on Theodicy, and other subjects. On Empirical Psychology also I contributed various articles, and at last became associated with Herr Karl Philipp Moritz in the editorship of the periodical *Magazin zur Erfahrungsseelenkunde.*

So much with regard to the events which have occurred in my life, and the communication of which, I thought, might be not without use. I have not yet reached the haven of rest; but

Quo nos fata trahunt retrahuntque sequamur.

4. *REFORM JUDAISM*

For many Jews, the struggle for emancipation necessitated internal reform of Jewish life. The Jewish economic posture would have to change; Jewish manners and culture would have to be updated; even Jewish religious life would have to adapt to eighteenth- and nineteenth-century standards. In fact, as emancipation progressed, the need for ritual reform became even more painfully obvious, as a means of stemming the rising tide of conversion and defection.

Israel Jacobson (1768–1828), a rich philanthropist and the so-called founder of Reform Judaism, first introduced ritual reforms at the school ("Jacobsonschule") he founded in Seesen in 1801. By 1808 Jacobson was supervising Westphalian Jewry's consistory system—introduced by Napoleon to organize and control Jewish life—and his religious program included German prayers, German hymns, a sermon in German by Jacobson himself, and quiet, decorous worship. These innovations proved so popular that Jacobson built a "Temple" in Seesen with his own funds, placed an organ inside, and introduced the first modern service in full form. The "Festival of the Jewish Reformation," or dedication of the Temple, was celebrated on

July 17, 1810, and included a German sermon, a choir, congregational singing in German, group prayers in unison, and Israel Jacobson himself in Protestant clerical garb (selection 4a).

By 1819 the first Reform prayer book, edited by Meyer Bresselau and Seckel Fraenkel, was in use in the Hamburg Temple. It was printed from left to right to resemble other German books, included translations at the bottom of the page, and recast the prayers for Jewish national restoration in universal terms so as to suggest a general redemption for all mankind rather than the redemption of Israel alone. These reformers also replaced the traditional prayer for the coming of the messiah by a prayer for an era of justice and brotherhood by translating *go'el* ("redeemer") as "redemption."

The Society of the Friends of Reform (Verein der Reformfreunde), founded by laymen in Frankfurt in November, 1842, published the most radical statement of principles yet proposed. The society's position was affirmed and radically expanded by the founding in 1845 of the Association for the Reform of Judaism (Genossenschaft für Reform in Judenthum) which established a congregation and published a prayer book. The ritual of the association was almost completely in the vernacular, this worship was conducted without head covering, and it was shifted from Saturday to Sunday (selection 4b).

The major pioneer and theoretician of Reform in Germany, Abraham Geiger (1810–1874), published a prayer book in Berlin in 1870. While significantly expanding and clarifying early Reform prayer books, its changes are already presaged in the Bresselau and Fraenkel as well as the Association's prayer book, while the principles which he includes (drawn from an 1869 Denkschrift or memoir) have their heart in the Frankfort statement. They are, however, not only the clearest examples of Reform thought in the latter half of the nineteenth century in Germany, but of enormous importance in their influence upon the principles of American Reform Judaism (selection 4c).

Selections 4a and 4b are taken from W. G. Plaut's *The Rise of Reform Judaism: A Sourcebook of its European Origins* (New York, 1963), and selection 4c comes from Jakob J. Petuchowski's *Prayerbook Reform in Europe* (New York, 1968). Reprinted by permission of the World Union for Progressive Judaism.

4a. Israel Jacobson, "A Dedication Address"

THE DEDICATION CEREMONY

The many hundreds of persons who had been invited came from Brunswick, Kassel, Halberstadt, Göttingen, Goslar, Helmstädt, and all surrounding places. Most of them had arrived in Seesen on the previous day, the sixteenth day of July. Some of them lodged in the ample buildings of the president [Jacobson], and others, for whom there was not enough room, were put up in the inn, and all costs were borne by Mr. Jacobson. In the evening he entertained everyone for dinner.

On the day of the dedication itself, on the seventeenth of July, at 7:00 in the morning, lovely music resounded from the roof of the temple (which was flat like a platform) and announced to the city the approaching festivities. At 8:00, all who had come to participate in the festivities assembled in the school hall of the well-known educational institution which President Jacobson had founded in Seesen. One could see persons of distinguished rank, scholars, Jewish, Protestant, and Catholic clergymen, officials, businessmen of all kinds, all walking together in complete concord, and uniform tolerance seemed to permeate all members of this numerous company. Here friends met, acquaintances and comrades from university days who had not seen each other for a long time and found each other unexpectedly here. The manifold and different groups in this large assembly were most interesting. Everyone found something to talk about.

At 9:00, the ringing of bells announced that the ceremonies would begin. Someone explained in a loud voice how the procession from the hall into the temple would take place and what the celebration itself would consist of. Thereafter, everyone began the solemn processional under the ringing of bells. The procession was led by two flags and by the students of the Jacobson Institute and the teachers. Then followed President Jacobson, the Prefect of the Department of Oker, Mr. Hanneberg, and the clerics and lay members of the Israelite Consistory from Kassel. Then came all the rabbis present, walking in pairs, in their clerical robes, and the Christian clergymen similarly. The mayor of the town and the deputy mayor came in their robes, the Count of Brabeck, public officials of the kingdom who were present, and all the other invited persons appeared in their best clothes. Finally, there came many other people from all classes and all faiths, who had come from the entire surroundings to observe the festivities. In solemn silence the long procession went from the auditorium of the school into the halls, through the doors into the street, and again through the doors of another house, and through this house into the court to the temple. Special admission cards had been printed for this festival in order to preserve order, and they had been distributed amongst all the participants in the procession.

After the procession had entered the temple proper, there came from the organ loft lovely music by sixty to seventy musicians and singers, and this put all hearts into the most solemn mood. After everyone had taken his seat, a cantata composed especially for this celebration by Dr. Heinroth, one of the teachers in the Jacobson Institute, was sung splendidly to the accompaniment of the rousing sound of the instruments.

The Jewish ritual now began, with Mr. Jacobson himself being the chief officiant and the rabbis assisting him. At the end, President Jacobson gave an address, which we print further on in excerpt. After the scrolls of the Torah, which were elaborately ornamented, had been taken from the Ark with great ceremony, they were carried around the temple seven times, preceded by boys with burning wax candles. Then several chapters of the Pentateuch were read, first in Hebrew and at once in German, publicly and with a loud voice. Mr. Schott, director of the educational institution, then mounted the rostrum and talked to the assembled multitude. Then came a chorale accompanied by organ and full orchestra, and this was sung first in Hebrew and then also in German. At the end of this song, in the singing of which the Christians and Israelites participated with deep emotion, Church Counselor Heinemann delivered an address befitting the occasion. After this address there were further songs by the choir.

The Temple was richly and tastefully illuminated. Its architectural beauty, its decorations and guilded pieces visible on all sides to the eye, the graceful columns and antique chandeliers, the flower garlands which hung everywhere, the colorful mixture of people, all this presented a most beautiful and interesting view. At the end of the service, President Jacobson elaborately entertained a table of two hundred in the school auditorium, in adjoining rooms for his seventy musicians, and in other rooms for an additional one hundred persons. The students of the Institute ate in the open, in the courtyard.

The festivities were original and unique. Where would one have seen a similar day on which Jews and Christians celebrated together in a common service in the presence of more than forty clergymen of both religions, and then sat down to eat and rejoice together in intimate company?

THE DEDICATION ADDRESS

It has been left to the tolerance of our days to bring about and to make possible that which only a little while ago would have appeared impossible. In building this edifice, it has not been my intent to bring about a complete religious unification of all religions. One accomplishes nothing at all if one desires everything or too much at one time. What is needed is gradual and slow development as is demonstrated by nature itself, when it brings forth its greater spiritual and physical accomplishments. Any divergence from this wise procedure of our common mother Nature which human stubbornness or frivolity might suggest, would only be followed by failures or even by the very opposite of that which was desired. What I had in mind when I first thought about building this temple was *your* religious education, my Israelite brothers, *your* customs, *your* worship, etc. Be it far from me that I should have any secret intention to undermine the pillars of your faith, to diminish our old and honored principles through the glitter of new opinions, or that, because of some hidden vanity, I should become a traitor to both our religion and you. You know my faithful adherence to the faith of my fathers. I need not protest it. My actions will witness for me more than my words. But if I do seek here first some rapprochement between you and our Christian neighbors, I would ask more for your gratitude and honest help than for your criticism or even opposition. For your true and progressive enlightenment depends upon this rapprochement. On it depends the education of your spirit for true religiosity and, at the same time also, your future greater political welfare. Who would dare to deny that our service is sickly because of many useless things, that in part it has degenerated into a thoughtless recitation of prayers and formulae, that it kills devotion more than encourages it, and that it limits our religious principles to that fund of knowledge which for centuries has remained in our treasure houses without increase and without ennoblement. On all sides, enlightenment opens up new areas for development. Why should we alone remain behind?

Let us be honest, my brothers. Our ritual is still weighted down with religious customs which must be rightfully offensive to reason as well as to our Christian friends. It desecrates the holiness of our religion and dishonors the reasonable man to place too great a value upon such customs; and on the other hand, he is greatly honored if he can increasingly encourage himself and his friends to realize their dispensability. Our ecclesiastical office, the Israelite Consistory, is willing to help us, is greatly concerned with the improvement of our synagogues and schools, spreads more correct principles abroad, and will, without partisanship, do the best for us even if at the moment we cannot see the flowers or fruits of these efforts.

And you, my highly honored other friends, who in name and in some aspects are different from my faith, I hope I have the full agreement of your sympathetic hearts in the principles I have set forth of the intent of this temple building, and of the hope for a happier future for my compatriots. There is nothing in this intent that in any way contradicts the principles of pure religion, of the demands of general morality, of reason, or of your own humanitarian attitude. I turst, therefore, that you will be far from receiving my brothers coldly. I trust that you will not reject them, as did your forebears only too often, but rather, that you will solicitously stretch out your hand to us in that rapprochement which I have sketched in its ideological outline, and for the sake of which partially I have dedicated this temple. Accept, therefore, my deepest and most devoted thanks for your warm interest in this rare celebration which you have so obviously manifested for me and my friends through your precious presence and through the expression of your sentiments.

And Thou, O God, whose mighty hand has lifted up our people once again after such long debasement, just as it happened once after a long imprisonment; Thou, O God, whose goodness has made it possible to complete the work of several years and bring it to a happy ending—grant unto us further, we pray, that we might sense the glorious traces of Thy love, of Thy benevolence, of Thy protection, both in the faith of our compatriots as in the results of this temple building. But with this confidence let us not be guilty of the indolence of delay, of the embarrassment of indecisiveness, of the mystical hope of the superstitious, and merely hope for Thine assistance. May we, conscious of our dignity, never forget *man,* the high destiny of a being whom Thou hast gifted with reason and freedom, that he might think for himself, act for himself, and whom Thou didst destine not to be a soulless machine in the plan of Thy creation. Let us never despair of the good cause of religion and mankind. Let us not lose heart when new obstacles will be thrust across our path, when we find that any beginning, like the uplifting and enlightenment of a dispersed people, can proceed but slowly and with many difficulties, and can mature only after centuries. Above all, O God, make us vividly conscious that we are brothers with all the adherents of other divine teachings; that we are descendants of one humanity which adores Thee as their common Father; that we are brothers who must learn love and gentle tolerance; brothers, finally, who under Thy guidance walk toward a common goal and who, in the end, when the mist will have been dispelled from before our eyes and all the errors gone from our spirit and all doubts removed from our reason, will meet each other on one and the same road. Amen.

4b. The Association for the Reform of Judaism

PROCLAMATION OF THE ASSOCIATION

Our inner faith, the religion of our hearts, is no longer in harmony with the external forms of Judaism. We want a positive religion; we want Judaism. We hold fast to the spirit of Holy Writ, which we acknowledge as a witness of divine revelation. We hold fast to everything by which God is truly honored in ways rooted in the spirit of our religion. We hold fast to the conviction that Judaism's teaching of God is eternally true; we hold fast to the promise that this teaching will someday become the possession of all mankind. But we want to understand the Sacred Scriptures according to the letter. We can no longer pray honestly for a Messianic kingdom on earth which shall bring us back to the homeland of our forefathers, pretending that we would return to it from a strange land—the very fatherland to which we are tied with all the bonds of love! We can no longer recognize a code as an unchangeable lawbook which maintains with unbending insistence that Judaism's task is expressed by forms which originated in a time which is forever past and which will never return. We who are deeply committed to the sacred content of our religion cannot hope to sustain it in its inherited form, and even less can we hope to hand it on to our descendants. Thus, placed between the graves of our fathers and the cradles of our children, we are stirred by the trumpet sound of our time. It calls us to be the last of a great inheritance in its old form, and at the same time, the first who, with unswerving courage and bound together as brothers in word and deed, shall lay the cornerstone of a new edifice for us and for the generations to come.

FROM THE INTRODUCTION TO THE BERLIN PRAYER BOOK

As we present a revised edition of our prayer book to the members of our association, we deem it to be our duty to sketch briefly the principal points of view on which this revision is based.

The Chosen People

To start with, the way and manner in which the chosenness and priestly vocation of Israel were expressed in our public prayers until now, seemed to require a thorough reform which would be adequate to our religious convictions. The chosenness of Israel as a holy priest-people and as God's own possession appears in our Holy Scriptures as a firmly established historic fact. But on closer examination, this has validity only as a *subjective* fact in the religious consciousness of the Jewish people. To a certain degree, the Jewish people had a full right to consider itself God's chosen people with whom God had entered into an intimate convenant, and whom He had distinguished with a call to priestly service. This was the degree in which it felt itself more enlightened and morally more developed than all pagan nations. It believed itself to be in the exclusive possession of a purified idea of God and of a moral life task to be holy even as God is holy, and thus truly closer to God and more intimately bound to Him than all other pagan peoples. In this sense we still consider it to be true that Israel *was* a chosen people, and that this well-founded conviction of its chosenness worked for the salvation and enlightenment of mankind. But as an *objective* fact, with all its important consequences for our religion, this chosenness has lost its validity. The concept of tribal holiness and of a special vocation arising from this has become entirely foreign to us, as has the idea of an intimate covenant between God and Israel which is to remain significant for all eternity. Human character and dignity, and God's image within us—these alone are for us signs of chosenness. We consider man as chosen and closer to God as he exemplifies these gifts and witnesses to them through virtue and righteousness. In such a sense we may occasionally mention Israel's choice in our prayers, in order to urge ourselves on to noble humanity and true brotherly love, and thus to distinguish ourselves, not as a people, but as human beings and as a congregation who stand together in their devotion to a worthy life.

Revelation

Closely connected with this concept of Israel's choice and holiness is the idea of revelation, which in our prayers has received a formulation which in every way reflects our religious convictions. Revelation to us is the divine illumination of the spirit of our fathers which does not exceed the natural limits of human ability and which is, therefore, capable of continued development. Consequently, when our sacred texts speak of a revelation which many of our fathers received in the course of supernatural events, we can only consider such texts, in accordance with our religious convictions, as a living expression of *subjective* faith. This feeling, filled with the power of inner truth, invested our fathers with a sense of blessing, but as for us, we must deny its objective factuality. Our ancestors and all of Jewish antiquity were thoroughly convinced that God, of whose holy being and will they had the noblest conception, had illumined their spirit and had revealed to them the highest truths. They felt this so deeply that they could speak of the act of revelation only with a living sense of *immediacy*. To the degree that this conviction had living reality for them, this sense of immediacy was heightened greatly. According to the extensive description in the Holy Scriptures, the Decalogue was revealed at Sinai with the greatest solemnity. This is testimony for us that our forefathers had, as we have, a sense of the infinitely higher importance of these cornerstones of all moral knowledge, when compared to all other laws and ordinances. The Ten Commandments are not more important and holy because they were revealed with greater solemnity; the reverse is true: they were revealed with greater solemnity because they are in themselves more important and holy for the human spirit. The divinely illumined human spirit is and remains the last source of judgment to decide which revelation is of greater or smaller importance.

Our Heritage

The congruence of our feelings and knowledge with that of our most ancient ancestors forms the spiritual bond and historic connection between them and us. This allows us to view and revere the heritage they bequeathed us as *the inheritance of our fathers,* and to call the universal God, the Father of all men, whom our ancestors knew and loved (and whom to know and love they taught us), "God of our Fathers," "Shield of Abraham," "Saviour of Jacob." Hence our prayers quote whole passages from the Bible in which our ancestors' faith in an immediate, apparently supernatural revelation is expressed vividly and with great force. But these citations are given a place only because the warm vital thrust of our fathers' conviction can thus retain its influence on our sense of worshipfulness; there is no yielding in this of any religious conviction on our part. However, such poetry must not sully the purity and clarity of our religious consciousness, lest a grievous contradiction accompany us from the synagogue out into life itself and spoil for our sobered spirit what poetry gained for our warmly aroused sentiment.

Old and New Prayers

What we have said applies to the old prayers as well as to those which have been reshaped to resemble their old examples. Everywhere the national and dogmatically narrow aspects must give way to the living flow of purely human, truly religious thoughts. For a noble, truthful, pious soul, the thought of the Father of all mankind is more stirring than that of a God of Israel. The image of God, imprinted upon every human being as a covenant-sign of divine love, has more poetry than the chosenness of Israel. The general love of neighbor and brother, deeply imbedded in every man, has more attraction than a particular ceremonial law. The universal human bond sanctifies more than does an exclusive pact between Jehovah and his firstborn son Israel. All these ideas were deeply rooted in the subjectivity of the Jewish people and had their great historic importance for the development of the human race. For the preacher they provide a treasure of religious thoughts and truths as well as suggestive homilies, but they must not confuse and confound the simple sensibilities of the worshiper. Rather, prayer should be like a clear, transparent mirror of the sea in which the sentiment of the worshiper can reflect itself. Man lives primarily in the present, and its mode of thought and expression are most familiar to him. What is presented to him out of the past should facilitate and not obscure his understanding of the present.

As concerns newly created prayers, they all belong to the religious spirit of the present, to which Judaism owes its reawakening and its revitalization. They belong to the genius of the modern era which has regenerated and rebuilt Judaism from the ground up. Our sense of belonging to this faith is one of pride and joy, for Judaism has passed through the process of purification and has retained its sustaining power despite all the destructive battles which were waged against it from various sides, by the forces of stagnation as well as those of *negation.* This is perhaps a fitting place to say frankly that Judaism hides within its bosom a treasure of ideas and sentiments which has not yet been unlocked, for it is enclosed in forms and symbols which must be completely abandoned so that those deeply hidden ideas and sentiments may rise again in their primal force. Some think that it is these symbols and forms which one must trustingly preserve, so that in practicing them one may acquire the hidden kernel. It is precisely the position of Reform that one must indeed value the kernel in its full worth, but can gain access to it only through shucking the husk. The symbols and forms and the whole history of Judaism must serve as a lamp so that, by its light eternal, ideas may be distinguished from ephemeral forms. Only those forms will be granted a relative religious value which are suitable for the exposition of an idea and for the awakening of sentiment. The diligent reader of these prayers to whom the reforming movements of the last decades are familiar, will find that in this fine book the greatest achievements in this area, the high ideals and sentiments, are brought together, which, in the purifying struggle on the battlefield of science, have proved themselves as the ideals and sentiments of the genuine Jewish spirit. We call special attention to those prayers which contain thoughts of the holiness of God and man, the priestly vocation of Israel, the purified Messianic idea, and others.

May this prayer book, its contents refined, continue to awaken and maintain the spirit of true religiosity in our congregation and our whole community of coreligionists. We remain bound to them in spirit and in love. May it be witness to the purity of our striving.

Berlin, October, 1848

THE COMMITTEE OF EDITORS
In behalf of the Representatives of the
Association for the Reform of Judaism

PASSOVER PRAYER

Reader: Our God and God of our fathers! Thou hast chosen Israel from among all nations, hast graced us with Thy love, hast sanctified us by Thy Commandments, and hast dedicated us to Thy service and called us to carry Thy name through the whole earth.

Thou hast given us the Feast of Passover so that, filled with joyous gratitude, we should remember the mercy which Thou didst show to our fathers. Thou didst take from their shoulders the hard yoke of Egypt's slavery and didst lead them from servitude to freedom and knowledge. But to us Thou gavest this festival so that we might increasingly share in this freedom, which is ours because of our fathers; that we might unswervingly hold fast to the teachings of eternal truth which Thou didst proclaim for them and for all coming generations.

Lord, we thank Thee for the freedom which Thou hast given to our fathers and to us. But with our gratitude, let there also arise to Thee our fervent supplication for the welfare of our distant brethren who are still oppressed by persecutions, as they were centuries ago; who, abandoned to hatred and despotism, cry out in their bitter oppression. O Father of Mankind, let the sun of Thy love illumine and warm the hearts of those who still nourish hatred and contempt against their brothers of different faiths; who believe that they serve Thee, Almighty Father, when they threaten those with ruination who pray to Thee in a manner different from theirs. Make strong the faith and confidence of our persecuted brethren; uphold them in their certainty that Thou canst never be far from those who look to Thee and hold fast to Thy pure law.

But into the heart of the free man plant Thou obedience to Thy will; let him hearken to the teachings of virtue which Thou didst write into his heart and which Thou didst proclaim to us in Thy revelation. Make us firm in our reverence to these teachings, and keep us from the delusion that through license we can honor the right to inner freedom. Help us to be worthy sons of freedom, so that we may use it for Thy glory, for the sake of our fatherland, and for our own welfare.

Choir: Praise the Lord, all ye nations,
Praise Him, all ye peoples,
For His mercy and truth
Endure forever.
Halleluyah!

4c. Abraham Geiger, "Preface to the Frankfurt Prayerbook"

The prayerbook appearing herewith hardly needs to be commended and introduced to the public for which it is meant. The liturgical question has already for years occupied one of the foremost positions in the consideration of the task of adapting the historical form of Judaism to the demands of the present. It is unlikely to lose this favored position for a long time to come. The worship service is the bond which binds the congregation. It is meant to be the expression of religious conviction, as alive in the individual as in the group. It must not deny the connection with the totality of the historical past; yet it must, at the same time, nourish the religious needs of the present. The demands made upon a prayerbook for our time are, therefore, so manifold, and proceed from such divergent points of view, that the publication of a prayerbook which could satisfy *all congregations* simply cannot be undertaken. The divergences between the various congregations, corresponding to the divergent needs felt within them, will not cease for a long time yet. Perhaps the colorful multiplicity may even increase for a while. But this must not lead us astray; and it must not fill us with the fear of a split. Gradually, the mutual coming together will again take place. In some congregations the questions reach the level of consciousness later than in others. Still, their time comes, too. And the arrangements of congregations which have progressed earlier then serve as an example for their own improvements. Once the necessity for the one or the other improvement has come to the fore, the need for further reforms will soon be felt, and general unanimity will increasingly come about.

Those are looks into the future. For the immediate present, the prayerbook which we offer here does not claim to meet all the demands. However, it does make its appearance in the confident hope that is will offer guidance to those congregations in which there is an awareness of the task of the present, guidance as to how the newly awakened needs can be satisfied.

The prayerbook has not been modeled according to the theory of an individual. It has its roots in history, and in the expressed invitations of large congregations. It is, therefore, primarily offered to the latter. But, as a new edition of a liturgical arrangement which for sixteen years has already been at home in, and beloved by, many circles, it could also expect the satisfaction of old, and the winning of new, friends.

For many years already, the lack of a well-arranged prayerbook, particularly for New Year and the Day of Atonement, had been felt by the congregation of Frankfurt on the Main. Finally, the decision was reached to add this part to the prayerbook for Sabbath and festivals, printed in 1860. An agreement about the manner of execution was reached when men of knowledge and zeal on the board of the congregation themselves seriously undertook to represent this idea. The commission of experts, appointed for this purpose, soon convinced itself that a *complete* work would have to be produced. The daily service and domestic devotions must not be missing. And the services for Sabbath and festivals were also in need of a more convenient arrangement and of a uniform revision. Thus the commission's deliberations were spread over the entire field. Out of the thorough discussions of the commission, there emerged a plan which, according to well-considered guiding principles, showed the necessary respect for the existing practice, removed the contradiction between it and the newly prevailing views, and gave expression to the true religious feelings. The principles were then formulated. They were combined in a memoir, and were approved by the administration already in June, 1869, as was the plan of the new prayerbook based upon them, in October of the same year.

To the Worthy Authorities of the Congregation I herewith submit the extensive plan, worked out in twenty-three sessions of the commission, appointed by you, for the composition of a new prayerbook.

The principles which guided the commission in its conclusions, and which the commission applied with conscientious care to the consideration and determination of every single point, are adequately apparent in an examination of the submitted plan. However, it would considerably facilitate and shorten the deliberations if, at the request of the commission, I were briefly to set forth those principles here.

1. The prayerbook, by and large, should retain its customary character. It should continue to express in a precise form its connection with the whole history of Judaism. Consequently, in its essential components, the worship service remains in Hebrew. The traditional Hebrew expression, though here and there not free from a certain Oriental extravagance, is, on the whole, to remain untouched.

2. Nevertheless, particularly on the distinguished days, the service must contain a few *German* prayers and meditations. Furthermore, the Hebrew text must be accompanied by a *German adaptation.* This must not, in rigid fear, force a Hebrew coloration upon the language of our fatherland. Rather should it, with all preservation of the original fervor, appeal to the soul through its accustomed sound.

3. Special care must be taken that the *duration* of the service be reduced to that degree which facilitates an uninterrupted devotion. Therefore, unnecessary repetitions as well as unessential prayers and those without content must be omitted. Even the heaping up of valuable prayers must be avoided. Rather must their impressiveness be heightened by rotation and by their distribution over various occasions.

4. With all respectful retention of Judaism's historical elements, religious *concepts* which have had a temporal validity, but which have been displaced by *a progressively purer conception,* must not be retained in a one-sided and sharp accentuation. Rather must they be either totally removed or recast into a form which does not contradict the purer conception.

5. Consequently,

(i) *Highly materialistic descriptions of the Deity,* as they occur in the *piyutim,* must be removed;

(ii) The enumeration of the various *angelic* orders and the depiction of their activity cannot be admitted;

(iii) The belief in immortality must not content itself with the one-sided formulation of a *physical resurrection.* It must, instead, be expressed in a manner which also includes the concept of spiritual continuity.

6. Concerning, in particular, *the position of Israel in world history,* this must be strongly articulated in the following direction: Judaism is the religion of truth and of light. Israel received his task, and continues to be the bearer and herald of this doctrine. To this is related his confidence that this doctrine will progressively become the common possession of the entire educated world, thereby enlarging Israel to include all of mankind. Forms of expression which tend to narrow or obscure this lofty thought are unsuitable.

7. Consequently, the *national aspect* of Israel must recede into the background:

(i) The *separation* between Israel and the other peoples, which existed at one time, has no right to be expressed in prayer. Rather ought there to be an expression of the joy that such barriers are increasingly falling.

(ii) The exalted feeling of a noble spiritual vocation must avoid any appearance of *overbearance,* and must shun any side glances at *"other peoples."*

(iii) The look into the future should arouse the happy hope in the *unification of all mankind,* in truth, in justice, and in peace. However, wholly faded from our consciousness is the belief in the *restoration of a Jewish State in Palestine,* and, correspondingly, in the *building of a temple* in Jerusalem to serve as the point of unification for Israel. The same applies to the belief in the *Ingathering of the Dispersed* and to everything connected with such a restoration of vanished circumstances. The expression of such a hope in prayer, the petition for its realization, would be a blatant untruth.

8. Similarly, that conception, which envisages our worship service as again becoming a *sacrificial service,* is irreconcilable with the whole progress of the times.

Even if it be assumed that, in ancient times, sacrifice was an adequate expression of the adoration of God, sacrifice has long since made way for a more spiritual worship service, and its reintroduction is unthinkable.

Passages which only remotely remind us of ancient human sacrifice, regarded as an abomination by the Judaism of all periods, must be totally removed from the prayerbook.

But *animal sacrifices,* too, no longer have a right to be represented as a desired institution of the future. Just as little *does the memory of them, of the way in which, at one time, they were offered,* contain the least element of religious edification. Of this, too, the prayerbook must remain free.

On the execution of those essential principles, the commission bases the proposals which it has submitted. The commission is convinced that the prayerbook, presented in this form, will, at one and the same time, not be bereft of the suggestions of past tradition, and yet also do justice to the needs of the present.

Most respectfully submitted to the worthy authorities of the congregation,

Dr. Abraham Geiger, Rabbi

Frankfurt on the Main, June 8, 1869

Just as there was agreement among the members of the commission, and approval on the part of the administration of the congregation, concerning the guiding principles and the plan based upon them, so, too, have the most important German prayers (which are to be recited aloud, and which are considered as part of the public worship service) been determined in common consultations. However, I bear sole responsibility for the German prayers which are recited silently, as well as for the translations, the domestic devotions, and the occasional prayers. Essentially, they follow the edition of the Breslau prayerbook of sixteen years ago. But, in view of the experience gained during that time span, they have frequently been formulated with greater precision and in a more appropriate form. In this connection, the *Collection of Prayers and Psalms for Israelites,* published in 1847, by Auerbach and Jost, has been particularly useful; and some complete passages have been taken from there almost verbatim.

The congregation of Frankfurt is important enough to issue its own prayerbook, which is in accord with the views prevalent in its midst. But it may hope, in view of the influence which it exerts, and in view of the homogeneous character which many of the intelligent congregations of South-West Germany share with it, that the liturgical arrangement which it has introduced will also find admission elsewhere.

The prayerbook offers itself no less to the Eastern congregations of our fatherland—particularly in view of the fact that, in essence, it proceeds from the same principles which, sixteen years ago, guided the edition of the Breslau prayerbook. The latter is now out of print. With the attachment which it found in Breslau, and with the positive reception and adoption which it found in many other congregations, the need for a new edition was daily felt to be more urgent. After the plan of this new edition had been made public, many congregations in Germany as well as in America voiced their desire to introduce the new prayerbook after its appearance. In order to facilitate this wider distribution, still another aspect had to be taken into consideration.

The divergences between the so-called *German* rite, prevailing in the South West, and the *Polish* rite, prevailing in the East of our fatherland, do not, indeed, rest upon any difference of principles. There would be no inherent objection to a compromise between them. However, in the historical evolution of the Jewish worship service, several passages have remained foreign to the German rite, passages which, in the Polish rite, have achieved a standing of respect, having endeared themselves to those accustomed to the Polish rite. The congregations following the German rite would regard it as just as unfounded to be asked to adopt those passages as the congregations following the Polish rite would consider it unjustified to be deprived of those old components, against which there could be no well-founded objection. To give a single example, the German rite does not know of a Memorial Service on the last days of the great festivals, whereas the Polish rite regards this service as a deeply felt need of the heart. For the Day of Atonement, the German rite, at best, has introduced this service after the Musaph prayers, whereas, in the Polish rite, it precedes the Musaph service. Particularly in the case of the High Holy Days, New Year and the Day of Atonement, the soulful character of which has also been carried over into the excellent prayers customary on those days, there are many divergences between the rites, and a mutual accommodation would be beset by many peculiar difficulties. That is why it seemed in order, as far as the first part of the prayerbook is concerned, to label some passages as belonging solely to the German rite, and others as exclusive components of the Polish rite. But it also seemed in order to publish the second part, containing the services for New Year and the Day of Atonement, in two entirely separate editions. In this way, each of the two rites retained its fundamental character to the extent to which it could be reconciled with the guiding principles.

Thus may this prayerbook begin its journey into the congregations and into the homes with the happy confidence that it will not lack divine blessing. May it be granted the ability to contribute its share to the exaltation of devotion in our synagogues, in order that true piety be aroused and revived in Israel among both young and old!

Geiger

Berlin, July 25, 1870

5. *WISSENSCHAFT DES JUDENTHUMS*

Wissenschaft des Judenthums, or the Science of Judaism, was a movement which emerged in the early nineteenth century. The challenge of majority culture and signs of German Jewish disaffection caused a small but talented group of scholars to reinvestigate the nature of the Jewish past. Led by a circle of gifted researchers, Wissenschaft burst into Berlin (Eduard Gans, 1798–1839, and Leopold Zunz, 1794–1886), Galicia (Nachman Krochmal, 1785–1840), France (Salomon Munk, 1803–1867), Italy (Samuel David Luzzatto, 1800–1865), and other centers of Jewry. A confluence of philological, historical, and philosophic investigations of Jews and Judaism produced the movement, and it was raised to a scholarly discipline by Zunz's *Liturgic Addresses of the Jews (Die gottesdienstlichen Vorträge der Juden, historisch entwickelt)* in 1832—the first important product of the application of academic criteria to the study of Jewish history within the Wissenschaft group. Written to prove that the sermon had historical justification within Judaism, Zunz's work was utilized, as was much of the Wissenschaft output, to buttress the position of Reform Judaism. Indeed, much of the Wissenschaft historical research only encouraged every shade of Reform to assert its continuity with the past.

Born in Frankfurt on the Main in 1810, Abraham Geiger (d. 1874) attended the universities of Heidelberg and Bonn, was ordained, and in 1840 (after a long and bitter struggle) was elected a rabbi in the large community of Breslau. An innovator in liturgy and practice, Geiger was one of many Jewish scholars in Germany motivated to undertake a wide number of Jewish historical studies. He produced important studies in biblical philology, medieval Hebrew poetry, rabbinic literature, Jewish historiography, and contemporary theology, founded two scholarly journals, and provided —through a synthesis of Hegelian philosophy and Jewish history—the most important philosophical grounding for the practical activities of German Reform Judaism. Geiger was particularly representative of the Science of Judaism in his determination to describe the historic course of Judaism through its achievements, ideas, and personalities.

Abraham Geiger, A *General Introduction to the Science of Judaism*

(Lectures delivered by Geiger at the Academy for the Science of Judaism, Berlin, 1872–1874)

PREFACE

The introduction to the Science of Judaism which is to be given here aims at bringing about a full understanding of the religious thought and ideal content which pervades Judaism and which dwells within it as its unique life-giving force. The only method by which such understanding can be acquired is the study of the manner in which the idea first entered into the physical world, of the way in which it has found expression in language and literature and in which it has manifested itself in practice in the course of history. Only when the spiritual motive behind Judaism has thus been traced inductively will it be possible for us to gain a true conception of its full content and its philosophical and religio-ethical tenets. It is true that they will then be isolated from the time-bound forms in which they have been expressed at various periods, but they will still bear within themselves vital forces which have not yet achieved their full development. The Science of Judaism may thus be divided into three aspects:

1. Philological
2. Historical, particularly as regards the history of Jewish literature and culture
3. Philosophical and religious

To begin with, there will be some who will count against Judaism the fact that it has a philological aspect at all, which is supposed to be no less important than its history, and who will view this as proof of its narrowness. There will be those who will compare Judaism with Christianity. They will point out that, while Christianity has exerted some influence on the development, or rather on the style, of language, it did not make its appearance in a language of its own, but in Greek which was then the idiom of world culture. The fact that, soon thereafter, Christianity came to employ Latin, the tongue of the Romans who held sway over the civilized world, will be taken as an indication of the universal nature of this faith. On closer examination, however, one will find that what seemed an advantage for Christianity is actually a shortcoming and that what first appeared to be a weakness of Judaism is actually one of its strong points.

A new idea can originate only in a strong personality. It is only by a strong individual that a universally acceptable idea can be conceived. It will then mature into consummate expression only in one who is especially qualified and endowed for this purpose by his active participation in the general natural tendencies of mankind. Wherever a superior form of development of the universal human type is in evidence it will manifest itself in superior, distinctive individuality. In such persons the idea which can embrace all of mankind will shine forth in the form of a conviction that pervades all of that person's life; the idea will carry with it the demand that everyone else allow himself to be imbued with it to the same extent and also the awareness that this demand is possible of fulfillment especially here. This conviction will dominate such an individual. Moreover, while the conviction will, on the one hand, constitute the whole essence of the individual, his personality, sharp and distinct as it is, will, on the other hand, impress the seal of its subjective nature on the idea. It is impossible to separate the two influences from one another.

If this is true with regard to one individual, it must certainly be even more so in the case of a whole nation. It is only in a nation with special potentialities that science, art, and religion will manifest themselves in a refined form. Just because they are so completely dominated by the idea, the people, its views, and its language will also impress their full individual character upon the thoughts and creations which are supposed to represent that which is universally human. Only a people which has a healthy vitality and which constitutes a closed entity will be able to produce ideas that are viable, comprehensive, and of abiding value. These ideas will, of necessity, bear the imprint of the definite and unique physiognomy of that people. This physiognomy is the vessel that will contain the idea and will of necessity limit its manifestations. It will detract nothing, however, from the general validity of its contents. Thus the idea must come to the fore in full individual definiteness and in accordance with the language and concepts of the people with whom it originated; indeed, it must come forth as the particular expression of that people. Only later may it become transfigured into a greater spirituality, as it becomes independent of the soil in which it first matured. If it is not to fall victim to that curse which adheres to every unhealthy outgrowth of romanticism, it must not be the product of vague and hazy perceptions. Thus, we will not cast aspersions on the universal value of ancient Greek art just because its themes were derived from mythology and its characters bear Greek features. True, the artist of today no longer carves idols, nor does he mold his figures in terms of Greek beauty, but the fact remains that the idea of art was fully realized by the ancient Greeks and this will be understood by everyone who is receptive to it.

The strength of Judaism lies precisely in the fact that it has grown out of a full national life and that it possesses both a language and a history as a nation. The idea of Judaism was an all-embracing one. Hence, if it was not to be a drifting shadow, it had to find expression in a healthy national individualism which, on the one hand, saw all of mankind epitomized within itself, but, on the other hand, sought to embrace all the world of mankind beyond its own confines. Thus it is a strong point of Judaism that it originally revealed itself in a language which was entirely imbued with the idea and which was the noblest fruit of a full national life. Judaism was not, however, dependent upon language and nationality; indeed, it survived in all its vitality even after being deprived of both. When its vessel was smashed, its survival was not affected thereby. Because it always had to engage in violent struggle,

Judaism remained a closed and separate entity; and yet it has succeeded in transmitting its basic ideals to mankind as a universal heritage. And when the artificial barriers fall, it will continue to retain its universality throughout the course of history. Let us, therefore, look back with joy on our former life as a nation, as being an essential transitional era in our history, and on our language, through which the life of that Jewish nation had taken root in spiritual soil!

Christianity put in its very first appearance as a universalist faith; but precisely in this lack of a national origin and individual language lies its weakness. Its concepts and sentiments are characterized by great vagueness; they conflict with every definite national trait. They are mere phantoms which deny all real life. Dreams of a disembodied existence, they widen the chasm between body and soul and view the destruction of all things physical as the greatest attainable bliss. Christianity arose under the influence of the disintegration of noble civilizations, the Jewish and the Greek; it was garbed in decaying languages; it had the seeds of morbidity implanted in it, as it were—a morbid state under which it labors to this day. Christianity is the true mother of mysticism and romanticism. Judaism, on the other hand, is lucid, concrete, vital, and affirmative. Judaism is permeated with spirituality; it does not deny the earthy world, but transfigures it instead. It is rooted in one particular people with a language and history of its own, and yet it embraces all of mankind.

. . . The Science of Judaism is the study of the particular orientation of the spiritual life through which, within one particular sphere, Judaism was founded, developed, broadcast, and preserved in full vigor down to our time. Our interest in this spiritual force grows as we perceive that it did not operate within narrow limits and far away from the world of reality. On the contrary, its spiritual power has manifested itself almost at all times in the very midst of the mightiest spiritual movements in world history, at the very focal points of important cultural developments. It was, in fact, receptive to stimuli emanating from the centers of culture, so that it never shut them out; but it was not absorbed by them. It succeeded rather in assimilating them to its own manner, thus giving evidence of its independent vitality. This evidence is corroborated even more effectively by the telling influence which the spirit of Judaism has continuously exerted on human progress as a whole and which—as its vitality permits us to hope—it will continue to exercise in the future. At three important crossroads in world history, Judaism had an important part in guiding the development of spiritual and intellectual life. At the close of the era of antiquity, Judaism gave birth to

Christianity; during the Middle Ages, it brought Islam to life and nourished it with its essential content; and at the opening of the modern era, it provided the intellectual background for Spinoza and thus the first momentum for a complete revolution in the theories of philosophy. These worldwide forces did not continue to have an effect on Judaism, but the spirit of Judaism continued to be manifest within them. It is significant, too, that Judaism survived and took root in those countries which long before had produced the first fruits of civilization: Egypt, Phoenicia, Syria, Assyria and Babylonia. Judaism maintained the closest possible ties with these countries and thus certainly was in no position to ward off their intellectual influences. Nevertheless, Judaism remained independent of them. True, at a later date, it was exposed to the influences of Parsism which it assimilated in a fashion which was its very own; subsequently, it united with Hellenism to give birth to Alexandrianism; and, eventually, it developed its own fullest potential in closest union with Arab civilization. It was in this manner that Judaism made its contribution to the cultural movement and communicated to medieval Christianity the intellectual heritage of antiquity which it had rescued from oblivion in the Arab era. Hence the hope is quite justified that the time may not be distant when Judaism will once more impregnate and so transform the world of ideas, and at the same time independently assimilate the variety of outside cultural elements to which it is exposed.

Through this highly effective activity on the part of Judaism, both in giving and in receiving, the content as well as the scope of its "science" has develop into a mighty system. . . . All of the individual parts thereof constitute member organisms of one great whole. None of these may be ignored; by the same token, no one such element may be emphasized at the expense of the others. The sole task of the specialists, therefore, is to analyze the individual facets and then to relate them to the whole.

Even as any vital and viable idea falls into a threefold organic division of its own, so this entire wealth of material, too, may be separated into three major categories.

The idea became manifest in the physical world with all the vigor and freshness of youthful strength; however, it remained confined inside the framework of the time and the space within which it was born. In naïve elation at its victory it overlooked the limitations inherent in it, and, as it soared upward, it bore with it upon its wings the dust of the earthly conditions under which it had first come into being. . . . Its eyes were trained upon the Utopian heights from which it felt called upon to envelop all things below, and yet it found itself compelled to go on existing within the narrow bounds of limited lowlands. It had the ability creatively to reflect a perfect image, and yet it remained so deeply rooted in its native soil that it could not detach itself from it.

Thus Judaism became firmly consolidated. Next, it sought to penetrate all outside conditions, to transform them. But, instead, it was itself modified and influenced by the very conditions which it had sought to affect. The further it reached out, the more one-sided it became; it dissipated its strength and lost its intensity. The spiritual wealth which it gained was not always genuine, and the idea which inspired it grew superficial and was eventually spent, dissipated.

And then it attained the third phase. At this point it pulled itself together and reverted to its former intrinsic character; but with the difference that now it was changed by a wealth of experiences and acquisitions which it then purified and transfigured.

. . . Language is the articulation of the national idea; history is the idea in action. Language is more vital and more immediate than history; like a garment, it covers the whole spirit at one time. However, its first outpouring is connected with a definite stage of the people's development. Thereafter it will at best no longer be the expression of the spirit but only its handy tool; in most instances it declines and becomes petrified. History is different. History does not reflect the spirit completely and all at once; it is dependent also on many factors which lie outside the spirit of the nation to which it belongs. But it is precisely by means of struggle, by development, by conflict, and by victory or defeat that the strength or the impotence of the spirit is revealed. Particularly in the case of Judaism, we find that history revealing an inexhaustible wealth of possibilities for the unfolding and molding of spiritual and intellectual life.

It is self-evident that history, as an essential component of the Science of Judaism, can only be a study of the history of spiritual achievements. The outer facets of its history have value only as substrata, as conditions under which achievements could come into being and which either hindered or furthered the growth of such achievements. It should be remembered, however, that it is inherent in the very nature of the Jews that their history should primarily be a spiritual one and, as such, a process that helped shape the entire world, and that it should not be expressed either in civic policy or primarily in political or communal life. The Jews remain in a state of inner division which in turn gives rise to inner struggle and feats of spiritual heroism. Such, in fact, is the fate of all highly gifted peoples. The empire of the ancient Greeks fell, after their short-lived world supremacy, their unity having been forged by the Macedonians, the most primitive tribe in their midst. As for the Italians, who are now in the process of being welded into one united nation by the crude Piedmontese, they have yet to prove whether, as a united nation with a capital in Rome, they will be able to regain that historical significance which we must admit they had attained during the Middle Ages. It was not despite their own inner division, but, in fact, just because of it, that the Germans were able to give birth to the greatest discoveries, . . . to the free spirit of the Reformation and to the glory of a literature of worldwide import. It is our wish that the new united Reich, led by its imperial dynasty, may be able to record similar achievements. Such, too, has been the history of Judaism, and it is precisely to its independence from political status that Judaism owes its survival. Anything that enters into the life of a nation as a sudden thing, instead of as a tender sapling, gradually growing into a strong plant, is no longer history. Judaism, on the other hand, has sprouted into full bloom from the tenderest of seedlings; with this fact it demonstrates that it has a genuine history.

. . . As part of the Science of Judaism, a study of its history will, of course, remain subject to all those laws which history recognizes as science. Scientific, critical study must not be hindered by dogmatic assumptions. Judaism has no cause to fear an unbiased critical examination.

. . . The history of Judaism is wonderfully unique in that it spans a period extending from remote antiquity down to the immediate present. It is therefore not mere curiosity which acts as a spur to its study, not merely the desire to eavesdrop on the mystery of the origins of Judaism, but at least equally the desire to detect the extent to which all of its later development was essentially already inherent in the growth and flowering process of the original seeds. These beginnings are hidden, modestly and shamefacedly, in dim obscurity; the scholar, however, cannot avoid this difficulty, but must remain dependent upon these prehistorical phenomena. Without the revelation which only such study of the ancient history of Judaism, even though the results may be mere approximations, affords, he can never succeed in gaining the proper insight into Judaism's subsequent history which lies more fully recorded before him.

The history of Judaism may be divided into four periods.

The first period is that of *Revelation,* of vigorous creation, unfettered and unhindered. It was an era of free, creative formation from within. This period extends to the close of the biblical era, which cannot be said to have ended at the time of Exile, for its outgrowths continued well beyond that date.

The second period is the era during which all this biblical material was processed, shaped, and molded for life; it was then that Judaism took root in the spiritual heritage of the past and at the same time still maintained a certain degree of freedom in its approach to that heritage. This was the period of *Tradition,* which extended from the time of the completion of the Bible to the completion of the Babylonian Talmud.

The third period is characterized by toilsome preoccupation with the heritage as it then stood. The spiritual heritage was guarded and preserved, but no one felt authorized to reconstruct it or to develop it further. No one dared go beyond the limits set long before. This was the period of rigid *Legalism,* of casuistry, the era which was devoted to the summing up of what had been handed down by tradition. It extended from the time of the completion of the Babylonian Talmud down into the middle of the eighteenth century.

The fourth period, the era of liberation, has been marked by an effort to loosen the fetters of the previous era by means of the use of reason and historical research. However, the bond with the past has not been severed. What is being attempted is solely to revitalize Judaism and to cause the stream of history to flow forth once again. This is the era of *Critical Study,* our own modern era.

THE PERIOD OF REVELATION

. . . Corresponding to the outwardly discernible course of history there is also an inner, spiritual history, namely, that of religious development. As a consequence of the growth of a sharply defined national consciousness . . . which tended more and more to work for segregation and for the exclusion of all foreign admixtures, the Deity which this nation worshiped also had to assume a unique position. This of course did not necessarily exclude the recognition of other national deities; it was thought that the god Khemosh had the same relationship to the nation under his rule as Yahweh had to the people of Israel. But the other deities were regarded only as alien gods, as hostile beings which would be overcome by the God of Israel. The concept of God did not immediately take shape as a pure ideal of one God for the entire universe, a Supreme Being who could neither be pictured nor perceived by the physical senses. Nevertheless, this idea of a God superior to all other gods already bore within itself the seeds of a more mature concept toward which it then evolved, slowly but inevitably.

We have hardly any records to supply us with information concerning that time when the Reubenites first settled in the territory east of the river Jordan. In all likelihood their religious views differed little from those of the neighboring tribes. Nor do we have any definite records of the time of the first settlements in the territory west of the Jordan. The mode of divine worship there was still harsh and cruel—crude, in keeping with the character of these tribes—but it clearly tended to weld them into one single unit. Gradually, certain places, particularly Beersheba, gained prominence as exclusive sites for the worship of God. We must assume that in those days such practices as human sacrifice and the worship of wells and trees were the custom; the worship of God, however, sought to entrench itself in a form clearly separated from the religious rites of alien tribes, though without attaining complete purity just yet. Here, too, we have no reliable historical records to serve us as an introduction to the thinking that prevailed in the midst of those tribes.

In all likelihood it was only with the immigration of additional tribes, such as those of Manasseh and Ephraim, who came west from Egypt through the land east of the Jordan River, that the religious picture took on a purer form; this change may well have come to pass even prior to their movement to the west. From then on a milder character, the product of a higher civilization, came to permeate the religious views of this region. Although it still survived for some time, the practice of human sacrifice as part of the official religious ritual was now opposed, and the primitive practice of offering one's children, and one's sons in particular, to the Deity was replaced by the milder custom of circumcision. The precise extent to which the influence of Egyptian civilization made its weight felt here and in other similar instances is difficult to determine. . . .

Men like Elijah and Elisha, whose personalities, though enveloped in a veil of pious legend, still rate high above those of their peers, whose excesses of sensuality were the vogue in their day, were stern in their determined fight against tyranny and lack of principle. But even greater were those prophets, such as Hosea, Amos, and others, who did not stand out by virtue of miraculous acts but who had a powerful effect upon the spirit of the people by their high ideals of religion and ethics. The priestly class, too, a numerous and powerful body in Israel, was affected by this progressive process of purification. Now there came about a wonderful amalgamation of the old and the new into a single whole. The ceremonial of priesthood and sacrifices now stood side by side with religious requirements of great refinement and purity. The feeling of revulsion at any other mode of worship went hand in hand with the retention of institutions originally derived from alien cultures. These institutions were now Israelized, as it were, and were themselves rendered holy thereby. . . .

The entire body of strictly historical narrative came into being at a later date, during the era of the kingdom of Judea which saw nothing but apostasy and impious idol worship in the neighboring kingdom of Israel. Next to the prophets of the kingdom of Israel, the earlier components of the first four books of the Pentateuch are the only sources that can provide us with a faithful reflection of the thinking which prevailed then in the northern kingdom. There all of ancient history becomes a mirror of the present. From the very outset, Ephraim is given a place of prominence, without, however, detracting in any manner from the historic significance of Judah. Both the migration to Egypt and the Exodus thence are recorded here as events involving the entire nation. Whatever statutes and institutions had been in force at the time of the writing of this literature were ascribed to a lawgiver who had lived in days of antiquity. This lawgiver, however, was in turn assisted by a priestly caste which was almost equal to him, and at times even above him in rank. With this in mind, it should not come as a surprise to us that sacrifices and the priesthood should still have taken up so much space in this important portion of Hebraic literature.

Judah's development was much more gradual; but in the long run it had greater permanence. More and more, there evolved a discipline in which the existence of one officially recognized Temple only and of a continuous dynasty of rulers forced the priesthood into a secondary position. This in turn gave rise to the evolution of simpler customs, that slowly gained in purity and refinement as time went by. It was only after the fall of the kingdom of Israel in the north that Judah developed a literature of its own, though this literature was then all the more magnificent in its maturity. Personalities like Isaiah, Micah, Jeremiah, and others showed a clarity of thought and boldness of prophetic vision such as had never been given expression in the kingdom of Israel. Here we find a noble kind of nationalism which, though it emphasized the doctrine of the Chosen People, was deeply rooted in a higher mission and in the calling of that People to translate this mission into living reality. It is here that the concept of One Sole Invisible God, who cannot be represented by a physical image, acquires a stronger conviction and a more definite expression.

. . . Eventually, the whole Jewish concept of history and of religious life and law had to adapt itself to the views that prevailed in the kingdom of Judah. Along with the original literary creations which were completely pervaded by this spirit, the traditions and ritual practices already in existence had to undergo a transformation in keeping with the new spirit which now gained the upper hand. The entire historical account, particularly that of the divided state, underwent a thorough revision, in keeping with changed conditions. The history of the northern kingdom of Israel now was represented as that of a state which had no right to exist and was torn asunder by eternal dissension because it had rejected its rightful Ruler and the one true faith. Only a very few true accounts of this era may have found their way into the historical books of the Bible as they now stand; and even there they are immured within the framework of the new interpretation. Some such ancient components have been preserved from the pre-Davidic era and from that of David and Solomon; but these are surrounded by accretions and changes from which the original accounts are yet to be clearly distinguished. . . .

THE PERIOD OF TRADITION

The spirit of the nation, with its intuitive genius, forged steadily ahead and created new things, out of its own resources, in ever-increasing perfection until it reached its zenith. Then everything came to a standstill: now its primary concern became, not to create new things, but to preserve the acquired heritage, to collect it, sift it, supplement it, and adapt it for every conceivable situation in life, an effort which might entail complete change in one instance, and the ferreting out and confirmation of the smallest and pettiest details in another. In the history of any nation, this could be an era of great significance, in which ideal concepts receive their full embodiment and thus firmly establish the life of that nation upon a bedrock of ideals. Just the same, the original creative force will be missed, and in instances in which the times by their very nature make growth and development a pressing necessity, that development will appear to be narrowly confined . . . manifesting itself in superficial breadth rather than in the dimension of inner depth. This will be particularly true when circumstances from without do not permit spiritual progress and when, in fact, pressure from without and lack of free self-determination have an unfavorable effect on the spirit. Such was the situation of the Jews under Persian rule.

At that time, the people could lead a marginal existence at best. No impetus toward regeneration emanated from the Persian empire which, after the advent to power of Cyrus, had fallen prey itself to the spiritual indolence typical of great empires of Asia. . . . Though the book of Esther may contain little material of actual historical value, it does serve as evidence of the things that the people recalled most clearly of the rule of Persia; their situation was precarious, dependent on transient moods and caprice, and the spirit atrophied. The language in which this book is written and the attitude which it reflects match one another. Given such conditions it was inevitable that Judea, though it did not entirely fade away, should suffer from a state of creeping paralysis.

The situation changed, however, when Greek civilization attained world supremacy. It is true, of course, that by that time Greece, too, had passed its zenith. Macedonia, which then occupied the position of political leadership, was the least cultured part of Greece. Moreover, this vast expansion of the new empire, of necessity, caused the spirit of its civilization to become superficial and to degenerate. . . .

After the fall of the empire of Alexander it was Egypt, strongly Hellenized, that exercised the most powerful influence upon the Jews. A great number of them lived there; these Jews were completely assimilated into the Egyptian state; but they maintained the closest of ties with Judea, both nationally and religiously speaking. . . . Alexandria had become a haven for the Jews who had been immigrating there for centuries from the wasted and impoverished land of Judea. Here and in other places, there came into being great Jewish communities whose language, education, and ideology were a mixture of those of Greece and Egypt. . . . It was only in their religion that they remained in close touch with their native land, with Jerusalem, its center, and with the Holy Temple there. Hence these Jewish communities serve as the first example of a religion outgrowing the confines of territory and nationality. Quite the same is true of the Greco-Jewish colonies which existed during the era of the Second Jewish Commonwealth. Thus we see that this phenomenon, to which Christianity has proudly pointed as proof of its spiritual might transcending all national boundaries, had been manifest in Judaism at least three centuries prior to the birth of the Christian faith.

EVALUATION OF THE TALMUD

Intellectual life at the academies of Palestine was characterized by dull languor. The Jerusalem Gemara is bare, meager, and sober, though not lacking in legendary superstition. But the reliable references and reports about antiquity which it has preserved for us are of great historic value. . . .

The Babylonian Gemara, by contrast, is bubbling over with life; in the academies of Babylonia the scholars plunged into their new studies with youthful avidity, though at times with a passion which overreached the goals that had been set. Its statutes and interpretations were accepted as sacred, and though they changed a good deal in both language and content during their progress through time and space, no one dared question them. For this reason the reports and traditions contained in it are much less reliable [than those in the Jerusalem text] and must therefore be studied with critical caution. A legalistic methodology with hair-splitting casuistry now gained the upper hand. . . .

It is not known how and when the Jerusalem Gemara was completed. The fact is that it was not concluded at all; it stopped abruptly as a result of the gradual decline of the academies in Palestine, probably as early as the fourth century. The Babylonian Talmud was not concluded until the end of the fifth century. In this way everything was rigidly fixed and flexibility came to an end. For the past fourteen centuries the Talmud has had Judaism within its tight clasp and still does so, no matter how frequently modern scientific study might have tried to uproot it, nor will it lose its dominance until we ourselves have entirely outgrown the Middle Ages.

This much is sure: The Talmud is not by any means identical with the Science of Judaism, nor does it contain that Science, either basically or specifically. The Talmud is, however, an important historical document, spanning an era of approximately seven centuries, which gives a clear idea of both the evolution of Judaism and the factors inhibiting its growth. It contains, for example, a good deal that is important for a full understanding of the Bible and of its history. But the Talmud must be examined only by the light of critical study, for we are dealing here with reports which, in part, have adopted foreign components even in the process of oral transmission and, in part, have moved in the course of time into an entirely different perspective. This is an extensive task for critical study, but it is a rewarding one. Halakah, both old and new, Mishnah, and reinterpretation in the Gemara are developments within a narrow sphere. Of more basic significance than any of these is the contrast between Pharisaism and Sadducism. The equality (to which the Pharisees aspired) has deprived us of our freedom in this respect, and our longing for the restoration of the old state of affairs has almost robbed us of our liberty in theory as well. . . .

THE PERIOD OF RIGID LEGALISM (FROM THE SIXTH CENTURY TO THE MIDDLE OF THE EIGHTEENTH CENTURY)

It is interesting to note that the era of inner legalistic rigidity in Jewish Law was, at the same time, a period of lively interest and participation on the part of the Jews in general culture. It is quite true that the motives for intellectual activity did not originate from within; nor was intellectual energy free and able to work on its own heritage and to transform it. However, it was determined all the more to seize upon problems of a more general nature and sought to penetrate them in response to even the slightest stimulus in that direction.

Indeed, with the standstill in the development of the Babylonian Talmud, an era of rigidity had set in. The Babylonian Talmud had not reached a natural conclusion, but had come to an abrupt ending by a cutting of the thread, as it were, by persecution and by the decline of the great academies in Persia. The cause of this petrification lay not in any total exhaustion of Judaism's vital energy. Proof for this is in the intellectual life of the world. But petrification may set in also when natural development is impeded by obstacles from without, or when the inner motivations that formerly engendered it have come to an end. For either of these makes it impossible to forge a new link in the chain of vital evolution. Tradition then continues to exist as binding, but it no longer possesses full intrinsic justification. This is exactly what happened in Judaism. Oppression weighed heavily upon it and hindered free study and inquiry. The motivations which had obtained in the older days, namely, the internal conflicts within the nation and the attainment of priestly consecration for the group as a whole, were no longer present. The statutes which had resulted from them now remained as mere time-honored customs which had to find support from tradition and interpretation and were viewed as inviolable. That which in earlier days had been a means to an end had now become an end in itself. There was nothing that could be done against statutes and interpretations which were posited as divinely handed-down tradition. Of course, some opposition to the untenable nature of such tortuous interpretation gradually stirred, but it could not make any real headway.

Perhaps, had circumstances permitted continued and undisturbed evolution, the awareness of this artificiality might have become stronger and made for change. But paralysis of thought, brought about by the force of unfavorable circumstances, did not permit such a development. Thus tradition had to remain, and it became more and more inflexible and rigid as the years went on. . . .

C. The New Anti-Semitism

6. IDEOLOGICAL SPOKESMEN

All through the nineteenth century, European society was wracked by the convulsions of rapid change. The liberal ideals of the French Revolution were seen by some as the beginning of a glorious new epoch in human history and by others as a disaster of unprecedented proportions. By the 1870s, the benefits extended to European Jewry were being challenged in some quarters. Voices began to attack the granting of political and social rights to the Jews and to question the Jewish response to these rights. It was suggested that the Jews, despite their newfound equality, had remained clannishly separate and had continued to live by disreputable economic practices; alternatively it was argued that the Jews had assimilated too fully and formed the vanguard of the corrosive forces disintegrating traditional European civilization (i.e., liberalism, finance capitalism, revolutionary socialism).

One of the most influential spokesmen for these anti-Jewish views was the respected German politician and historian, Heinrich von Treitschke (1834–1896). In 1879 Treitschke published in the *Preussische Jahrbucher* a deliberately provocative essay on the Jews. He began with the simple assumption that the popular anti-Jewish agitation had to be seen as symptomatic of a profound concern with the Jews. "Are these outbreaks of a deep, long-suppressed anger really only a momentary outburst, as hollow and irrational as the Teutonic anti-Semitism of 1819? No—the instinct of the masses has in fact clearly recognized a great danger, a serious sore spot of the new German national life." The remainder of the essay is then devoted to an analysis of the problemmatic aspects of German-Jewish life. Treitschke's study was widely read and debated; because of the author's prestige, it could not be ignored or dismissed. Key intellectuals, Jewish and non-Jewish alike, challenged Treitschke's contentions. Obviously anti-Semitism had become a meaningful issue on the political and cultural scene.

Not all the antipathy toward the Jews was channeled into the relatively dispassionate and rational arguments of academicians. There was a vigorous and irrational hate literature developing as well. The most well known of these late-nineteenth-century tracts is the alleged *Protocols of the Meetings of the Learned Elders of Zion.* Purporting to represent the minutes of the gatherings of an international Jewish conspiracy, this repeatedly exposed forgery reflects the rampant fears of worldwide Jewish links, of Jewish economic success, of Jewish political liberalism, of Jewish intellectual and cultural influence. Often disregarded as a silly fraud, the *Protocols* have been translated into a number of languages and have done untold harm.

The Treitschke selection is taken from "A Word about Our Jewry," translated by Helen Lederer, edited by Ellis Rivkin. Copyright 1958 by the Hebrew Union College Press. Reprinted with permission of the Hebrew Union College. The excerpts from the *Protocols* are reprinted from Herman Bernstein, *The Truth about "The Protocols of Zion"* (New York, 1935), an elaborate unmasking of the literary sources of the forgery.

6a. Heinrich von Treitschke, "A Word about Our Jewry"

Among the symptoms of a great change in mood in the German nation, none appears so strange as the violent movement against the Jews. Until a few months ago, the notorious "reverse Hep-Hep call" was still dominant in Germany. About the national shortcomings of the Germans, the French, and all other nations everybody could freely say the worst things; but if somebody dared to speak in just and moderate terms about some undeniable weakness of the Jewish character, he was immediately branded as a barbarian and a religious persecutor by nearly all of the newspapers. Today we have already come to the point where the majority of the Breslau voters —obviously not in wild excitement but with quiet deliberation—conspired not to elect a Jew to the diet under any circumstances. Anti-Semitic societies are formed, the "Jewish Question" is discussed in noisy meetings, a flood of anti-Semitic pamphlets appears on the market. There is only too much of dirt and brutality in these doings, and it is impossible to suppress one's disgust when one notices that some of these incendiary pamphlets obviously come from Jewish pens. It is well known that since Pfefferkorn and Eisenmenger there were always many former Jews among the most fanatical Jew-baiters. But is there really nothing but mob brutality and business envy at the bottom of this noisy activity? Are these outbreaks of a deep, long-suppressed anger really only a momentary outburst, as hollow and irrational as the Teutonic anti-Semitism of 1819? No—the instinct of the masses has in fact clearly recognized a great danger, a serious sore spot of the new German national life; the current word "the German Jewish question" is more than an empty phrase.

If the English and the French talk with some disdain of the prejudice of the Germans against the Jews we must reply to them: "You don't know us; you live in happier circumstances which make the rise of such 'prejudices' impossible." The number of Jews in Western Europe is so small that they cannot have any noticeable influence upon the morality of the nation. But our country is invaded year after year by multitudes of assiduous pant-selling youths from the inexhaustible cradle of Poland, whose children and grandchildren are to be the future rulers of Germany's exchanges and Germany's press. This immigration grows visibly in numbers and the question becomes more and more serious how this alien nation can be assimilated. The Jews of the Western and Southern European countries belong mostly to the Spanish branch which looks back on a comparatively proud history and which always adjusted comparatively easily to the Western way of life. In fact, the great majority of them have become good Frenchmen, Englishmen, Italians, as far as can be expected from a people of such pure blood and such distinct peculiarity. We Germans, however, have to deal with Jews of the Polish branch, which bears the deep scars of centuries of Christian tyranny. According to experience they are incomparably more alien to the European, and especially to the German national character.

What we have to demand from our Jewish fellow citizens is simple: that they become Germans, regard themselves simply and justly as Germans, without prejudice to their faith and their old sacred past which all of us hold in reverence; for we do not want an era of German-Jewish mixed culture to follow after thousands of years of German civilization. It would be a sin to forget that a great number of Jews, baptized and unbaptized, Felix Mendelssohn, Veit, Riesser, and others, not to mention the ones now living, were

Germans in the best sense of the word, men in whom we revere the noble and fine traits of the German spirit. At the same time it cannot be denied that there are numerous and powerful groups among our Jews who definitely do not have the goodwill to become simply Germans. It is painful enough to talk about these things. Even conciliatory words are easily misunderstood here. I think, however, some of my Jewish friends will admit, with deep regret, that recently a dangerous spirit of arrogance has arisen in Jewish circles and that the influence of Jewry upon our national life, which in former times was often beneficial, has recently often been harmful. I refer the reader to *The History of the Jews* by Graetz. What a fanatical fury against the "arch-enemy" Christianity, what deadly hatred just of the purest and most powerful exponents of German character, from Luther to Goethe and Fichte! And what hollow, offensive self-glorification! Here it is proved with continuous satirical invective that the nation of Kant was really educated to humanity by the Jews only, that the language of Lessing and Goethe became sensitive to beauty, spirit, and wit only through Börne and Heine! Is there any English Jew who would dare to slander in such manner the land which guards and protects him? And this stubborn contempt for the German goyim is not at all the attitude of a single fanatic. There is no German city which does not count many honest, respectable Jewish firms among its merchants. But it cannot be denied that the Jews have contributed their part to the promoting business with its dishonesty and bold cupidity, that they share heavily in the guilt for the contemptible materialism of our age which regards every kind of work only as business and threatens to suffocate the old simple pride and joy the German felt in his work. In many thousands of German villages we have the Jewish usurer. Among the leading names of art and science there are not many Jews. The greater is the number of Semitic hustlers among the third-rank talents. And how firmly this bunch of litterateurs hangs together! How safely this insurance company for immortality works, based on the tested principle of mutuality, so that every Jewish poetaster receives his one-day fame, dealt out by the newspapers immediately and in cash, without delayed interest.

The greatest danger, however, is the unjust influence of the Jews in the press—a fateful consequence of our old narrow-minded laws which kept the Jews out of most learned professions. For ten years public opinion in many German cities was "made" mostly by Jewish pens. It was a misfortune for the Liberals, and one of the reasons of the decline of the party, that their papers gave too much scope to the Jews. The present weakness of the press is the necessary reaction against this unnatural state of things. The little man is firmly convinced now that the Jews write everything in the newspapers and he will not believe anything they say any longer. Our newspapers owe much to the Jewish talent. The acuteness and nimble quickness of the Jewish mind found the arena of the press always a congenial field. But here, too, the effect was two-edged. Börne was the first to introduce into our journalism the peculiar shameless way of talking about the fatherland offhand and without any reverence, like an outsider, as if mockery of Germany did not cut deeply into the heart of every individual German. To this was added that unfortunate busybody "me-too" attitude, which has to have a hand in everything and does not even refrain from passing judgment on the inner affairs of the Christian churches. What Jewish journalists write in mockery and satirical remarks against Christianity is downright revolting, and such blasphemies are offered to our people as the newest acquisitions of "German" enlightenment! The moment emancipation was gained the Jews insisted boldly on their "certificate," demanded literal parity in everything, forgetful of the fact that we Germans are, after all, a Christian nation and the Jews are only a minority. It has happened that the removal of Christian pictures was demanded, and even the celebration of the Sabbath in mixed schools.

If we consider all this—and much more could be added—then the noisy agitation of the moment appears only as a brutal and spiteful but natural reaction of the Germanic national consciousness against an alien element which has usurped too much space in our life. It has at least the one involuntary merit of having liberated us from the ban of a tacit falsehood. It is already a gain that an evil which everybody sensed but which nobody wanted to touch is now discussed openly. Let us not deceive ourselves: The movement is deep and strong. A few jokes about the words of wisdom from the mouths of Christian-Socialist soapbox orators will not be sufficient to suppress it. Even in the best-educated circles, among men who would reject with horror any thought of Christian fanaticism or national arrogance, we hear today the cry, as from one mouth, "The Jews are our misfortune!"

There can be no talk among the intelligent of an abolition or even a limitation of the Emancipation. That would be an open injustice, a betrayal of the fine traditions of our state, and would accentuate rather than mitigate the national contrasts. What made the Jews of France and England harmless and often beneficent members of society was at the bottom nothing but the energy of the national pride and the firmly rooted national way of life of these two nations which look back on centuries of national culture. Ours is a young nation. Our country still lacks national style, instinctive pride, a firmly developed individuality; that is the reason why we were defenseless against alien manners for so long. But we are in the process of acquiring these qualities, and we can only wish that our Jews recognize in time the change which is now occurring in Germany as a necessary consequence of the foundation of the German state. In some places there are Jewish societies against usury which silently do much good. They are the work of intelligent Israelites who have recognized that their fellow Jews must adjust to the customs and ideas of their Christian fellow citizens. Much remains to be done in this direction. It is not possible to change the hard German heads into Jewish heads. The only way out therefore is for our Jewish fellow citizens to make up their minds without reservations to be Germans, as many of them have done already long ago, to their advantage and ours. There will never be a complete solution. There has always been an abyss between Europeans and Semites, since the time when Tacitus complained about the *odium generis humani.* There will always be Jews who are nothing else but German-speaking Orientals. There will also always be a specifically Jewish education; and, as a cosmopolitan power, it has a historical right to existence. But the contrast can be mitigated if the Jews, who talk so much about tolerance, become truly tolerant themselves and show some respect for the faith, the customs, and the feelings of the German people which has long ago atoned for old injustice and given them human and civil rights. The lack of such respect in many of our Jewish fellow citizens in commerce and literature is the basic reason for the passionate anger in our days.

It is not a pleasant sight, this raging and quarreling, this boiling up of unfinished ideas in our new Germany. But we cannot help our being the most passionate of all nations, although we called ourselves phlegmatics so often. New ideas never broke through in our country other than under bad convulsions. May God grant that we come out of the ferment and unrest of these exciting years with a stricter concept of the state and its obligations and with a more vigorous national consciousness.

6b. *The Protocols of the Elders of Zion*

PROTOCOL NO. 1

. . . Putting aside fine phrases we shall speak of the significance of each thought: by comparisons and deductions we shall throw light upon surrounding facts.

What I am about to set forth, then, is our system from the two points of view, that of ourselves and that of the goyim (i.e., non-Jews).

It must be noted that men with bad instincts are more in number than the good, and therefore the best results in governing them are attained by violence and terrorization, and not by academic discussions. Every man aims at power, everyone would like to become a dictator if only he could, and rare indeed are the men who would not be willing to sacrifice the welfare of all for the sake of securing their own welfare.

What has restrained the beasts of prey who are called men? What has served for their guidance hitherto?

In the beginnings of the structure of society they were subjected to brutal and blind force; afterward—to Law, which is the same force, only disguised. I draw the conclusion that by the law of nature right lies in force.

Political freedom is an idea but not a fact. This idea one must know how to apply whenever it appears necessary with this bait of an idea to attract the masses of the people to one's party for the purpose of crushing another who is in authority. This task is rendered easier if the opponent has himself been infected with the idea of freedom, *so-called liberalism,* and, for the sake of an idea, is willing to yield some of his power. It is precisely here that the triumph of our theory appears: the slackened reins of government are immediately, by the law of life, caught up and gathered together by a new hand, because the blind might of the nation cannot for one single day exist without guidance, and the new authority merely fits into the place of the old already weakened by liberalism.

In our day the power which has replaced that of the rulers who were liberal is the power of Gold. Time was when Faith ruled. The idea of freedom is impossible of realization because no one knows how to use it with moderation. It is enough to hand over a people to self-government for a certain length of time for that people to be turned into a disorganized mob. From that moment on we get internecine strife which soon develops into battles between classes, in the midst of which states burn down and their importance is reduced to that of a heap of ashes.

Whether a state exhausts itself in its own convulsions, whether its internal discord brings it under the power of external foes—in any case it can be accounted irretrievably lost: *it is in our power.* The despotism of capital, which is entirely in our hands, reaches out to it a straw that the state, willy-nilly, must take hold of: if not—it goes to the bottom.

Should anyone of a liberal mind say that such reflections as the above are immoral I would put the following questions: If every state has two foes and if in regard to the external foe it is allowed and not considered immoral to use every manner and art of conflict, as for example to keep the enemy in ignorance of plans of attack and defense, to attack him by night or in superior numbers, then in what way can the same means in regard to a worse foe, the destroyer of the structure of society and the commonweal, be called immoral and not permissible?

Is it possible for any sound logical mind to hope with any success to guide crowds by the aid of reasonable counsels and arguments, when any objection or contradiction, senseless though it may be, can be made and when such objection may find more favor with the people, whose powers of reasoning are superficial? Men in masses and the man of the masses, being guided solely by petty passions, paltry beliefs, customs, traditions, and sentimental theorism, fall a prey to party dissension, which hinders any kind of agreement even on the basis of a perfectly reasonable argument. Every resolution of a crowd depends upon a chance or packed majority, which, in its ignorance of political secrets, puts forth some ridiculous resolution that lays in the administration a seed of anarchy.

The political has nothing in common with the moral. The ruler who is governed by the moral is not a skilled politician, and is therefore unstable on his throne. He who wishes to rule must have recourse both to cunning and to make-believe. Great national qualities, like frankness and honesty, are vices in politics, for they bring down rulers from their thrones more effectively and more certainly than the most powerful enemy. Such qualities must be the attributes of the kingdoms of the goyim, but we must in no wise be guided by them.

Our right lies in force. The word "right" is an abstract thought and proved by nothing. The word means no more than: Give me what I want in order that thereby I might have a proof that I am stronger than you.

Where does right begin? Where does it end?

In any state in which there is a bad organization of authority, an impersonality of laws and of the rulers who have lost their personality amid the flood of rights ever multiplying out of liberalism, I find a new right—to attack by the right of the strong, and to scatter to the winds all existing forces of order and regulation, to reconstruct all institutions, and to become the sovereign lord of those who have left to us the rights of their power by laying them down voluntarily in their liberalism.

Our power in the present tottering condition of all forms of power will be more invincible than any other, because it will remain invisible until the moment when it has gained such strength that no cunning can any longer undermine it.

Out of the temporary evil we are now compelled to commit will emerge the good of an unshakable rule, which will restore the regular course of the machinery of the national life, brought to naught by liberalism. The result justifies the means. Let us, however, in our plans, direct our attention not so much to what is good and moral as to what is necessary and useful.

Before us is a plan in which is laid down strategically the line from which we cannot deviate without running the risk of seeing the labor of many centuries brought to naught.

In order to elaborate satisfactory forms of action it is necessary to have regard to the rascality, the slackness, the instability of the mob, its lack of capacity to understand and respect the conditions of its own life, or its own welfare. It must be understood that the might of a mob is blind, senseless, and unreasoning force ever at the mercy of a suggestion from any side. The blind cannot lead the blind without bringing them into the abyss; consequently, members of the mob, upstarts from the people even though they should be as a genius for wisdom, yet having no understanding of the political, cannot come forward as leaders of the mob without bringing the whole nation to ruin.

Only one trained from childhood for independent rule can have understanding of the words that can be made up of the political alphabet.

A people left to itself, i.e., to upstarts from its midst, brings itself to ruin by party dissensions excited by the pursuit of power and honors and disorders arising therefrom. Is it possible for the masses of the people calmly and without petty jealousies to form judgments, to deal with the affairs of the country, which cannot be mixed up with personal interests? Can they defend themselves from an external foe? It is unthinkable, for a plan broken up into as many parts as there are heads in the mob, loses all homogeneity, and thereby becomes unintelligible and impossible of execution.

It is only with a despotic ruler that plans can be elaborated extensively and clearly in such a way as to distribute the whole properly among the several parts of the machinery of the state: from this the conclusion is inevitable that a satisfactory form of government for any country is one that concentrates in the hands of one responsible person. Without an absolute despotism there can be no existence for civilization which is carried on not by the masses but by their guide, whosoever that person may be. The mob is a savage and displays its savagery at every opportunity. The moment the mob seizes freedom in its hands it quickly turns to anarchy, which in itself is the highest degree of savagery.

Behold the alcoholized animals, bemused with drink, the right to an immoderate use of which comes along with freedom. It is not for us and ours to walk that road. The peoples of the goyim are bemused with alcoholic liquors; their youth has grown stupid on classicism and from early immorality, into which it has been inducted by our special agents—by tutors, lackeys, governesses in the houses of the wealthy, by clerks and others, by our women in the places of dissipation frequented by the goyim. In the number of these last I count also the so-called "society ladies," voluntary followers of the others in corruption and luxury.

Our countersign is—Force and Make-believe. Only force conquers in political affairs, especially if it be concealed in the talents essential to statesmen. Violence must be the principle, and cunning and make-believe the rule for governments which do not want to lay down their crowns at the feet of agents of some new power. This evil is the one and only means to attain the end, the good. Therefore we must not stop at bribery, deceit, and treachery when they should serve toward the attainment of our end. In politics one must know how to seize the property of others without hesitation if by it we secure submission and sovereignty.

Our state, marching along the path of peaceful conquest, has the right to replace the horrors of war by less noticeable and more satisfactory sentences of death, necessary to maintain the terror which tends to produce blind submission. Just but merciless severity is the greatest factor of strength in the state: not only for the sake of gain but also in the name of duty, for the sake of victory, we must keep to the program of violence and make-believe. The doctrine of squaring accounts is precisely as strong as the means of which it makes use. Therefore it is not so much by the means themselves as by the doctrine of severity that we shall triumph and bring all governments into subjection to our super-government. It is enough for them to know that we are merciless for all disobedience to cease.

Far back in ancient times we were the first to cry among the masses of the people the words "Liberty, Equality, Fraternity," words many times repeated since those days by stupid poll parrots who from all sides round flew down upon these baits and with them carried away the well-being of the world, true freedom of the individual, formerly so well guarded against the pressure of the mob. The would-be wise men of the goyim, the intellectuals, could not make anything out of the uttered words in their abstractness; did not note the contradiction of their meaning and interrelation; did not see that in nature there is no equality, cannot be freedom; that Nature herself has established inequality of minds, of characters, and capacities, just as immutably as she has established subordination to her laws; never stopped to think that the mob is a blind thing, that upstarts elected from among it to bear rule are, in regard to the political, the same blind men as the mob itself, that the adept, though he be a fool, can yet rule, whereas the nonadept, even if he were a genius, understands nothing in the political—to all these things the goyim paid no regard; yet all the time it was based upon these things that dynastic rule rested: the father passed on to the son a knowledge of the course of political affairs in such wise that none should know it but members of the dynasty and none could betray it to the governed. As time went on the meaning of the dynastic transference of the true position of affairs in the political was lost, and this aided the success of our cause.

In all corners of the earth the words "Liberty, Equality, Fraternity" brought to our ranks, thanks to our blind agents, whole legions who bore our banners with enthusiasm. And all the time these words were cankerworms at work boring into the well-being of the goyim, putting an end everywhere to peace, quiet, solidarity, and destroying all the foundations of the goy states. As you will see later, this helped us to our triumph; it gave us the possibility, among other things, of getting into our hands the master card—the destruction of the privileges, or in other words of the very existence of the aristocracy of the goyim, that class which was the only defense peoples and countries had against us. On the ruins of the natural and genealogical aristocracy of the goyim we have set up the aristocracy of our educated class headed by the aristocracy of money. The qualifications for this aristocracy we have established in wealth, which is dependent upon us, and in knowledge, for which our learned elders provide the motive force.

Our triumph has been rendered easier by the fact that in our relations with the men whom we wanted we have always worked upon the most sensitive chords of the human mind, upon the cash account, upon the cupidity, upon the insatiability for material needs of man; and each one of these human weaknesses, taken alone, is sufficient to paralyze initiative, for it hands over the will of men to the disposition of him who has bought their activities.

The abstraction of freedom has enabled us to persuade the mob in all countries that their government is nothing but the steward of the people who are the owners of the country, and that the steward may be replaced like a worn-out glove.

It is this possibility of replacing the representatives of the people which has placed them at our disposal, and, as it were, given us the power of appointment.

PROTOCOL NO. 2

It is indispensable for our purpose that wars, so far as possible, should not result in territorial gains: war will thus be brought on to the economic ground, where the nations will not fail to perceive in the assistance we give the strength of our predominance, and this state of things will put both sides at the mercy of our international *agentur;* which possesses millions of eyes ever on the watch and unhampered by any limitations whatsoever. Our international rights will then wipe out national rights, in the proper sense of right, and will rule the nations precisely as the civil law of states rules the relations of their subjects among themselves.

The administrators, whom we shall choose from among the public, with strict regard to their capacities for servile obedience, will not be persons trained in the arts of government, and will therefore easily become pawns in our game in the hands of men of learning and genius who will be their advisers, specialists bred and reared from early childhood to rule the affairs of the whole world. As is well known to you, these specialists of ours have been drawing to fit them for rule the information they need from our political plans, from the lessons of history, from observations made of the events of every moment as it passes. The goyim are not guided by practical use of unprejudiced historical observation, but by theoretical routine without any critical regard for consequent results. We need not, therefore, take any account of them—let them amuse themselves until the hour strikes, or live on hopes of new forms of enterprising pastime, or on the memories of all they have enjoyed. For them let that play the principal part which we have persuaded them to accept as the dictates of science (theory). It is with this object in view that we are constantly, by means of our press, arousing a blind confidence in these theories. The intellectuals of the goyim will puff themselves up with their knowledge and without any logical verification of it will put into effect all the information available from science, which our *agentur* specialists have cunningly pieced together for the purpose of educating their minds in the direction we want.

Do not suppose for a moment that these statements are empty words: think carefully of the successes we arranged for Darwinism, Marxism, Nietzsche-ism. To us Jews, at any rate, it should be plain to see what a disintegrating importance these directives have had upon the minds of the goyim.

It is indispensable for us to take account of the thoughts, characters, tendencies of the nations in order to avoid making slips in the political and in the direction of administrative affairs. The triumph of our system, of which the component parts of the machinery may be variously disposed according to the temperament of the peoples met on our way, will fail of success if the practical application of it be not based upon a summing up of the lessons of the past in the light of the present.

In the hands of the states of today there is a great force that creates the movement of thought in the people, and that is the press. The part played by the press is to keep pointing out requirements supposed to be indispensable, to give voice to the complaints of the people, to express, and to create discontent. It is in the press that the triumph of freedom of speech finds its incarnation. But the goyim states have not known how to make use of this force; and it has fallen into our hands. Through the press we have gained the power to influence while remaining ourselves in the shade; thanks to the press we have got the gold in our hands, notwithstanding that we have had to gather it out of oceans of blood and tears. But it has paid us, though we have sacrificed many of our people. Each victim on our side is worth in the sight of God a thousand goyim.

7. *THE DREYFUS AFFAIR*

The anti-Jewish agitation of the late nineteenth century was not confined to literary treatises. Anti-Jewish organizations were created; anti-Semitic political parties were formed; overt violence occasionally broke out. The event around which much of the anti-Jewish activity coalesced was the

Dreyfus Affair. Beginning with the search for a spy on the French General Staff and the unjust conviction of Captain Alfred Dreyfus, the affair became a national *cause célèbre,* deeply fragmenting French society over issues of justice, national honor, the reputation of the army, the role of the Church, and the position of French Jewry.

The first selection below comes from the pen of Alfred Dreyfus himself. In 1899, upon his return from imprisonment, Dreyfus published a set of memoirs, based on a diary composed on the living hell of Devil's Island and expanded with suitable background material. In our selection, we see first the prosperous and happy young captain, successful in his military career (an unusual calling for a Jew) and sublimely unaware of the dangers lurking in his path. We sense the total shock of the accusation and conviction, the incredible humiliation of his public degradation, the unflinching loyalty to his wife and family whose honor he must redeem, and the unflagging faith that France—his glorious France—would inevitably redress such a monstrous miscarriage of justice.

All of the activity that brought Dreyfus back to France, eventually set him free, and finally led to his exoneration was unknown to the prisoner languishing on Devil's Island. A major turning point in the campaign for revision came on January 13, 1898, when the brilliant and controversial novelist Émile Zola challenged the French army and the government with his scandalous indictment "J'Accuse." Blazoned across the front page of the newspaper *L'Aurore,* "J'Accuse" was meant to force the Dreyfus case out of the military courts and into civil litigation. This it did—and more. It brought Zola a conviction for slander and temporary flight to England; it resulted in a wave of riots against the Jews; and it ultimately turned the tide in favor of Alfred Dreyfus's retrial and exculpation.

The first selection is taken from the English translation of Dreyfus's memoirs, entitled *Five Years of My Life 1894–1899* (New York, 1901). "J'Accuse" is reprinted from Louis L. Snyder's useful collection of source materials, *The Dreyfus Case: A Documentary History,* © 1973 Rutgers University, the State University of New Jersey. Reprinted by permission of the Rutgers University Press, New Brunswick, New Jersey.

7a. Alfred Dreyfus, *Five Years of My Life*

1

I was born at Mulhouse, in Alsace, the 9th of October, 1859. My childhood passed quietly under the gentle influence of my mother and my sisters, and of a father deeply devoted to his children, and under the careful protection of brothers older than myself.

My first sad impression, of which the painful souvenir has never faded from my memory, was the war of 1870. On the conclusion of peace, my father chose to remain a Frenchman, and we were obliged to leave Alsace. I went to Paris to continue my studies.

In 1878 I entered the École Polytechnique, which I left in 1880 to enter as pupil sublieutenant of artillery at the Military School of Fontainebleau. The 1st of October, 1882, I was appointed lieutenant in the 31st Regiment of Artillery, in garrison at Le Mans. At the end of the year 1883 I was classed in the horse batteries of the first division of Independent Cavalry at Paris.

On the 12th of September, 1889, I was promoted captain in the 21st Regiment of Artillery, detached as assistant at the Central School of Military Pyrotechny at Bourges. In the course of the winter I became engaged to be married to Mdlle. Lucie Hadamard, who became my devoted and heroic wife.

During my engagement I prepared myself for the École Supérieure de Guerre, which I entered on the 20th of April, 1890. The next day I was married. I left the École Supérieure de Guerre in 1892 with the note "very good" and the brevet of staff officer. My class number on leaving the school entitled me to a subordinate place on the General Staff, which I entered on the 1st of January, 1893.

A brilliant and facile career was opened to me; the future appeared under bright auspices. After the day's labors I tasted the repose and the charms of family life. Interested in all the manifestations of the human mind, I delighted in reading during the pleasant evenings passed at my own fireside. My wife and I were perfectly happy, and our first child enlivened our home. I had no worldly anxieties; the same profound affection united me with the members of my own and my wife's family. All that renders life happy seemed to smile upon me.

2

The year 1893 passed without any occurrence of note; my daughter Jeanne came to shed a new ray of sunshine in our home.

The year 1894 was to be the last of my service on the General Staff of the army. During the last quarter of that year I was designated for the regulation period of service in a regiment of infantry stationed at Paris.

I commenced my duties on October 1st; on Saturday, the 13th of October, 1894, I received an official note requesting me to go on the following Monday morning at nine o'clock to the War Department, to be present at the general inspection, it being expressly enjoined upon me to appear in mufti. The hour named seemed to me very early for the general inspection, which ordinarily takes place in the evening, and the order to appear in civilian dress also surprised me. But after remarking these singularities when I read the official note, I attached little importance to them and forgot them speedily.

On Sunday evening my wife and I dined as usual at the house of her parents, which we left full of gaiety, and lighthearted as we always were after an evening passed in the family circle.

On Monday morning I took leave of those dear to me. My little son Pierre, then three and a half years old, who was accustomed to go with me to the door when I went out, accompanied me that morning as usual. This circumstance became one of my keenest remembrances in my misfortunes. Often in my nights of agony and despair I have recalled the moment when I had clasped my child in my arms for the last time, and that recollection seemed to endow me with renewed strength and will.

The morning was fine and cool, the sun had risen above the horizon, dissipating the thin, light fog, and everything indicated a splendid day. As I arrived at the War Office a short time in advance, I strolled for some moments before the building, and then went up to the offices. Upon entering I was received by Commandant Picquart, who seemed to be waiting for me, and who at once took me into his private room. I was surprised to see none of my comrades, as officers are always assembled in groups at the general inspection. After a few minutes of trivial conversation, Commandant Picquart conducted me to the private office of the Chief of the General Staff.

My surprise was great upon entering. Instead of meeting the Chief of the General Staff, I was received by Commandant du Paty de Clam, in uniform. Three persons in civilian dress, who were completely unknown to me, were also present. These three men were M. Cochefert, Chief of the Secret Police, his secretary, and M. Gribelin, Keeper of the Records. Commandant du Paty came up to me and said in a trembling voice, "The general is coming; whilst you are waiting, as I have a letter to write and have a sore finger, will you kindly write it for me?" However singular this request, made in such circumstances, I at once assented. I sat down at a little table already prepared, and Commandant du Paty seated himself close to me, following my hand with his eye. After first directing me to fill up an inspection form, he dictated to me a letter in which certain passages recalled the letter of accusation, which I heard of afterward, and which was known by the name of the "Bordereau." In the course of the dictation the commandant said sharply, "You tremble." I did not tremble. At the court-martial of 1894 he explained this brusque exclamation, saying that he had noticed that I did not tremble during the dictation, and that he had consequently thought I was playing a part, and had therefore endeavored to shake my self-assurance. This vehement remark surprised me greatly, as well as the hostile attitude of Commandant du Paty. But as there was no suspicion in my mind, I supposed he was finding fault with my handwriting. My fingers were cold, as the temperature outside was chilly, and I had only been for a few moments in a warm room. I therefore replied to him, "My fingers are half frozen."

As I continued to write without emotion, Commandant du Paty tried a fresh maneuver, and said to me violently, "Pay attention; it is a serious matter." Though surprised at conduct as rude as it was unexpected, I said nothing, and simply endeavored to write better. From that moment Commandant du Paty, as he stated before the court-martial of 1894, considered that I had all my presence of mind, and that it was useless to continue the experiment any further. The scene of the dictation had been arranged in advance in every detail, but the result had not answered the expectations of those who had devised it.

As soon as the dictation was finished Commandant du Paty rose, and, placing his hand on my shoulder, exclaimed in a loud voice, "In the name of the law, I arrest you. You are accused of the crime of high treason!" Had a thunderbolt fallen at my feet the effect produced upon me could not have been more violent. I stammered a few disconnected words, protesting against an infamous accusation which nothing in my life could justify. . . .

5

The degradation took place on Saturday, the 5th of January. I underwent the horrible torture without breaking down.

Previously to the terrible ordeal I waited for an hour in the garrison adjutant's room at the École Militaire. During those trying moments I summoned all my strength; the remembrance of the fearful months which I had just passed came back to me. In broken accents I recalled the last visit which Commandant du Paty de Clam had made to me at the prison. I protested against the vile accusation which had been brought against me. I reminded those around me that I had again written to the Minister to assure him of my innocence. By distorting the words I then uttered, Captain Le-Brun Renault, with a strange lack of conscientious scruples, afterward gave currency to the story of a so-called confession, of which I first learned even the existence only in January, 1899. If I had been informed of it before my departure from France, which took place in February, 1895, that is to say more than seven weeks after my public degradation had taken place, I should have endeavored to stifle this fable at the outset.

After the interval of waiting, I was conducted by an officer and four men to the center of the square.

Nine o'clock struck. General Barras, who commanded the squad of execution, gave the order to shoulder arms.

I was suffering martyrdom, but I straightened myself and made a supreme effort to rally my strength, trying to sustain myself by the remembrance of my wife and children. Immediately after the formal reading of the sentence I exclaimed to the troops:

"Soldiers, an innocent man is degraded. Soldiers, an innocent man is dishonored! *Vive la France! Vive l'armée!*"

An adjutant of the Republican Guard came up to me and rapidly tore the buttons from my coat, the stripes from my trousers, and the marks of my rank from my cap and coat sleeves, and then broke my sword across his knee. . . . I saw all these emblems of honor fall at my feet. Then, in the midst of my agony, but with head erect, I shouted again and again to the soldiers and the assembled people, "I am innocent!"

The parade continued. I was compelled to march round the entire square. I heard the howls of a deluded mob; I could feel the shudder with which it looked upon me in the belief that the condemned man in their presence was a traitor to his country, and I made a superhuman effort to create in their hearts the commiseration due to an innocent man unjustly condemned.

The march round the square was at last completed, the torture was over as I thought, but in truth the agony of that memorable day had only just begun.

I was handcuffed, and was taken in the prison van to the common lockup on the other side of the Alma bridge. . . .

On reaching the end of the bridge I saw through the grated ventilator of the van the windows of the house where many pleasant years of my life had been passed, and where all my happiness was centered. My anguish at this pathetic sight was unspeakable.

On arriving at the lockup, in my torn and ragged uniform, I was dragged from room to room, searched, photographed, and measured. At length, toward noon, I was taken to the Santé prison and locked in a convict's cell. . . .

6

I left the Santé prison on January 17, 1895. As usual in the evening, I had put my cell in order and lowered my couch, and I went to bed at the regular hour, nothing having transpired to give me the slightest hint of my impending removal. I had even been told during the day that my wife had received permission to see me two days later, as she had not been able to come for nearly a week.

Between ten and eleven o'clock at night I was suddenly awakened and told to prepare at once for my departure. I had only time to dress myself hastily. The delegate of the Minister of the Interior, who, with three wardens, had charge of the transfer, showed revolting brutality. He had me hurriedly handcuffed while I was scarcely dressed, and gave me no time even to pick up my eyeglasses. The cold that night was terrible. I was taken to the Orléans railway station in a prison van, and then brought in a roundabout way to the freight entrance, where were waiting the cars built specially for the transportation of convicts on their way to the penal colonies of Guiana or New Caledonia. The cars are divided into narrow cells, each barely accommodating a man in sitting posture, and when the door is closed it is impossible to stretch one's legs. I was locked up in one of these cells, my wrists handcuffed, and with irons on my ankles. The night was horribly long; all my limbs were benumbed. The next morning I was trembling with fever, and able to obtain only, after many demands, a little black coffee with some bread and cheese.

At last, toward noon, the train arrived at La Rochelle. Our departure from Paris was not publicly known, and if on arriving the authorities had embarked me at once for the Île de Ré, I should have passed unrecognized.

But there were at the station a few loungers who were in the habit of coming to see the arrival of the convicts on their way to the Île de Ré. The wardens thought it best to wait until the onlookers had gone. But every few minutes the chief warden was called away from the train by the delegate of the Ministry of the Interior, and then would return to give mysterious orders to the other guards.

Each of these wardens went out in his turn and came back bustlingly, now closing one grating and now another, and whispering in each other's ears. It was clear that this singular maneuvering would end by attracting the attention of the curious, who would say, "There must be an important prisoner in the van, and as he has not been taken out, let us wait and see him." Then once the wardens and delegate lost their heads. It seemed that someone had been indiscreet, that my name was pronounced. The news spread abroad and the crowd increased rapidly. I had to remain all the afternoon in the car, hearing the crowd outside, which was becoming more turbulent as time went on. At last, at nightfall, I was taken from the car, and as soon as I appeared the clamor redoubled and blows fell on and around me. The crowd made sudden and angry rushes. I stood impassive in the midst of this throng, for a moment even almost alone, ready to deliver up my body to the fury of the mob. But my soul was my own, and I understood only too well the outraged feelings of these poor deluded people. I should have wished only, in leaving my body to their mercy, to have cried out to them their pitiful error. I pushed away the wardens who came to my assistance, but they answered that they were responsible for me. How heavy, then, is the responsibility weighing on those others, who, torturing a man, have also abused the confidence of an entire nation.

At last I got to the carriage which was to take me away, and after an exciting journey we came to the port of La Palice, where I was embarked in a longboat. The intense cold had continued and my body was benumbed, my head on fire, and my hands and ankles bruised by the irons. The trip lasted an hour.

On my arrival at the Île de Ré in the black night, I was marched through the snow to the prison, where I was received brutally by the governor. At the bureau of registry they stripped and searched me. Finally, toward nine o'clock, crushed in body and soul, I was led to the cell which I was to occupy. A guard room adjoined my cell, with which it communicated by means of a large grated transom opening above my bed. Night and day, two wardens, relieved every two hours, were on guard at this window, and had strict orders not to lose sight of my slightest movement.

The governor of the prison notified me the same evening that when I had interviews with my wife they would take place at the bureau of registry, in his presence, that he would be placed between my wife and myself, separating one from the other, and that I should not have the right to embrace her, nor even to approach her.

Each day during my stay at the Île de Ré, after the walk I was allowed to take in the yard adjoining my cell, I was stripped and searched. A high wall completely separated the yard from the buildings and courtyards occupied by convicts.

But when I went to the yard for my daily walk, all the guards were stationed as sentries along its walls. . . .

MY DIARY

(To be placed in the possession of my wife)

Sunday, April 14, 1895

Today I begin the diary of my miserable and terrible life. Indeed, it is only today that I have had paper at my disposal; every sheet is numbered and initialed, so that I cannot conceal or abstract any portion of it. I am responsible for the use made of it! But what could I do with it? Of what use could it be to me? To whom should I give it? What secret have I to confide to paper? Each of these questions is an enigma!

Until now I have had faith in reason, I have believed in the logic of things and events, I have trusted in human justice! Nothing strange or extravagant has found an abiding place in my mind. Oh, what a crumbling away of all my beliefs and all sound reason!

What fearful months I have passed, what sorrowful months still await me!

I had decided to kill myself after my iniquitous condemnation. To be convicted of the most infamous crime a man can commit, on the strength of a doubtful piece of paper, the handwriting of which was an imitation of my own, or which resembled it—this certainly is enough to drive to despair a man who holds honor to be above all else. My dear wife, so devoted and courageous, has taught me in this time of disaster that, since I am innocent, I have no right to abandon her or voluntarily give up the struggle. I feel that she is right and that my duty is clearly indicated; but yet I am afraid—yes, afraid—of the terrible moral sufferings I shall have to endure. Physically, I felt myself strong, my conscience was pure and unsullied, and endowed me with more than human strength; but my physical and mental tortures have been greater even than I expected, and today I am bowed down in body and soul.

However, I have yielded to my wife's entreaties, and have the courage to live! I have undergone the most horrible ordeal that can be inflicted on a soldier—an ordeal worse than any death; then, step by step, I have traversed the hideous path which has brought me hither, passing through the Santé prison and the convict depot of the Île de Ré, enduring without flinching the insults and cries of the mob, but leaving a fragment of my heart at every turn of the road.

My conscience bore me up; my reason told me each day that the truth at last must burst forth triumphant; in a century like ours the light cannot long be suppressed; but alas! each day brought with it a fresh disappointment. The light not only did not break forth, but everything was done to prevent it from appearing.

I was, and am still, kept in the strictest close confinement; all my correspondence is read and closely examined at the Ministry of the Interior in Paris, and often not forwarded. I have even been forbidden to write to my wife of the investigations which I wished to advise her to have made. It was impossible for me to defend myself.

I thought that, once in my exile, I might find, if not rest—that never can be mine until my honor has been vindicated—at least some tranquillity of mind and body which might permit me to wait for the day of rehabilitation. What a new and bitter disappointment!

After a voyage of fifteen days, shut up in a cage, I first spent four days in the roadstead of the Îles du Salut, without going on deck, under a tropical sun. My brain nearly gave way with suffering and despair.

When I was landed, I was locked in a cell of the prison, with closed shutters, prohibited from speaking to anyone, alone with my thoughts, subjected to the regimen of a convict. My letters had first to be sent to Cayenne. I do not know if they have yet been forwarded.

I remained thus for a month, locked in my cell, without once leaving it, in spite of all the bodily fatigues of my painful journey. Several times I nearly lost my reason; I had congestion of the brain, and my horror of life was such that the thought came to me to refuse medical aid, and thus court the welcome death which would end my martyrdom. This would indeed have been deliverance and the cessation of my long agony, for I should not have broken my promise, and my death would have been only natural.

The remembrance of my wife and of my duty toward my children has given me the strength to nerve myself once more. I must not counteract her efforts and abandon her in her mission of seeking out the truth and the true culprit. For this reason I asked to see the doctor, in spite of my strong repugnance to every new face.

At last, after thirty days of close confinement, they came to remove me to the Île du Diable, where I shall enjoy a semblance of liberty. By day, I shall be able to walk about in a space a few hundred yards square, followed at every step by the wardens; at nightfall (between six and half-past six o'clock) I shall be locked in my hut, four yards square, closed by an iron door, before which relays of wardens watch me all the night long.

A chief and five wardens have been charged with this service and with guarding me; my rations are half a loaf of bread a day, two thirds of a pound of meat three times a week, and on other days tinned bacon or spiced meats. To drink I have water.

What a terrible existence of constant suspicion, of ceaseless vigilance, endured by a man who cherishes his honor as dearly as does any man in the world!

And still I never receive any news of my wife and children, though I have learned that since March 9, nearly three weeks ago, there have been letters for me at Cayenne. I have asked that telegrams may be sent to Cayenne and to France for news of my dear ones. There is no answer.

Oh, how I long to live until the day of rehabilitation, to let the world know my sufferings and give peace to my aching heart. Shall I bear up until that day dawns? I often have doubts, my heart is so broken and my health so shaken.

Sunday night, April 14–15, 1895

It is impossible for me to sleep. This cage, before which the guard walks up and down like a phantom in my dreams, the torment of the vermin which infest me, the smoldering in my heart that I, who have always and everywhere done my duty, should be in this horrible place—all this excites and agitates my nerves, which are already shattered, and drives away sleep. When shall I again pass a calm and tranquil night? Perhaps not until I am in the grave, when I shall sleep the sleep that is everlasting. How sweet it will be to think no longer of human vileness and cowardice!

The ocean, which I hear moaning beneath my little window, has always for me a strange fascination. It soothes my thoughts as it did before, but now they are very bitter and somber. It recalls dear memories to mind, the happy days I have passed at the seaside, with my wife and darling children.

I have again the violent sensation which I felt on the ship, of being drawn almost irresistibly toward the sea, whose murmuring waves seem to call to me, like some great comforter. This mysterious influence of the sea over me is powerful; on the voyage from France I had to close my eyes and call up the image of my wife to avoid yielding to it.

Where are the bright dreams of my youth and the ambitions of my manhood? Nothing longer lives within me; my brain wanders under the stress of my thoughts. What is the hidden mystery of this drama? Even now I comprehend nothing of what has passed. To be condemned without palpable proof, on the strength of a forged scrap of handwriting! Whatever the soul and conscience of a man may be, is there not more than enough here to demoralize him?

The sensitiveness of my nerves, after all this torture, has become so acute that each new impression, even from without, produces on me the effect of a deep wound. . . .

10

On Monday, June 8, 1899, half an hour after noon, the chief warden entered my hut precipitately and handed me the following note:

"Be good enough to let Captain Dreyfus know immediately of the order of the Court of Cassation. The Court quashes and annuls the sentence pronounced on December 22, 1894, against Alfred Dreyfus by the first court-martial of the Military Government of Paris, and orders that the accused shall be tried before a court-martial at Rennes, etc., etc.

"The present decision is to be printed and transcibed in the Book of Records of the first court-martial of the Military Government of Paris, on the margin of the annulled sentence. In virtue of this decision, Captain Dreyfus ceases to be subjected to the convict regimen; he becomes a simple prisoner under arrest, and is restored to his rank and allowed to again wear his uniform.

"See that the prison authorities cancel the commitment and withdraw the military guard from the Ile du Diable. At the same time, have the prisoner taken into custody by the commandant of the troops and replace the wardens by a squad of gendarmes, who will do guard duty on the Île du Diable, according to the regulations of military prisons.

"The cruiser *Sfax* leaves Port-de-France today, with orders to take the prisoners from the Île du Diable and bring him back to France.

"Communicate to Captain Dreyfus the details of the decision and the departure of the *Sfax*."

My joy was boundless, unutterable. At last, I was escaping from the rack to which I had been bound for five years, suffering martyrdom for the sake of my dear ones, for my children. Happiness succeeded the horror of that inexpressible anguish. The day of justice was at last dawning for me. After the Court's decision, I thought that everything was going to be terminated speedily; that there was no further question of anything but mere formality.

Of my own story I knew nothing. As I said, I was still back in 1894, with the Bordereau as the only document in my case, with the sentence of the court-martial, the terrible parade of degradation, and its attendant cries of death from a deluded people. I believed in the loyalty of General de Boisdeffre; I believed in the head of the state, Félix Faure; I thought both eager for justice and truth. After that, a veil had been interposed before my eyes, and had become more impenetrable every day. The few facts I had gleaned during the last month remained incomprehensible to me. I had learned the name of Esterhazy, the forgery of Lieutenant-Colonel Henry, and his suicide. I had only had official relations with the heroic Lieutenant-Colonel Picquart. The grand struggle undertaken by a few great minds, full of the love of truth, was utterly unknown to me. . . .

7b. Émile Zola, "J'Accuse!"

LETTER TO M. FÉLIX FAURE, PRESIDENT OF THE REPUBLIC

MONSIEUR LE PRÉSIDENT:

Will you permit me, in my gratitude for the kindly welcome that you once extended to me, to have a care for the glory that belongs to you, and to say to you that your star, so lucky hitherto, is threatened with the most shameful, the most ineffaceable, of stains?

You have emerged from base calumnies safe and sound; you have conquered hearts. You seem radiant in the apotheosis of that patriotic *fête* which the Russian alliance has been for France, and you are preparing to preside at the solemn triumph of our Universal Exposition, which will crown our great century of labor, truth, and liberty. But what a mud stain on your name—I was going to say on your reign—is this abominable Dreyfus affair! A council of war has just dared to acquit an Esterhazy in obedience to orders, a final blow at all truth, at all justice. And now it is done! France has this stain upon her cheek; it will be written in history that under your presidency it was possible for this social crime to be committed.

Since they have dared, I too will dare. I will tell the truth, for I have promised to tell it, if the courts, once regularly appealed to, did not bring it out fully and entirely. It is my duty to speak; I will not be an accomplice. My nights would be haunted by the specter of the innocent man who is atoning, in a faraway country, by the most frightful of tortures, for a crime that he did not commit.

And to you, *Monsieur le Président,* will I cry this truth, with all the force of an honest man's revolt. Because of your honor I am convinced that you are ignorant of it. And to whom then shall I denounce the malevolent gang of the really guilty, if not to you, the first magistrate of the country?

First, the truth as to the trial and conviction of Dreyfus.

A calamitous man has managed it all, has done it all—Colonel du Paty de Clam, then a simple major. He is the entire Dreyfus case; it will be fully known only when a sincere investigation shall have clearly established his acts and his responsibilities. He appears as the most heady, the most intricate, of minds, haunted with romantic intrigues, delighting in the methods of the newspaper novel, stolen papers, anonymous letters, meetings in deserted spots, mysterious women who peddle overwhelming proofs by night. It is he who conceived the idea of dictating the *bordereau* to Dreyfus; it is he who dreamed of studying it in a room completely lined with mirrors; it is he whom Major Forzinetti represents to us armed with a dark lantern, trying to gain access to the accused when asleep, in order to throw upon his face a sudden flood of light, and thus surprise a confession of his crime in the confusion of his awakening. And I have not to tell the whole; let them look, they will find. I declare simply that Major du Paty de Clam, entrusted as a judicial officer with the duty of preparing the Dreyfus case, is, in the order of dates and responsibilities, the first person guilty of the fearful judicial error that has been committed.

The *bordereau* already had been for some time in the hands of Colonel Sandherr, director of the bureau of information, who since then has died of general paralysis. "Flights" have taken place; papers have disappeared, as they continue to disappear even today; and the authorship of the *bordereau* was an object of inquiry, when little by little an *a priori* conclusion was arrived at that the author must be a staff officer and an officer of artillery—clearly a double error, which shows how superficially this *bordereau* had been studied, for a systematic examination proves that it could have been written only by an officer of troops. So they searched their own house; they examined writings; it was a sort of family affair—a traitor to be surprised in the war offices themselves, that he might be expelled therefrom. I need not again go over a story already known in part. It is sufficient to say that Major du Paty de Clam enters upon the scene as soon as the first breath of suspicion falls upon Dreyfus. Starting from that moment, it is he who invented Dreyfus; the case becomes his case; he undertakes to confound the traitor, and induce him to make a complete confession. There is also, to be sure, the minister of war, General Mercier, whose intelligence seems rather inferior; there is also the Chief of Staff, General de Boisdeffre, who seems to have yielded to his clerical passion, and the sub-Chief of Staff, General Gonse, whose conscience has succeeded in accommodating itself to many things. But at bottom there was at first only Major du Paty de Clam, who leads them all, who hypnotizes them—for he concerns himself also with spiritualism, with occultism, holding converse with spirits. Incredible are the experiences to which he submitted the unfortunate Dreyfus, the traps into which he tried to lead him, the mad inquiries, the monstrous fancies, a complete and torturing madness.

Ah! this first affair is a nightmare to one who knows it in its real details. Major du Paty de Clam arrests Dreyfus, puts him in close confinement; he runs to Mme. Dreyfus, terrorizes her, tells her that, if she speaks, her husband is lost. Meantime the unfortunate was tearing his flesh, screaming his innocence. And thus the examination went on, as in a fifteenth-century chronicle, amid mystery, with a complication of savage expedients, all based on a single childish charge, this imbecile *bordereau,* which was not simply a vulgar treason, but also the most shameless of swindles, for the famous secrets delivered proved, almost all of them, valueless. If I insist, it is because here lies the egg from which later was to be hatched the real crime, the frightful denial of justice, of which France lies ill. I should like to show in detail how the judicial error was possible; how it was born of the machinations of Major du Paty de Clam; how General Mercier and Generals de Boisdeffre and Gonse were led into it, gradually assuming responsibility for this error, which afterward they believed it their duty to impose as sacred truth, truth beyond discussion. At the start there was, on their part, only carelessness and lack of understanding. At worst we see them yielding to the religious passions of their surroundings, and to the prejudices of the *esprit de corps*. They have suffered folly to do its work.

But here is Dreyfus before the council of war. The most absolute secrecy is demanded. Had a traitor opened the frontier to the enemy in order to lead the German emperor to Notre Dame, they would not have taken stricter measures of silence and mystery. The nation is awestruck; there are whisperings of terrible doings, of those monstrous treasons that excite the indignation of History, and naturally the nation bows. There is no punishment severe enough; it will applaud even public degradation; it will wish the guilty man to remain upon his rock of infamy, eaten by remorse. Are they real then—these unspeakable things, these dangerous things, capable of setting Europe aflame, which they have had to bury carefully behind closed doors? No, there was nothing behind them save the romantic and mad fancies of Major du Paty de Clam. All this was done only to conceal the most ridiculous of newspaper novels. And, to assure one's self of it, one need only study attentively the indictment read before the council of war.

Ah! the emptiness of this indictment! That a man could have been condemned on this document of a prodigy is iniquity. I defy honest people to read it without feeling their hearts leap with indignation and crying out their revolt at the thought of the unlimited atonement yonder, on Devil's Island. Dreyfus knows several languages—a crime; no compromising document was found on his premises—a crime; he sometimes visits the neighborhood of his birth—a crime; he is industrious, he is desirous of knowing everything—a crime; he does not get confused—a crime; he gets confused—a crime. And the simplicities of this document, the formal assertions in the void! We were told of fourteen counts, but we find, after all, only one—that of the *bordereau*. And even as to this we learn that the experts were not in agreement; that one of them, M. Gobert, was hustled out in military fashion, because he permitted himself to arrive at another than the desired opinion. We were told also of twenty-three officers who came to overwhelm Dreyfus with their testimony. We are still in ignorance of their examination, but it is certain that all of them did not attack him, and it is to be remarked, furthermore, that all of them belonged to the war offices. It is a family trial; there they are all at home; and it must be remembered that the staff wanted the trial, sat in judgment at it, and has just passed judgment a second time.

So there remained only the *bordereau,* concerning which the experts were not in agreement. It is said that in the council chamber the judges naturally were going to acquit. And, after that, how easy to understand the desperate obstinacy with which, in order to justify the conviction, they affirm today the existence of a secret overwhelming document, a document that cannot be shown, that legitimates everything, before which we must bow, an invisible and unknowable god. I deny this document; I deny it with all my might. A ridiculous document, yes, perhaps a document concerning little women, in which there is mention of a certain D——— who becomes too exacting; some husband doubtless, who thinks that they pay him too low a price for his wife. But a document of interest to the national defense the production of which would lead to a declaration of war tomorrow! No, no; it is a lie; and a lie the more odious and cynical because they lie with impunity, in such a way that no one can convict them of it. They stir up France; they hide themselves behind her legitimate emotion; they close mouths by disturbing hearts, by perverting minds. I know no greater civic crime.

These, then, *Monsieur le Président,* are the facts which explain how it was possible to commit a judicial error; and the moral proofs, the position of Dreyfus as a man of wealth, the absence of motive, this continual cry of innocence, complete the demonstration that he is a victim of the extraordinary fancies of Major du Paty de Clam, of his clerical surroundings, of that hunting down of the "dirty Jews" which disgraces our epoch.

And we come to the Esterhazy case. Three years have passed; many consciences remain profoundly disturbed, are anxiously seeking, and finally become convinced of the innocence of Dreyfus.

I shall not give the history of M. Scheurer-Kestner's doubts, which later became convictions. But, while he was investigating for himself, serious things were happening to the staff. Colonel Sandherr was dead, and Lieutenant-Colonel Picquart had succeeded him as Chief of the Bureau of Information. And it is in this capacity that the latter, in the exercise of his functions, came one day into possession of a letter-telegram addressed to Major Esterhazy by an agent of a foreign power. His plain duty was to open an investigation. It is certain that he never acted except at the command of his superiors. So he submitted his suspicions to his hierarchical superiors, first to General Gonse, then to General de Boisdeffre, then to General Billot, who had succeeded General Mercier as Minister of War. The famous Picquart documents, of which we have heard so much, were never anything but the Billot documents—I mean, the documents collected by a subordinate for his minister, the documents which must be still in existence in the war department. The inquiries lasted from May to September, 1896, and here it must be squarely affirmed that General Gonse was convinced of Esterhazy's guilt, and that General de Boisdeffre and General Billot had no doubt that the famous *bordereau* was in Esterhazy's handwriting. Lieutenant-Colonel Picquart's investigation had ended in the certain establishment of this fact. But the emotion thereat was great, for Esterhazy's conviction inevitably involved a revision of the Dreyfus trial; and this the staff was determined to avoid at any cost.

Then there must have been a psychological moment, full of anguish. Note that General Billot was in no way compromised; he came freshly to the matter; he could bring out the truth. He did not dare, in terror undoubtedly, of public opinion, and certainly fearful also of betraying the entire staff, General de Boisdeffre, General Gonse, to say nothing of their subordinates. Then there was but a minute of struggle between his conscience and what he believed to be the military interest. When this minute had passed, it was already too late. He was involved himself; he was compromised. And since then his responsibility has only grown; he has taken upon his shoulders the crime of others, he is as guilty as the others, he is more guilty than they, for it was in his power to do justice, and he did nothing. Understand this; for a year General Billot, Generals de Boisdeffre and Gonse have known that Dreyfus is innocent, and they have kept this dreadful thing to themselves. And these people sleep, and they have wives and children whom they love!

Colonel Picquart had done his duty as an honest man. He insisted in the presence of his superiors, in the name of justice; he even begged of them; he told them how impolitic were their delays, in view of the terrible storm which was gathering, and which would surely burst as soon as the truth should be known. Later there was the language that M. Scheurer-Kestner held likewise to General Billot, adjuring him in the name of patriotism to take the matter in hand, and not to allow it to be aggravated till it should become a public disaster. No, the crime had been committed; now the staff could not confess it. And Lieutenant-Colonel Picquart was sent on a mission; he was farther and farther removed, even to Tunis, where one day they even wanted to honor his bravery by charging him with a mission which would surely have led to his massacre in the district where the Marquis de Morès met his death. He was not in disgrace; General Gonse was in friendly correspondence with him; but there are secrets which it does one no good to find out.

At Paris the truth went on, irresistibly, and we know in what way the expected storm broke out. M. Mathieu Dreyfus denounced Major Esterhazy as the real author of the *bordereau,* at the moment when M. Scheurer-Kestner was about to lodge a demand for a revision of the trial with the keeper of the seals. And it is here that Major Esterhazy appears. The evidence shows that at first he was dazed, ready for suicide or flight. Then suddenly he determines to brazen it out; he astonishes Paris by the violence of his attitude. The fact was that aid had come to him; he had received an anonymous letter warning him of the intrigues of his enemies; a mysterious woman had even disturbed herself at night to hand to him a document stolen from the staff, which would save him. And I cannot help seeing here again the hand of Lieutenant-Colonel du Paty de Clam, recognizing the expedients of his fertile imagination. His work, the guilt of Dreyfus, was in danger, and he was determined to defend it. A revision of the trial—why, that meant the downfall of the newspaper novel, so extravagant, so tragic, with its abominable *dénouement* on Devil's Island. That would never do. Thenceforth there was to be a duel between Lieutenant-Colonel Picquart and Lieutenant-Colonel du Paty de Clam, the one with face uncovered, the other masked. Presently we shall meet them both in the presence of civil justice. At bottom it is always the staff defending itself, unwilling to confess its crime, the abomination of which is growing from hour to hour.

It has been wonderingly asked who were the protectors of Major Esterhazy. First, in the shadow, Lieutenant-Colonel du Paty de Clam, who devised everything, managed everything; his hand betrays itself in the ridiculous methods. Then there is General de Boisdeffre, General Gonse, General Billot himself, who are obliged to acquit the major, since they cannot permit the innocence of Dreyfus to be recognized, for, if they should, the war offices would fall under the weight of the public contempt. And the beautiful result of this prodigious situation is that the one honest man in the case, Lieutenant-Colonel Picquart, who alone has done his duty, is to be the victim, the man to be derided and punished. O justice, what frightful despair grips the heart! They go so far as to say that he is a forger; that he manufactured the telegram, to ruin Esterhazy. But, in heaven's name, why? For what purpose? Show a motive. Is he, too, paid by the Jews? The pretty part of the story is that he himself was an anti-Semite. Yes, we are witnesses of this infamous spectacle—the proclamation of the innocence of men ruined with debts and crimes, while honor itself, a man of stainless life, is stricken down. When a society reaches that point, it is beginning to rot.

There you have, then, *Monsieur le Président,* the Esterhazy case—a guilty man to be declared innocent. We can follow the beautiful business, hour by hour, for the last two months. I abridge, for this is but the résumé of a story whose burning pages will someday be written at length. So we have seen General de Pellieux, and then Major Ravary, carrying on a rascally investigation whence knaves come transfigured and honest people sullied. Then they convened the council of war.

How could it have been expected that a council of war would undo what a council of war had done?

I say nothing of the choice, always possible, of the judges. Is not the superior idea of discipline, which is in the very blood of these soldiers, enough to destroy their power to do justice? Who says discipline says obedience. When the Minister of War, the great chief, has publicly established, amid the applause of the nation's representatives, the absolute authority of the thing judged, do you expect a council of war formally to contradict him? Hierarchically that is impossible. General Billot conveyed a suggestion to the judges by his declaration, and they passed judgment as they must face the cannon's mouth, without reasoning. The preconceived opinion that they took with them to their bench is evidently this: "Dreyfus has been condemned for the crime of treason by a council of war; then he is guilty, and we, a council of war, cannot declare him innocent. Now, we know that to recognize Esterhazy's guilt would be to proclaim the innocence of Dreyfus." Nothing could turn them from that course of reasoning.

They have rendered an iniquitous verdict which will weigh forever upon our councils of war, which will henceforth tinge with suspicion all their decrees. The first council of war may have been lacking in comprehension; the second is necessarily criminal. Its excuse, I repeat, is that the supreme chief had spoken, declaring the thing judged unassailable, sacred and superior to men, so that inferiors could say naught to the contrary. They talk to us of the honor of the Army; they want us to love it, to respect it. Ah! certainly, yes, the Army which would rise at the first threat, which would defend French soil; that Army is the whole people, and we have for it nothing but tenderness and respect. But it is not a question of that Army, whose dignity is our special desire, in our need of justice. It is the sword that is in question; the master that they may give us tomorrow. And piously kiss the sword hilt, the god? No!

I have proved it, moreover; the Dreyfus case was the case of the war offices, a staff officer, accused by his staff comrades, convicted under the pressure of the Chiefs of Staff. Again I say, he cannot come back innocent, unless all the staff is guilty. Consequently the war offices, by all imaginable means, by press campaigns, by communications, by influences, have covered Esterhazy only to ruin Dreyfus a second time. Ah! with what a sweep the Republican Government should clear away this band of Jesuits, as General Billot himself calls them! Where is the truly strong and wisely patriotic minister who will dare to reshape and renew all? How many of the people I know are trembling with anguish in view of a possible war, knowing in what hands lies the national defense! And what a nest of base intrigues, gossip, and dilapidation has this sacred asylum, entrusted with the fate of the country, become! We are frightened by the terrible light thrown upon it by the Dreyfus case, this human sacrifice of an unfortunate, of a "dirty Jew." Ah! what a mixture of madness and folly, of crazy fancies, of low police practices, of inquisitorial and tyrannical customs, the good pleasure of a few persons in gold lace, with their boots on the neck of the nation, cramming back into its throat its cry of truth and justice, under the lying and sacrilegious pretext of the *raison d'état!*

And another of their crimes is that they have accepted the support of the unclean press, have suffered themselves to be championed by all the knavery of Paris, so that now we witness knavery's insolent triumph in the downfall of right and of simple probity. It is a crime to have accused of troubling France those who wish to see her generous, at the head of the free and just nations, when they themselves are hatching the impudent conspiracy to impose error, in the face of the entire world. It is a crime to mislead opinion, to utilize for a task of death this opinion that they have perverted to the point of delirium. It is a crime to poison the minds of the little and the humble, to exasperate the passions of reaction and intolerance, while seeking shelter behind odious anti-Semitism, of which the great liberal France of the rights of man will die, if she is not cured. It is a crime to exploit patriotism for works of hatred, and, finally, it is a crime to make the sword the modern god, when all human science is at work on the coming temple of truth and justice.

This truth, this justice, for which we have so ardently longed—how distressing it is to see them thus buffeted, more neglected and more obscured. I have a suspicion of the fall that must have occurred in the soul of M. Scheurer-Kestner, and I really believe that he will finally feel remorse that he did not act in a revolutionary fashion, on the day of interpellation in the Senate, by thoroughly ventilating the whole matter, to topple everything over. He has been the highly honest man, the man of loyal life, and he thought that the truth was sufficient unto itself, especially when it should appear as dazzling as the open day. Of what use to overturn everything, since soon the sun would shine? And it is for this confident serenity that he is now so cruelly punished. And the same is the case of Lieutenant-Colonel Picquart, who, moved by a feeling of lofty dignity, has been unwilling to publish General Gonse's letters. These scruples honor him the more because, while he remained respectful of discipline, his superiors heaped mud upon him, working up the case against him themselves, in the most unexpected and most outrageous fashion. Here are two victims, two worthy people, two simple hearts, who have trusted God, while the devil was at work. And in the case of Lieutenant-Colonel Picquart we have seen even this ignoble thing—a French tribunal, after suffering the reporter in the case to arraign publicly a witness and accuse him of every crime, closing its doors as soon as this witness has been introduced to explain and defend himself. I say that is one crime more, and that this crime will awaken the universal conscience. Decidedly, military tribunals have a singular idea of justice.

Such, then, is the simple truth, *Monsieur le Président,* and it is frightful. It will remain a stain upon your presidency. I suspect that you are powerless in this matter—that you are the prisoner of the constitution and of your environment. You have nonetheless a man's duty, upon which you will reflect, and which you will fulfill. Not indeed that I despair, the least in the world, of triumph. I repeat with more vehement certainty; truth is on the march, and nothing can stop it. Today sees the real beginning of the affair, since not until today have the positions been clear: on one hand, the guilty, who do not want the light; on the other, the doers of justice, who will give their lives to get it. When truth is buried in the earth, it accumulates there, and assumes so mighty an explosive power that, on the day when it bursts forth, it hurls everything into the air. We shall see if they have not just made preparations for the most resounding of disasters, yet to come.

But this letter is long, *Monsieur le Président,* and it is time to finish.

I accuse Lieutenant-Colonel du Paty de Clam of having been the diabolical workman of judicial error—unconsciously, I am willing to believe—and of having then defended his calamitous work, for three years, by the most guilty machinations.

I accuse General Mercier of having made himself an accomplice, at least through weakness of mind, in one of the greatest iniquities of the century.

I accuse General Billot of having had in his hands certain proofs of the innocence of Dreyfus, and of having stifled them; of having rendered himself guilty of his crime of *lèse-humanité* and *lèse-justice* for a political purpose, and to save the compromised staff.

I accuse General de Boisdeffre and General Gonse of having made themselves accomplices in the same crime, one undoubtedly through clerical passion, the other perhaps through that *esprit de corps* which makes the war offices the Holy Ark, unassailable.

I accuse General de Pellieux and Major Ravary of having conducted a rascally inquiry—I mean by that a monstrously partial inquiry, of which we have, in the report of the latter, an imperishable monument of naïve audacity.

I accuse the three experts in handwriting, Belhomme, Varinard, and Couard, of having made lying and fraudulent reports, unless a medical examination should declare them afflicted with diseases of the eye and of the mind.

I accuse the war offices of having carried on in the press, particularly in *L'Éclair* and in *L'Écho de Paris,* an abominable campaign, to mislead opinion and cover up their faults.

I accuse, finally, the first council of war of having violated the law by condemning an accused person on the strength of a secret document, and I accuse the second council of war of having covered this illegality, in obedience to orders, in committing in its turn the judicial crime of knowingly acquitting a guilty man.

In preferring these charges, I am not unaware that I lay myself liable under Articles 30 and 31 of the press law of July 29, 1881, which punishes defamation. And it is willfully that I expose myself thereto.

As for the people whom I accuse, I do not know them, I have never seen them, I entertain against them no feeling of revenge or hatred. They are to me simple entities, spirits of social ill-doing. And the act that I perform here is nothing but a revolutionary measure to hasten the explosion of truth and justice.

I have but one passion, the passion for the light, in the name of humanity which has suffered so much, and which is entitled to happiness. My fiery protest is simply the cry of my soul. Let them dare, then, to bring me into the Assize Court, and let the investigation take place in the open day.

I await it.

Accept, *Monsieur le Président,* the assurance of my profound respect.

ÉMILE ZOLA

D. The Slumbering Giant: Eastern European Jewry

8. POGROMS

Alexander II, Czar of Russia, was assassinated on March 13, 1881. The bomb that exploded in St. Petersburg shook the whole empire. Immediately the nation was in mourning, and the air was filled with fear as well as sadness. Jews were particularly fearful, for they were quickly pointed to as possible conspirators. During April, 1881, a wave of pogroms erupted in the Ukraine and swept over the neighboring provinces as well. They began in Elisavetgrad on April 27, 1881, and were immediately followed by more extensive pogroms at Kiev and Odessa in May and in Warsaw in December. During an eighteen-month period in 1881–1882, Jews were attacked in at least 167 towns in southwestern Russia; the damage to 20,000 Jewish homes and stores reached $80 million while the livelihoods of perhaps 100,000 Jews were impaired.

Aided by striking apathy on the part of the local officials and police as well as regional military forces, these pogroms were only a prelude to violent attacks on Kishinev's Jews in April, 1903. There, about 50 Jews were killed, 86 seriously wounded, hundreds hurt, and perhaps 500–1,000 shops plundered or destroyed. This mass violence peaked in more than a hundred Jewish communities during the revolutionary year of 1905. On October 31 alone, at least 300 Jews were slain in Odessa and perhaps 1,000 Jews died during this wave of assaults. The riots culminated in Bialystok on June 14–16, 1906, where more than 100 Jews were killed and extensive damage to homes and shops was incurred.

The news of the Kishinev massacres, more so than all the others, spread quickly not only through Russia but through Europe and America as well. Chaim Nachman Bialik (1873–1934), the most celebrated Hebrew poet of modern times, was sent by the Jewish Historical Commission in Odessa to interview survivors of the pogroms and to record his reflections of the disaster. The result was his poem "The City of Slaughter" (B'Ir Ha-Haregah)—an almost Isaianic indictment of his people. While not sparing the Gentiles, and contrasting the calm rising of the sun "just as nothing were" to the immense slaughter, Bialik reprimands the Jews for their cowardice, impotence, and resignation. For countless Jews, ever since the poem's publication in 1904, it has signaled a turning point from centuries of Jewish passivity toward a more active defense of Jewish rights and lives.

The first selection below is Helena Frank's translation of Bialik's poem from *Selected Poems: Chaim Nachman Bialik,* copyright 1972 by the Union of American Hebrew Congregations. Reprinted with permission of the U.A.H.C. "The History of My Dovecot" is abridged and reprinted by permission of Schocken Books Inc. from *Benya Krik, the Gangster and Other Stories,* by Isaac Babel, edited by Avrahm Yarmolinsky, copyright © 1948, 1969 by Schocken Books Inc.

8a. Chaim Nachman Bialik, "The City of Slaughter"

Of steel and iron, cold and hard and dumb,
Now forge thyself a heart, O man! and come
And walk the town of slaughter.
Thou shalt see
With walking eyes, and touch with conscious hands,
On fences, posts, and doors,
On paving in the street, on wooden floors,
The black, dried blood, commingled here and there
With brains and splintered bone.
And thou shalt wander in and out of ruins
Of broken walls, doors wrenched from off their hinges,
Stoves overturned, dilapidated hearths,
And singed beams laid bare, and half-burnt bricks,
Where axe and flame and iron yesternight
Danced a wild dance and led the bloody revel.
Then, creep to attics, clamber over roofs,
Peep in where all the black and yawning holes
Appear like ragged wounds that neither wait

Nor hope for healing more in all this world.
Outside, the sultry air is thick with feathers,
And thou shalt think to wade as in a river,
A flow of human sweat, the sweat of anguish.
Thou stumblest over heaps of goods and chattels—
They're just whole lives of men, whole lives of men,
Like broken potsherds, past all mending ever—
Thou walkest, runnest, fallest in the wreckage,
In cushions, tinsel, linings, silk and satin,
All dragged and rent and torn to bits and trampled—
They're holidays and Sabbaths, joy of feast days—
And scarfs and prayer books, parchments, scraps of Torah,
The white and holy wrappings of thy soul.
Look, look! they fold themselves about thy feet,
They kiss thy very footmarks in the dust . . .
Thou fleest! whither? back to light and air?
Run, run! the sky will laugh thee, man, to scorn!
The sun will blind thee with its glowing spears,
Acacias hung with tassels white and green
Will poison thee with smells of blood and flowers,
And blossoms and feathers fall on thee in showers.
A thousand, thousand shivered bits of glass
Shall twinkle in thy dazzled eyes—behold!
For now is given thee a wondrous thing,
A twofold gift, a slaughter and a spring!
The garden blossomed and the sun shone bright,
The *Shochet* slaughtered!
The knife was sharp and glistened, from the wound
Flowed blood and gold.
Thou seek'st the shelter of a court! in vain!
A heap of refuse. They beheaded twain:
A Jew—his dog, with hatchets, yesterday,
Toward the center of the court. This morning
A hungry pig came by and dragged them hither,
And routed, grunting, in their mingled blood.
Let be! tomorrow there will fall a shower
And wash the blood into the drain, and stifle
Its cry to heaven for vengeance; some, maybe,
Has sunk already deep, deep down, and feeds

The thorny tangle of a crooked hedge.
And calmly, like today and yesterday.
The sun will rise tomorrow, in the east,
Its splendor not diminished in the least,
And just as nothing were, pursue its way . . .
Go, half distraught, and scramble to a garret,
And there remain alone in musty gloom.
Alone? the fear of death is breathing round thee!
It fans the dark with black and chilly feathers
And lifts each single hair upon thy head.
Look, here and here, and in between the rafters,
Are eyes and eyes that gaze at thee in silence,
The eyes of martyred souls,
Of hunted, harried, persecuted souls,
Who've huddled all together in the corner,
And press each other closer still and quake;
For here it was the sharpened axes found them,
And they have come to take another look,
And in the apple of each staring eye
To glass once more the picture of their end,
Of all the terror of their savage death,
Of all the suff'ring of their dreary lives
And, trembling like a crowd of startled doves,
They flutter in a cluster to the ceiling,
And thence they gaze at thee with dumb, wild eyes,
That follow thee and ask the old, old question,
The one that never yet has reached to heaven,
And never will:
For what, for what? and once again, for what?
Yes, strain thy neck . . . behold, there is no heaven!
There's nothing but a roof of blackened tiles.
Thence hangs a spider—go and ask the spider!
She saw it all, and she's a living witness,
The old gray spider spinning in the garret.
She knows a lot of stories—bid her tell them!
A story of a belly stuffed with feathers,
Of nostrils and of nails, of heads and hammers.
Of men who, after death, were hung head downward,
Like geese, along the rafter.

A story of a suckling child asleep,
A dead and cloven breast between its lips,
And of another child they tore in two,
Thus cutting short its last and loudest scream,
For "Ma–" was heard, but "Mama" never finished.
And many, many more such fearful stories
That beat about thy head and pierce thy brain,
And stab the soul within thee, does she know.
And, stifling down the sob within thy throat,
Thou rushest headlong down the stairs and out–
To see again the world of ev'ry day,
The usual sun, outpouring unashamed
A wealth of beams at every guilty threshold,
And lavish of its store on worse than swine.

Descend into the vale where smiles a garden,
Where in the garden stands a silent shed.
As though they slept upon their sleeping victims
Like vampires drunk with blood,
Behold a heap of cartwheels piled together,
And bent and broken, splashed with blood and marrow.
And some there are with open spikes that point
Like murd'rous fingers clutching at a throat.
Yet wait without! When fiery and bloody
The sun has set beneath the western sky,
Then steal thee thief-like back into the shed,
And fall a prey to terror . . .
To terror! see, it hovers in the air
And clings about the walls and soaks the stillness.
Hush, listen well! the wheels begin to move,
Torn shreds of limbs are live again beneath them,
They twitch convulsively in blood, their own, they anguish.
A quiet groan, a rattle in the throat
Of one not killed outright, a last low sigh,
A smothered scream, and then a grind of teeth,
All this is there alive beneath the wheels,
And fastens on the beams and on the rafters,
And squeezes in at ev'ry crack and hole,
Or else hangs midway in the shudd'ring air,

A canopy above thy sickened head.
A speechless woe, because beyond all words,
Trouble and sorrow infinite . . . but hush,
There's someone else beside thee, slowly feeling
His way in darkness and with closed eyes.
And, sunk in great abysses of distress,
He stretches out before him two thin hands
Toward the depth obscure, alive with fears
And probes the darkness with his ten blind fingers,
But seeking for no outlet . . .
'Tis he, 'tis himself, the voiceless Spirit
Of Pain, a captive of his own accord,
And one who, pitiless, condemned himself
To endless ages of unuttered woe.
And hov'ring in the shed around you twain
Is *Na-venad,* the Homeless One, who rests not,
And never finds a corner or a foothold.
A stable Presence, weary, deathly weary
O pitiful! 'twere fain to weep, and cannot,
To give one cry, but one, and still is silent,
And chokes and struggles, with the tears unshed,
And spreads its pinions o'er the slaughtered martyrs,
And hides away its face, dissolved in sorrow,
And weeps within itself without a language.
Hush, go thou softly now and shut the doors,
And eye to eye remain with it alone,
And let its burning wrongs and aching griefs
Forever interpenetrate thy soul.
When all within thy soul has died to silence,
Go, touch its wounds, and they will live and speak.
Then bear its woes' remembrance in thy breast
To all the confines of the whole wide world,
And seek a name for them, and find it never . . .
Now go without the town when none may see thee,
And steal thee softly to the place of burial;
And stand beside the martyrs' new-made graves,
And stand and look and let thine eyelids fall—
And turn to stone.
Thy heart shall fail within thee, but thine eye

Burn hot and tearless as the desert sand.
Thy mouth shall open to shriek aloud for vengeance,
And dumb as are the tombstones shalt thou stand.
Go, look and look, behold them where they lie
Like butchered calves, and yet thou hast no tear
To give to them, as I have no reward.
For I have hither come, O ye dead bones,
To beg of you, forgive Me!
Forgive your God, you that have been shamed forever!
For all your dark and bitter lives forgive Me,
And for your ten times dark and bitter death!
For when you stand tomorrow at My threshold,
When you remind Me, when you ask for payment,
I shall but answer you: "Come, see, I've nothing.
It cries to heaven, I hear it, but I've nothing.
For I am poor myself, I'm beggared also.
And woe and woe and woe is all My worlds!
Let all the seven heavens moan for pity.
To bring such sacrifices all for nothing,
To live such lives and die such deaths for nothing,
Not knowing to what end, for what, for what!
Her head enwrapped in clouds, my old Shechinah
Shall sit for evermore and weep for shame;
And night by night I too will lean from heaven
And Myself mourn upon your graves.
The shame is very great and great the anguish,
And which is greater, say thou, son of man!
No, best keep silent, be a speechless witness,
And testify with words to having found Me
In poverty and having seen My woe.
Yet, son of man, departing take with thee
A portion of My sorrow and My care,
And mingle it with wrath and cast it from thee
To fill the lap of corpses still alive."

What now? go back and gaze on leaves and grass?
The fresh and fragrant message of the spring
Steals in upon thine heart and there awakes
A longing for a new and freer life . . .

The grass is grave-grass, man, and smells of death.
Tear out a handful, fling it down behind thee,
And say, with closed eyes:
"My people is as grass pluckt up, and how
Shall that which has no root revive and live?"
Come, look no more, come back to those yet living.
Today's a fast day, come where stands the *shul,*
And plunge thy soul in tears, their sea of tears.
Thou hear'st the lamentations and the moans
From open mouths, from out between locked teeth.
The rent and quiv'ring sounds, like things alive,
Unite, and—hearken! now they rise again
In one despairing wail of misery,
That tosses still between a damp, dark ceiling
And upturned faces all awry with pain.
A sudden horror chills you to the bone:
Thus wails a people only that is lost,
Whose soul is dust and ashes, and its heart
A scorched desert. . . .
No root of hatred, not a blade of vengeance,
For hark, they beat the breast and cry, *Ashamnu!*
They pray of Me forgiveness for their sin.
Their sin? the sin of shadows on the wall,
The sin of broken pots, of bruised worms!
What will they? why stretch out their hands to Me?
Has none a fist? And where's a thunderbolt
To take revenge for all the generations,
To blast the world and tear the heavens asunder
And wreck the universe, My throne of glory?
And hear, thou son of man!
When next the reader cries upon the platform,
"Arise, O God, avenge the slaughtered victims,
Avenge Thy holy ones, the pious graybeards,
The suckling children, God, the little children!"
And all the people cry with him together,
And when, like thee, the very pillars tremble,
I will be cruel to thee, very cruel,
For thou shalt have no single tear to shed;
And should a cry arise in thee, I'll choke it,

Between thy teeth, if need be, I will choke it.
I will not have thee mourn as do the others.
The tear unshed, that bury in thyself,
Deep down within thy heart, and build a tower
Of gall and hatred round it; let it lie
A serpent in a nest and men shall suck
And pass its venom on,
With thirst and hunger still unsatisfied.
And when the day of retribution comes,
Then break the wall and let the serpent out,
And like a poisoned arrow shoot it forth
With hunger raging and with thirsty fang,
And pierce thy race, thine own race, through the heart!

Tomorrow, son of man, go pace the street:
Behold a market full of living ware,
Of bruised and beaten, half-dead human cattle,
With bent and twisted backs,
Of skin and bones tied up in rags,
Of maimed and crippled children, and of women
All spent and parched, and these,
Like locusts or the latter summer flies,
Besiege the doors and windows, ev'ry gateway,
And stretch out crooked hands with fest'ring wounds
(The hands have only lately learned to beg),
Each crying out his merchandise of woe:
"A groschen for a wound, a groschen for a wound!
A groschen for a violated daughter!
A groschen for a grandsire done to death,
And for a son, a boy just ripening to marriage!"
Go, tramping pedlars, seek the field of victims,
And dig white bones from out your new-made graves,
And fill your baskets, ev'ryone his basket.
Go out into the world, and drag them with you,
From town to town, wherever there's a market,
And spread them out before the strangers' windows,
And sing hoarse beggar-songs, and ask for pity!
And beg your way, and trade as heretofore
In flesh and blood, your own. . . .

Now flee, O son of man, forever flee,
And hide thee in the desert—and go mad!
There rend thy soul into a thousand pieces,
And fling thy heart to all wild dogs for food!
The burning stones shall hiss beneath thy tears,
And stormy winds shall swallow up thy cry!

8b. Isaac Babel, "The History of My Dovecot"

FOR MAXIM GORKY

As a child, I very much wanted to have a dovecot. In my whole life I never wanted anything more. I was nine when Father promised to give me money to buy the lumber and three pairs of pigeons. This was in 1904. I was studying for the *gymnasia* entrance examination. We were living in Nikolaev, in the province of Kherson. This province exists no longer, our city now being part of the Odessa Region. . . .

But our happy days came later. They came for my mother when she was beginning to get used to making sandwiches for me to take to school, or when she was shopping for my school supplies: a pen-and-pencil case, a penny bank, a school knapsack, new books in stiff bindings, and notebooks with glossy covers. No one in the world feels the fascination of new things more strongly than do children. A child thrills to their smell like a dog on a hare's trail, and knows an ecstasy which, when we grow up, is called inspiration. And this pure, childish delight in owning things that had the aroma of tender dampness and freshness peculiar to new things was communicated to my mother. It took us a month to get used to the pen-and-pencil case and to the unforgettable morning twilight when I would have tea on the edge of a large lamp-lit table and gather my books into my school knapsack; it took us a month to get used to our happy life, and only after the first half-term did I remember about the pigeons.

I had everything ready for them—one rouble fifty and a dovecot that Grandfather Shoyl had made out of a box. The dovecot was painted brown. It had nests for twelve pairs of pigeons, carved ledges on the roof, and a special grating of my own invention to help me decoy strange birds. Everything was ready. On Sunday, October 20, I was about to set out for Okhotnitzky Square, but a sudden calamity barred my way.

My admission to the second year of high school, of which this is the story, occurred in the autumn of the year 1905. Czar Nicholas was then granting a constitution to the Russian people, and orators in shabby overcoats climbed up on the low pillars near the city hall and made speeches. There was shooting on the streets at night and Mother wouldn't hear of my going to Okhotnitzky Square. Early in the morning of October 20, our neighbors' boys were flying kites right opposite the police station, and our water carrier had knocked off work and was promenading up and down the street, his hair greased and his face red. Then we saw the sons of Kalistov, the baker, drag out a leather-upholstered horse, and start doing gymnastics in the middle of the street. No one interfered with them; in fact Semernikov, the policeman, egged them on to jump higher. Semernikov was wearing a silk belt and his boots had a higher polish than they had ever known. It was this policeman in plain clothes who frightened my mother most of all. That was the reason why she was reluctant to let me go, but I made my way to the street through the backyard, and ran to Okhotnitzky Square, which was far beyond the railway station.

Ivan Nikodimich, pigeon seller, sat in his usual place on the square. In addition to pigeons, he had rabbits for sale and a peacock. The peacock, its dazzling tail spread out, sat on a perch and moved its dispassionate, exquisite little head from side to side. A twisted cord was attached to one of its legs, and the end of it was held down by Ivan Nikodimich's rush chair.

As soon as I got there I bought from the old man a pair of reddish-blue pigeons with sumptuous ragged tails, and a pair of crowned pigeons, and tucked them away in a bag in my bosom. I still had forty kopecks left, but the old man would not let me have a pair of pigeons of the Krukov breed at that price. I loved the short, granular, friendly bills of the Krukov pigeons. Forty kopeks was a fair price, but the trader held out for more and averted from me his sallow face consumed by the solitary passions of the bird-catcher. After considerable bargaining, seeing that there were no other buyers, Ivan Nikodimich gave in. I had my way, and yet it all turned out badly.

At noon or a little later a man in felt boots crossed the square. He walked lightly on swollen legs and his animated eyes were blazing in his wasted face.

"Ivan Nikodimich," he said as he passed by the bird-catcher, "pack up your things; over in the city the Jerusalem gentry are being given the constitution. On the fish market Grandfather Babel has been done in. . . ."

Having spoken, he strode on lightly among the bird cages, like a barefoot plowman walking along the edge of a field.

"Bad business," muttered Ivan Nikodimich after him; "bad business," he shouted more severely, and began to gather up the rabbits and the peacock and shoved the Krukov pigeons at me, accepting forty kopecks. I tucked them away in my bosom and watched the people running from the marketplace. The last one to leave was the peacock perched on Ivan Nikodimich's shoulder. He sat there like the sun in the moist autumnal sky; he sat as July sits on the pink riverbank, red-hot July in the long, cool grass. With my eyes I followed the old man, his cobbler's chair and the darling cages, wrapped up in gay rags. The marketplace was by now deserted, and the shooting sounded close-by.

Then I ran toward the railway station, crossed the square that suddenly fell away from me, and flew into a deserted side street covered with yellow trampled earth. At the far end of the street sat legless Makarenko in his wheelchair; he used to wheel himself around town in this chair and sell cigarettes from a tray. Boys in our street bought cigarettes from him, the children liked him. I made straight for him when I ran into the side street.

"Makarenko," I said, breathless with running, and I patted the cripple's shoulder. "Have you seen my grandfather Shoyl?"

The cripple made no answer. His coarse face, a thing of red fat that spoke of fists and iron, was translucent. He was fidgeting in his wheelchair in great excitement, and his wife, Katyusha, her cotton-padded rump turned to us, was sorting out objects that lay on the ground.

"What have you counted?" asked the cripple, and shrank away from the woman, as though he knew beforehand that her answer would be unbearable.

"Gaiters, fourteen," said Katyusha, without straightening up, "quilt covers, six; now I am counting the mobcaps."

"Mobcaps!" shouted Makarenko, choked and made a sound like a sob. "Looks like God has elected me, Katerina, to be the scapegoat. People are carrying away whole bolts of linen, everybody else gets his cut, and we get mobcaps."

And indeed, a woman came running along the lane, a beauty, her face aflame. She was carrying several Turkish fezzes under one arm and a bolt of cloth under the other. In a blissful, frantic voice, she was calling to her children who had strayed off; a silk dress and a pale-blue blouse floated in the air, like appendages of her flying form, and she paid no attention to Makarenko who followed her in his wheelchair. The cripple lagged behind her, the wheels rattled, he kept working the levers feverishly, but could not keep up with her.

"Missus," he screamed at the top of his voice, "for God's sake, Missus, where did you get that calico?"

But the woman with the floating dress was gone. A rickety old wagon came round the corner from the opposite direction. A peasant lad was standing in it.

"Where's everybody?" asked the lad and lifted a red rein above the jades who were leaping in their collars.

"Everybody's on Cathedral Street," said Makarenko imploringly, "everybody's there, my good fellow; whatever you pick up—bring it all here, I'll buy everything."

Hearing the name of the street, the lad wasted no time. He bent over the front of the wagon and whipped up his piebald jades. The horses, like calves, heaved their filthy hindquarters, and broke into a gallop. The yellow lane was again deserted; then the legless man turned his quenched eyes on me.

"Is it that God has elected me?" he said apathetically. "Am I then the son of man?" And Makarenko stretched out toward me a paralytic's hand stained with leprosy.

"What have you got in that bag?" he asked me, and took the bag that had been warming my heart.

The cripple plunged his heavy hand into the bag and pulled a reddish-blue pigeon out into the light. Its claws turned up, the bird lay in his palm. "Pigeons," said Makarenko and, grinding his wheels, rolled over to me. "Pigeons," he repeated, like an inevitable echo, and hit me on the cheek.

He struck me with full force, his fist clutching the pigeon and the bird was crushed against my temple. Katyusha's cotton-padded rump spun in my pupils, and I fell to the ground in the new coat which was part of my school uniform.

"Their seed must be destroyed," said Katyusha, straightening her back over the mobcaps. "I hate their seed and their stinking men. . . ."

She said other things about our seed, but I heard no more. I lay on the ground and the entrails of the crushed bird trickled down my temple. They trickled down my cheeks, wriggling, splashing, blinding me. A tender bluish gut of the pigeon crept down my forehead, and I shut the eye which could still see, so as not to behold the world spread out before me. It was small and terrible. Before my eyes lay a pebble weathered to the semblance of the face of an old woman with a large jaw, also a piece of rope and a bunch of feathers, still breathing. My world was small and terrible. I shut my eyes so as not to see it and I pressed against the earth that lay under me in reassuring muteness. This trampled earth was so utterly unlike our life and the threat of examinations in our life. Somewhere far away disaster was riding across it on a white horse, but the noise of the hoofs was growing fainter, ceased, and finally stillness, the bitter stillness that sometimes strikes down children in distress, suddenly obliterated the dividing line between my trembling body and the immobile earth. My earth smelled of moist bowels, of graves, of flowers. I became aware of its odors and broke into tears that had no terror in them.

Then I walked along a strange street piled with white boxes. I walked alone on a sidewalk swept clean as if it were Sunday, and I cried bitterly, unstintedly, satisfyingly, as I was never to cry again in my whole life. The wires, turned white, hummed overhead, a fidgety little mutt ran in front of me, and in a side street a young peasant with a vest on was smashing a window in Hariton Efrussi's house. He was using a mallet and swinging his whole body with it, and, sighing, he beamed in all directions, smiling a good-natured smile of intoxication, sweat, and spiritual vigor. The whole street was filled with the crackling, crunching, singing of the scattering splinters. The peasant was swinging his mallet simply that he might sway his body, sweat, and shout extraordinary words in a strange, non-Russian tongue. He shouted and chanted them and kept tearing open his blue eyes, until a church procession entered the street on its way from the city hall. Old men with dyed beards carried in their hands a portrait of a combed and curled Czar, banners with images of sepulchral saints waved over the procession, and fiery old women surged forward uncontrollably. The peasant in the vest, catching sight of the procession, pressed the mallet to his breast and ran after the banners, and I, having waited till the procession had gone past, made my way home.

It was empty, our house. The white doors were wide open; the grass around the dovecot was trampled. Kuzma alone had not deserted the courtyard. Kuzma, the gatekeeper, sat in the shed on Shoyl's corpse, laying out the body.

"The wind carries you about like a bad chip of wood," said the old man, catching sight of me, "you've been gone a dog's age. . . . The people here have gone and finished off our grandfather."

Kuzma sniffled, turned away, and started taking a perch out of a rip in grandfather's trousers. Two perches had been stuck into Grandfather: one into a rip in his trousers, the other into his mouth, and though Grandfather was dead, one perch was still alive and twitching.

"They've done for our grandfather and nobody else," said Kuzma, throwing the perch to the cat; "he cursed the hell out of the lot of them, he sure blasted them, the good man. You ought to get five-kopeck pieces for his eyes."

But at the time, being only ten years old, I did not know what dead people wanted with five-kopeck pieces.

"Kuzma," I said in a whisper, "save us."

And going up to the gatekeeper, I threw my arms around his old stooped back with one shoulder higher than the other, and I caught sight of Grandfather from behind this friendly back. Shoyl lay on the floor, which was strewn with sawdust, his chest crushed, his beard sticking up, his bare feet thrust into coarse shoes. His legs, spread wide apart, were dirty, purple, dead. Kuzma bustled about the corpse, he tied up the jaw and kept looking for something else to do for the deceased. He bustled about as though he had just acquired a new possession, and only quieted down after he had combed out the dead man's beard.

"He cursed the hell out the whole lot," he said with a smile, and eyed the corpse lovingly. "If it had been just Tartars, he'd have chased them off, but then those Russians came up, and their women too. Russians just can't bear to forgive anybody, I know Russians."

The gatekeeper strewed more sawdust around the deceased, removed his carpenter's apron, and took me by the hand.

"Let's go to your father," he muttered, squeezing my hand tighter; "your father has been looking for you since morning; let's go, or it'll be the death of him." And I went with Kuzma to the tax inspector's house, where my parents had hidden when they ran away from the pogrom.

9. *THE GREAT MIGRATION*

Mass emigration of Jews from Russia began just after the Elisavetgrad pogrom of spring, 1881; for most of these emigrants the longed-for refuge was America. Between 1881 and 1900 some half-million Jews entered the United States from Eastern Europe; by the coming of World War I another million and a quarter had arrived. Coming from Russia, Poland, Lithuania, Hungary, Romania, and adjacent territories, they overwhelmed and transformed the approximately 250,000 Jews already here in 1880 and constituted the bulk of the almost four million Jews in the United States by 1925.

The majority of these immigrants came to the United States via the route of Mary (*née* Mashke in 1881) Antin; from the towns and villages of the Russian Pale to the German-Russian border and then through Germany to ports such as Hamburg or Bremen—the final stop before reaching America. Along the way Mary's mind, yet that of a child, vividly records the hardships of the journey: the confusion of being surrounded by an advice shouting crowd as one grasps the steamer ticket sent from the new land, the control stations at the German border with their customary medical inspections, the turmoil and travail of the hurried train ride, and the sensations of being "herded at the stations, packed in the cars, and driven from place to place like cattle."

The following selection is Chapter 8 of Mary Antin's autobiographical best seller, *The Promised Land* (Boston, 1912).

Mary Antin, *The Promised Land*

THE EXODUS

On the day when our steamer ticket arrived, my mother did not go out with her basket, my brother stayed out of heder, and my sister salted the soup three times. I do not know what I did to celebrate the occasion. Very likely I played tricks on Deborah, and wrote a long letter to my father.

Before sunset the news was all over Polotzk that Hannah Hayye had received a steamer ticket for America. Then they began to come. Friends and foes, distant relatives and new acquaintances, young and old, wise and foolish, debtors and creditors, and mere neighbors—from every quarter of the city, from both sides of the Dvina, from over the Polota, from nowhere—a steady stream of them poured into our street, both day and night, till the hour of our departure. And my mother gave audience. Her faded kerchief halfway off her head, her black ringlets straying, her apron often at her eyes, she received her guests in a rainbow of smiles and tears. She was the heroine of Polotzk, and she conducted herself appropriately. She gave her heart's thanks for the congratulations and blessings that poured in on her; ready tears for condolences; patient answers to monotonous questions; and handshakes and kisses and hugs she gave gratis.

What did they not ask, the eager, foolish, friendly people? They wanted to handle the ticket, and Mother must read them what is written on it. How much did it cost? Was it all paid for? Were we going to have a foreign passport or did we intend to steal across the border? Were we not all going to have new dresses to travel in? Was it sure that we could get kosher food on the ship? And with the questions poured in suggestions, and solid chunks of advice were rammed in by nimble prophecies. Mother ought to make a pilgrimage to a "Good Jew"—say, the Rebbe of Lubavitch—to get his blessing on our journey. She must be sure and pack her prayer books and Bible, and twenty pounds of zwieback at the least. If they did serve trefah on the ship, she and the four children would have to starve, unless she carried provisions from home.—Oh, she must take all the featherbeds! Featherbeds are scarce in America. In America they sleep on hard mattresses, even in winter. Haveh Mirel, Yachne the dressmaker's daughter, who emigrated to New York two years ago, wrote her mother that she got up from childbed with sore sides, because she had no featherbed.—Mother mustn't carry her money in a pocketbook. She must sew it into the lining of her jacket. The policemen in Castle Garden take all their money from the passengers as they land, unless the travelers deny having any.

And so on, and so on, till my poor mother was completely bewildered. And as the day set for our departure approached, the people came oftener and stayed longer, and rehearsed my mother in long messages for their friends in America, praying that she deliver them promptly on her arrival, and without fail, and might God bless her for her kindness, and she must be sure and write them how she found their friends.

Hayye Dvoshe, the wig-maker, for the eleventh time repeating herself, to my mother, still patiently attentive, thus:

"Promise me, I beg you. I don't sleep nights for thinking of him. Emigrated to America eighteen months ago, fresh and well and strong, with twenty-five ruble in his pocket, besides his steamer ticket, with new phylacteries, and a silk skullcap, and a suit as good as new—made it only three years before—everything respectable, there could be nothing better;—sent one letter, how he arrived in Castle Garden, how well he was received by his uncle's son-in-law, how he was conducted to the baths, how they bought him an American suit, everything good, fine, pleasant;—wrote how his relative promised him a position in his business—a clothing merchant is he—makes gold—and since then not a postal card, not a word, just as if he had vanished, as if the earth had swallowed him. *Oi, weh!* what haven't I imagined, what haven't I dreamed, what haven't I lamented! Already three letters have I sent—the last one, you know, you yourself wrote for me, Hannah Hayye, dear—and no answer. Lost, as if in the sea!"

And after the application of a corner of her shawl to eyes and nose, Hayye Dvoshe, continuing:

"So you will go into the newspaper, and ask them what has become of my Möshele, and if he isn't in Castle Garden, maybe he went up to Balti-moreh—it's in the neighborhood, you know—and you can tell them, for a mark, that he has a silk handkerchief with his monogram in Russian, that his betrothed embroidered for him before the engagement was broken. And may God grant you an easy journey, and may you arrive in a propitious hour, and may you find your husband well, and strong, and rich, and may you both live to lead your children to the wedding canopy, and may America shower gold on you. Amen."

The weeks skipped, the days took wing, an hour was a flash of thought; so brimful of events was the interval before our departure. And no one was more alive than I to the multiple significance of the daily drama. My mother, full of grief at the parting from home and family and all things dear, anxious about the journey, uncertain about the future, but ready, as ever, to take up what new burdens awaited her; my sister, one with our mother in every hope and apprehension; my brother, rejoicing in his sudden release from heder; and the little sister, vaguely excited by mysteries afoot; the uncles and aunts and devoted neighbors, sad and solemn over their coming loss; and my father away over in Boston, eager and anxious about us in Polotzk—an American citizen impatient to start his children on American careers—I knew the minds of every one of these, and I lived their days and nights with them after an apish fashion of my own.

But at bottom I was aloof from them all. What made me silent and big-eyed was the sense of being in the midst of a tremendous adventure. From morning till night I was all attention. I must credit myself with some pang of parting; I certainly felt the thrill of expectation; but keener than these was my delight in the progress of the great adventure. It was delightful just to be myself. I rejoiced, with the younger children, during the weeks of packing and preparation, in the relaxation of discipline and the general demoralization of our daily life. It was pleasant to be petted and spoiled by favorite cousins and stuffed with belated sweets by unfavorite ones. It was distinctly interesting to catch my mother weeping in corner cupboards over precious rubbish that could by no means be carried to America. It was agreeable to have my Uncle Moses stroke my hair and regard me with affectionate eyes, while he told me that I would soon forget him, and asked me, so coaxingly, to write him an account of our journey. It was delicious to be notorious through the length and breadth of Polotzk; to be stopped and questioned at every shop door, when I ran out to buy two kopecks' worth of butter; to be treated with respect by my former playmates, if ever I found time to mingle with them; to be pointed at by my enemies as I passed them importantly on the street. And all my delight and pride and interest were steeped in a super-feeling, the sense that it was I, Mashke, *I myself*, that was moving and acting in the midst of unusual events. Now that I was sure of America, I was in no hurry to depart, and not impatient to arrive. I was willing to linger over every detail of our progress, and so cherish the flavor of the adventure.

The last night in Polotzk we slept at my uncle's house, having disposed of all our belongings, to the last three-legged stool, except such as we were taking with us. I could go straight to the room where I slept with my aunt that night, if I were suddenly set down in Polotzk. But I did not really sleep. Excitement kept me awake, and my aunt snored hideously. In the morning I was going away from Polotzk, forever and ever. I was going on a wonderful journey. I was going to America. How could I sleep?

My uncle gave out a false bulletin, with the last batch that the gossips carried away in the evening. He told them that we were not going to start till the second day. This he did in the hope of smuggling us quietly out, and so saving us the wear and tear of a public farewell. But his ruse failed of success. Half of Polotzk was at my uncle's gate in the morning, to conduct us to the railway station, and the other half was already there before we arrived.

The procession resembled both a funeral and a triumph. The women wept over us, reminding us eloquently of the perils of the sea, of the bewilderment of a foreign land, of the torments of homesickness that awaited us. They bewailed my mother's lot, who had to tear herself away from blood relations to go among strangers; who had to face gendarmes, ticket agents, and sailors, unprotected by a masculine escort; who had to care for four young children in the confusion of travel, and very likely feed them trefah or see them starve on the way. Or they praised her for a brave pilgrim, and expressed confidence in her ability to cope with gendarmes and ticket agents, and blessed her with every other word, and all but carried her in their arms.

At the station the procession disbanded and became a mob. My uncle and my tall cousins did their best to protect us, but we wanderers were almost torn to pieces. They did get us into a car at last, but the riot on the station platform continued unquelled. When the warning bell rang out, it was drowned in a confounding babel of voices—fragments of the oft-repeated messages, admonitions, lamentations, blessings, farewells. "Don't forget—" "Take care of—" "Keep your tickets—" "Möshele—newspapers!" "Garlick is best!" "Happy journey!" "God help you!" "Goodbye! Goodbye!" "Remember—"

The last I saw of Polotzk was an agitated mass of people, waving colored handkerchiefs and other frantic bits of calico, madly gesticulating, falling on each other's necks, gone wild altogether. Then the station became invisible, and the shining tracks spun out from sky to sky. I was in the middle of the great, great world, and the longest road was mine.

Memory may take a rest while I copy from a contemporaneous document the story of the great voyage. In accordance with my promise to my uncle, I wrote, during my first months in America, a detailed account of our adventures between Polotzk and Boston. Ink was cheap, and the epistle, in Yiddish, occupied me for many hot summer hours. It was a great disaster, therefore, to have a lamp upset on my writing table, when I was near the end, soaking the thick pile of letter sheets in kerosene. I was obliged to make a fair copy for my uncle, and my father kept the oily, smelly original. After a couple of years' teasing, he induced me to translate the letter into English, for the benefit of a friend who did not know Yiddish; for the benefit of the present narrative, which was not thought of thirteen years ago. I can hardly refrain from moralizing as I turn to the leaves of my childish manuscript, grateful at last for the calamity of the overturned lamp.

Our route lay over the German border, with Hamburg for our port. On the way to the frontier we stopped for a farewell visit in Vilna, where my mother had a brother. Vilna is slighted in my description. I find special mention of only two things, the horsecars and the bookstores.

On a gray wet morning in early April we set out for the frontier. This was the real beginning of our journey, and all my faculties of observation were alert. I took note of everything—the weather, the trains, the bustle of railroad stations, our fellow passengers, and the family mood at every stage of our progress.

The bags and bundles which composed our traveling outfit were much more bulky than valuable. A trifling sum of money, the steamer ticket, and the foreign passport were the magic agents by means of which we hoped to span the five thousand miles of earth and water between us and my father. The passport was supposed to pass us over the frontier without any trouble, but on account of the prevalence of cholera in some parts of the country, the poorer sort of travelers, such as emigrants, were subjected, at this time, to more than ordinary supervision and regulation.

At Versbolovo, the last station on the Russian side, we met the first of our troubles. A German physician and several gendarmes boarded the train and put us through a searching examination as to our health, destination, and financial resources. As a result of the inquisition we were informed that we would not be allowed to cross the frontier unless we exchanged our third-class steamer ticket for second-class, which would require two hundred rubles more than we possessed. Our passport was taken from us, and we were to be turned back on our journey.

My letter describes the situation:

> We were homeless, houseless, and friendless in a strange place. We had hardly money enough to last us through the voyage for which we had hoped and waited for three long years. We had suffered much that the reunion we longed for might come about; we had prepared ourselves to suffer more in order to bring it about, and had parted with those we loved, with places that were dear to us in spite of what we passed through in them, never again to see them, as we were convinced—all for the same dear end. With strong hopes and high spirits that hid the sad parting, we had started on our long journey. And now we were checked so unexpectedly but surely, the blow coming from where we little expected it, being, as we believed, safe in that quarter. When my mother had recovered enough to speak, she began to argue with the gendarme, telling him our story and begging him to be kind. The children were frightened and all but I cried. I was only wondering what would happen.

Moved by our distress, the German officers gave us the best advice they could. We were to get out at the station of Kibart, on the Russian side, and apply to one Herr Schidorsky, who might help us on our way.

The letter goes on:

> We are in Kibart, at the depot. The least important particular, even, of that place, I noticed and remembered. How the porter—he was an ugly, grinning man—carried in our things and put them away in the southern corner of the big room, on the floor; how we sat down on a settee near them, a yellow settee; how the glass roof let in so much light that we had to shade our eyes because the car had been dark and we had been crying; how there were only a few people besides ourselves there, and how I began to count them and stopped when I noticed a sign over the head of the fifth person—a little woman

with a red nose and a pimple on it—and tried to read the German, with the aid of the Russian translation below. I noticed all this and remembered it, as if there were nothing else in the world for me to think of.

The letter dwells gratefully on the kindness of Herr Schidorsky, who became the agent of our salvation. He procured my mother a pass to Eidtkuhnen, the German frontier station, where his older brother, as chairman of a well-known emigrant aid association, arranged for our admission into Germany. During the negotiations, which took several days, the good man of Kibart entertained us in his own house, shabby emigrants though we were. The Schidorsky brothers were Jews, but it is not on that account that their name has been lovingly remembered for fifteen years in my family.

On the German side our course joined that of many other emigrant groups, on their way to Hamburg and other ports. We were a clumsy enough crowd, with wide, unsophisticated eyes, with awkward bundles hugged in our arms, and our hearts set on America.

The letter to my uncle faithfully describes every stage of our bustling progress. Here is a sample scene of many that I recorded:

> There was a terrible confusion in the baggage room where we were directed to go. Boxes, baskets, bags, valises, and great, shapeless things belonging to no particular class, were thrown about by porters and other men, who sorted them and put tickets on all but those containing provisions, while others were opened and examined in haste. At last our turn came, and our things, along with those of all other American-bound travelers, were taken away to be steamed and smoked and other such processes gone through. We were told to wait till notice should be given us of something else to be done.

The phrases "we were told to do this" and "told to do that" occur again and again in my narrative, and the most effective handling of the facts could give no more vivid picture of the proceedings. We emigrants were herded at the stations, packed in the cars, and driven from place to place like cattle.

> At the expected hour we all tried to find room in a car indicated by the conductor. We tried, but could only find enough space on the floor for our baggage, on which we made-believe sitting comfortably. For now we were obliged to exchange the comparative comforts of a third-class passenger train for the certain discomforts of a fourth-class one. There were only four narrow benches in the whole car, and about twice as many people were already seated on these as they were probably supposed to accommodate. All other space, to the last inch, was crowded by passengers or their luggage. It was very hot and

close and altogether uncomfortable, and still at every new station fresh passengers came crowding in, and actually made room, spare as it was, for themselves. It became so terrible that all glared madly at the conductor as he allowed more people to come into that prison, and trembled at the announcement of every station. I cannot see even now how the officers could allow such a thing; it was really dangerous.

The following is my attempt to describe a flying glimpse of a metropolis:

Toward evening we came into Berlin. I grow dizzy even now when I think of our whirling through that city. It seemed we were going faster and faster all the time, but it was only the whirl of trains passing in opposite directions and close to us that made it seem so. The sight of crowds of people such as we had never seen before, hurrying to and fro, in and out of great depots that danced past us, helped to make it more so. Strange sights, splendid buildings, shops, people, and animals, all mingled in one great, confused mass of a disposition to continually move in a great hurry, wildly, with no other aim but to make one's head go round and round, in following its dreadful motions. Round and round went my head. It was nothing but trains, depots, crowds—crowds, depots, trains—again and again, with no beginning, no end, only a mad dance! Faster and faster we go, faster still, and the noise increases with the speed. Bells, whistles, hammers, locomotives shrieking madly, men's voices, peddlers' cries, horses' hoofs, dogs' barkings—all united in doing their best to drown every other sound but their own, and made such a deafening uproar in the attempt that nothing could keep it out.

The plight of the bewildered emigrant on the way to foreign parts is always pitiful enough, but for us who came from plague-ridden Russia the terrors of the way were doubled.

In a great lonely field, opposite a solitary house within a large yard, our train pulled up at last, and a conductor commanded the passengers to make haste and get out. He need not have told us to hurry; we were glad enough to be free again after such a long imprisonment in the uncomfortable car. All rushed to the door. We breathed more freely in the open field, but the conductor did not wait for us to enjoy our freedom. He hurried us into the one large room which made up the house, and then into the yard. Here a great many men and women, dressed in white, received us, the women attending to the women and girls of the passengers, and the men to the others.

This was another scene of bewildering confusion, parents losing their children, and little ones crying; baggage being thrown together in one corner of the yard, heedless of contents, which suffered in consequence; those white-clad Germans shouting commands, always accompanied with "Quick!

> Quick!"—the confused passengers obeying all orders like meek children, only questioning now and then what was going to be done with them.
>
> And no wonder if in some minds stories arose of people being captured by robbers, murderers, and the like. Here we had been taken to a lonely place where only that house was to be seen; our things were taken away, our friends separated from us; a man came to inspect us, as if to ascertain our full value; strange-looking people driving us about like dumb animals, helpless and unresisting; children we could not see crying in a way that suggested terrible things; ourselves driven into a little room where a great kettle was boiling on a little stove; our clothes taken off, our bodies rubbed with a slippery substance that might be any bad thing; a shower of warm water let down on us without warning; again driven to another little room where we sit, wrapped in woollen blankets till large, coarse bags are brought in, their contents turned out, and we see only a cloud of steam, and hear the women's orders to dress ourselves—"Quick! Quick!" or else we'll miss—something we cannot hear. We are forced to pick out our clothes from among all the others, with the steam blinding us; we choke, cough, entreat the women to give us time; they persist, "Quick! Quick!—or you'll miss the train!"—Oh, so we really won't be murdered! They are only making us ready for the continuing of our journey, cleaning us of all suspicions of dangerous sickness. Thank God!

In Polotzk, if the cholera broke out, as it did once or twice in every generation, we made no such fuss as did these Germans. Those who died of the sickness were buried, and those who lived ran to the synagogues to pray. We travelers felt hurt at the way the Germans treated us. My mother nearly died of cholera once, but she was given a new name, a lucky one, which saved her; and that was when she was a small girl. None of us were sick now, yet hear how we were treated! Those gendarmes and nurses always shouted their commands at us from a distance, as fearful of our touch as if we had been lepers.

We arrived in Hamburg early one morning, after a long night in the crowded cars. We were marched up to a strange vehicle, long and narrow and high, drawn by two horses and commanded by a mute driver. We were piled up on this wagon, our baggage was thrown after us, and we started on a sight-seeing tour across the city of Hamburg. The sights I faithfully enumerate for the benefit of my uncle include little carts drawn by dogs, and big cars that run of themselves, later identified as electric cars.

The humorous side of our adventures did not escape me. Again and again I come across a laugh in the long pages of the historic epistle. The description of the ride through Hamburg ends with this:

> The sight-seeing was not all on our side. I noticed many people stopping to look at us as if amused, though most passed by us as though used to such sights. We did make a queer appearance all in a long row, up above people's heads. In fact, we looked like a flock of giant fowls roosting, only wide awake.

The smiles and shivers fairly crowded each other in some parts of our career.

> Suddenly, when everything interesting seemed at an end, we all recollected how long it was since we had started on our funny ride. Hours, we thought, and still the horses ran. Now we rode through quieter streets where there were fewer shops and more wooden houses. Still the horses seemed to have but just started. I looked over our perch again. Something made me think of a description I had read of criminals being carried on long journeys in uncomfortable things—like this? Well, it was strange—this long, long drive, the conveyance, no word of explanation; and all, though going different ways, being packed off together. We were strangers; the driver knew it. He might take us anywhere—how could we tell? I was frightened again as in Berlin. The faces around me confessed the same.
>
> Yes, we are frightened. We are very still. Some Polish women over there have fallen asleep, and the rest of us look such a picture of woe, and yet so funny, it is a sight to see and remember.

Our mysterious ride came to an end on the outskirts of the city, where we were once more lined up, cross-questioned, disinfected, labeled, and pigeonholed. This was one of the occasions when we suspected that we were the victims of a conspiracy to extort money from us; for here, as at every repetition of the purifying operations we had undergone, a fee was levied on us, so much per head. My mother, indeed, seeing her tiny hoard melting away, had long since sold some articles from our baggage to a fellow passenger richer than she, but even so she did not have enough money to pay the fee demanded of her in Hamburg. Her statement was not accepted, and we all suffered the last indignity of having our persons searched.

This last place of detention turned out to be a prison. "Quarantine" they called it, and there was a great deal of it—two weeks of it. Two weeks within high brick walls, several hundred of us herded in half a dozen compartments—numbered compartments—sleeping in rows, like sick people in a hospital; with rollcall morning and night, and short rations three times a day; with never a sign of the free world beyond our barred windows; with anxiety and longing and homesickness in our hearts, and in our ears the unfamiliar voice of the invisible ocean, which drew and repelled us at the same time.

The fortnight in quarantine was not an episode; it was an epoch, divisible into eras, periods, events.

> The greatest event was the arrival of some ship to take some of the waiting passengers. When the gates were opened and the lucky ones said goodbye, those left behind felt hopeless of ever seeing the gates open for them. It was both pleasant and painful, for the strangers grew to be fast friends in a day, and really rejoiced in each other's fortune; but the regretful envy could not be helped either.

Our turn came at last. We were conducted through the gate of departure, and after some hours of bewildering maneuvers, described in great detail in the report to my uncle, we found ourselves—we five frightened pilgrims from Polotzk—on the deck of a great big steamship afloat on the strange big waters of the ocean.

For sixteen days the ship was our world. My letter dwells solemnly on the details of the life at sea, as if afraid to cheat my uncle of the smallest circumstance. It does not shrink from describing the torments of seasickness; it notes every change in the weather. A rough night is described, when the ship pitched and rolled so that people were thrown from their berths; days and nights when we crawled through dense fogs, our foghorn drawing answering warnings from invisible ships. The perils of the sea were not minimized in the imaginations of us inexperienced voyagers. The captain and his officers ate their dinners, smoked their pipes, and slept soundly in their turns, while we frightened emigrants turned our faces to the wall and awaited our watery graves.

All this while the seasickness lasted. Then came happy hours on deck, with fugitive sunshine, birds atop the crested waves, band music and dancing and fun. I explored the ship, made friends with officers and crew, or pursued my thoughts in quiet nooks. It was my first experience of the ocean, and I was profoundly moved.

> Oh, what solemn thoughts I had! How deeply I felt the greatness, the power of the scene! The immeasurable distance from horizon to horizon; the huge billows forever changing their shapes—now only a wavy and rolling plain, now a chain of great mountains, coming and going farther away; then a town in the distance, perhaps, with spires and towers and buildings of gigantic dimensions; and mostly a vast mass of uncertain shapes, knocking against each other in fury, and seething and foaming in their anger; the gray sky, with its mountains of gloomy clouds, flying, moving with the waves, as it seemed, very near them; the absence of any object besides the one ship; and the deep, solemn groans of the sea, sounding as if all the voices of the world had been

turned into sighs and then gathered into that one mournful sound—so deeply did I feel the presence of these things, that the feeling became one of awe, both painful and sweet, and stirring and warming, and deep and calm and grand.

I would imagine myself all alone on the ocean, and Robinson Crusoe was very real to me. I was alone sometimes. I was aware of no human presence; I was conscious only of sea and sky and something I did not understand. And as I listened to its solemn voice, I felt as if I had found a friend, and knew that I loved the ocean. It seemed as if it were within as well as without, part of myself; and I wondered how I had lived without it, and if I could ever part with it.

And so suffering, fearing, brooding, rejoicing, we crept nearer and nearer to the coveted shore, until, on a glorious May morning, six weeks after our departure from Polotzk, our eyes beheld the Promised Land, and my father received us in his arms.

10. THE SOCIALIST UTOPIA

Some young East European Jews rejected emigration as the solution to Jewish woes. For them, the time had come to stand and fight, to join the battle to transform the backward society of Russia into a socialist utopia. The cradle of the Jewish socialist movement was Vilna, the birthplace of Abraham Cahan (1860–1951). Few Jews were represented in general revolutionary and socialist movements during Cahan's school years, but one, Aaron Samuel Liebermann (1845–1880), had some influence upon young Abe. Liebermann attempted to spread socialist ideas among Jewish workers in Vilna, using as his vehicle the Hebrew language, and to establish contacts with major Russian revolutionaries. The type of harassment Cahan so vividly describes in the following selection was to force many like Liebermann to emigrate to America.

Cahan, even after the assassination of Alexander II in 1881, "regarded himself as a human being, not as a Jew." Yet his active involvement with Jews and in matters Jewish while still in Russia was to be crucial for his subsequent career. The events in the selection highlight a brief period during 1881–1882, but give some insight into the emerging Jewish radicalism. By 1882 Cahan was in the United States and almost overnight became the central figure in the Lower East Side Yiddish-speaking ghetto of New York City. A fiery labor organizer and spokesman for socialist causes, the leading journalist on the Lower East Side, and the first and most effective Jewish writer of fiction of his generation, Cahan signals the opening of the era of Jewish socialism in both Russia and the United States.

The selection below is taken from Abraham Cahan's memoirs, translated into English as *The Education of Abraham Cahan* (Philadelphia, 1969).

The Education of Abraham Cahan

Soon after the execution of the two terrorists, the revolutionaries shocked the world with their most daring deed: the assassination of Alexander II.

On the Sunday when it happened—March 1, according to the old Russian calendar—I was studying Gerd's *Botany,* with the aim of memorizing some forty dry pages. I had neglected to do Lavrov's assignments. I sat staring at the first page, overwhelmed to the point of depression by the task ahead of me.

"If only something would happen so that there would be no lesson tomorrow!" I thought to myself. Then it happened. A miracle! A student entered the class and announced: "The director requests that you close your books and come out into the corridor."

After all four classes had assembled, the director emerged from the teachers' room. Solemnly he announced, "There will be no lessons tomorrow. Our Czar is dead."

Two students pinched me. They knew I was one of "those." This was their way of congratulating me. We returned to our classrooms. Some students in the other classes who suspected my true role wanted to come into our room but my classmates kept them out. A servant in our room, told the Czar was dead, barked back, "If there is a mud puddle, devils will be found."

For me this meant that the Russian people were ripe for revolution. Nevertheless we took no chances and waited for him to leave. Then I announced that I wanted to see someone. It was almost ten o'clock and the gate was locked. With the help of my classmates I was able to get out through one of the high windows in the mess hall.

I ran to Sokolov's place. He was not at home. Two young men and a young lady were talking about things that had nothing to do with the great event of the day. I told them what had happened. We tried to guess the details of the event.

The door flew open and in stumbled Eltchik, breathlessly mumbling "Killed, killed, at last!" Then Sokolov arrived. And others. But no one knew the details. All I would be able to report to my classmates would be the consensus that the Czar's sudden death meant he had been assassinated.

The next morning at dawn we began to rehearse a requiem under Eban's direction. We were given black armbands and led off to join Jewish students from other schools assembling at the big synagogue. There we sang an "El Molei Rachamim" (God is Full of Mercy) and Eban's requiem for the Czar. Two gymnasium students who belonged to our group motioned to me and made fun of our armbands.

That day, *Vilenski Viestnik* carried a dispatch from Petersburg with the following story.

The Czar was traveling from the Winter Palace to the riding academy. He was going by way of the Catherine Canal route. Suddenly a bomb exploded, smashing the Czar's carriage. The Czar, however, was not hurt. Some people were holding a young man dressed like a concierge. The Czar approached and asked his name.

An officer came running toward the Czar.

"How do you feel, Your Majesty?"

"Thank God I am well. But look. . . ." he said, pointing to the wounded.

"Don't be in such a hurry to thank God!" the young concierge commented as the Czar turned to go back to the carriage. His Majesty had taken only a few steps when a second explosion rang out. This time he fell to the ground in a cloud of smoke. His legs had been blown off and he screamed, "Home. . . . Home. . . . To die!"

A few hours later he was dead.

In the wake of the assassination, censorship was forgotten. Every day the press blazoned a new sensation. One of the first of these was the report that explosive equipment had been found in a cheese shop on Little Sadova Street. Wires had been strung from the shop to the middle of the street where a dynamite contraption was found buried in the earth. It was primed to rip the street. The shop was owned by a couple named Kobozev.

In his regular Sunday visits to the riding academy, the Czar moved along one of two alternate routes. This time he had gone along the canal. At other times he would come along Little Sadova Street. By either route, the Czar was destined to die.

Every Petersburg concierge was a police spy. Even though the Kobozevs dressed plainly and lived simply, their concierge had noticed that they were often visited by students and that the wife smoked cigarettes. He spent one entire day keeping them under surveillance.

He told the police about his suspicions. They sent a detective to investigate. In the guise of a health inspector, he gained entrance to the shop, was cordially received by Kobozev who even served him a drink. There was nothing suspicious about this couple, the detective reported.

The day after the assassination, the shop remained closed. The concierge called the police who broke down the door and dicovered the truth. Even the couch on which the detective had sat was mined.

On Tuesday, March 15, we were taken to the most important Russian church in the city. There, together with other students and teachers, we swore loyalty to the new Czar, Alexander III. I had trouble suppressing laughter when one of the students whom I recognized from Sokolov's place, made the sign of the fig instead of saluting. . . .

Shortly after the assassination there was a pogrom against the Jews in Elisavetgrad. No one could foresee the tragedy to which it was a prelude. It was to become the first of a series of pogroms leading in turn to the mass migration of Jews to America.

Even though the pogrom brought dread into the heart of every Jew, I must admit that the members of my group were not disturbed by it. We regarded ourselves as human beings, not as Jews. There was only one remedy for the world's ills and that was socialism. . . .

Ossip Tsilshtein and I were assigned to the same public school in Velizh. Shortly before the end of the vacation period we set out together on the overnight journey by train to Vitebsk. We traveled the eighty versts from there to Velizh by carriage, changing horses four times and driven in the end by a teamster who spurred the animals on by howling like a wolf.

Our school was a new one. In addition to Ossip and myself the faculty included only the teacher-principal who had arrived a week earlier to put things in order. We decided to spend the night at an inn and to meet him at the school in the morning.

I arose early and looked out the window. In the bright sunlight I saw that we were surrounded on all sides by an expanse of mud and puddles such as I had never seen before. Nonetheless, after breakfast we donned our brown teacher's frock coats and our distinctive hats with their teacher's badge and set out from the center of the town.

The shopkeepers hurried to their doorways to look us over as we leaped across puddles and skirted muddy patches on the way to the school, which we found on a second floor over a row of shops.

Our principal, in his twenties, looked healthy enough but clearly lacked charm and idealism. He had graduated from the Institute four years earlier, a member of the school's first class. Throughout his four years he had been a top student—good memory, good marks.

But he was all innocence and had the heart of a petty official. Later, after he married a pretty girl, his family, his respectability, and his money constituted his total concern. Stingy, sly, superstitious, he never held a book in his hand and instead boasted of the bargains in eggs, potatoes, or beets he had managed to get in the day's marketing for his family. His talents were more suitable for a shopkeeper than for a teacher.

By comparison, Tsilshtein was an avid reader and showed good style in his writing. He was neat and punctual and even somewhat elegant and romantic. If our principal would have made a fine shopkeeper, Tsilshtein would have been a proper singer, composer, or pianist. He taught the preparatory class while I assisted the principal in the three other grades. Tsilshtein rated ten rubles a week, I received eight.

At the school, the principal had the better living quarters. Mine was a single small room near the classrooms. I felt deprived of the privacy I needed and arranged to move in with Tsilshtein when he found good quarters.

It was not easy to adjust to Velizh and its people. The natives rolled their *r*'s in a way that grated on my ears. Their cooking was impossible. The Gentiles were Byelo-Russians and in speech and dress were close to pure Russian. On Sundays, the marketplace was aflame with red blouses and provided a pleasant sight.

The Jews of Velizh were of the hasidic sect. Their fanaticism created a thick cloud of superstition such as I had never encountered in Vilna. Velizh was not far distant from Lubavitz and its famous rabbi—the center of Hasidism. In Velizh a man's wife followed him at a distance. To stroll together was a sign of moral laxness.

I was very homesick during my first days in Velizh.

One principle of the revolutionaries was to mingle with the people. Therefore I decided to attend services at the synagogue. On our second or third Sabbath in Velizh, Tsilshtein and I set out for the most important prayer house in the town, fully aware of the fact that in view of the old-fashioned piety of the city our education branded us as Gentiles and that our absence, in any case, would not be noted.

But when we entered the synagogue, the congregation welcomed us as important guests. We were given seats in the most important pews. Then we were called forward to the reading of the Law.

When my turn came, I read the Haftorah. I read the text well but I had trouble chanting the notes. I had last read from the Haftorah some eight years earlier, at my bar mitzvah. In short, I was out of practice and doing a poor job of it, so that I began to fumble my words.

The congregation was following my every word and tone. I began to burn with blushing. When it was done I couldn't look anyone in the face. The next morning I met one of my new young friends and he greeted me with "Eh, Panie Cahan, that was some job you put together." The derisive sarcasm behind his smile and compliment was not lost on me. It echoed in my mind for a long time. I turned from the synagogue to other ways of meeting the people.

The Dvina flows from Velizh to Vitebsk and on to Riga and the sea. It was the waterway for shipping logs to Riga. The major industry of the city centered on lumber drawn from the surrounding forests. The wealthiest Jewish families, the Berlins and the Zarkhis, were in lumber. The townspeople bragged that "Chaim Berlin owns more land than the King of Denmark."

He lived in the old-fashioned manner. His coachman was an old Jew with sidelocks who wore a yarmulke under his hat. I once saw him waiting for his employer. Seated atop a carriage, he held his whip in one hand and in the other a book of psalms from which he was reading with evident fervor.

I was invited to tutor one of the Zarkhi youngsters. I found the household steeped in the ignorance of the Middle Ages. The youngster was arrogant and when the mother bargained with me over my fee as if I were a peasant selling her a wagon load of weed, I made some excuse and departed.

Tsilshtein and I struck up friendships with the sons-in-law who had married into these families. I grew less lonely. But life was neither easy nor agreeable, and school didn't help.

The students, hasidic boys with long, curled sidelocks, all answered, as if in a wry joke, to the most purely Russian names. I would call out the famous Russian name, "Lomonosov!" and a twelve-year-old hasidic boy, his nose in need of a handkerchief, would rise.

I bemoaned my fate as a teacher. I found consolation in counting the days to Passover when I would go home for the holiday.

We found living quarters with the Yatskevitch family. Old Dr. Yatskevitch was the owner of our school building. His home was on a quiet street with gardens and wooden houses. We rented a wing of three rooms and an attic which had been occupied by a son, Heinrich, who was preparing to enter a university.

As we inspected the apartment I spotted photographs of radical writers—Pisarev, Dobrolyubov, Lassalle—on the tables. Later, when we met Heinrich, our first conversation was full of caution. He turned out to be a member of the Vitebsk revolutionary group. I showed him the books and magazines I had brought with me from Vilna.

He showed me a picture of Chernishevsky and a copy of an illegal book entitled *Slovo V'Veliki Piatok,* written especially for distribution in the villages. It was written in the vernacular of the peasant and in the manner of a religious tract but its content was really revolutionary.

I was as happy with our new apartment as a young lad with his first pair of long trousers. I put my books and my rare magazines in their places, feeling certain that in so isolated a town as Vilezh, the police would not recognize their true nature.

I began a heavy reading program. I undertook to learn French. On the Sukkot holiday, we visited two school friends in nearby Nevel where we were the center of much attention. We were invited for meals and social events, and when we walked in the street we were followed. A marriage broker haunted us until we left for home.

Through the Yatskevitch family we came to know the Lochov family, large landowners who often sent their carriage to bring us to their estate where we sometimes spent an entire weekend. Mrs. Lochov was a clever, dark-haired widow with two daughters and a son. The older daughter was solemn, the younger lighthearted, and the son, Kolia, was good-natured and hotheaded by turns. The estate was managed by a hired German manager who spoke little Russian.

Their home was warmed by open hospitality. The younger daughter was in the care of a Gentile governess, a girl who was a member of the Vitebsk revolutionary group. Both Mrs. Lochov and her daughters sympathized with our revolutionary ideals. Once, when we were riding in their carriage, a member of our Vitebsk group handed me a copy of the first volume of Karl Marx's *Capital* in a Russian translation. I spent that night absorbing the profundity of its philosophy.

Our group in Velizh included Gentiles and Jews, among them some teachers from nearby villages. The trusted ones would meet in our apartment for discussions and debates. We would also forward copies of *The Will of the People,* which I would in some cases send through the mails by inserting them into other merchandise like socks or underwear. I also made a few dozen copies of Chernishevsky's picture. Later we sold these to raise money for our revolutionary Red Cross. On New Year's Day we went to Sivetz and sang songs for the peasant children.

We had a second group of visitors to our apartment whom we kept distinct from the trusted group. These were the emancipated Jewish youngsters who wanted a place where they could smoke a cigarette on the Sabbath or hear the challenging talk of freethinkers.

Dr. Yatskevitch had long ago retired form medical practice. He now lived on the rents from his properties. He was an ardent Polish patriot who could not speak a single word of Polish.

He suffered from alcoholism. For several days he would be dead drunk. Then he would go into a nervous drying-out period when he twitched and trembled like a spastic paralytic. The entire process would then be repeated.

He sent his servant, Maria, for me one time and I found him drunk. When he saw me he pressed my hand and began to heave with heartbreaking sobs, calling me by my Russianized name. "Avram Safonovitch, to this day there are no sewers in Warsaw." And he wept bitterly.

His older unmarried daughter never lost her sense of humor. Frequently she played the piano for us. The instrument was aged and its keys were dry and yellow, which was how her playing of light classics sounded.

Maria, the old Gentile servant, was devoted to us. We stirred some maternal instinct in her pious soul. She had nursed the Yatskevitch children from babyhood. Perhaps it was our excellent Russian speech or our government garb that did it. But for whatever reason, she baked special dishes for Tsilshtein and me.

With these friends, afloat on the tide of socialist moral purpose, my self-confidence grew. I had already ceased to be disturbed by the condition of my eyes. But I could not altogether escape a dandified awareness of my attractive frock coat, with its brass buttons. I felt elevated by the many acquaintances I had made in the Gentile world. When I caught myself with this thought, I berated myself, somewhat halfheartedly, as a pious Jew does when he catches himself thinking sinful thoughts.

Shortly after my arrival in Velizh I was published for the first time. The article, dealing with the need for a technical school in Velizh, was printed in *Russky Yevrey (The Russian Jew)*, a Russian-language weekly about Jewish affairs. It was not a very important article and revealed no great talent. But word spread through the town that "Cahan, the teacher, writes for the Russian papers."

Afterward, when I read a piece in *Russky Yevrey* or *Razsvet* or even in my *Sovremennik*, I was aware that I differed from other readers. I was a reader who was also a published writer. I dreamed of bigger articles by me.

I was pleased. But I was also far from satisfied. There were hours and days when Velizh seemed to be an unbearable burden. The prospect of life as a teacher in an isolated province depressed me. I lusted for life. I had dreams to fulfill. In my frustration I occasionally fell into melancholia.

I was homesick for Vilna. And I was homesick for the bigger world I had not yet come to know. Even in my most happy moods I could not accept my role as teacher in Velizh and continuously there rang in my head the question, "How can I get out of here?"

Shortly before Purim I received the following letter from my mother:

> Your darkly charming friend who teaches Rivka caught a cold. The funeral has already taken place. He was buried deep, deep, deep. The cold is great; take care of yourself, my son! Do not go outside without your muffler.

This was not my mother's usual way of writing, and besides the cold weather had ended. The message she was in fact sending was that Rabinovitch, my dark friend who shared quarters with Badanes, had been arrested.

Soon there was another letter, this one about our fellow institutnik Stotchik, a member of the Vilna group. It was from Trotsky and Yunovitch, now teaching in Nevel, who took the precaution of informing us about the arrest of Stotchik in Homel by writing to us about it on an open postcard and registering their "surprise" over the fact that he had turned out to be "that kind of person."

I had written often to Stotchik. I assumed he had burned all my letters just as I had burned all of his. He was taken to Number 14, the political prison in Vilna, and there, alone in his cell, he hanged himself with a bed sheet.

I lay on my bed, reading. Alone, I fell into an uneasy sleep. Suddenly I awoke, worried at once over the forbidden materials still in our tiny bedroom. I gathered these together, wrapped them in a single package, and gave them to Maria, telling her someone would call for it. Back in my room, I dozed off again. I dreamed I heard footsteps of several persons and awoke with a start. Before me I saw a company of uninvited guests: the chief of Velizh gendarmes, the assistant bailiff, and several gendarmes and detectives. They searched the apartment. The chief had received a tip from Vitebsk.

He was a fat fellow with swollen feet and seemed to be permanently out of breath. He couldn't bend over, even to spit. In addition, he was as ignorant as a peasant. He picked up my copy of Marx's *Capital.* Ten years later even schoolchildren would know about this book. But at this time only those in the movement knew its significance. It had not been banned.

He pointed to the subtitle, *A Critique of Political Economy.*

"What does this mean?" he asked, pointing to the word "political."

"Oh, this is a book about business," I answered, pointing to the words "economy" and "capital."

As each book was examined and approved it was piled onto the table until there was one big heap. Toward the end I spotted two books, one of them Tsilshtein's diary, still to be examined. I pushed the two into the pile of examined books.

I had packed up the portrait of Chernishevsky in the package I gave to Maria. The chief pointed to the portrait of Lassalle. I told him it was the picture of a German scholar.

Then they were finished. Evidently, the chief was convinced that I was not "one of those."

"You must have enemies in Vitebsk."

"It looks like it," I answered, grasping at the excuse.

The true nature of my books and pictures escaped him. He indicated he thought the tip had come from someone in Vitebsk who resented my lack of religion. He had only done his duty.

Starikovitch, the assistant bailiff, was intelligent and warmhearted. He may not have known Marx. But he told the bailiff about Lassalle's picture and the following day the bailiff said to Meyerson, who tutored his children, "Tell Cahan not to think he fooled Starikovitch like he fooled the chief of gendarmes. Starikovitch knows who that smart German Jew Lassalle is."

The bailiff never missed an opportunity to ridicule the chief of the gendarmes.

A few days later I was searched again. This time they got me in class while I was teaching. In they marched with their gleaming uniforms, their spurs and swords clanking.

"Send the children home and come with us," the chief commanded in a tone that seemed to add sarcastically, "You and your false information and your pious Jews! Now I know what you really are."

I was marched out of the school into the marketplace, causing a sensation among the shopkeepers and their customers, while my children ran through the streets shouting that their teacher had murdered the Czar.

This time I stood by while for more than three hours they searched our apartment again, reexamining everything carefully. They took the twenty-three issues of *Sovremennik* and finally instructed me to appear for further questioning in the evening.

At headquarters that evening, I was examined by the chief and the assistant prosecuting attorney for the Velizh district; the latter did most of the questioning. Because his wife was the daughter of an aristocratic land-owning family, he too put on an aristocratic air and addressed me in a cold, baronial manner that was as highly polished as his fingernails.

In the absence of a stenographer, a petty officer with a huge moustache set down an account of the proceeding in a large, round hand. The fat chief smiled humbly as he tried to help the prosecutor with the questioning, especially when a stern tone was needed.

It was clear to me that they had found one of my letters at Stotchik's place. They wanted to know how I had first met Sokolov. I said I had met him in Oszmiana where he was a postmaster. I had never been in Oszmiana in my life.

I told them that I had visited his quarters to see one of his students and that in my letter I had asked him to introduce a certain young Jewess to Sokolov's sister. She wanted information about Bestuzhev's university for women. I took advantage of their own ignorance and acted confused when they read off a list of names.

When the interrogation ended I was warned not to leave the city. I was told I would be kept under surveillance. I was to be taken to Vitebsk for further questioning.

The Lochovs were also searched. In Kolia's room they found a letter from Morozov in which he detailed plans for spreading propaganda in the villages. The Lochov family was placed under house arrest.

Tsilshtein remained loyal and the Meyersons continued their friendship. But I began to sense a spreading coldness toward me among the townspeople—as if I had a communicable disease. Velizh became unbearable. The question was: Do I wait until they take me to Vitebsk or do I disappear now?

In lighter moments I felt I was not yet in grave danger. They had found nothing. The most I could get was five years in Siberia where I would be in good company among the many educated persons already in exile. I could expect occasional help from my uncle in Petersburg. The five years would pass in reading and studying—a fate that seemed preferable to a lifetime of teaching in a small, provincial town.

On the other hand, I could take off for Switzerland or Paris. In both places there were Russian revolutionaries, many of them famous. In either place I could study and continue my revolutionary activities as an exile, working for the day when I would return to my country as an "illegal."

If I was to run, it must be done at once, before the Vilna prosecutor received Velizh papers and the falsehoods in my statements would be revealed. Otherwise, my fate would be to be taken without delay to the notorious Number 14 jail in Vilna where I was certain to find Rabinovitch, Sokolov and others of our group already under arrest.

Meanwhile, because he was trustworthy, I dispatched young Selig Meyerson, a clever lad, to Vilna with the purpose of exchanging information with comrades who were still free. I needed more information if I was to hold my ground in further questioning.

But despite his resourcefulness, Selig encountered difficulty in Vilna. Some of those for whom he searched were out of the city. So he was told. Others had been arrested. He got to Menaker, who apparently could not be reassured that Selig was my messenger. On his return he reported that it was his impression that the arrests had destroyed our group. I decided to disappear.

It was not a difficult thing to do. The police were certain I could not escape and for this reason their close surveillance was not very close.

I told the Meyersons of my plan to disappear from Velizh. They were all eager to help. Old man Yosef Moshe, at the prospect of saving a Jew from the hands of "those gentiles," suddenly seemed twenty years younger.

A barge from Vitebsk had been trapped in the river by the ice. Now its captain was preparing to return to Vitebsk. Old Meyerson's plan was to put me on board. No sooner said than done! Meyerson bargained with the captain to take on a young merchant who had to leave town secretly. The captain asked no questions.

The plan was for me to hide out until, at the given signal, I would come to a nearby bridge and remain under it until given the sign to come aboard. I would be put into an empty case, then covered with a pile of sacks.

Old Meyerson treated me like a father, addressed me with the familiar "du" and supplied me with an alias. "You must forget that you are Cahan. From now on you are Lifshitz. Nu, so who are you?"

"Lifshitz," I answered with a smile.

"It's not a joke. Don't forget your new name. And don't become confused when you answer."

I raised 200 rubles for my journey to the border. Then I arranged for Tsilshtein to keep our light burning all night, to pretend the next morning that he was searching for me, and then to inform the police that I had not been home all night and that he could not find me.

The plan was for me to arrive before dawn in Vitebsk, take the six o'clock train for Kursk where I would transfer to the Warsaw train. While the police would be looking for me in Sivetz and other nearby areas, I would be with Dr. Yatshevitch's son in Warsaw.

We were to sail in the afternoon. I received word that all was in readiness. The trouble was that on the bridge, under which I was to hide pending the signal to come aboard, were the mayor, the precinct police captain, and scores of others, who had come not to trap me but to witness a major event—the sailing of the first barge liberated by the thaw. The captain waited, lost patience, and set off without me.

I was in real trouble. But there was old Meyerson, unable to understand the meaning of despair. He sent one of his sons across the river. Soon the son returned with his mission accomplished. He had purchased a new rowboat. He had hired two Byelo-Russians as oarsmen. Under cover of the darkness I was to set out with them at ten o'clock that evening. They were to row me to Vitebsk. My heart sang within me. . . .

I traveled from Vitebsk to Orsha by wagon, then across the Dnieper to Mohilev by steamboat. On the boat a young glover from Kovno sat next to me. He shared his chicken and his jokes with me. I wasn't prepared when he suddenly asked me who I was and what my business was in Mohilev.

"I'm arranging a match for my brother," I told him.

Then I let my imagination roam free and described all of the fictitious details.

He scrutinized my sidelocks and began to laugh.

"Such a yeshiva boy and they send you to inspect the bride and bargain for the dowry?"

"Don't believe it, then!"

"Oho, he is insulted!" He apologized.

He was a Jew trying to be friendly. Too friendly. I decided to lose him in Mohilev. We arrived at nine in the evening. He was clucking over me like a mother hen. He was going to take me to one of his relatives for the night.

At one of the street crossings I asked him to wait a moment. I went into a courtyard, doubled back across an alley, came around a sidewall, and crouched under a gate.

Soon he was shouting with all of his might. I could see him from my hiding place.

"Lifshitz! Lifshitz!" For ten minutes he continued to search and to shout. Then I heard him mutter to himself, "That's a yeshiva boy for you! Hold him by the hand and still he gets lost! Such a genius they send to investigate the bride and the dowry!"

He was gone. Lifshitz had arrived in Mohilev. I decided to stay until after the Passover holiday. . . .

Elia introduced me to a friend named Trufonov whose parents lived in Nevel. Trufonov was so homesick that when he heard from Elia that Cahan had visited his parents and that I looked like Cahan, there seemed to be a special bond between us. Once, he mentioned his brother-in-law, Spokoiny, who lived in Nevel.

I had spent many hours with Spokoiny. He was the first to tell me about the Jewish theater. Such a theater was not permitted in Vilna. But the governor of Vitebsk did allow Goldfaden's troupe to play in that city. The troupe toured through Russia.

Eight months earlier, in the summer of 1881, they had performed on Krestovsky Island in Petersburg. I was then visiting my uncle. But I had so little interest in the Yiddish theater that I attended not a single performance.

Intellectual Jews looked upon the Yiddish theater with disdain. The Russian-Jewish weeklies, *Russky Yevrey, Razsvet,* and *Voschod,* ridiculed its scripts and its actors.

The Yiddish theater had not achieved a very high standing. But this was not the most important reason for their attacks. The intellectuals were ashamed of everything that was Yiddish. Had anyone ever spoken to them of Yiddish literature they would have laughed at him.

There was a recognized and respected literature in Hebrew. But Yiddish theater or literature? That was a joke. And Yiddish actors were considered to be clowns.

But Spokoiny had described some of the things done in the Yiddish theater. And he had sung for us some of Goldfaden's songs. I even learned some of the melodies. Now, as Trufonov spoke of these things, the warmth of my memories strengthened our friendship.

One day he confided in me. There was a man named Belkin now in Mohilev looking for young people to go to Palestine.

"I tell you this because you are no ordinary person. Do you really think I believe this story about your running away from prison? Who are you?"

He assured me I could trust him with my secret. But I insisted there was no secret. I asked him to introduce me to Belkin.

Following the terrorist conspiracy of the Will of the People party, which resulted in the assassination of Alexander II, pogroms against the Jews broke out in southern Russia. Suddenly it became clear to many young intellectual Jews that Russia was not their homeland and that a true home must be found for the Jews. But where? The Russian weekly publications on Jewish affairs debated whether it should be America or Palestine.

In Kiev, a group of students entered a synagogue crowded with weeping, mourning Jews. One of them named Aleinikoff rose and spoke in Russian to the congregation.

"We are your brothers," he said. "We are Jews, just as you are. Until now we thought of ourselves as Russians, not as Jews. Now we regret it. The events of these last weeks—the pogroms in Elisavetgrad, in Balta, here in Kiev, and in other cities have shown us how tragic has been our mistake. Yes, we are Jews."

These words had a stunning effect on the congregation. And this event was the beginning of the nationalist movement among the young Jewish intellectuals in Russia. The Kiev student group consisted of those who favored America as the land to which Jews should look for a new home.

Some were so deeply moved that they stopped talking in Russian and began to use only Yiddish with which they had become unfamiliar. Many discarded their Russianized names and assumed their Jewish ones. Yakov became Yankel again and Natasha answered only when addressed as Ethel.

But I must admit that these new nationalists comprised only a small group. And Jewish revolutionaries who fell in with the nationalist movement also comprised a small group. The reasons for this may seem unbelievable. Among the Jewish revolutionaries were some who considered the anti-Semitic massacres to be a good omen. They theorized that the pogroms were an instinctive outpouring of the revolutionary anger of the people, driving the Russian masses against their oppressors. The uneducated Russian people knew that the Czar, the officials, and the Jews sucked their blood, they argued. So the Ukrainian peasants attacked the Jews, the "percentniks." The revolutionary torch had been lit and would next be applied to the officials and the Czar himself. This was the reasoning of some revolutionaries—Jews and non-Jews.

Members of the underground Will of the People party, which had engineered the assassination, released a proclamation addressed to the Ukrainian pogrom makers. In it they enunciated this theory and urged the pogrom makers to continue their revolutionary work. The proclamation appeared in issue Number 6 of their official party organ. It pointed out that the Jews were not the only ones deserving of their "justice." One of the group that composed the proclamation was a Jew.

Vilna and Vitebsk were distant from the regions in which the pogroms occurred, so that we heard only echoes of those events. But I remember that before my departure from Vilna to Velizh one of the members of our group discussed with me, on the basis of an article we had read, how the pogroms had been directed against the exploiters and how this would be the start of a revolution that would ultimately destroy capitalists, oppression, and robbery.

I was at the time young and immature, despite my wide reading and my deep feelings. My theories and opinions were not based on facts, logic, or experience. The truth is that much of the revolutionary party then consisted of inexperienced youngsters, and even our leaders, with more knowledge and experience, were young.

The revolutionaries had hoped that the bomb which killed Alexander would touch off a revolution. They were ready to believe that the pogroms that followed their act of terror were the beginning of that uprising. It had merely taken an unpredictable turn: instead of an attack on government centers it had turned into an attack on the Jews. But they assured themselves that this was only the beginning.

Some of the revolutionaries had a different explanation. They were certain that the government itself had set off the pogroms in order to save the throne from a revolutionary upheaval. In this way it had sidetracked the course of revolution. By making the Jews the scapegoats, it had confused the common people so that in the end the peasants were certain that the Jews and not the Czar were the cause of their troubles. Blinded by anti-Semitism, the peasant lost sight of the true cause of his misery—a despotic, thieving government. The pogroms were the Czar's lightning rod.

Almost everywhere, government officials encouraged new acts of violence instead of arresting and punishing the pogrom makers. There were rare exceptions. Generally, the police quietly stood aside. Nor was there any official denial that the Czar had ordered the pogroms against the Jews. In many cases it was clear that pogrom leaders were government agents masquerading as peasants.

It makes no sense to believe that the government itself organized the pogroms to save itself from the people's wrath. But once the pogroms were launched, the government made the most of them. There is no question that then many government agents helped the pogrom makers.

The first pogrom, the one in Elisavetgrad, resulted from an accidental argument between a Jewish innkeeper and a drunken peasant. It became the model for the other attacks on Jews that followed immediately. The robberies and outrages had a single style; it was clear that the same hand had guided the bloodbaths everywhere.

Two groups emerged. One believed that a new home for the Jews should be started in America, the land of rich resources and opportunity. The other urged a return to Palestine, the historical home of the Jewish people. Belkin was a pioneer of this pro-Palestine movement.

I had been cut off from my friends and had no one with whom I could discuss such matters. Belkin carried a book into which he wrote the names of candidates for Palestine. He was a doer of deeds, an idealist, almost one of "ours." Perhaps he could advise me.

When I met him the next day I liked him at once. He was earnest and not a huckster. He left off propagandizing when he realized almost at once that he was getting nowhere with me. After we had talked for an hour I trusted him enough to tell him that I could not subscribe to the Palestine idea, that I was first of all a socialist and was anxious to get to Switzerland.

He argued that all I could work for, in that case, would be to return to Russia someday as an "illegal," with false papers. Sooner or later I would be arrested. I would give my life for what? he asked. For a Russian people who made pogroms on Jews?

In Palestine, he continued, I could work for the fulfillment of an ideal of happiness and security for our people and without risking my life. Or, if I was so determined to serve my socialist ideal, why must I go to Switzerland? Why not to America? Many socialists were heading for America where they planned to establish communist colonies.

But I longed to work in behalf of the freedom of the Russian people. If they were only permitted to learn, to understand the truth, I pleaded, everything would be different. There would be no more pogroms and Jews and Gentiles would be free and equal.

Later, I could not forget what he had told me about America. I imagined a wonderful communist life in that far-off country, a life without "mine" and "thine." I had thought until now that such a dream of equality could be realized only in the distant future. In America it could become a reality now.

I had read of Robert Owen's attempt to establish a colony. Like others, it had failed. The new Jewish colonies would endure because they would be based on sound socialist ideas. Pro-Palestine Belkin had made a pro-American out of me.

From him I learned that thousands of Jewish immigrants were assembling in Brody in Galicia with the idea of getting to America and that there were many socialists among them.

It was held against the Jews that so many of them were tradesmen, moneylenders, small businessmen, whereas the most honorable pursuit should be agriculture. The lands in which Jews had settled had held this belief for generations. The early Russian revolutionaries idolized the tiller of the soil.

Jews were not allowed to be farmers. They were only allowed to trade with those who worked the soil. Now both groups of immigrants were determined to change the Jews into tillers of the earth; their great ideal was to work the land.

It was more than thirty years before I saw Belkin again. By that time he had helped to establish the first colonies in Palestine. But that night, after he gave me a warm goodbye and his wishes for a successful journey, I paced my room in a fever. America! To go to America! To reestablish the Garden of Eden in that distant land. My spirit soared. All my other plans dissolved. I was for America! . . .

I worried about my parents. Eleven years later I learned that the police and gendarmes had come to the house in Strashuner's courtyard and searched every corner, every piece of furniture and pillow for secret literature or any letters I might have left behind. Tsilshtein, home for the holiday, had already informed them that I had departed from Velizh.

As I prepared to leave for America I longed to send word to them. A young man from Zhitomir, staying at the inn, was leaving for Petersburg. I wrote a letter which pretended to be from him to my parents and asked him to mail it from some point en route.

I wrote:

> I am a good friend of your son. I have received a letter from him from Paris. He writes that he arrived safely and has excellent prospects. He will study at the university in Paris. He sends his warmest regards and assures you that he is well and in good circumstances. He is happy and promises to write all the details in a future letter.

The young man promised to mail the letter at the Dinaburg station. A heavy load was lifted from my heart.

My last evening in Mohilev! I had become very much a part of the family. The three weeks had passed like a dream. Now, suddenly, the dream was ended. I had not thought when I left Velizh that I was starting such a long journey. This was the point at which I was cutting myself off from my past, from those I loved. Would I ever see them again?

Elia was also embarking on a trip. He was going to Nevel with a brief stop in Vitebsk. I wrote a letter which I planned to drop into Elia's trunk when no one was around. I wrote:

> Dear Friend, I put this letter in your trunk under these things in order that you do not find it until you arrive in Nevel. Until now, I denied my identity, but you were right. Tell my friends where you saw me and tell them that I am gone from Russia.

The next day the place was in an uproar. I carried the letter in my pocket and never got the chance to drop it in the trunk.

Elia was going only to the next province. But Mrs. Machover and the children fussed over him as if he too were heading for America—packing and repacking.

Then it was time to go. "Be well! Go in good health! Have a good trip!" They swarmed around Elia and me—he the hero of his family, I the hero of all the others who had gathered.

An insignificant detail! A young man leaves for America! Can any of my young readers understand the importance and the drama of this departure?

We arrived at the pier.

"May God help you! Write us how things are in America! Maybe someday we will come over also!"

Elia boarded his steamer, bound for Nevel; I ascended mine, going to Kiev. The name of my ship was *Marusia.*

11. THE ZIONIST DREAM

Leo (Yehudah Leib) Pinsker, a progressive and highly educated Russian Jew, was the son of Simcha Pinsker, an excellent Hebrew scholar and authority on the medieval Karaite sect. He was born in Tomashov, Poland, in 1821, spent his childhood in Odessa, received his M.D. degree at Moscow University, helped found the first Russian Jewish weekly *Razsvet (Dawn),* and was a distinguished physician in Odessa until his death in 1891.

Together with Moses Hess's *Rome and Jerusalem* (1862) and Theodore Herzl's *The Jewish State* (1896), Pinsker's *Auto-Emancipation* ranks as one of the classical works of Zionism. And like Hess and particularly Herzl, Pinsker was more than merely a theoretician; after the pogroms and May Laws of 1881–1882 he associated himself prominently with, and became chairman of the first international assembly of, the Hoveve Tziyon (Lovers of Zion) at their 1884 conference, became the first chairman or president of the Lovers of Zion Committee in Odessa, labored in the cause of the colonization of Palestine, and eventually became the symbolic head of Lovers of Zion.

Published anonymously in German in Berlin, the center of modern Jewish assimilation, Pinsker's essay, as those of Hess and Herzl, was addressed to, and largely ignored by, Occidental Jews, although it was enthusiastically applauded and vigorously condemned in Russian Jewish communities. Pinsker argued that the civil emancipation of the Jew in Western Europe was a delusion, for hatred of the Jew had its source in a deep-rooted natural feeling or psychic disorder. Emancipation, an activity of reason, cannot control psychosis, and hence the hope of the Jews was to be found not in the emancipation of Jews by others, but in self-emancipation.

Pinsker's conceptual framework, metaphors, definitions, and analysis contrast significantly in their biological emphasis with Herzl's political categories. Pinsker puts his argument in the language of current scientific terminology, arguing that the Jews are a biological entity, a race that cannot be assimilated. This entity is abnormal or aberrant, and, as such, causes irrational fear among non-Jews. Anti-Semitism, in its modern guises, is of a piece with medieval demonology, and Pinsker treats it as a typical pathological case. A partial remedy for the illnesses of both the non-Jewish majority and the Jewish minority would be the normalization of relationships; for Pinsker this meant the development of Jewish statehood. By the second edition of his essay Pinsker was arguing that the country in which the self-emancipated Jew should live must be Palestine.

The following condensation is from the translation of *Auto-Emancipation* published in Washington, D.C., in 1944 by the Zionist Organization of America.

Leo Pinsker, *Auto-Emancipation: An Appeal to His People by a Russian Jew*

That hoary problem, subsumed under the Jewish question, today, as ever in the past, provokes discussion. Like the squaring of the circle it remains unsolved, but unlike it, continues to be the ever-burning question of the day. That is because the problem is not one of mere theoretical interest: it renews and revives in everyday life and presses ever more urgently for solution.

This is the kernel of the problem, as we see it: *the Jews comprise a distinctive element among the nations under which they dwell, and as such can neither assimilate nor be readily digested by any nation.*

Hence the solution lies in finding a means of so readjusting this exclusive element to the family of nations, that the basis of the Jewish question will be permanently removed.

This does not mean, of course, that we must think of waiting for the age of universal harmony.

No previous civilization has been able to achieve it, nor can we see even in the remote distance, that day of the Messiah, when national barriers will no longer exist and all mankind will live in brotherhood and concord. Until then, the nations must narrow their aspirations to achieve a tolerable *modus vivendi.*

The world has yet long to wait for eternal peace. Meanwhile nations live side by side in a state of relative peace, secured by treaties and international law, but based chiefly on the fundamental equality between them.

But it is different with the people of Israel. There is no such equality in the nations' dealings with the Jews. The basis is absent upon which treaties and international law may be applied: mutual respect. Only when this basis is established, when the equality of Jews with other nations becomes a fact, can the Jewish problem be considered solved.

An equality of this kind did exist in the now long forgotten past, but unfortunately, under present conditions, the prospect that will readmit the Jewish people to the status of nationhood is so remote as to seem illusory. It lacks most of the essential attributes by which a nation is recognized. It lacks that autochthonous life which is inconceivable without a common language and customs and without cohesion in space. The Jewish people has no fatherland of its own, though many motherlands; no center of focus or gravity, no government of its own, no official representation. They home everywhere, but are nowhere at home. The nations have *never* to deal with a Jewish nation but always with mere *Jews*. The Jews are not a nation because they lack a certain distinctive national character, inherent in all other nations, which is formed by common residence in a single state. It was clearly impossible for this national character to be developed in the Diaspora; the Jews seem rather to have lost all remembrance of their former home. Thanks to their ready adaptability, they have all the more easily acquired characteristics, not inborn, of the people among whom fate has thrown them. Often to please their protectors, they recommend their traditional individuality entirely. They acquired or persuaded themselves into certain cosmopolitan tendencies which could no more appeal to others than bring satisfaction to themselves.

In seeking to fuse with other peoples they deliberately renounced to some extent their own nationality. *Yet nowhere did they succeed in obtaining from their fellow citizens recognition as natives of equal status.*

But the greatest impediment in the path of the Jews to an independent national existence is that they do not feel its need. Not only that, but they go so far as to deny its authenticity.

In the case of a sick man, the absence of desire for food is a very serious symptom. It is not always possible to cure him of this ominous loss of appetite. And even if his appetite is restored, it is still a question whether he will be able to digest food, even though he desire it.

The Jews are in the unhappy condition of such a patient. We must discuss this most important point with all possible precision. We must prove that the misfortunes of the Jews are due, above all, to their lack of desire for national independence; and that this desire must be awakened and maintained in time if they do not wish to be subjected forever to disgraceful existence—in a word, we must prove that *they must become a nation.*

In the seemingly irrelevant circumstances, that the Jews are not regarded as an independent nation by other nations, rests in part the secret of their abnormal position and of their endless misery. Merely to belong to this people is to be indelibly stigmatized, a mark repellent to non-Jews and painful to the Jews themselves. However, this phenomenon is rooted deeply in human nature.

Among the living nations of the earth the Jews are as a nation long since dead.

With the loss of their country, the Jewish people lost their independence, and fell into a decay which is not compatible with existence as a whole vital organism. The state was crushed before the eyes of the nations. But after the Jewish people had ceased to exist as an actual state, as a political entity, they could nevertheless not submit to total annihilation—they lived on spiritually as a nation. The world saw in this people the uncanny form of one of the dead walking among the living. The ghostlike apparition of a living corpse, of a people without unity or organization, without land or other bonds of unity, no longer alive, and yet walking among the living—this spectral form without precedence in history, unlike anything that preceded or followed it, could but strangely affect the imagination of the nations. And if the fear of ghosts is something inborn, and has a certain justification in the psychic life of mankind, why be surprised at the effect produced by this dead but still living nation?

A fear of the Jewish ghost has passed down the generations and the centuries. First a breeder of prejudice, later in conjunction with other forces we are about to discuss, it culminated in Judeophobia.

Judeophobia, together with other symbols, superstitions, and idiosyncrasies, has acquired legitimacy among all the peoples of the earth with whom the Jews had intercourse. Judeophobia is a variety of demonopathy with the distinction that it is not peculiar to particular races but is common to the whole of mankind, and that this ghost is not disembodied like other ghosts but partakes of flesh and blood, must endure pain inflicted by the fearful mob who imagines itself endangered.

Judeophobia is a psychic aberration. As a psychic aberration it is hereditary, and as a disease transmitted for two thousand years it is incurable.

It is this fear of ghosts, the mother of Judeophobia, that has evoked this abstract, I might say Platonic hatred, thanks to which the whole Jewish nation is wont to be held responsible for the real or supposed misdeeds of its individual members, and to be libeled in so many ways, to be buffeted about so shamefully.

Friend and foe alike have tried to explain or to justify this hatred of the Jews by bringing all sorts of charges against them. They are said to have crucified Jesus, to have drunk the blood of Christians, to have poisoned wells, to have taken usury, to have exploited the peasant, and so on. These and a thousand and one other charges against an entire people have been proved groundless. They showed their own weakness in that they had to be trumped up wholesale in order to quiet the evil conscience of the Jew-baiters, to justify the condemnation of an entire nation, to demonstrate the necessity of burning the Jew, or rather the Jewish ghost, at the stake. He who tries to prove too much proves nothing at all. Though the Jews may justly be charged with many shortcomings, those shortcomings are, at all events, not such great vices, not such capital crimes, as to justify the condemnation of the entire people. In individual cases, indeed, these accusations are contradicted by the fact that the Jews get along fairly well with their Gentile neighbors. This is the reason that the charges preferred are usually of the most general character, made up out of whole cloth, based to a certain extent on *a priori* reasoning, and true at best in individual cases, but not admitting of proof as regards the whole people.

In this way have Judaism and anti-Semitism passed for centuries through history as inseparable companions. Like the Jewish people, the real wandering Jew, anti-Semitism, too, seems as if it would never die. He must be blind indeed who will assert that the Jews are not *the chosen people,* the people chosen for universal hatred. No matter how much the nations are at variance in their relations with one another, however diverse their instincts and aims, they join hands in their hatred of the Jews; on this one matter all are agreed. The extent and the manner in which this antipathy is shown depends of course upon the cultural status of each people. The antipathy as such, however, exists in all places and at all times, whether it appears in the form of deeds of violence, as envious jealousy, or under the guise of tolerance and protection. To be robbed as a Jew or to be protected as a Jew is equally humiliating, equally destructive to the self-respect of the Jews.

Having analyzed Judeophobia as a hereditary form of demonopathy, peculiar to the human race, and having represented anti-Semitism as proceeding from an inherited aberration of the human mind, we must draw the important conclusion that we must give up contending against these hostile impulses as we must against every other inherited predisposition. This view is especially important because it should persuade us that polemics is useless and that we should abstain from it as a waste of time and energy, for against superstition even the gods contend in vain. Prejudice or instinctive ill-will is not moved by rational argument, however forceful and clear. These sinister powers must either be kept within bounds by force like every other blind natural force or simply evaded.

In human psychology, then, we find the roots of the prejudice against the Jewish nation; but there are other factors not less important which render impossible the fusion or equalization of the Jews with the other peoples to be considered.

No people, generally speaking, likes foreigners. Ethnologically, this cannot be brought as a charge against any people. Now, is the Jew subject to *this* general law to the same extent as the other nationalities? Not at all! The aversion which meets the foreigner in a strange land can be repaid in equal coin in his home country. The non-Jew pursues his own interest in a foreign country openly and without giving offense. It is everywhere considered natural that he should fight for these interests, alone or in conjunction with others. The foreigner has no need to *be,* or to *seem* to *be,* a patriot. But as for the Jew, not only is he not a native in his own home country, but he is also not a foreigner; he is, in very truth, the stranger *par excellence.* He is regarded as neither friend nor foe but an alien, of whom the only thing known is that he has no home.

One *distrusts* the foreigner but does not *trust* the Jew. The foreigner has a claim to hospitality, which he can repay in the same coin. The Jew can make no such return; consequently he can make no claim to hospitality. He is not a guest, much less a welcome guest. He is more like a beggar; and what beggar is welcome? He is rather a refugee; and where is the refugee to whom a refuge may not be refused?

The Jews are aliens who can have no representatives, because they have no country. Because they have none, because their home has no boundaries within which they can be entrenched, their misery too is boundless. The *general law* does not apply to the Jews as true aliens, but there are everywhere *laws for the Jews,* and if the general law is to apply to them, a special and explicit bylaw is required to confirm it. Like the Negroes, like women, and unlike all free peoples, they must be *emancipated.* If, unlike the Negroes, they belong to an advanced race, and if, unlike women, they can produce not only women of distinction, but also distinguished men, even men of greatness, then it is very much the worse for them.

Since the Jew is nowhere at home, nowhere regarded as a native, he remains an alien everywhere. That he himself and his ancestors as well are born in the country does not alter this fact in the least.

In the great majority of cases, he is treated as a stepchild, as a Cinderella; in the most favorable cases he is regarded as an adopted child whose rights may be questioned; *never* is he considered a legitimate child of the fatherland.

The German proud of his Teutonism, the Slav, the Celt, not one of them admits that the Semitic Jew is his equal by birth; and even if he be ready, as a man of culture, to admit him to all civil rights, he will never quite forget that his fellow citizen is a Jew. The *legal emancipation* of the Jews is the culminating achievement of our century. But *legal* emancipation is not *social* emancipation, and with the proclamation of the former the Jews are still far from being emancipated from their exceptional *social position.*

The emancipation of the Jews is required as a postulate of *logic,* of *law,* and of *enlightened national interest,* but it can never be a spontaneous expression of human *feeling.* Far from owing its origin to spontaneous *feeling,* it is *never a matter of course;* and it has never yet taken root so deeply that further discussion of it becomes unnecessary. In any event, whether emancipation was undertaken from spontaneous impulse or from conscious motives, it remains a rich gift, a splendid alms, willingly or unwillingly flung to the poor, humble beggars whom no one, however, cares to shelter, because a homeless, wandering beggar wins confidence or sympathy from none. The Jew is not permitted to forget that the daily bread of civil rights must be given him.

So long as this people produces in accordance with its nature, vagrant nomads; so long as it cannot give a satisfactory account of whence it comes and whither it goes; so long as the Jews themselves prefer not to speak in Aryan society of their Semitic descent and prefer not to be reminded of it; so long as they are persecuted, tolerated, protected, or emancipated, the stigma attached to this people, which forces it into an undesirable isolation from all nations, cannot be removed by any sort of legal emancipation.

This degrading dependence of the ever alien Jew upon the non-Jew is reinforced by another factor, which makes amalgamation of the Jews with the original inhabitants of a land absolutely impossible. In the great struggle for existence, civilized peoples readily submit to laws which help to transform their struggle into a peaceful competition, a noble emulation. In this respect a distinction is usually made between the native and the foreigner, the first, of course, always receiving the preference. Now, if this distinction is drawn even against the foreigner of equal birth, how harshly is it applied to the ever alien Jew! The beggar who dares to cast longing eyes upon a country not his own is in the position of a young virgin's suitor, guarded against him by jealous relatives! And if he nevertheless prosper and succeed in plucking a flower here and there from its soil, woe to the ill-fated man! He must expect the fate of the Jews of Spain and Russia.

The Jews, moreover, do not suffer only when they meet with notable success. Wherever they are congregated in large numbers, they must, by their very preponderance, hold an advantage in competition with the non-Jewish population. Thus, in the western provinces we see the Jews squeezed together, leading a wretched existence in dreadful poverty, while charges of Jewish exploitation are continually pressed.

To sum up then, to the living the Jew is a corpse, to the native a foreigner, to the homesteader a vagrant, to the proprietary a beggar, to the poor an exploiter and a millionaire, to the patriot a man without a country, for all a hated rival.

This *natural antagonism* is the source of numberless misunderstandings, accusations, and reproaches which both parties rightfully or wrongfully hurl at each other. Instead of realizing their own position and adopting a rational line of conduct, the Jews appeal to eternal justice, and fondly imagine that the appeal will have some effect. And whereas the non-Jew should simply plead superior strength, the historical prerogative of the strong over the weak, he seeks to justify his attitude by a mass of accusations which, on closer examination, prove to be baseless or negligible. The impartial thinker, who does not desire to judge and interpret the affairs of this world according to the principles of some Utopian Arcadia, but would merely ascertain the facts in order to draw a conclusion of practical value, will not seriously charge either of the parties with responsibility for this antagonism. To the Jews, however, he will say: "You are *foolish,* because you stand there nonplussed and expect of human nature something which it has never produced—humanity. You are also contemptible, because you have no real self-estimation and no national *self-respect.*"

National self-respect! Where can we find it? It is precisely the great misfortune of our race that we do not constitute a nation, but are merely Jews. We are a flock scattered over the whole face of the earth, and no shepherd to protect us and bring us together. At best we attain the rank of goats, which in Russia are mated with racehorses. And that is the highest reach of our ambition!

It is true that those who claim to sympathize with us have always taken good care that we should have no respite in which to recover our self-respect. As individual Jews, but not as a Jewish nation, we have carried on for centuries the hard and unequal struggle for existence. Each man singly has sequestered his genius and energy for a little oxygen and a morsel of bread, moistened with tears. We did not succumb in this desperate struggle. We waged the most glorious of all guerrilla struggles with the peoples of the earth, who with one accord wished to destroy us. But the war we have waged—and God knows how long we shall continue to wage it—has not been for a fatherland, but for the wretched maintenance of millions of "Jew peddlers."

The nations of the earth could not destroy us bodily, yet they were able to suppress in us every sense of national independence. So now we look on with fatalistic indifference when in many countries we are refused such recognition as would not lightly be denied to Zulus. In the Diaspora we maintained our individual life, and proved our power of resistance, but we broke the common tie of national consciousness. Seeking to maintain our material existence, we were compelled very often to forget our moral dignity. We did not perceive that unworthy tactics, though forced upon us, have lowered us still more in the eyes of our opponents, that we were only the more exposed to humiliating contempt and outlawed existence, which has at length become our baleful heritage. In the great, wide world there was no place for us. We pray only for a little place somewhere to lay our weary head to rest. And as our claims diminished, our dignity vanished away.

We were the shuttlecock which the peoples tossed in turn to one another. The cruel game was equally amusing whether we were caught or thrown, and was enjoyed all the more as our national respect became more elastic and yielding in the hands of the peoples. Under such circumstances, how could there be any question of national self-determination, of a free, active development of our national force or of our native genius?

By the way, our enemies did not fail to make capital of this trait, though irrelevant, in order to prove our inferiority. One would think that a man of genius among them grew as blackberries on the hedges. The wretches! They mock the eagle who once soared to heaven and saw Divinity itself, because he can no longer fly after his wings are broken! Even so we have remained on the level with the great peoples of civilization. Grant us but our independence, allow us to take care of ourselves, give us but a little strip of land like that of the Serbians and Romanians, give us a chance to lead a national existence and then prate about our lacking manly virtues! *Today we live under the weight of evils you have brought upon us. What we lack is not genius but self-consciousness, an appreciation of our value as men of which we were deprived by you!*

When we are ill-used, robbed, plundered, and dishonored, we dare not defend ourselves, and, worse still, we take it almost as a matter of course. When our face is slapped, we soothe our burning cheek with cold water; and when a bloody wound has been inflicted, we apply a bandage. When we are turned out of the house which we ourselves built, we beg humbly for mercy, and when we fail to reach the heart of our oppressor we move on in search of another exile.

When an idle spectator on the road calls out to us: "You poor Jewish devils are certainly to be pitied," we are most deeply touched; and when a Jew is said to be an honor to his people, we are foolish enough to be proud of it. We have sunk so low that we become almost jubilant when, as in the West, a small fraction of our people is put on an equal footing with non-Jews. But he who must be *put* on a footing stands but weakly. If no notice is taken of our descent and we are treated like others born in the country, we express our gratitude by actually turning renegades. For the sake of the comfortable position we are granted, for the fleshpots which we may enjoy in peace, we persuade ourselves, and others, that we are no longer Jews, but full-blooded citizens. Idle delusion! Though you prove yourselves patriots a thousand times, you will still be reminded at every opportunity of your Semitic descent. This fateful *memento mori* will not prevent you, however, from accepting the extended hospitality, until some fine morning you find yourself crossing the border and you are reminded by the mob that you are, after all, nothing but vagrants and parasites, without the protection of law.

But even humane treatment does not prove that we are welcome.

Indeed, what a pitiful figure we cut! We are not counted among the nations, neither have we a voice in their councils, even when the affairs concern us. Our fatherland—the other man's country; our unity—dispersion; our solidarity—the battle against us; our weapon—humility; our defense—flight; our individuality—adaptability; our future—the next day. What a miserable role for a nation which descends from the Maccabees!

Do you wonder that a people which allowed itself for dear life's sake to be trampled upon, and has learned to love these very feet that trample upon them, should have fallen into the utmost contempt!

Our tragedy is that we can neither live nor die. We cannot die despite the blows of our enemies, and we do not wish to die by our own hand, through apostasy or self-destruction. Neither can we live; our enemies have taken care of that. We will not recommence life as a nation, live like the other peoples, thanks to those overzealous patriots, who think it is necessary to sacrifice every claim upon independent national life to their loyalty as citizens—which should be a matter of course. Such fanatical patriots deny their ancient national character for the sake of any other nationality, whatever it may be, of high rank or low. But they deceive no one. They do not see how glad one is to decline Jewish companionship.

Thus for eighteen centuries we have lived in disgrace, without a single earnest attempt to shake it off!

We know well the great martyrology of our people and we would be the last to place the responsibility upon our ancestors. The demands of individual self-preservation necessarily suppress in the germ every national thought, every united movement. If the non-Jewish peoples, thanks to our dispersion, deserved to strike through each of us the whole Jewish people, we had the resistance to survive as a people, but we were left too powerless to raise ourselves and carry on an active struggle in our own behalf. Under the pressure of the hostile world we have lost in the course of our long exile all self-confidence, all initiative.

Moreover, the belief in a Messiah, in the intervention of a higher power to bring about our political resurrection, and the religious assumption that we must bear patiently divine punishment, caused us to abandon every thought of our national liberation, unity, and independence. Consequently, we have renounced the idea of a nationhood and did so the more readily since we were preoccupied with our immediate needs. Thus we sank lower and lower. The people *without a country forgot their country*. Is it not high time to perceive the disgrace of it all?

Happily, matters stand somewhat differently now. The events of the last few years in *enlightened* Germany, in Romania, in Hungary, and especially in Russia, have effected what the far bloodiest persecutions of the Middle Ages could not. The national consciousness which until then had lain dormant in sterile martyrdom awoke the masses of the Russian and Romanian Jews and took form in an irresistible movement toward Palestine. Mistaken as this movement has proved to be by its results, it was, nevertheless, a right instinct to strike out for home. The severe trials which they have endured have now provoked a reaction quite different from the fatalistic submission to a divine condign punishment. Even the unenlightened masses of the Russian

Jews have not entirely escaped the influences of the principles of modern culture. Without renouncing Judaism and their faith, they revolted against undeserved ill-treatment which could be inflicted with impunity only because the Russian Government regards the Jews as aliens. And the other European governments—why should they concern themselves with the citizens of a state in whose internal affairs they have no right to interfere?

Today, when our kinsmen in a small part of the earth are allowed to breathe freely and can feel more deeply for the sufferings of their brothers; today, when a number of other subject and oppressed nationalities have been allowed to regain their independence, we, too, must not sit a moment longer with folded hands; we must not consent to play forever the hopeless role of the "Wandering Jew." It is a truly hopeless one, leading to despair.

When an individual finds himself despised and rejected by society, no one wonders if he commits suicide. But where is the deadly weapon to give the *coup de grace* to the scattered limbs of the Jewish nation, and then who would lend his hand to it? The destruction is neither possible nor desirable. Consequently, we are bound by duty to devote all our remaining moral force to reestablishing ourselves as a living nation, so that we may ultimately assume a more fitting and dignified role among the family of the nations.

If the basis of our argument is sound, if the prejudice of mankind against us rests upon anthropological and social principles, innate and ineradicable, we must look no more to the slow progress of humanity. And we must learn to recognize that as long as we lack a home of our own, such as the other nations have, we must resign forever the noble hope of becoming the equals of our fellowmen. We must recognize that before the great idea of human brotherhood will unite all the peoples of the earth, millennia must elapse; and that meanwhile a people which is at home everywhere and nowhere, must everywhere be regarded as alien. The time has come for a sober and dispassionate realization of our true position.

With unbiased eyes and without prejudice we must see in the mirror of the nations the tragicomic figure of our people, which with distorted countenance and maimed limbs helps to make *universal* history without managing properly its *own* little history. We must reconcile ourselves once and for all to the idea that the other nations, by reason of their inherent *natural* antagonism, will forever reject us. We must not shut our eyes to this natural force which works like every other elemental force; we *must* take it into account. We must not *complain* of it; on the contrary, we are *in duty bound* to take courage, to rise, and to see to it that we do not remain forever the Cinderella, the butt of the peoples.

We are no more justified in leaving our national fortune in the hands of the other peoples than we are in making them responsible for our national misfortune. The human race, including ourselves, has hardly reached the first stage of the interminable road to perfection in human conduct, providing the goal is to be reached at all. We must, therefore, abandon the delusion that we are fulfilling by our dispersion a Providential mission, a mission in which no one believes, an honorable post which we, to speak frankly, would gladly resign, if the odious epithet "Jew" could only be blotted out of the memory of man.

We must seek our honor and our salvation not in self-deceptions, but in the restoration of our national ties. Hitherto the world has not considered us as a firm of standing, and consequently we enjoyed no genuine credit.

If other national movements which have risen before our eyes were their own justification, can it still be questioned whether the Jews have a similar right? They play a larger part in the life of the civilized nations, and they have rendered greater service to humanity; they have a greater past and history, a common, unmixed descent, an indestructible vigor, an unshakable faith, and an unexampled martyrology; the peoples have sinned against them more grievously than against any other nation. Is not that enough to make them capable and worthy of possessing a fatherland?

The struggle of the Jews for national unity and independence as an established nation not only possesses the inherent justification that belongs to the struggle of every oppressed people, but it is also calculated to win the support of the people by whom we are now unwanted. This struggle must become an irresistible factor of contemporary international politics and destined for future greatness.

At the very outset we expect a great outcry. Most Jews, grown timid and skeptical, will declare the early activities to be the unconscious convulsions of a crushed organism and certainly its execution and achievement is sure to encounter the gravest of difficulties and perhaps will be possible only after superhuman efforts. But since the Jews have no other way out of their desperate position, it would be cowardly to shrink from it in the face of heavy odds. But "faint heart never won fair lady"—and, indeed, what have we to lose? At the worst, we shall continue to be in the future what we have been in the past, what we are too cowardly to resolve that we will be no longer: *eternally despised Jews.*

We have lately had very bitter experiences in Russia. We are both too many and too few; too many in the southwestern provinces, in which the Jews are allowed to reside, and too few in all the other provinces, where they are forbidden. If the Russian Government, and the Russian people as well, realized that an equal distribution of the Jewish population would benefit the entire country, we might have been spared all our sufferings. Unfortunately, Russia cannot and will not realize this. That is not our fault, neither is it a consequence of the low cultural state of the Russian people. We have found our bitterest opponents, indeed, in a large part of the press, which might be supposed to possess education; the unfortunate situation of the Russian Jews is due, rather, purely and simply to the operation of those *general forces,* a consequence of human nature which we have previously discussed. And since it is not to be our mission to reform mankind, we must see what *we* have to do for ourselves under the circumstances.

Such being the situation, we shall forever remain a burden to the rest of the population, parasites who can never secure their favor. The apparent fact that we can mix with nations only slightly offers a further obstacle to the establishment of amicable relations. Therefore, we must see to it that the *surplus,* the unassimilable residue, is removed and elsewhere provided for. The burden is ours alone. If the Jews could be equally distributed among all the peoples of the earth, perhaps there would be no Jewish question. But this is not possible. Nay, there can be no more doubt that an immigration of the Jews *en masse* into the most progressive countries would be declined with emphasis.

We say this with a very heavy heart; but we must admit the truth. And it is necessary to know the facts if we would improve our position.

Moreover, it would be a misfortune if we were unwilling to profit by the testimony of our experience which has practical value, the most important being the constantly growing conviction that we are nowhere at home, and that we must at last look for a *home,* if not a *country* of our own.

Another conclusion is that the sorry upshot of the Russian and Romanian emigration is ascribable solely to the important fact that we were taken unawares; we had made no provision for the principal needs, a refuge and a systematic organization of emigration. When thousands were seeking new homes we forgot to provide for that which no villager forgets when he wants to move—the small matter of suitable new lodgings.

If we would have a secure home, give up our endless life of wandering and rise to the dignity of a nation in our own eyes and in the eyes of the world, we must, above all, not dream of restoring ancient Judaea. We must not attach ourselves to the place where our political life was once violently interrupted and destroyed. The goal of our present endeavors must be not the "Holy Land," but a land of our own. We need nothing but a large tract of land for our poor brothers, which shall remain our property and from which no foreign power can expel us. There we shall take with us the most sacred possessions which we have saved from the shipwreck of our former country, the *God-idea* and the *Bible.* It is these alone which have made our old fatherland the Holy Land, and not Jerusalem or the Jordan. Perhaps the Holy Land will again become ours. If so, all the better, but *first of all,* we must determine—and this is the crucial point—what country is accessible to us, and at the same time adapted to offer the Jews of all lands who must leave their homes a secure and indisputed refuge, capable of productivization. . . .

The Jews are not a living nation; they are everywhere aliens; therefore they are despised.

The civil and political emancipation of the Jews is not sufficient to raise them in the estimation of the peoples.

The proper, the only solution, is in the creation of a Jewish nationality, of a people living upon its own soil, the auto-emancipation of the Jews; their return to the ranks of the nations by the acquisition of a Jewish homeland.

We must not persuade ourselves that humanity and enlightenment alone can cure the malady of our people.

The lack of national self-respect and self-confidence, of political initiative and of unity, are the enemies of our national renaissance.

That we may not be compelled to wander from one exile to another, we must have an extensive, productive land of refuge, a *center* which is our own.

The present moment is the most favorable for this plan.

The international Jewish question must have a national solution. Of course, our national regeneration can only proceed slowly. *We* must take the first step. Our *descendants* must follow us at a measured and not overpreipitant speed.

The national regeneration of the Jews must be initiated by a congress of Jewish notables.

No sacrifice should be too great for this enterprise which will assure our people's future, everywhere endangered.

The financial execution of the undertaking does not present insurmountable difficulties.

Help yourselves, and God will help you!

12. *AMERICA! AMERICA!*

The "Bintel Brief"—letters from the Lower East Side to the *Jewish Daily Forward*—provide one of the most sensitive and vivid records of immigrant adaptation, a record equaled only by the magnificent pictorial legacy of Byron, Hine, Austen, and Riis and the immediacy of articles which appeared in the New York *Times,* New York *Tribune, Evening Post,* and the Yiddish press.

Here one senses the maelstrom of conflicting reactions to the new homeland: enthusiasm for expanded economic opportunities, excitement over political equality, and occasional yearning for the familiar warmth of the land left behind. The letters also remind us that the immigrants' difficulties certainly did not end when they disembarked in the United States. Quarantine, customs, medical examinations, boards of inquiry, and suspicion of becoming a public charge were to be endured at Castle Garden or Ellis Island while inefficient organizations, fraud, victimization, inferior lodgings, and even "white slavery" were lurking on the shore of the mainland.

"Bintel Brief" challenge the popular and prevailing notion of immigrant orthodoxy as expressed in a typical history of the Jews: "The immigrants from eastern Europe hailed from three political jurisdictions, Russia, Austria-Hungary and Rumania, but their major cultural possession, the Orthodox faith . . . was common to all of them." There is some truth in this but not much; while the importance of religion to these newcomers cannot be doubted, they subordinated religious commitments to ethnic ones, dedicated themselves to radicalism with the same enthusiasm as did non-Jewish socialists, and were to be shaped at least as much by American influences as by those of Europe. Scores of letters pose the dilemma of Jewish radicals whose antireligious tactics promised support in Russia but who are faced with a middle-class America where religion was quite respectable.

Lower East Side Jewish immigrant letters also demonstrate that, as with all other immigrant groups, intra-ethnic tension was abundant. No more than southern Italians were East European Jews a unity; Galizianers and Litvaks had their troubles not only with the new land but with each other.

The selections that follow come from I. Metzker, ed. *A Bintel Brief: Sixty Years of Letters from the Lower East Side to the Jewish Daily Forward* (Garden City, N.Y., 1971). Copyright © 1971 by Doubleday & Company, Inc., and used by permission of Doubleday & Company, Inc.

A Bintel Brief

1906

Esteemed Editor,

I hope that you will advise me in my present difficulty.

I am a "greenhorn," only five weeks in the country, and a jeweler by trade. I come from Russia, where I left a blind father and a stepmother. Before I left, my father asked me not to forget him. I promised that I would send him the first money I earned in America.

When I arrived in New York I walked around for two weeks looking for a job, and the bosses told me it was after the season. In the third week I was lucky, and found a job at which I earn eight dollars a week. I worked, I paid my landlady board, I bought a few things to wear, and I have a few dollars in my pocket.

Now I want you to advise me what to do. Shall I send my father a few dollars for Passover, or should I keep the little money for myself? In this place the work will end soon and I may be left without a job. The question is how to deal with the situation. I will do as you tell me.

Your thankful reader,

I.M.

ANSWER:
The answer to this young man is that he should send his father the few dollars for Passover because, since he is young, he will find it easier to earn a living than would his blind father in Russia.

1906

Worthy Editor,

I am a workingman from Bialystok, and there I belonged to the Bund. But I had to leave Bialystok, and later came to Minsk where I worked and joined the Socialist-Revolutionaries. What convinced me to join this organization is this: in Minsk there was a Bundist demonstration that was attacked by the police. They beat up the demonstrators brutally, and arrested many of them. The prisoners were lashed so severely that many of them became ill. One worker from Dvinsk was sentenced to fifty lashes, which caused him to develop epilepsy and while working in a factory he would suddenly fall in a fit.

When we, his co-workers, saw this, it aroused in us a desire for revenge against Czar Nicholas and his tyrannical police force. But when there was a convention of the Bund at that time, and they declared a policy against revenge, many of our Bund members joined the Socialist-Revolutionaries. I wanted to enter the militant organization, but war was declared against Japan and since I was a reservist, I began to get mail from home advising me to flee to America. I let myself be talked into it and left.

I have been in the country now two years, and life is not bad. I work in a jewelry store, for good wages. But my heart will not remain silent within me over the blood of my brothers being spilled in Russia. I am restless because of the pogroms that took place in Bialystok, where I left old parents and a sister with three small children. I haven't heard from them since the pogrom and don't know if they're alive. But since they lived in the vicinity of the "Piaskes" where the Jewish defense group was located, it's possible they are alive.

Now I ask your advice. I cannot make up my mind whether to fulfill my duty to my parents and sister and bring them to America, if I hear from them, or to go back to Russia and help my brothers in their struggle.

If I had known what was going to happen there, I would not have gone to America. I myself had agitated that one should not leave for America but stay and fight in Russia till we were victorious. Now I feel like a liar and a coward. I agitated my friends, placed them in the danger of soldiers' guns and bullets. And I myself ran away.

Respectfully,
M.G.

ANSWER:
If one were to ask us the question before leaving Russia, we would not advise him to leave the revolutionary battlefields. Since the writer of the letter is already here and speaks of his two duties, we would like to tell him that the Assistance Movement in America is developing so rapidly that everyone who wants to be useful will be able to do enough here. He should bring his parents and sister here, and become active in the local movement.

1906

Dear Editor,

I am a girl from Galicia and in the shop where I work I sit near a Russian Jew with whom I was always on good terms. Why should one worker resent another?

But once, in a short debate, he stated that all Galicians were no good. When I asked him to repeat it, he answered that he wouldn't retract a word, and that he wished all Galician Jews dead.

I was naturally not silent in the face of such a nasty expression. He maintained that only Russian Jews are fine and intelligent. According to him, the *Galitzianer* are inhuman savages, and he had the right to speak of them so badly.

Dear Editor, does he really have a right to say this? Have the Galician Jews not sent enough money for the unfortunate sufferers of the pogroms in Russia? When a Gentile speaks badly of Jews, it's immediately printed in the newspapers and discussed hotly everywhere. But that a Jew should express himself so about his own brothers is nothing? Does he have a right? Are Galicians really so bad? And does he, the Russian, remain fine and intelligent in spite of such expressions?

As a reader of your worthy newspaper, I hope you will print my letter and give your opinion.

With thanks in advance,
B.M.

ANSWER:
The Galician Jews are just as good and bad as people from other lands. If the Galicians must be ashamed of the foolish and evil ones among them, then the

Russians, too, must hide their heads in shame because among them there is such an idiot as the acquaintance of our letter writer.

1906

Dear Editor,

I join all the others who marvel at your "Bintel Brief," where almost everyone who has something on his conscience, or a secret, can express himself. I, too, wish to get something off my chest, and I want your advice.

I came to America as a *shokhet.* The ship I was on sank. I was among the lucky ones who were rescued, but my valise with my possessions, including the papers that certified that I am a *shokhet,* was lost.

Since I could no longer be a *shokhet,* I became a shirt-maker. Later I worked my way up and became a cloak-maker. But I was not satisfied because the physical labor and the degradation we had to endure in the shops was unbearable.

Within a few years two of my brothers came from Europe. We stayed together and we all worked in a shirt shop. Several times we tried contracting, but it didn't work out. At that time, white collars for shirts came into fashion. We had to sew on neckbands, to which the white collars were buttoned. This became a nuisance that delayed the work. Imagine having to cut out a band to fit each shirt we made. This wasn't easy, and the boss gave us the job of making the bands at home, as night work.

In short, one of us got an idea. Since the whole trade found the neckbands a problem, why not make the neckbands for all the manufacturers? Said and done! It worked out well. They snatched the bands from our hands and we were very busy. We were the only ones in the line from the start, and we prospered. Later a few more shops opened, but that didn't bother us because the trade grew even bigger.

Now we have a huge factory with our names on a big sign on the front of the building. But the bands that gave us our start are no longer made by us alone. We have many workers but have paid little attention to them since we were so involved with making our fortune.

In time I began to read your newspaper and, out of curiosity, even the "Bintel Brief," to see what was going on in the world. As I read more and more about the troubles, my conscience awoke and I began to think: "Robber, cold-blooded robber." My conscience spoke to me: "Just look at your workers, see how pale and thin and beaten they look, and see how healthy and ruddy your face and hands are."

This conscience of mine has a strong voice. It yells at me just as I yell at my workers, and scolds me for all my offenses against them. It will be enough for me to give just a few samples of my evil deeds: The clock in our shop gets "fixed" twice a day; the hands are moved back and forth. The foreman has on his table a stick like a conductor's baton and when someone says a word during working hours he hears the tick-tock of that stick. Our wages are never under two dollars or over seven dollars a week.

My conscience bothers me and I would like to correct my mistakes, so that I will not have to be ashamed of myself in the future. But do not forget that my brothers do not feel as I do, and if I were to speak to them about all this they would consider me crazy. So what is left for me to do? I beg you, worthy Editor, give me a suggestion.

Yours sincerely,
B.

ANSWER:
We are proud and happy that through the *Forward* and the "Bintel Brief" the conscience of this letter writer was aroused. We can only say to the writer that he must not muffle the voice of his conscience. He will lose nothing, but will gain more and more true happiness.

1908

Worthy Mr. Editor,

Please help us decide who is right in the debate between friends, whether a Socialist and freethinker should observe *yohrzeit?*

Among the disputants there is a Socialist, a freethinker, who observes his mother's *yohrzeit* in the following manner: He pays a pious man to say the Kaddish prayer for the dead, and burns a *yohrzeit* candle in his home. He himself doesn't say Kaddish, because he doesn't believe in religion. But his desire to respect the memory of his mother is so strong that it does not prevent him from performing this religious ceremony.

Among the debaters there are those who do not want to know of such an emotion as honoring the dead. But if one does desire to do so, one should say Kaddish himself, even if he does not believe in it.

Therefore, our first question is: Can we recognize the beautiful human emotion of honoring the dead, especially when it concerns one so near as a mother? The second question: If so, should the expression of honor be in keeping with the desires of the honored? Third: Would it be more conscientious and righteous if the freethinker said Kaddish himself, or if he hired a pious man to do it for him?

Being convinced that this matter interests a great number of people, we hope you, Mr. Editor, will answer us soon.

With regards,
The Debating Group

ANSWER:
Honoring a departed one who was cherished and loved is a gracious sentiment and a requisite for the living. And everyone wants to be remembered after his death. Socialists and freethinkers observe the anniversaries of their great leaders—just recently they commemorated the twenty-fifth anniversary of the death of Karl Marx.

Saying Kaddish is certainly a religious rite, and to pay someone to say Kaddish is not the act of a freethinker. But we can understand the psychology of a freethinker who feels that hiring someone else is not as much against his own convictions as to say Kaddish himself.

1909

Dear Editor,

We, the undersigned, appeal to you to use your worthy newspaper to help save a family from going under.

This is about a family from Yekaterinaslav, Russia, who suffered greatly from the pogroms. The father and a child were murdered, the mother was crippled, a twenty-year-old boy had his head split open, and a sixteen-year-old boy had his arm broken.

The survivors of the family, the mother and three children, came to America, and lived in New Britain, Connecticut. Here the mother was forced to place one child in a Catholic orphanage and give the other two to good people. The older boy, whose head had been split by the hoodlums, had a recurrence of the effects of the blow and was taken into government hospital in New York for cure. Then the authorities decided that he has to be sent back to Russia—to the city where his father and brother had been murdered. His crippled mother intends to go with him, but she is desolate because she has to leave the other children behind.

What will become of this unfortunate's children who remain alone in New Britain? What will happen to the child in the Catholic orphanage? We appeal to all Yekaterinaslaver societies and individuals to help save this family. The boy has been in the country over two years and something must be done to stop his being sent back. If this can't be done, it must at least be made possible for the mother and son to leave the country with a little money for the first piece of bread, because they don't have a red cent.

The boy is in the Staten Island Hospital and will be sent away any day now. *Landsleit* and friends, do your duty to this family that is so alone [here the name of the woman is given].

With friendly regards,
Your Reader From New Britain, Connecticut.

ANSWER:
In this answer it is stated that a reporter from the *Forward* visited the family and verified that the condition was even worse than was described in the letter.

In the answer, the Jews and Jewish organizations are scolded for neglecting these victims of the pogrom for so long, and for not seeing to it that the child was at least placed in a Jewish orphanage. Attention is also called to all those active in Jewish organizations and to the Hebrew Immigrant Aid Society. They can still influence the authorities to keep the young man from being sent back. The Jewish welfare organization and the family's *landsleit* are ordered to act immediately on this case to help the unfortunates.

1909

Dear Mr. Editor,

I was born in a small town in Russia, and until I was sixteen I studied in Talmud Torahs and yeshivas, but when I came to America I changed quickly. I was influenced by the progressive newspapers, the literature, I developed spiritually and became a freethinker. I meet with freethinking, progressive people, I feel comfortable in their company and agree with their convictions.

But the nature of my feelings is remarkable. Listen to me: Every year when the month of Elul rolls around, when the time of Rosh Hashanah and Yom Kippur approaches, my heart grows heavy and sad. A melancholy descends on me, a longing gnaws at my breast. At that time I cannot rest, I wander about through the streets, lost in thought, depressed.

When I go past a synagogue during these days and hear a cantor chanting the melodies of the prayers, I become very gloomy and my depression is so great that I cannot endure it. My memory goes back to my happy childhood years. I see clearly before me the small town, the fields, the little pond and the woods around it. I recall my childhood friends and our sweet childlike faith. My heart is constricted, and I begin to run like a madman till the tears stream from my eyes and then I become calmer.

These emotions and these moods have become stronger over the years and I decided to go to the synagogue. I went not in order to pray to God but to heal and refresh my aching soul with the cantor's sweet melodies, and this had an unusually good effect on me.

Sitting in the synagogue among *landsleit* and listening to the good cantor, I forgot my unhappy weekday life, the dirty shop, my boss, the bloodsucker, and my pale sick wife and my children. All of my America with its hurry-up life was forgotten.

I am a member of a Progressive Society, and since I am known there as an outspoken freethinker, they began to criticize me for going to the synagogue. The members do not want to hear of my personal emotions and they won't understand that there are people whose natures are such that memories of their childhood are sometimes stronger than their convictions.

And where can one hide on Yom Kippur? There are many of us, like me. They don't go to work, so it would be good if there could be a meeting hall where they could gather to hear a concert, a lecture, or something else.

What is your opinion of this? Awaiting your answer, I remain,

Your reader,
S.R.

ANSWER:

No one can tell another what to do with himself on Yom Kippur. If one is drawn to the synagogue, that is his choice. Naturally, a genuinely sincere freethinker is not drawn to the synagogue. The writer of this letter is full of memories of his childhood days at home, and therefore the cantor's melodies influence him so strongly. Who among us isn't moved by a religious melody remembered from his youth? This, however, has no bearing on loyalty to one's convictions. On Yom Kippur, a freethinker can spend his time in a library or with friends. On this day he should not flaunt himself in the eyes of the religious people. There is no sense in arousing their feelings. Every man has a right to live according to his beliefs. The pious man has as much right to his religion as the freethinker to his atheism. To parade one's acts that insult the religious feeling of the pious, especially on Yom Kippur, the day they hold most holy, is simply inhuman.

1909

Dear Editor,

Please print my letter and give me an answer. You might possibly save my life with it. I have no peace, neither day nor night, and I am afraid I will go mad because of my dreams.

I came to America three years ago from a small town in Lithuania, and I was twenty years old at that time. Besides me, my parents had five more unmarried daughters. My father was a Hebrew teacher. We used to help out by plucking chickens, making cigarettes, washing clothes for people, and we lived in poverty. The house was like a Gehenna. There was always yelling, cursing, and even beating of each other. It was bitter for me till a cousin of mine took pity on me. He sent a steamship ticket and money. He wrote that I should come to America and he would marry me.

I didn't know him, because he was a little boy when he left our town, but my delight knew no bounds. When I came to him, I found he was a sick man, and a few weeks later he died.

Then I began to work on ladies' waists. The "pleasant" life of a girl in the dreary shop must certainly be familiar to you. I toiled, and like all shopgirls, I hoped and waited for deliverance through a good match.

Landsleit and matchmakers were busy. I met plenty of prospective bridegrooms, but though I was attractive and well built, no one grabbed me. Thus a year passed. Then I met a woman who told me she was a matchmaker and had many suitors "in stock." I spilled out all my heartaches to her. First she talked me out of marrying a work-worn operator with whom I would have to live in poverty, then she told me that pretty girls could wallow in pleasure if they made the right friends. She made such a connection for me. But I had not imagined what that meant.

What I lived through afterward is impossible for me to describe. The woman handed me over to bandits, and when I wanted to run away from them they locked me in a room without windows and beat me savagely.

Time passed and I got used to the horrible life. Later I even had an opportunity to escape, because they used to send me out on the streets, but life had become meaningless for me anyway, and nothing mattered anymore. I lived this way for six months, degraded and dejected, until I got sick and they drove me out of that house.

I appealed for admission into several hospitals, but they didn't want to take me in. I had no money, because the rogues had taken everything from me. I tried to appeal to *landsleit* for help, but since they already knew all about me, they chased me away. I had decided to throw myself into the river, but wandering around on the streets, I met a richly dressed man who was quite drunk. I took over six hundred dollars from him and spent the money on doctors, who cured me.

Then I got a job as a maid for fine people who knew nothing about my past, and I have been working for them for quite a while. I am devoted and diligent, they like me, and everything is fine.

A short time ago the woman of the house died, but I continued to work there. In time, her husband proposed that I marry him. The children, who are not yet grown up, also want me to be their "mother." I know it would be good for them and for me to remain there. The man is honest and good; but my heart won't allow me to deceive him and conceal my past. What shall I do now?

Miserable

ANSWER:
Such letters from victims of "white slavery" come to our attention quite often, but we do not publish them. We are disgusted by this plague on society, and dislike bringing it to the attention of our readers. But as we read this letter we felt we dare not discard it, because it can serve as a warning for other girls. They must, in their dreary lives, attempt to withstand these temptations and guard themselves from going astray.

This letter writer, who comes to us with her bitter and earnest tears, asking advice, has sufficient reason to fear that if the man finds out about her past he will send her away. But it is hard to conceal something that many people know. Such a thing cannot be kept secret forever. When the man finds out about it from someone else, he would feel that she had betrayed him and it would be worse.

Therefore, "Honesty is the best policy." She should tell him the truth, and whatever will be, will be.

E. World War I and Its Aftermath

13. THE RENEWAL OF WISSENSCHAFT DES JUDENTHUMS

Despite the turmoil of World War I and the post-war years, or perhaps to some extent because of it, Jewish life underwent remarkable intellectual and cultural ferment. The variety of movements created during the nineteenth century showed fresh vitality, intensifying old programs and moving in new directions as well. One of the most striking manifestations of this groping and creativity was the renewal of Wissenschaft des Judenthums, particularly in Germany. Out of this renewal came a galaxy of distinguished scholars and important contributions toward understanding the richness and complexity of the Jewish past. This Wissenschaft des Judenthums moved far beyond the cloistered walls of the academy, bearing an important message for a large number of perplexed modern Jews as well. Through the efforts of leaders like Franz Rosenzweig and Martin Buber, the insights of the academicians were translated into an idiom understandable to Jews searching for a meaningful sense of identity.

Franz Rosenzweig (1886–1929), a decisive figure in this movement, was an extraordinary man. Raised in assimilated surroundings in Cassel, Germany and immersed in the study of medicine, modern history and philosophy from 1905–1912, he was on the verge of conversion when suddenly struck by the meaning of his Jewishness. A brilliant thinker and expositor, he led a talented group in the quest for a fuller understanding of the Jewish past and its implications for a Jewish future. Afflicted by a debilitating paralysis (lateral sclerosis), he became a symbol of unyielding will and resolve to all who knew him, particularly as head of the Lehrhaus (Free Jewish House of Study). The accompanying lecture sums up much of

Rosenzweig's thinking on Jewish education and introduces us to the program of his vital and influential circle.

The following selection is taken from *Franz Rosenzweig: His Life and Thought,* presented by Nahum N. Glatzer, copyright © 1953, 1961 by Schocken Books Inc. Reprinted by permission of Schocken Books Inc.

Franz Rosenzweig, "On Jewish Learning"

FROM THE DRAFT OF THE ADDRESS AT THE OPENING OF THE FREIES JUDISCHES LEHRHAUS IN FRANKFURT

Today, as the Lehrhaus opens its doors to carry on the series of Jewish adult education courses which were held here during the past winter and summer, I shall not attempt to emulate the revered man whose splendid address launched our last winter's activities by taking a subject from the vast field of Jewish scholarship. Nor would you expect it of me, younger and unknown as I am. I intend only to give you an account of the task we have set ourselves and the goals we have in mind, and I shall try to formulate these in the simplest of words.

Learning—there are by now, I should say, very few among you unable to catch the curious note the word sounds, even today, when it is used in a Jewish context. It is to a book, the Book, that we owe our survival—that Book which we use, not by accident, in the very form in which it has existed for millennia: it is the only book of antiquity that is still in living use as a scroll. The learning of this book became an affair of the people, filling the bounds of Jewish life, completely. Everything was really within this learning of the Book. There have been "outside books," but studying them was looked upon as the first step toward heresy. Occasionally such "outside" elements—Aristotle, for example—have been successfully naturalized. But in the past few centuries the strength to do this would seem to have petered out.

Then came the Emancipation. At one blow it vastly enlarged the intellectual horizons of thought and soon, very soon afterwards, of actual living.

Jewish "studying" or "learning" has not been able to keep pace with this rapid extension. What is new is not so much the collapse of the outer barriers; even previously, while the ghetto had certainly sheltered the Jew, it had not shut him off. He moved beyond its bounds, and what the ghetto gave him was only peace, home, a home for his spirit. What is new, is not that the Jew's feet could now take him farther than ever before—in the Middle Ages the Jew was not an especially sedentary, but rather a comparatively mobile element of medieval society. The new feature is that the wanderer no longer returns at dusk. The gates of the ghetto no longer close behind him, allowing him to spend the night in solitary learning. To abandon the figure of speech—he finds his spiritual and intellectual home outside the Jewish world.

The old style of learning is helpless before this spiritual emigration. In vain have both Orthodoxy and Liberalism tried to expand into and fill the new domains. No matter how much Jewish Law was stretched, it lacked the power to encompass and assimilate the life of the intellect and the spirit. The *mezuzah* may have still greeted one at the door, but the bookcase had, at best, a single Jewish corner. And Liberalism fared no better, even though it availed itself of the nimble air squadron of ideas rather than trying to master life by engaging it in hand-to-hand combat with the Law. There was nothing to be done apparently, except dilute the spirit of Judaism (or what passed for it) as much as possible in order to stake off the whole area of intellectual life; to fill it in the true sense was out of the question. High-sounding words were always on tap, words that the Judaism of old had had, but which it was chary of uttering for fear of dulling their edges with too frequent use. High-sounding words, like "humanity," "idealism," and so forth, which those who mouthed them thought as encompassing the whole world. But the world resists such superficial embraces. It is impossible to assimilate to Judaism a field of intellectual and spiritual life through constantly reiterating a catch-word and then claiming it to have kinship with some Jewish concept or other. The problems of democracy, for instance, cannot be Judaized merely by referring to the sentence in the Torah: "One law and one ordinance shall be both for you and for the stranger that sojourneth with you" (Num. 15:16), nor those of socialism by citing certain social institutions or social programs in ancient Israel. If we insist on trying, so much the worse for us! For the great, the creative spirits in our midst, have never allowed themselves to be deceived. They have left us. They went everywhere, they found their own spiritual homes, and they created spiritual homes for others. The Book around which we once gathered stands forlorn in this world, and even for those who regard it as a beloved duty to return to it at regular intervals, such a return is nothing but a turning away from life, a turning one's back on life. Their world remains un-Jewish even when they still have a Jewish world to return to. "Learning"—the old form of maintaining the relationship between life and the Book—has failed.

Has it really? No, only in the old form. For down at heel as we are, we should not be a sign and a wonder among the peoples, we should not be the eternal people, if our very illness did not beget its own cure. It is now as it has always been. We draw new strength from the very circumstance that seemed to deal the death blow to "learning," from the desertion of our scholars to the realms of the alien knowledge of the "outside books," from the transformation of our erstwhile *talmide hakhamim* into the instructors and professors of modern European universities. A new "learning" is about to be born—rather, it has been born.

It is a learning in reverse order. A learning that no longer starts from the Torah and leads into life, but the other way round: from life, from a world that knows nothing of the Law, or pretends to know nothing, back to the Torah. That is the sign of the time.

It is the sign of the time because it is the mark of the men of the time. There is no one today who is not alienated, or who does not contain within himself some small fraction of alienation. All of us to whom Judaism, to whom being a Jew, has again become the pivot of our lives—and I know that in saying this here I am not speaking for myself alone—we all know that in being Jews we must not give up anything, not renounce anything, but lead everything back to Judaism. From the periphery back to the center; from the outside, in.

This is a new sort of learning. A learning for which—in these days—he is the most apt who brings with him the maximum of what is alien. That is to say, *not* the man specializing in Jewish matters; or, if he happens to be such a specialist, he will succeed, not in the capacity of a specialist, but only as one who, too, is alienated, as one who is groping his way home.

It is not a matter of pointing out relations between what is Jewish and what is non-Jewish. There has been enough of that. It is not a matter of apologetics, but rather of finding the way back into the heart of our life. And of being confident that this heart is a Jewish heart. For we are Jews.

That sounds very simple. And so it is. It is really enough to gather together people of all sorts as teachers and students. Just glance at our prospectus. You will find, listed among others, a chemist, a physician, a historian, an artist, a politician. Two-thirds of the teachers are persons who, twenty or thirty years ago, in the only century when Jewish learning had become the monopoly of specialists, would have been denied the right of teaching in a Jewish House of Study. They have come together here as Jews. They have come together in order to "learn"—for Jewish "learning" includes Jewish "teaching." Whoever teaches here—and I believe I may say this in the name of all who are teaching here—knows that in teaching here he need sacrifice nothing of what he is. Whoever gathers—and all of us are "gatherers"—must seize upon that which is to be gathered wherever he finds it. And more than this: he must seize upon himself as well, wherever he may find himself. Were we to do otherwise we should continue in the errors of a century and perpetuate the failure of that century: the most we could do would be to adorn life with a few "pearls of thought" from the Talmud or some other source, and—for the rest—leave it just as un-Jewish as we found it. But no: we take life as we find it. Our own life and the life of our students; and gradually (or, at times, suddenly) we carry this life from the periphery where we found it to the center. And we ourselves are carried only by a faith which certainly cannot be proved, the faith that this center can be nothing but a Jewish center.

This faith must remain without proof. It carries further than our word. For we hail from the periphery. The oneness of the center is not something that we possess clearly and unambiguously, not something we can be articulate about. Our fathers were better off in that respect. We are not so well off today. We must search for this oneness and have faith that we shall find it. Seen from the periphery, the center does not appear invariably the same. In fact, the center of the circle looks different from each point of the periphery. There are many ways that lead from the outside in. Nevertheless, the inside is oneness and harmony. In the final analysis, everyone here should be speaking about the same thing. And he who speaks as he should, will in the end really have spoken about exactly what everyone else has spoken about. Only the outset, only the point of departure, will be different for everyone.

So, and only so, will you be able to understand the divisions and contrasts in our prospectus. The contrasts are put in solely for the purpose of being bridged. Today what is classical, historical, and modern in Judaism may be placed side by side, but this ought not to be so and in the future will not be so. It is up to us to discover the root-fibers of history in the classical phase, and its harvest in the modern. Whatever is genuinely Jewish must be all three simultaneously. Such has been the case in Judaism in all its productive periods. And we shall leave it to those who stand on the outside to consider contrasts such as that between the Torah and the Prophets, between Halakhah and Haggadah, between world and man, as real contrasts which cannot be reconciled. So far as we are concerned, which one of us is not certain that there could be no Torah without the prophetic powers of Moses, father of all prophets before him and after him? And—on the other hand—that there could be no prophets without the foundation of a Law and an order from which their prophecy derived its rule and measure? As for any contrast between Halakhah and Haggadah—every page of the Talmud shows the student that the two are inseparably intertwined, and every page of Jewish history confirms that the same minds and hearts are preoccupied with both: scholarly inquiry and meditation, legal decision *and* scriptural exegesis. And, finally, the Jewish world! Who could imagine that it would be possible to build it up without man, Jewish man! And what—in the long run—will become of Jewish man if, no matter where he lives, he is not surrounded by an atmosphere Jewish to some degree, by a Jewish world?

So, all of this hangs together. More than that: it is one and the same within itself, and as such it will be presented to you here. You should regard every individual aspect, every individual lecture or seminar you attend, as a part of the whole, which is offered to you only for the sake of the whole.

It is in this sense that now, at the opening of the new term in this hall, I bid you welcome. May the hours you spend here become hours of remembrance, but not in the stale sense of a dead piety that is so frequently the attitude toward Jewish matters. I mean hours of another kind of remembrance, an inner remembering, a turning that, believe me, will and must become for you a returning home. Turn into yourself, return home to your innermost self and to your innermost life.

14. *WESTERN EUROPE: THE NAZIS*

A large number of antidemocratic parties emerged in Germany in the years after World War I, a bloody frenzy of a war which exacerbated nationalistic and chauvinistic feelings. One such party, the National Socialists German Workers' party (Nazis), was organized in 1919 and combined the two most popular creeds of the time, nationalism and socialism. Adolf Hitler (1889–1945), the son of a minor Austrian customs official, left

Vienna for Munich in 1913, enlisted in the German army in 1914, and became Nazi party member number 55 after the war. Two strong influences, detailed in his writings, worked upon the young Hitler: the pan-Germanism rampant in his hometown and the anti-Semitism of Vienna. Both were embodied in Karl Lueger, mayor of Vienna, and Hitler acknowledged that it was observation of political activity in Vienna, especially the successful use of anti-Semitism as a political tool by Lueger, that enabled him to grasp most clearly the potential of anti-Semitism as a unifying force in Germany.

In 1923, after the failure of an uprising *(putsch)* which he led in Munich, Hitler was imprisoned. During his stay in prison, he dictated the first volume of *Mein Kampf (My Struggle)*, a book that was to serve as the fundamental text of the Nazi movement. The war, then the inflation that followed in its wake, and the crash of '29, which ended the decade, destroyed all sense of cohesion, continuity, certainty, and confidence. The German middle class —insecure and fearful of being dragged down into the proletariat, excited by Nazi expressions of elemental forces and ideals, and propelled by an image, nay, an "honorable title," of themselves as "barbarians" who shall "rejuvenate the world"—swept Hitler into power in 1933. The eventual result of this triumph was extraordinary suffering for Germany and her neighbors, the destruction of one third of world Jewry, and the liquidation of age-old Jewish settlements throughout Central and Eastern Europe.

It is easy, but dangerous, to dismiss Hitler as a madman. He combined in one person many of the suspicions, grievances, and animosities that had plagued Western civilization for more than a century, including anti-Semitism, anti-intellectualism, antiliberalism, and anti-industrialism. Few modern leaders, if any, have united these sentiments so persuasively and so destructively.

The following selections are from Hitler's *Mein Kampf,* translated by Ralph Manheim (Boston, 1943). Reprinted by permission of Houghton Mifflin Company.

Adolf Hitler, *Mein Kampf*

Today it is difficult, if not impossible, for me to say when the word "Jew" first gave me ground for special thoughts. At home I do not remember having heard the word during my father's lifetime. I believe that the old gentleman would have regarded any special emphasis on this term as cultural backwardness. In the course of his life he had arrived at more or less cosmopolitan views which, despite his pronounced national sentiments, not only remained intact, but also affected me to some extent.

Likewise at school I found no occasion which could have led me to change this inherited picture.

At the Realschule, to be sure, I did meet one Jewish boy who was treated by all of us with caution, but only because various experiences had led us to doubt his discretion and we did not particularly trust him; but neither I nor the others had any thoughts on the matter.

Not until my fourteenth or fifteenth year did I begin to come across the word "Jew," with any frequency, partly in connection with political discussions. This filled me with a mild distaste, and I could not rid myself of an unpleasant feeling that always came over me whenever religious quarrels occurred in my presence.

At that time I did not think anything else of the question.

There were few Jews in Linz. In the course of the centuries their outward appearance had become Europeanized and had taken on a human look; in fact, I even took them for Germans. The absurdity of this idea did not dawn on me because I saw no distinguishing feature but the strange religion. The fact that they had, as I believed, been persecuted on this account sometimes almost turned my distaste at unfavorable remarks about them into horror.

Thus far I did not so much as suspect the existence of an organized opposition to the Jews.

Then I came to Vienna.

Preoccupied by the abundance of my impressions in the architectural field, oppressed by the hardship of my own lot, I gained at first no insight into the inner stratification of the people in this gigantic city. Notwithstanding that Vienna in those days counted nearly two hundred thousand Jews among its two million inhabitants, I did not see them. In the first few weeks my eyes and my senses were not equal to the flood of values and ideas. Not until calm gradually returned and the agitated picture began to clear did I look around me more carefully in my new world, and then among other things I encountered the Jewish question.

I cannot maintain that the way in which I became acquainted with them struck me as particularly pleasant. For the Jew was still characterized for me by nothing but his religion, and therefore, on grounds of human tolerance, I maintained my rejection of religious attacks in this case as in others. Consequently, the tone, particularly that of the Viennese anti-Semitic press, seemed to me unworthy of the cultural tradition of a great nation. I was oppressed by the memory of certain occurrences in the Middle Ages, which I should not have liked to see repeated. Since the newspapers in question did not enjoy an outstanding reputation (the reason for this, at that time, I myself did not precisely know), I regarded them more as the products of anger and envy than the results of a principled, though perhaps mistaken, point of view.

I was reinforced in this opinion by what seemed to me the far more dignified form in which the really big papers answered all these attacks, or, what seemed to me even more praiseworthy, failed to mention them; in other words, simply killed them with silence.

I zealously read the so-called world press *(Neue Freie Presse, Wiener Tageblatt,* etc.) and was amazed at the scope of what they offered their readers and the objectivity of individual articles. I respected the exalted tone, though the flamboyance of the style sometimes caused me inner dissatisfaction, or even struck me unpleasantly. Yet this may have been due to the rhythm of life in the whole metropolis.

Since in those days I saw Vienna in that light, I thought myself justified in accepting this explanation of mine as a valid excuse.

But what sometimes repelled me was the undignified fashion in which this press curried favor with the Court. There was scarcely an event in the Hofburg which was not imparted to the readers either with raptures of enthusiasm or plaintive emotion, and all this to-do, particularly when it dealt with the "wisest monarch" of all time, almost reminded me of the mating cry of a mountain cock.

To me the whole thing seemed artificial.

In my eyes it was a blemish upon liberal democracy.

To curry favor with this Court and in such indecent forms was to sacrifice the dignity of the nation.

This was the first shadow to darken my intellectual relationship with the "big" Viennese press.

As I had always done before, I continued in Vienna to follow events in Germany with ardent zeal, quite regardless whether they were political or cultural. With pride and admiration, I compared the rise of the Reich with the wasting away of the Austrian state. If events in the field of foreign politics filled me, by and large, with undivided joy, the less gratifying aspects of internal life often aroused anxiety and gloom. The struggle which at that time was being carried on against William II did not meet with my approval. I regarded him not only as the German Emperor, but first and foremost as the creator of a German fleet. The restrictions of speech imposed on the Kaiser by the Reichstag angered me greatly because they emanated from a source which in my opinion really hadn't a leg to stand on, since in a single session these parliamentarian imbeciles gabbled more nonsense than a whole dynasty of emperors, including its very weakest numbers, could ever have done in centuries.

I was outraged that in a state where every idiot not only claimed the right to criticize, but was given a seat in the Reichstag and let loose upon the nation as a "lawgiver," the man who bore the imperial crown had to take "reprimands" from the greatest babblers' club of all time.

But I was even more indignant that the same Viennese press which made the most obsequious bows to every rickety horse in the Court, and flew into convulsions of joy if he accidentally swished his tail, should, with supposed concern, yet, as it seemed to me, ill-concealed malice, express its criticisms of the German Kaiser. Of course it had no intention of interfering with conditions within the German Reich—oh, no, God forbid—but by placing its finger on these wounds in the friendliest way, it was fulfilling the requirements of journalistic truth, etc. And now it was poking this finger around in the wound to its heart's content.

In such cases the blood rose to my head.

It was this which caused me little by little to view the big papers with greater caution.

And on one such occasion I was forced to recognize that one of the anti-Semitic papers, the *Deutsches Volksblatt,* behaved more decently.

Another thing that got on my nerves was the loathsome cult for France which the big press, even then, carried on. A man couldn't help feeling ashamed to be a German when he saw these saccharine hymns of praise to the "great cultural nation." This wretched licking of France's boots more than once made me throw down one of these "world newspapers." And on such occasions I sometimes picked up the *Volksblatt,* which, to be sure, seemed to me much smaller, but in these matters somewhat more appetizing.

I was not in agreement with the sharp anti-Semitic tone, but from time to time I read arguments which gave me some food for thought.

At all events, these occasions slowly made me acquainted with the man and the movement, which in those days guided Vienna's destinies: Dr. Karl Lueger and the Christian Social party.

When I arrived in Vienna, I was hostile to both of them.

The man and the movement seemed "reactionary" in my eyes.

My common sense of justice, however, forced me to change this judgment in proportion as I had occasion to become acquainted with the man and his work; and slowly my fair judgment turned to unconcealed admiration. Today, more than ever. I regard this man as the greatest German mayor of all times.

How many of my basic principles were upset by this change in my attitude toward the Christian Social movement!

My views with regard to anti-Semitism thus succumbed to the passage of time, and this was my greatest transformation of all.

It cost me the greatest inner soul struggles, and only after months of battle between my reason and my sentiments did my reason begin to emerge victorious. Two years later, my sentiment had followed my reason, and from then on became its most loyal guardian and sentinel.

At the time of this bitter struggle between spiritual education and cold reason, the visual instruction of the Vienna streets had performed invaluable services. There came a time when I no longer, as in the first days, wandered blindly through the mighty city; now with open eyes I saw not only the buildings but also the people.

Once, as I was strolling through the Inner City, I suddenly encountered an apparition in a black caftan and black hair locks. Is this a Jew? was my first thought.

For, to be sure, they had not looked like that in Linz. I observed the man furtively and cautiously, but the longer I stared at this foreign face, scrutinizing feature for feature, the more my first question assumed a new form:

Is this a German?

As always in such cases, I now began to try to relieve my doubts by books. For a few hellers I bought the first anti-Semitic pamphlets of my life. Unfortunately, they all proceeded from the supposition that in principle the reader knew or even understood the Jewish question to a certain degree. Besides, the tone for the most part was such that doubts again arose in me, due in part to the dull and amazingly unscientific arguments favoring the thesis.

I relapsed for weeks at a time, once even for months.

The whole thing seemed to me so monstrous, the accusations so boundless, that, tormented by the fear of doing injustice, I again became anxious and uncertain.

Yet I could no longer very well doubt that the objects of my study were not Germans of a special religion, but a people in themselves; for since I had begun to concern myself with this question and to take cognizance of the Jews, Vienna appeared to me in a different light than before. Wherever I went, I began to see Jews, and the more I saw, the more sharply they became distinguished in my eyes from the rest of humanity. Particularly the Inner City and the districts north of the Danube Canal swarmed with a people which even outwardly had lost all resemblance to Germans.

And whatever doubts I may still have nourished were finally dispelled by the attitude of a portion of the Jews themselves.

Among them there was a great movement, quite extensive in Vienna, which came out sharply in confirmation of the national character of the Jews: this was the *Zionists.*

It looked, to be sure, as though only a part of the Jews approved this viewpoint, while the great majority condemned and inwardly rejected such a formulation. But when examined more closely, this appearance dissolved itself into a unsavory vapor of pretexts advanced for mere reasons of expedience, not to say lies. For the so-called liberal Jews did not reject the Zionists as non-Jews, but only as Jews with an impractical, perhaps even dangerous, way of publicly avoiding their Jewishness.

Intrinsically they remained unalterably of one piece.

In a short time this apparent struggle between Zionistic and liberal Jews disgusted me; for it was false through and through, founded on lies and scarcely in keeping with the moral elevation and purity always claimed by this people.

The cleanliness of this people, moral and otherwise, I must say, is a point in itself. By their very exterior you could tell that these were no lovers of water, and, to your distress, you often knew it with your eyes closed. Later I often grew sick to my stomach from the smell of these caftan-wearers. Added to this, there was their unclean dress and their generally unheroic appearance.

All this could scarcely be called very attractive; but it became positively repulsive when, in addition to their physical uncleanliness, you discovered the moral stains on this "chosen people."

In a short time I was made more thoughtful than ever by my slowly rising insight into the type of activity carried on by the Jews in certain fields.

Was there any form of filth or profligacy, particularly in cultural life, without at least one Jew involved in it?

If you cut even cautiously into such an abscess, you found, like a maggot in a rotting body, often dazzled by the sudden light—a kike!

What had to be reckoned heavily against the Jews in my eyes was when I became acquainted with their activity in the press, art, literature, and the theater. All the unctuous reassurances helped little or nothing. It sufficed to look at a billboard, to study the names of the men behind the horrible trash they advertised, to make you hard for a long time to come. This was pestilence, spiritual pestilence, worse than the Black Death of olden times, and the people was being infected with it! It goes without saying that the lower the intellectual level of one of these art manufacturers, the more unlimited his fertility will be, and the scoundrel ends up like a garbage separator, splashing his filth in the face of humanity. And bear in mind that there is no limit to their number; bear in mind that for one Goethe Nature easily can foist on the world ten thousand of these scribblers who poison men's souls like germ-carriers of the worse sort, on their fellowmen.

It was terrible, but not to be overlooked, that precisely the Jew, in tremendous numbers, seemed chosen by Nature for this shameful calling.

Is this why the Jews are called the "chosen people"?

I now began to examine carefully the names of all the creators of unclean products in public artistic life. The result was less and less favorable for my previous attitude toward the Jews. Regardless how my sentiment might resist, my reason was forced to draw its conclusions.

The fact that nine tenths of all literary filth, artistic trash, and theatrical idiocy can be set to the account of a people, constituting hardly one hundredth of all the country's inhabitants, could simply not be talked away; it was the plain truth.

And I now began to examine my beloved "world press" from this point of view.

And the deeper I probed, the more the object of my former admiration shriveled. The style became more and more unbearable; I could not help rejecting the content as inwardly shallow and banal; the objectivity of exposition now seemed to me more akin to lies than honest truth; and the writers were—Jews.

A thousand things which I had hardly seen before now struck my notice, and others, which had previously given me food for thought, I now learned to grasp and understand.

I now saw the liberal attitude of this press in a different light; the lofty tone in which it answered attacks and its method of killing them with silence now revealed itself to me as a trick as clever as it was treacherous; the transfigured raptures of their theatrical critics were always directed at Jewish writers, and their disapproval never struck anyone but Germans. The gentle pinpricks against William II revealed its methods by their persistency, and so did its commendation of French culture and civilization. The trashy content of the short story now appeared to me as outright indecency, and in the language I detected the accents of a foreign people; the sense of the whole thing was so obviously hostile to Germanism that this could only have been intentional.

But who had an interest in this?

Was all this a mere accident?

Gradually I became uncertain.

The development was accelerated by insights which I gained into a number of other matters. I am referring to the general view of ethics and morals which was quite openly exhibited by a large part of the Jews, and the practical application of which could be seen.

Here again the streets provided an object lesson of a sort which was sometimes positively evil.

The relation of the Jews to prostitution and, even more, to the white-slave traffic, could be studied in Vienna as perhaps in no other city of Western Europe, with the possible exception of the southern French ports. If you walked at night through the streets and alleys of Leopoldstadt, at every step you witnessed proceedings which remained concealed from the majority of the German people until the war gave the soldiers on the eastern front occasion to see similar things, or, better expressed, forced them to see them.

When thus for the first time I recognized the Jew as the coldhearted, shameless, and calculating director of this revolting vice traffic in the scum of the big city, a cold shudder ran down my back.

But then a flame flared up within me. I no longer avoided discussion of the Jewish question; no, now I sought it. And when I learned to look for the Jew in all branches of cultural and artistic life and its various manifestations, I suddenly encountered him in a place where I would least have expected to find him.

When I recognized the Jew as the leader of the Social Democracy, the scales dropped from my eyes. A long soul struggle had reached its conclusion.

Even in my daily relations with my fellow workers, I observed the amazing adaptability with which they adopted different positions on the same question, sometimes within an interval of a few days, sometimes in only a few hours. It was hard for me to understand how people who, when spoken to alone, possessed some sensible opinions, suddenly lost them as soon as they came under the influence of the masses. It was often enough to make one despair. When, after hours of argument, I was convinced that now at last I had broken the ice or cleared up some absurdity, and was beginning to rejoice at my success, on the next day to my disgust I had to begin all over again; it had all been in vain. Like an eternal pendulum their opinions seemed to swing back again and again to the old madness.

All this I could understand: that they were dissatisfied with their lot and cursed the Fate which often struck them so harshly; that they hated the employers who seemed to them the heartless bailiffs of Fate; that they cursed the authorities who in their eyes were without feeling for their situation; that they demonstrated against food prices and carried their demands into the streets: this much could be understood without recourse to reason. But what inevitably remained incomprehensible was the boundless hatred they heaped upon their own nationality, despising its greatness, besmirching its history, and dragging its great men into the gutter.

This struggle against their own species, their own clan, their own homeland, was as senseless as it was incomprehensible. It was unnatural.

It was possible to cure them temporarily of this vice, but only for days or at most weeks. If later you met the man you thought you had converted, he was just the same as before.

His old unnatural state had regained full possession of him.

I gradually became aware that the Social Democratic press was directed predominantly by Jews; yet I did not attribute any special significance to this circumstance, since conditions were exactly the same in the other papers. Yet one fact seemed conspicuous: there was not one paper with Jews working on it which could have been regarded as truly national, according to my education and way of thinking.

I swallowed my disgust and tried to read this type of Marxist press production, but my revulsion became so unlimited in so doing that I endeavored to become more closely acquainted with the men who manufactured these compendiums of knavery.

From the publisher down, they were all Jews.

I took all the Social Democratic pamphlets I could lay hands on and sought the names of their authors: Jews. I noted the names of the leaders; by far the greatest part were likewise members of the "chosen people," whether they were representatives in the Reichsrat or trade-union secretaries, the heads of organizations or street agitators. It was always the same gruesome picture. The names of the Austerlitzes, Davids, Adlers, Ellenbogens, etc., will remain forever graven in my memory. One thing had grown clear to me: the party with whose petty representatives I had been carrying on the most violent struggle for months was, as to leadership, almost exclusively in the hands of a foreign people; for, to my deep and joyful satisfaction, I had at last come to the conclusion that the Jew was no German.

Only now did I become thoroughly acquainted with the seducer of our people.

A single year of my sojourn in Vienna had sufficed to imbue me with the conviction that no worker could be so stubborn that he would not in the end succumb to better knowledge and better explanations. Slowly I had become an expert in their own doctrine and used it as a weapon in the struggle for my own profound conviction.

Success almost always favored my side.

The great masses could be saved, if only with the gravest sacrifice in time and patience.

But a Jew could never be parted from his opinions.

At that time I was still childish enough to try to make the madness of their doctrine clear to them; in my little circle I talked my tongue sore and my throat hoarse, thinking I would inevitably succeed in convincing them how ruinous their Marxist madness was; but what I accomplished was often the opposite. It seemed as though their increased understanding of the destructive effects of Social Democratic theories and their results only reinforced their determination.

The more I argued with them, the better I came to know their dialectic. First they counted on the stupidity of their adversary, and then, when there was no other way out, they themselves simply played stupid. If all this didn't help, they pretended not to understand, or, if challenged, they changed the subject in a hurry, quoted platitudes which, if you accepted them, they immediately related to entirely different matters, and then, if again attacked, gave ground and pretended not to know exactly what you were talking about. Whenever you tried to attack one of these apostles, your hand closed on a jelly-like slime which divided up and poured through your fingers, but in the next moment collected again. But if you really struck one of these fellows so telling a blow that, observed by the audience, he couldn't help but agree, and if you believed that this had taken you at least one step forward, your amazement was great the next day. The Jew had not the slightest recollection of the day before, he rattled off his same old nonsense as though nothing at all had happened, and, if indignantly challenged, affected amazement; he couldn't remember a thing, except that he had proved the correctness of his assertions the previous day.

Sometimes I stood there thunderstruck.

I didn't know what to be more amazed at: the agility of their tongues or their virtuosity at lying.

Gradually I began to hate them.

All this had but one good side: that in proportion as the real leaders or at least the disseminators of Social Democracy came within my vision, my love for my people inevitably grew. For who, in view of the diabolical craftiness of these seducers, could damn the luckless victims? How hard it was, even for me, to get the better of this race of dialectical liars! And how futile was such success in dealing with people who twist the truth in your mouth, who without so much as a blush disavow the word they have just spoken, and in the very next minute take credit for it after all.

No. The better acquainted I became with the Jew, the more forgiving I inevitably became toward the worker.

In my eyes the gravest fault was no longer with him, but with all those who did not regard it as worth the trouble to have mercy on him, with iron righteousness giving the son of the people his just deserts, and standing the seducer and corrupter up against the wall.

Inspired by the experience of daily life, I now began to track down the sources of the Marxist doctrine. Its effects had become clear to me in individual cases; each day its success was apparent to my attentive eyes, and, with some exercise of my imagination, I was able to picture the consequences. The only remaining question was whether the result of their action in its ultimate form had existed in the mind's eye of the creators, or whether they themselves were the victims of an error.

I felt that both were possible.

In the one case it was the duty of every thinking man to force himself to the forefront of the ill-starred movement, thus perhaps averting catastrophe; in the other, however, the original founders of this plague of the nations must have been veritable devils; for only in the brain of a monster—not that of a man—could the plan of an organization assume form and meaning, whose activity must ultimately result in the collapse of human civilization and the consequent devastation of the world.

In this case the only remaining hope was struggle, struggle with all the weapons which the human spirit, reason, and will can devise, regardless on which side of the scale Fate should lay its blessing.

Thus I began to make myself familiar with the founders of this doctrine, in order to study the foundations of the movement. If I reached my goal more quickly than at first I had perhaps ventured to believe, it was thanks to my newly acquired, though at that time not very profound, knowledge of the Jewish question. This alone enabled me to draw a practical comparison between the reality and the theoretical flimflam of the founding fathers of Social Democracy, since it taught me to understand the language of the Jewish people, who speak in order to conceal or at least to veil their thoughts; their real aim is not therefore to be found in the lines themselves, but slumbers well concealed between them.

For me this was the time of the greatest spiritual upheaval I have ever had to go through.

I had ceased to be a weak-kneed cosmopolitan and become an anti-Semite.

Just once more—and this was the last time—fearful, oppressive thoughts came to me in profound anguish.

When over long periods of human history I scrutinized the activity of the Jewish people, suddenly there rose up in me the fearful question whether inscrutable Destiny, perhaps for reasons unknown to us poor mortals, did not with eternal and immutable resolve, desire the final victory of this little nation.

Was it possible that the earth had been promised as a reward to this people which lives only for this earth?

Have we an objective right to struggle for our self-preservation, or is this justified only subjectively within ourselves?

As I delved more deeply into the teachings of Marxism and thus in tranquil clarity submitted the deeds of the Jewish people to contemplation, Fate itself gave me its answer.

The Jewish doctrine of Marxism rejects the aristocratic principle of Nature and replaces the eternal privilege of power and strength by the mass of numbers and their dead weight. Thus it denies the value of personality in man, contests the significance of nationality and race, and thereby withdraws from humanity the premise of its existence and its culture. As a foundation of the universe, this doctrine would bring about the end of any order intellectually conceivable to man. And as, in this greatest of all recognizable organisms, the result of an application of such a law could only be chaos, on earth it could only be destruction for the inhabitants of this planet.

If, with the help of his Marxist creed, the Jew is victorious over the other peoples of the world, his crown will be the funeral wreath of humanity and this planet will, as it did thousands of years ago, move through the ether devoid of men.

Eternal Nature inexorably avenges the infringement of her commands.

Hence today I believe that I am acting in accordance with the will of the Almighty Creator: *by defending myself against the Jew, I am fighting for the work of the Lord. . . .*

In general the art of all truly great national leaders at all times consists among other things primarily in not dividing the attention of a people, but in concentrating it upon a single foe. The more unified the application of a people's will to fight, the greater will be the magnetic attraction of a movement and the mightier will be the impetus of the thrust. It belongs to the genius of a great leader to make even adversaries far removed from one another seem to belong to a single category, because in weak and uncertain characters the knowledge of having different enemies can only too readily lead to the beginning of a doubt in their own right.

Once the wavering mass sees itself in a struggle against too many enemies, objectivity will put in an appearance, throwing open the question whether all others are really wrong and only their own people or their own movement are in the right.

And this brings about the first paralysis of their own power. Hence a multiplicity of different adversaries must always be combined so that in the eyes of the masses of one's own supporters the struggle is directed against only one enemy. This strengthens their faith in their own right and enhances their bitterness against those who attack it.

That the old pan-German movement failed to understand this deprived it of success.

Its goal had been correct, its will pure, but the road it chose was wrong. It was like a mountain climber who keeps the peak to be climbed in view and who sets out with the greatest determination and energy, but pays no attention to the trail, for his eyes are always on his goal, so that he neither sees nor feels out the character of the ascent and thus comes to grief in the end.

The opposite state of affairs seemed to prevail with its great competitor, the Christian Social party.

The road it chose was correct and well chosen, but it lacked clear knowledge of its goal.

In nearly all the matters in which the pan-German movement was wanting, the attitude of the Christian Social party was correct and well planned.

It possessed the necessary understanding for the importance of the masses and from the very first day assured itself of at least a part of them by open emphasis on its social character. By aiming essentially at winning the small and lower middle classes and artisans, it obtained a following as enduring as it was self-sacrificing. It avoided any struggle against a religious institution and thus secured the support of that mighty organization which the Church represents. Consequently, it possessed only a single truly great central opponent. It recognized the value of large-scale propaganda and was a virtuoso in influencing the psychological instincts of the broad masses of its adherents.

If nevertheless it was unable to achieve its goal and dream of saving Austria, this was due to two deficiencies in its method and to its lack of clarity concerning the aim itself.

The anti-Semitism of the new movement was based on religious ideas instead of racial knowledge. The reason for the intrusion of this mistake was the same which brought about the second fallacy.

If the Christian Social party wanted to save Austria, then in the opinion of its founders it must not operate from the standpoint of the racial principle, for if it did a dissolution of the state would, in a short time, inevitably occur. Particularly the situation in Vienna itself, in the opinion of the party leaders, demanded that all points which would divide their following should be set aside as much as possible, and that all unifying conceptions be emphasized in their stead.

At that time Vienna was so strongly permeated especially with Czech elements that only the greatest tolerance with regard to all racial questions could keep them in a party which was not anti-German to begin with. If Austria were to be saved, this was indispensable. And so they attempted to win over small Czech artisans who were especially numerous in Vienna, by a struggle against liberal Manchesterism, and in the struggle against the Jews on a religious basis they thought they had discovered a slogan transcending all of old Austria's national differences.

It is obvious that combating Jewry on such a basis could provide the Jews with small cause for concern. If the worst came to the worst, a splash of baptismal water could always save the business and the Jew at the same time. With such a superficial motivation, a serious scientific treatment of the whole problem was never achieved, and as a result far too many people, to whom this type of anti-Semitism was bound to be incomprehensible, were repelled.

The recruiting power of the idea was limited almost exclusively to intellectually limited circles, unless true knowledge were substituted for purely emotional feeling. The intelligentsia remained aloof as a matter of principle. Thus the whole movement came to look more and more like an attempt at a new conversion of the Jews, or perhaps even an expression of a certain competitive envy. And hence the struggle lost the character of an inner and higher consecration; to many, and not necessarily the worst people, it came to seem immoral and reprehensible. Lacking was the conviction that this was a vital question for all humanity, with the fate of all non-Jewish peoples depending on its solution.

Through this halfheartedness the anti-Semitic line of the Christian Social party lost its value.

It was a sham anti-Semitism which was almost worse than none at all; for it lulled people into security; they thought they had the foe by the ears, while in reality they themselves were being led by the nose.

In a short time the Jew had become so accustomed to this type of anti-Semitism that he would have missed its disappearance more than its presence inconvenienced him.

If in this the Christian Social party had to make a heavy sacrifice to the state of nationalities, they had to make an even greater one when it came to championing Germanism as such.

They could not be "nationalistic" unless they wanted to lose the ground from beneath their feet in Vienna. They hoped that by a pussy-footing evasion of this question they could still save the Habsburg state, and by that very thing they encompassed its ruin. And the movement lost the mighty source of power which alone can fill a political party with inner strength for any length of time.

Through this alone the Christian Social party became a party like any other.

In those days I followed both movements most attentively. One, by feeling the beat of its innermost heart, the other, carried away by admiration for the unusual man who even then seemed to me a bitter symbol of all Austrian Germanism.

When the mighty funeral procession bore the dead mayor from the City Hall toward the Ring, I was among the many hundred thousands looking on at the tragic spectacle. I was profoundly moved and my feelings told me that the work, even of this man, was bound to be in vain, owing to the fatal destiny which would inevitably lead this state to destruction. If Dr. Karl Lueger had lived in Germany, he would have been ranked among the great minds of our people; that he lived and worked in this impossible state was the misfortune of his work and of himself.

When he died, the little flames in the Balkans were beginning to leap up more greedily from month to month, and it was a gracious fate which spared him from witnessing what he still thought he could prevent.

Out of the failure of the one movement and the miscarriage of the other, I for my part sought to find the causes, and came to the certain conviction that, quite aside from the impossibility of bolstering up the state in old Austria, the errors of the two parties were as follows:

The pan-German movement was right in its theoretical view about the aim of a German renascence, but unfortunate in its choice of methods. It was nationalistic, but unhappily not socialistic enough to win the masses. But its anti-Semitism was based on a correct understanding of the importance of the racial problem, and not on religious ideas. Its struggle against a definite denomination, however, was actually and tactically false.

The Christian Social movement had an unclear conception of the aim of a German reawakening, but had intelligence and luck in seeking its methods as a party. It understood the importance of the social question, erred in its struggle against the Jews, and had no notion of the power of the national idea.

If, in addition to its enlightened knowledge of the broad masses, the Christian Social party had had a correct idea of the importance of the racial question, such as the pan-German movement had achieved; and if, finally, it had itself been nationalistic, or if the pan-German movement, in addition to its correct knowledge of the aim of the Jewish question, had adopted the practical shrewdness of the Christian Social party, especially in its attitude toward socialism, there would have resulted a movement which even then in my opinion might have successfully intervened in German destiny.

If this did not come about, it was overwhelmingly due to the nature of the Austrian state.

Since I saw my conviction realized in no other party, I could in the period that followed not make up my mind to enter, let alone fight with, any of the existing organizations. Even then I regarded all political movements as unsuccessful and unable to carry out a national reawakening of the German people on a larger and not purely external scale.

But in this period my inner revulsion toward the Habsburg state steadily grew.

The more particularly I concerned myself with questions of foreign policy, the more my conviction rose and took root that this political formation could result in nothing but the misfortune of Germanism. More and more clearly I saw at last that the fate of the German nation would no longer be decided here, but in the Reich itself. This was true, not only of political questions, but no less for all manifestations of cultural life in general.

Also in the field of cultural or artistic affairs, the Austrian state showed all symptoms of degeneration, or at least of unimportance for the German nation. This was most true in the field of architecture. The new architecture could achieve no special successes in Austria, if for no other reason because since the completion of the Ring its tasks, in Vienna at least, had become insignificant in comparison with the plans arising in Germany.

Thus more and more I began to lead a double life; reason and reality told me to complete a school as bitter as it was beneficial in Austria, but my heart dwelt elsewhere.

An oppressive discontent had seized possession of me, the more I recognized the inner hollowness of this state and the impossibility of saving it, and felt that in all things it could be nothing but the misfortune of the German people.

I was convinced that this state inevitably oppressed and handicapped any really great German as, conversely, it would help every un-German figure.

I was repelled by the conglomeration of races which the capital showed me, repelled by this whole mixture of Czechs, Poles, Hungarians, Ruthenians, Serbs, and Croats, and everywhere, the eternal mushroom of humanity—Jews and more Jews.

To me the giant city seemed the embodiment of racial desecration.

The German of my youth was the dialect of Lower Bavaria; I could neither forget it nor learn the Viennese jargon. The longer I lived in this city, the more my hatred grew for the foreign mixture of peoples which had begun to corrode this old site of German culture.

The idea that this state could be maintained much longer seemed to me positively ridiculous.

Austria was then like an old mosaic; the cement, binding the various little stones together, had grown old and begun to crumble; as long as the work of art is not touched, it can continue to give a show of existence, but as soon as it receives a blow, it breaks into a thousand fragments. The question was only when the blow would come.

Since my heart had never beaten for an Austrian monarchy, but only for a German Reich, the hour of this state's downfall could only seem to me the beginning of the redemption of the German nation.

For all these reasons a longing rose stronger and stronger in me, to go at last whither since my childhood secret desires and secret love had drawn me.

I hoped someday to make a name for myself as an architect and thus, on the large or small scale which Fate would allot me, to dedicate my sincere services to the nation.

But finally I wanted to enjoy the happiness of living and working in the place which someday would inevitably bring about the fulfillment of my most ardent and heartfelt wish: the union of my beloved homeland with the common fatherland, the German Reich.

Even today many would be unable to comprehend the greatness of such a longing, but I address myself to those to whom Fate has either hitherto denied this, or from whom in harsh cruelty it has taken it away; I address myself to all those who, detached from their mother country, have to fight even for the holy treasure of their language, who are persecuted and tortured for their loyalty to the fatherland, and who now, with poignant emotion, long for the hour which will permit them to return to the heart of their faithful mother; I address myself to all these, and I know that they will understand me!

Only he who has felt in his own skin what it means to be a German, deprived of the right to belong to his cherished fatherland, can measure the deep longing which burns at all times in the hearts of children separated from their mother country. It torments those whom it fills and denies them contentment and happiness until the gates of their father's house open, and in the common Reich, common blood gains peace and tranquillity.

Yet Vienna was and remained for me the hardest, though most thorough, school of my life. I had set foot in this town while still half a boy and I left it a man, grown quiet and grave. In it I obtained the foundations for a philosophy in general and a political view in particular which later I only needed to supplement in detail, but which never left me. But not until today have I been able to estimate at their full value those years of study.

That is why I have dealt with this period at some length, because it gave me my first visual instruction in precisely those questions which belonged to the foundations of a party which, arising from smallest beginnings, after scarcely five years is beginning to develop into a great mass movement. I do not know what my attitude toward the Jews, Social Democracy, or rather Marxism as a whole, the social question, etc., would be today if at such an early time the pressure of destiny—and my own study—had not built up a basic stock of personal opinions within me.

For if the misery of the fatherland can stimulate thousands and thousands of men to thought on the inner reasons for this collapse, this can never lead to that thoroughness and deep insight which are disclosed to the man who has himself mastered Fate only after years of struggle.

15. *EASTERN EUROPE: THE BOLSHEVIKS*

Generally acknowledged to be the consummate prose writer to emerge from the Russian Revolution, Isaac Babel (1894–1941?), lived in Odessa, the center of Yiddish and Hebrew literature as well as of Jewish communal and political life in the early twentieth century. The son of a salesman of agricultural machines, who nourished in his son a passion for education, Babel rode with Budenny's Cossacks in the Revolution. Fighting alongside those very people who embodied all that the Jew feared, Babel was forced to live out the tensions he creates in his "Odessa stories" between Jewish values and the non-Jewish environment.

Babel plays off the physical against the intellectual constantly; Cossacks, brimming over with violence, passion, and sexuality, meeting a Jew, small in stature, with "spectacles on his nose and autumn in his soul." Babel's world is one of contrasts: the calm voice of a narrator against the tragic events around him; Gentiles being served gefilte fish rather than sausage; the lyricism of descriptive passages pertaining to nature with the crude eroticism and coarse vocabulary and behavior of his heroes; the traditional Sabbath meal blessings and the noise of war; gentle rabbis and Jewish robbers; and, implicitly, the disintegration of a way of life ("the native shtetl was dying").

In the following imaginatively rich and skillfully executed stories, Babel recounts the Russian Jews' encounter with the ruthlessness of Bolshevism—no longer the glory of an idealized past or future but rather the stench of poverty, disease, disintegration, and death. Transforming the chaos of his times into an art, Babel creates, through "simplicity born of complexity," a portrait of Jewish endurance, survival, and values against a backdrop of oppression and decay.

Isaac Babel, "The Revolution"

GEDALI

On Sabbath eves the thick sadness of memories torments me. On such evenings, long ago, my grandfather used to stroke the volumes of Ibn Ezra with his yellow beard. My grandmother, in a lace kerchief, would make magic over the Sabbath candles with her knotty fingers and sob sweetly. On those evenings my childish heart would rock like a little ship on enchanted waves. Oh, the moldered Talmuds of my childhood! Oh, the thick sadness of memories!

I roam through Zhitomir looking for a shy star. Beside the ancient synagogue, beside its yellow and indifferent walls, old Jews sell chalk, wicks, washing blue—Jews with prophets' beards and passionate rags on their sunken chests.

Here, before me, is the marketplace and the death of the marketplace. Killed is the fat soul of abundance. Dumb padlocks hang on the stalls and the granite of the pavement is as clean as the bald spot of a dead man. The shy star twinkles and goes out.

Success came to me later, success came just before sunset. Gedali's shop was tucked away in a row of closed stores. Dickens, where was your friendly shade that day? You would have seen in this old curiosity shop a pair of gilt slippers and ships' cables, an ancient compass and a stuffed eagle, a Winchester with the date 1810 engraved on it and a battered saucepan.

Old Gedali, the proprietor, walks around his treasures in the pink vacuum of evening, a little man in dark glasses and a green frock coat that reaches to the floor. He rubs his small white hands, plucks at his little gray beard, and, cocking his head, listens to invisible voices that float down to him.

This shop resembles the treasure box of a solemn boy with a craving for knowledge who will grow up to be a professor of botany. There are buttons in it and a dead butterfly, and the name of its tiny proprietor is Gedali. Everyone has left the marketplace, Gedali has stayed on. He slips in and out of a labyrinth of globes, skulls, and dead flowers, waving a bright duster of cock's feathers and flicking the dust off flowers that have died.

And now we sit on two empty beer barrels. Gedali twists and untwists his scanty beard. His high hat sways above us like a little black tower. Warm air floats past us. The sky changes color. Up above gentle blood flows from an overturned bottle, and a light odor of decay enfolds me.

"The Revolution—let us say aye to it, but are we to say nay to the Sabbath?" thus Gedali begins, winding about me the silken thongs of his cloudy eyes. "I cry yes to the Revolution; I cry yes to her, but she hides from Gedali and her only messengers are bullets. . . ."

"Sunlight does not enter closed eyes," I answer the old man. "But we will rip open the eyes that are closed."

"The Pole has closed my eyes," the old man says in a barely audible whisper. "The Pole, vicious dog that he is. He takes the Jew and tears out his beard, the cur! And now the vicious dog is getting a beating himself. That's fine, that's—Revolution. And then those who have given the Pole a beating say to me: 'Turn your gramophone over to us, Gedali, we're going to register it.' 'But I love music, madam,' I say to the Revolution. 'You don't know what you love, Gedali; I'm going to shoot you, and then you'll know. And I can't help shooting because I am the Revolution.' "

"She can't help shooting, Gedali," I say to the old man, "because she is the Revolution."

"But the Pole did his shooting, kind sir, because he was the Counterrevolution; you shoot because you are the Revolution. But surely the Revolution is joy. And joy doesn't like orphans in the house. Good deeds are done by good men. Revolution is the good deeds of good men. But good men do not kill. So it is bad men that are making the Revolution. But Poles, too, are bad men. Who, then, will tell Gedali which is Revolution and which is Counterrevolution. I used to study the Talmud, I love Rashi's commentaries and the books of Maimonides. And there are yet other men of understanding in Zhitomir. And here all of us, learned men, fall upon our faces and cry out at the top of our voices: 'Woe unto us, where is our sweet Revolution?' "

The old man fell silent. And we beheld the first star peeping along the Milky Way.

"The Sabbath has begun," Gedali brought out solemnly; "time for Jews to go to synagogue. . . . Mr. Comrade," he said, rising, and his high hat, like a black tower, swayed on his head, "bring a few good men to Zhitomir. Oh, they are scarce in our town, oh, how scarce! Bring good men and we'll turn all our gramophones over to them. We are no dunces. The International —we know what the International is. I want an International of good men, I want to have every soul registered and given the biggest ration. There, soul, take your fill, please, and enjoy life. The International, Mr. Comrade, you're the one who doesn't know what sauce goes with it."

"Gunpowder's the sauce that goes with it and it's spiced with the best blood. . . ."

And lo! the young Sabbath ascended its throne, coming out of the blue darkness.

"Gedali," I said, "today is Friday and it's already evening. Where can you get a Jewish cookie, a Jewish glass of tea, and in the glass of tea a little taste of that God who has been pensioned off?"

"Nowhere," Gedali answered me, hanging the padlock on his little treasure box, "nowhere. There is a tavern next door, and good people used to run it, but nobody eats there nowadays, they just weep."

He buttoned three bone buttons of his green frock coat, flicked himself with the cock's feathers, sprinkled a little water on his soft palms, and was gone—a tiny, lonely dreamer in a black top hat and with a large prayer book under his arm.

The Sabbath has begun. Gedali, founder of a Utopian International, has gone to synagogue to pray.

THE RABBI

". . . All are mortal. The mother alone is destined to eternal life. And when she passes on, she leaves a memory behind which no one as yet has dared to sully. The memory of the mother feeds our compassion even as the ocean, the boundless ocean feeds the rivers that carve the world. . . ."

Those were Gedali's words. He uttered them solemnly. The evening that was being snuffed out ensphered him in the pink haze of its sadness. The old man went on:

"The doors and windows of Hasidism, that passionate edifice, are smashed, but it is as deathless as the mother's soul. With empty eye sockets Hasidism still stands firmly at the crossroads swept by history's fierce winds."

Thus spoke Gedali and, having said his prayers in the synagogue, took me to see Rabbi Motele, the last of the Chernobyl dynasty.

Gedali and I walked up the main street. White churches gleamed in the distance like buckwheat fields. The wheel of a gun carriage groaned round the corner. Two pregnant Ukrainian women came out of a gateway, their coin necklaces jingling, and sat down on a bench. A shy star began to gleam on the sunset's orange battlefield, and peace, Sabbath peace, rested upon the crooked roofs of the Zhitomir ghetto.

"Here," whispered Gedali, pointing to a sprawling house with a shattered façade.

We entered a room, as stony and as naked as a morgue. Rabbi Motele sat at a table, surrounded by liars and madmen. He wore a sable *strammel* and a white robe belted with rope. He sat with closed eyes, digging his thin fingers into the yellow down of his beard.

"Where does the Jew come from?" he asked, and raised his eyelids.

"From Odessa," I answered.

"A pious city," said the rabbi with unusual vehemence, "the star of our exile and, against its will, the well of our misfortunes. What is the Jew's occupation?"

"I put the adventures of Hersh of Ostropol into verse."

"A mighty and worthy task," murmured the rabbi and dropped his eyelids. "The jackal howls when he is hungry, every fool has folly enough to be despondent, and alone the wise man rends the veil of being with laughter. . . . What did the Jew study?"

"The Torah."

"What is the Jew seeking?"

"Joy."

"Reb Mordkhe," said the zaddik, and shook his beard, "let the young man be seated at the table, let him eat with other Jews, this Sabbath eve, let him rejoice that he is alive and not dead, let him clap his hands when his neighbors dance, let him drink wine if he is given wine."

And Reb Mordkhe, an old buffoon, a hunchbacked old man, no taller than a boy of ten, with everted eyelids, darted up to me.

"Oh, my dear and so very young man," said the ragged Reb Mordkhe and winked at me, "how many rich fools have I known in Odessa, and how many penniless sages have I known in Odessa! Sit down at the table, young man, and drink the wine that won't be offered you. . . ."

We all seated ourselves side by side, the liars, the madmen, and the loafers. In the corner brawny Jews who looked like fishermen and apostles moaned over their prayer books. Gedali in his green frock coat was dozing against the wall like a bright-feathered bird. And suddenly behind his back I caught sight of a youth, a youth with the look of Spinoza, with Spinoza's powerful brow and with the sickly face of a nun. He was smoking and shivering, like an escaped prisoner whom his captors had brought back to his cell. Ragged Mordkhe stole up to him from behind, snatched the cigarette from his mouth, and ran to my side.

"That's Ilya, the rabbi's son," Mordkhe muttered hoarsely, and brought closer to me the bleeding flesh of his everted eyelids. "The accursed son, the last son, the disobedient son."

And Mordkhe shook his little fist threateningly at the youth and spat in his face.

"Blessed be the Lord," rang out the voice of Rabbi Motele Bratzlavsky, and he broke the bread with his monkish fingers. "Blessed be the God of Israel who has chosen us from among all the nations of the earth. . . ."

The rabbi blessed the food, and we sat down to eat. Beyond the window horses were neighing and Cossacks were shouting. The wilderness of war yawned beyond the window. The rabbi's son smoked one cigarette after another, through prayers and silence. When supper was over, I was the first to get up.

"My dear and so very young man," mumbled Mordkhe behind my back and tugged my belt, "if there were nobody in the world except the wicked rich and the penniless tramps, how would the saintly live?"

I gave the old man some money and went out into the street. I parted from Gedali and made my way back to the depot. In the propaganda train of the First Cavalry Corps there awaited me the glare of hundreds of lights, the magical brilliance of the radio station, the persistent pounding of printing presses, and my unfinished story for the paper, "The Red Cavalry Man."

THE RABBI'S SON

. . . Do you remember Zhitomir, Vasily? Do you remember the Teterev, Vasily, and that evening when the Sabbath, the young Sabbath tripped stealthily along the sunset, her little red heel treading on the stars?

The slender horn of the moon bathed its arrows in the black waters of the Teterev. Funny little Gedali, founder of the Fourth International, was taking us to Rabbi Motele Bratzlavsky's for evening service. Funny little Gedali swayed the cock's feathers of his high hat in the red haze of the evening. The candles in the rabbi's room blinked their predatory eyes. Bent over prayer books, brawny Jews were moaning in muffled voices, and the old buffoon of the zaddiks of Chernobyl jingled coppers in his torn pocket. . . .

. . . Do you remember that night, Vasily? Beyond the windows horses were neighing and Cossacks were shouting. The wilderness of war was yawning beyond the windows, and Rabbi Motele Bratzlavsky was praying at the eastern wall, his decayed fingers clinging to his *tales.* Then the curtain of the ark was drawn aside, and in the funereal light of the candles we saw the scrolls of the Torah gowned in purple velvet and light blue silk, and suspended above the Torahs the lifeless face, meek and beautiful, of Ilya, the rabbi's son, the last prince of the dynasty. . . .

Well, the day before yesterday, Vasily, the regiments of the Twelfth Army left the front at Kovel exposed. The victors' scornful cannonade thunderously broke out in the city. Our troops faltered and were thrown into confusion. The propaganda train started crawling away across the field's dead back. And a monstrous Russia in bast shoes shuffled past on either side of the cars, as incredible as a herd of lice. A typhus-ridden peasant mob trudged along, carrying on its shoulders the usual hump of soldiers' death. They jumped on the steps of our train and dropped off, knocked down by butt ends of rifles. They grunted, scratched themselves, and moved on in silence.

At the twelfth verst, having run out of potatoes, I tossed a batch of Trotsky's leaflets down to them. But only one of them stretched out a dirty, dead hand for a leaflet. And I recognized Ilya, the son of the rabbi of Zhitomir. I recognized him at once, Vasily. And it was so painful to see the prince, trouserless and doubled up under his soldier's pack, that, in defiance of the rules, we pulled him into our car. His bare knees, as helpless as a woman's, knocked against the rusty iron of the steps; two full-breasted typists in sailor suits dragged the long, bashful body of the dying man along the floor. We laid him on the floor of the editorial office. Cossacks, in red loose trousers, straightened what was left of his clothes. The girls, bearing down on their bandy legs, the legs of simpleminded females, stared drily at his private parts, the tender curly maleness of a spent Semite. And I who had seen him one night during my wanderings began to collect in a little box the scattered belongings of Bratzlavsky, Red Army man. There were all sorts of things here, helter-skelter—the instructions of a propagandist and the notebooks of a Jewish poet. Portraits of Lenin and Maimonides lay side by side: the gnarled iron of Lenin's skull and the dull silk of Maimonides' likeness. A lock of woman's hair lay in a volume of the resolutions of the Sixth Congress of the party, and crooked lines of Hebrew verse crowded the margins of Communist leaflets. Like a sad and niggardly rain they fell upon me—pages from the Song of Songs and revolver cartridges. The sad rain of sunset washed my dusty hair, and I said to the youth who lay there dying on a torn mattress:

"One Friday evening four months ago, Gedali who owns the curiosity shop took me to your father, Rabbi Motele, but you were not a member of the party then, Bratzlavsky. . . ."

"I was in the party," the boy answered, scratching his chest and writhing with fever, "but I couldn't leave my mother."

"And now, Ilya?"

"In a revolution a mother is a mere episode," he whispered, growing quieter. "My turn came, and the organization sent me to the front."

"And you found yourself in Kovel, Ilya?"

"I found myself in Kovel," he cried out in despair. "The rats exposed the front. I took command of a scratch regiment, but it was too late. I didn't have enough artillery."

He died before we reached Rovno. He died, the last prince, in the midst of verses, phylacteries, and foot clouts. We buried him near a forgotten railway station. And I, who am hardly able to hold the tempests of my imagination within this immemorial body, I was with my brother as he breathed his last.

16. THE UNITED STATES: EMERGING LEADERSHIP

Stephen S. Wise was born in 1874 in Budapest, Hungary, the son of a distinguished chief rabbi of Hungary. His family migrated to America in 1875, and Wise attended New York City public schools, graduated with honors from Columbia University, went to Vienna for rabbinical ordination and to Oxford for graduate study, and returned to America to serve as rabbi in New York (1893–1900), in Portland, Oregon (1900–1906; here he completed his Ph.D. thesis and translated the Book of Judges for the Jewish Publication Society's edition of the Holy Scriptures), and then of the Free Synagogue in New York.

As founder-rabbi of the Free Synagogue (which remained his rabbinate until his death in 1949), founder-president of the Jewish Institute of Religion (now merged with the Hebrew Union College), founder-chairman of the American Zionist Emergency Council, a founder and twice president of the

Zionist Organization of America, a founder and on several different occasions president of the American Jewish Congress, founder-president of the World Jewish Congress, and a leader in social reform (while yet in his twenties he was appointed Commissioner of Child Labor for the state of Oregon), Stephen Wise was an electrifying orator and the most well-known Jew in the world between the world wars.

The following selections, chapters 12 and 15 from Wise's autobiography, begin with his role in organizing a Jewish Congress which would adopt democratic methods in choosing the leaders of the Jewish community. While subordinating the role of Brandeis and others to his own in the founding of the Congress, Wise provides a rich description of the rise of community democracy, the accomplishments of the Congress at Versailles, the wide variety of liberal causes endorsed by the Congress in the 1920s and 1930s under Wise's presidency, the vigorous struggle waged by the Congress to expose and combat anti-Semitism, and the tortuous efforts to enroll American Jews in a protest campaign against the emerging Nazi terror.

Stephen Wise, *Challenging Years*

BATTLING FOR JEWISH DEMOCRACY

Throughout most of the life of the American Jewish Congress, it has been my privilege to serve as its president; and I find deep satisfaction in the great contributions the Congress has made to the security of Jewish life both here and abroad, to the struggle for the establishment of a Jewish national home, and to the realization of American democracy. Above all, the Congress finally and effectively shattered the dominance of paternalism and benevolent despotism in the internal affairs of the American Jewish community.

It should cause no surprise that so continuous and stern a battle has had to be waged within the Jewish community for democracy in the management of Jewish affairs. It is little more than a century, in many instances less, since

Jews, like most other human beings, dwelt in lands untouched by the spirit and methods of democracy. One of the results of the persecution of the Jews was the inevitable rise of a succession of individuals in all lands and ages who stood out as the intermediaries between their people and the sovereigns or authorities of one country or another, by whose grace and favor it alone was possible for Jews to live. Feuchtwanger's *Power* tells something of the series of Jewish ambassadors to whom the Germans gave the name, half-contemptuous and half-flattering, of *Hof-Jude,* paraphrased in Yiddish as *shtadlan.* Their function was to mediate between the non-Jewish oppressors and the Jewish oppressed—hardly conducive to a democratic attitude on the part of either the mediator above or the oppressed below.

The tradition was carried over to this country. Jews from Germany comprised the bulk of the American Jewish settlers during most of the nineteenth century. A number of wealthy and influential individuals occupied themselves with problems of philanthropy and relief and constituted themselves the spokesmen and representatives of the Jewish community whenever occasion required. The masses of Jews, their number growing as a result of the later Eastern European migration, had virtually no voice in the determination of the issues by which they were vitally affected.

But rumblings of discontent were being heard within the American Jewish community, which by 1900 had grown to two million and by 1910 to three million. The outbreak of the First World War lent impetus to the democratic stirrings of the Jewish masses. It was sensed at once that great things were at stake. American Jews had to face the problems of their fellow Jews which arose out of the war: (1) the desperate need in the war countries; (2) the grave threat to the populous Jewish belt in Eastern and Central Europe; (3) the hope that Palestine would somehow emerge as a Jewish land, an aspiration almost unanimously rejected by the men of wealth and influence who dominated the Jewish community. The masses of American Jews correctly felt that there could be no hope for the Jewish restoration of Palestine unless American Jewry was organized and united. To many of us it was clear that the demands of the Jewish people had to be formulated for the peace conferences that would follow the war. And we felt deeply that no persons or groups had a right to speak *for* American Jews unless they were prepared to speak *with* American Jews. In a word, the Jews of America had to take into their own hands the management of their own internal affairs. Needless to say, such views met with bitter opposition on the part of the highly benevolent "managers," who had come to believe that their dynasty was flawless and unchangeable.

The idea of an American Jewish Congress, uniting within a democratic framework all Jewish groups for common action on Jewish affairs, began to gather momentum. The concept, put forth by such persons as Nachman Syrkin, Gedaliah Bublick, and Baruch Zuckerman, was given its clearest formulation by Justice Brandeis. More than any other person, Brandeis recognized the inexorable necessity of ending the reign of the *Hof-Juden* in America and of substituting for it a democratic organization of Jewish life in a democratic land. He fully understood the part played by the "big business" of philanthropy in the management of Jewish affairs, but he deplored and resented the failure of those in control to invite the judgment and participation of those who were no less qualified to direct and control—namely the Jewish masses themselves. He developed the idea in a series of memorable addresses in the early years of the war. And the founding of the Congress was the result of the faith of a group of men led by Brandeis and Julian Mack, Felix Frankfurter and Pinchas Rutenberg, Louis Lipsky and Bernard Richards, Nathan Straus and myself, that American Jews, citizens of a great democracy, could be trusted, understandingly and with dignity, to make use of the normal instrumentalities of democratic life.

After a series of premeetings, the preliminary conference was held in Philadelphia on March 26, 1916. Mine was the historic privilege of delivering the keynote address. Brandeis, who had meanwhile been nominated by President Wilson for the Supreme Court, was not present at the conference. In my address I said:

> This day is destined to be memorable in the annals of Israel—the more because we are thinking not of ourselves alone, not for ourselves, but after the Jewish manner, of and for all Israel. . . .
>
> We again solemnly aver that a people is not worthy of respect which does not insist on the right to be heard touching its own affairs, but surrenders the right of judgment and decision to a company of men, however wise and benevolent, who substitute their own opinions and wishes for the convictions and determinations of the whole people. It were little less than a tragedy if the Jewish people, first among the peoples in democratic aim in this land, should succumb to the pressure exerted by those who for one reason or another are distrustful of the capacity of the many to manage their own affairs. . . .
>
> The world cannot be expected to assent to any program touching Israel's future as long as Israel does not unitedly deliberate and speak. Secrecy, always futile as a curative method, has proven disastrous in prolonging and intensifying Jewish woes. We now freely discuss our will where aforetime we furtively listened to the edict of others. A Congress means deliberation not agitation, discussion not division, enlightenment not secrecy. . . .

> We reject no leadership for we have known no leadership. Policies of inaction and aimlessness and timidity have presumed to erect themselves into leadership, tempered always by the grace of beneficence. With the substitution of inchoate purposelessness for the conscious direction of our affairs, we have been patient much too long. Accidentally and whimsically adopted policies have been set to do the work of undeviating principle. Such direction as has been has even lacked the merit of wise opportunism. We have had caution in the place of wisdom. We have had inaction erected into a program.
>
> The only program acceptable to the men in control of our affairs has been a program of palliation, as if nothing more than temporary relief could be hoped for Israel, wounded and oppressed. Relief, alas, is at times sorely needed, was never more needed than today. But relief is not to be exalted as the policy or program of a people unless these be hopeless beggars and that people adopt a program of relief as the only way out. Not relief but redress, not palliation but prevention, not charity but justice . . . is the only program worthy of a great and proud people.

The preliminary conference adopted the outlines of a program for the proposed American Jewish Congress, made provision for nationwide elections to the new body, and elected an Executive Committee whose duty was to push ahead with the plans. Discussions were carried on with other national organizations and, when the new Executive Committee met for its first session, virtually all national Jewish bodies were included. After extensive deliberation, an election system was evolved and elections held in the Jewish communities throughout the country on June 10, 1917. On that day, for the first time in modern Jewish history, 335,000 Jewish men and women went to the polls to choose their representatives to the first American Jewish Congress.

Originally, we had hoped to convene the Congress in the fall of 1917, but our entry into the war created new problems, and many counseled postponement. I put the matter squarely before President Wilson in a conference with him on June 29, 1917. He advised postponement, and we accepted his counsel. The President authorized me to say in a statement:

> While it may seem necessary to the gentlemen who have called the Congress to postpone it for some little time from the date fixed because of the urgency of public business, the President is persuaded that the American Jewish Congress will wisely and prudently serve Jewish interests, and that its deliberations and policies will be in accord with and helpful to the aims and policies of the American government.

Meanwhile, negotiations had been continuing between the Congress advocates and those who bitterly opposed the movement. Ultimately, the latter agreed to participate in the Congress provided it was to be regarded purely as a temporary, wartime body to be dissolved as soon as its function with regard to the peace conferences had been discharged. Because we felt the need of unity to be so urgent, we reluctantly accepted that condition.

The first session of the American Jewish Congress was finally convened in Philadelphia on Decenber 15–18, 1918. More than four hundred delegates were present, three hundred having been chosen in the nationwide elections and a hundred designated by national organizations. The participants included the most distinguished figures in American Jewish life and, to this day, I meet persons in all parts of the country whose proudest boast to me is that they were delegates to the founding session of the American Jewish Congress. The session adopted a program for submission to the Peace Conference which included the demand for full and equal civil, political, religious, and national rights for all citizens of any territory without distinction as to race or creed, autonomy in the management of their communal institutions by members of the various national and religious bodies, and recognition of the historic claim of the Jewish people to Palestine. The Congress program was thus a decisive victory for those of us who insisted that the rights of the Jews as a people and a nationality, no less than as individuals, had to be assured. It was no less a triumph for the Zionist cause. It was significant, even prophetic, I may add, that the Congress session adopted a resolution directing the American Jewish Congress "to take necessary and effective steps in cooperation with representative Jewish bodies in other countries for the convening of a World Jewish Congress."

The Congress elected a delegation to represent American Jewry at the Versailles Peace Conference consisting of Judge Julian Mack, as chairman, Louis Marshall, Colonel Harry Cutler, Jacob deHaas, Rabbi B. L. Levinthal, Joseph Barondess, Nachman Syrkin, Leopold Benedict, Bernard Richards, and myself.

I was already abroad, having left for London and Paris as soon as the war ended in order to begin discussions with Jewish and governmental leaders. Thus I was able to present to Mr. Balfour, as I have related elsewhere, the resolution of the Congress, the day after its adoption, calling on Britain to assume a trusteeship over Palestine. In Paris, the Congress delegation joined forces with and became part of the Comité des Délégations Juives which was made up, as far as war exigencies permitted, of democratically elected representatives of the Jewish populations of Europe.

When the delegation returned from Versailles it reported to a second session of the American Jewish Congress in Philadelphia on May 30 and 31, 1919. In the meantime, the struggle had been renewed between those who demanded the strict enforcement of the agreement that the Congress should terminate with the signing of the Peace Treaty and the many who recognized that the gains won by the Comité des Délégations Juives at the Peace Conference would hardly be permanent unless safeguarded through the unceasing vigilance of some democratically constituted body such as the Congress.

The Congress, adhering strictly to the original agreement, adjourned sine die. But a large body of delegates, myself among them, immediately reconvened in a "conference for the formation of an American Jewish Congress," determined that the gains we had made in bringing democracy into Jewish life should not be lost. Again, it was my privilege to sound the keynote. I warned that it was too late to return to "the undemocratic, un-American, un-Jewish method of dictation from above, however well-meaning in intent, however soft-spoken in manner."

The Conference elected an Executive Committee which was directed to convene a permanent Congress. Elections took place in May, 1922, and the first session of the permanent American Jewish Congress was held in Philadelphia in June.

The groups that had always opposed a democratic Jewish body withdrew from the Congress at the 1919 session. Since that time, they have for the most part continued resolutely to oppose and sabotage every effort to establish a representative Jewish body for the democratic management of the internal affairs of the Jewish community. Fortunately, as I see it, they have failed in these attempts.

During the 1920s, the Congress stood guard over situations affecting Jews in all parts of the world. It lent maximum support to the Zionist movement in the rebuilding of Palestine. It intervened promptly and energetically whenever the safety or security of Jews was threatened in any part of the world. It continually sought to widen the area of cooperation among Jews of all lands on their common problems. It gave fullest support to, and almost invariably took the initiative in, every effort to organize the American Jewish community on the broadest possible basis, efforts which in every instance were brought to naught by the opposition of the die-hard opponents of democratic organization. Above all, the Congress insisted at all times on full and frank public discussion of issues directly affecting the Jewish community, an insistence which, I am not unhappy to say, continued to earn for us the hostility of those who clung to the discredited belief in the efficacy of silence and secrecy touching grave issues in Jewish life.

I have dealt elsewhere in this volume with what I regard as the most historic achievements of the American Jewish Congress: the manner in which, for a decade, we rallied both Jews and non-Jews to an understanding of the menace of Hitler and fascism, and our leading role in the creation of the World Jewish Congress. There are two other equally historic contributions of which I would speak.

Early in the war, the leaders of the American and the World Jewish Congresses recognized the vast problems with which the Jewish people would be confronted at the end of the war. We were keenly aware of the fact that extensive research and preparation would be required in order intelligently to formulate the postwar demands and needs of the Jewish people. Accordingly, the American and World Jewish Congresses created the Institute of Jewish Affairs, headed by the distinguished international jurist, Dr. Jacob Robinson, and staffed by some of the most outstanding scholars in the Jewish world, many of whom had come from Europe at the outbreak of the war. During the war years, the Institute gathered a vast amount of data on every phase of the Jewish catastrophe and its implications. It devoted intensive study to all the problems likely to emerge at the end of the war—problems of relief and reparations, of indemnification and restitution, of the punishment of war criminals, of migration and the resettlement of refugees, of human rights and the international protection of minority groups. The researches of the Institute were published in a series of significant volumes and incorporated in memoranda and documents submitted to the Allied authorities, to various governments and international agencies, and, later, to the United Nations.

These materials provided the basis on which Jewish postwar claims were formulated. It is not too much to assert that concepts first formulated by the Institute have had a significant impact on the development of international policy on such fundamental problems as restitution, reparations, relief, the treatment of displaced persons, human rights, and the trials of war criminals. The formulation of these concepts was given great impetus by the War Emergency Conference of the World Jewish Congress held in Atlantic City on November 26–30, 1944. Despite the extraordinary difficulties created by the war, some 270 delegates representing Jewish communities of forty countries were present. In welcoming the delegates, I stated:

> This is not a relief conference. This is not a charity conference. . . . Even as we desire that the fullest justice shall be done to every people on earth, we shall be satisfied with nothing less than the fullest measure of justice to the people of Israel.

The resolutions adopted by the Emergency Conference, the most significant Jewish gathering held during the war, were soon recognized and accepted by Jews everywhere as the basic program for Jewish survival in the postwar world.

There is yet another major contribution of the American Jewish Congress which, I venture to predict, will prove to be a historic and enduring one, not only for American Jewry but for American democracy. Many of us in the Congress movement had long recognized that more than a decade of intensive worldwide fascist and anti-Semitic propaganda would leave a legacy of prejudice which it would prove extremely difficult to eradicate. Concepts of racism, already deeply imbedded in the thinking and practice of so many countries, including, unhappily, our own, had been strengthened and reinforced. It was clear that one of our major postwar responsibilities would be to do whatever we could to counter this threat not only to the security of the Jewish people but to the very fabric of the democratic system.

Throughout its history, the American Jewish Congress had always been actively concerned with anti-Semitism. But our concern was primarily with specific anti-Semitic incidents, movements, and outbreaks. Through various committees, we had continuously dealt with economic discrimination against Jews, particularly in the field of employment, and we had always been active with regard to any legislation that bore on Jewish interests, such as immigration. But it was obvious to us that the postwar situation would require a much more comprehensive and dynamic program, based on intensive scientific research and analysis.

My own interest and activity in the field of civil rights had gone back to the beginning of my participation in public affairs. But the American Jewish Congress—deeply involved in other issues—had never undertaken a large-scale program on behalf of civil and group rights as an integral part of its work.

As we began to devote ourselves intensively to these problems, we quickly realized that it would be futile to adopt the kinds of programs that had been generally employed to foster better intergroup understanding. Those programs, usually consisting of the widespread dissemination of literature and propaganda preaching goodwill, and the sponsoring of interfaith meetings and projects had proved almost wholly futile. What was required was a much more fundamental attack on the problem, based on modern concepts of social science and rooted in the recognition that the security of no group could be assured unless the full rights of all groups were safeguarded and extended. Accordingly, we set ourselves to devise a comprehensive program that would not be an anonymous and self-abasing plea for tolerance but a self-respecting and vigorous campaign for the equal rights of all people. In furthering this program we were extremely fortunate in enlisting the active and devoted services of two men of genius, brilliant and dedicated sons of the Jewish people, both of whom, alas, were far too soon to be taken from our midst—Professors Kurt Lewin and Alexander Pekelis.

Lewin, referred to by his professional colleagues as the "Einstein of modern psychology," had come to this country from Nazi Germany in 1933 to teach in American universities. Generally regarded as the foremost student of group psychology in the world, he had founded a research center for group dynamics at the Massachusetts Institute of Technology to train students in the new methods he had developed. He had written extensively on problems of Jewish education and published his now classic analysis of the phenomenon of self-hatred among minority groups. His increasing concern with the problem of Jewish survival brought him to the American Jewish Congress, for which he organized the Commission on Community Interrelations in 1944. Staffed by a group of highly skilled social psychologists and sociologists, the Commission began what is probably the most ambitious and what is likely to prove the most fruitful study of group tensions and group adjustment undertaken in this country. Lewin continued to serve the Commission actively as its chief consultant until his untimely and sudden death early in 1947, in the prime of his intellectual powers.

Alexander Pekelis was, beyond question, one of the most brilliant and creative men I have met in my lifetime. Russian born, German and Italian educated, he had been a distinguished professor of law in Italian universities until he was forced to flee in 1939. Arriving in this country in 1940, he soon embarked on what was to prove a meteoric career as a student at Columbia Law School and editor in chief of its *Law Review,* while at the same time serving as professor at the New School for Social Research. Within a short time, he had mastered the entire range of American history and law, and his papers and writings began to attract wide attention. Legal scholars have told me that they regarded him as the most creative and original legal mind in America. An ardent Zionist, and passionately dedicated to Jewish survival,

Pekelis was deeply concerned with every phase of Jewish life. When the American Jewish Congress organized its Commission on Law and Social Action in 1945, Pekelis accepted our invitation to become its active head. From his fertile brain there flowed the ideas and concepts that, applied by his colleagues, have won for the Commission acclaim as the most significant and productive body in its field in the United States. The Commission set for itself the task of surveying such major problem areas as discrimination in employment, education, and housing; racial segregation; and dissemination of racial propaganda through media of public communication. It then formulated in all of these fields comprehensive programs involving the promotion of legislation, test cases before the courts and administrative agencies, and social-action campaigns designed to transform public policy in these areas so as to protect the democratic and equal rights of all groups.

Pekelis's briefs written for the American Jewish Congress in many of these cases are regarded as masterpieces, his brief in a California case involving the segregation of Mexican-American children having been described as "the most important contribution to the socio-legal attack on segregation made in this country in twenty-five years." His briefs in the successful challenge of the American Jewish Congress to the New York *Daily News'* application for an FM radio license, on the grounds of its anti-Jewish and anti-Negro propaganda, resulted in wholly new concepts with regard to the public responsibilities of media of communication.

Pekelis, an inspiration to all of us, was killed in an air crash, returning from the World Zionist Congress in Switzerland in December, 1946. I shall always remember the day on board ship when I learned of his death as one of the saddest of my life. In his early forties at the time of his death, Pekelis was only at the beginning of what would have been a career of historic service to the Jewish people and democratic thought.

Fortunately, he had trained and taught his associates well, and they have continued his creative and pioneering work. From the Commission on Law and Social Action there have come campaigns such as that which led to the enactment in New York State of the first legislative measure in this country effectively to ban racial and religious discrimination in institutions of higher learning, and a long series of notable—and generally successful—interventions in the courts and administrative agencies in major test cases involving the rights not only of Jews, but of Negroes, Japanese, and other minority groups.

It was such pioneering activity by the American Jewish Congress which, I believe, was responsible for my appointment by President Truman to the

President's Commission on Higher Education, established in 1946 to survey the entire problem of higher education in the United States. I deem it a unique privilege to have served as a member of that body of distinguished public citizens and educators who produced so significant a report, later published under the title "Higher Education for American Democracy." My interest, I need hardly state, embraced all phases of the Commission's work. But I must confess that I was particularly concerned with the activity of the subcommittee, dealing with the problem of equalizing and expanding educational opportunity on which I served. This committee investigated the barriers to higher education imposed by financial circumstances, limitations of facilities, and discrimination because of race, color, or creed. I was able, as a result of the work of the American Jewish Congress, to bring to the attention of the Commission a large body of data and suggestions relating to the problem. It was extremely gratifying to me that the final report of the Commission spoke so forthrightly about the problem of discrimination and included many specific suggestions for its abolition, among them the passage of state legislation banning discriminatory admissions practices.

Though the enlarged work of the American Jewish Congress in this field is comparatively recent in origin, it has already had a very considerable impact on the programs of other bodies—both Jewish and non-Jewish—actively engaged in expanding the frontiers of democracy. Through the Commission on Law and Social Action, the Congress has greatly influenced American thinking on the approach to, and strategy in, the struggle for full equality. This, again, has been an outstanding example of the manner in which, as citizens and builders of American democracy, we Jews have taken our full part in shaping its affairs and in taking risks in the battle against privilege and inequality, not for ourselves chiefly or alone, but for all peoples and races in the land. . . .

RESISTANCE TO HITLERISM

On March 12, 1933, the Nazi swastika was proclaimed the official flag of the "New Germany." On March 27, the American Jewish Congress mobilized the first broad resistance movement to Hitlerism at a mass meeting held in Madison Square Garden, New York. That night, Bishops Manning and McConnell, Alfred E. Smith, John Haynes Holmes, Dr. S. Parkes Cadman, and William Green nobly uttered their abhorrence of Nazism, and together we lifted our voices seeking to forewarn Germany of what Hitler would inevitably mean.

As chairman of the meeting, I pointed out:

> A leader who sets out to divide his national home against itself may have election triumphs for an hour, but he is bound to go down in the end in moral defeat and in spiritual disaster.
>
> If it be true that we Jews stand among the objects of Hitlerite displeasure and ill-will, it is because you and I know that Hitlerism aims not at a change of government, but at a complete change of regime. He aims at the end of Democracy. He aims at the overthrow of Republicanism. He aims at the destruction of the parliamentary system, and Hitler is understanding enough to know that Jews are not fitful, expedient servants for an hour of Democracy and Republicanism. He knows that we Jews, after centuries of fire, have come to believe with all our hearts in the sacredness and in the perpetuity of democratic institutions and the democratic ideal.

At the mass meeting I sought to make clear that neither the Jews of the world nor the Jews of Germany demanded exceptional treatment or privileged position. We affirmed certain elementary axioms of civilization: the immediate cessation of anti-Semitic activity in Germany, including an end to the policy of racial discrimination against Jews and of their exclusion from the economic life of Germany; the safeguarding of Jewish life and the human rights of Jews; the revocation of all special measures already taken against Jewish nonnationals (East European Jews) and their equal treatment with all other nonnationals in Germany.

The protest of America on the Nazi terror against Jews was countered by the Nazi government with the announcement that the boycott against Jews in Germany was ordered because of the "atrocity propaganda" by Jews in America. However, as we soon learned from Germany, the opposite was true. One letter from Berlin dated April 2 reached me giving details of the horrors of April 1 for Jews throughout Germany. It added:

> Over here they have made the Jews and everyone else think that this boycott was only a retaliatory measure because of the action of the Jews in England and America and that nothing would have occurred otherwise. Lies—all lies. It was prepared months ago. I know! . . .
>
> They claim that all this was done in retaliation of what was done to Germany in foreign countries. Could any country in 48 hours have a complete list of every Jewish shop in Germany? This, mind you, included seamstresses, little shoemakers, tiny shops in basements that sell vegetables, and all this in the smallest hamlets and towns. You have no idea how all this was

organized to the nth degree. They had speakers in every factory throughout the country telling workmen and the masses that through a boycott instituted by the Jews against Germany they, the workmen, would be the ones to suffer and so they must help in rooting out these people and hitting them in their most vulnerable spot.

Thank God that the other countries know and, despite what this country is preaching that the mass meetings of the Jews in England and America has reacted injuriously to the Jews in Germany, I tell you this is not so. No matter how much they suffered in humiliation and insult last Saturday it is not one-hundredth of what we are all convinced was REALLY planned. According to their real program [the Boxheim documents and others] they had intended not only to close the shops but to plunder them everywhere and do a lot of other things far worse than what they did, and which they brag about as having been carried out in strictest discipline.

Hitler made the statement that the "People" wanted to carry all this through themselves and that only by organization and by their storm detachments and the regulations which they carried out to the letter were atrocities averted. That wasn't it. They were *afraid* now that the outside world knew to completely carry out what they had so systematically planned and organized—a huge program. They had to let their troopers loose but they limited their dirty work to only one day, ordering that the boycott should be over by 7 P.M.

And again from a Berlin lawyer who sent this message from Zurich:

It was only foreign protests, especially that of America, which prevented even more happenings, a greater number of kidnappings and bloody beatings and possibly one big general pogrom.

In contrast to these letters, on March 30, I received a cable from three former presidents of the German Zionist Federation stating that the situation was most serious and urging that I issue a statement denying that the anti-German boycott had been proclaimed by Jewish organizations.

The violence and insolence of a lengthy cable signed by the editors of a Jewish paper in Hamburg was such as to make me feel sure it was either sent under duress or directly by agents of the Nazi government. My suspicion about several such messages was later proven correct. This one, dated March 31, read:

. . . German Jews accuse you and associates to be fools of outside political influences. Your senseless overrating of own international importance and lack of judgment damage largely those you pretend to want to protect. . . . Better shut off your own limelight and useless meetings as surest means

> against anti-Semitism. German Jews who feel one with our great national ideas and keep tactful are treated with pronounced consideration from Gentile neighbors and present government officials. Please enlighten everyone about foregoing. This is your most important duty to repair your crimes against us.

We understood the plea and the plaint of our brother Jews in Germany. They were German patriots who loved their fatherland and had reason to love it. Some of their leaders were under the impact of panic and terror, others under some form of compulsion, in any event the compulsion of a great fear if not actual coercion. We had no quarrel with our Jewish brothers in Germany and their leaders, but their policy of uncomplaining assent and supercautious silence had borne evil fruit. They who had virtually been silent through the years of anti-Jewish propaganda could not be regarded by us as the wisest of counselors.

To those leaders of German Jewry who declared that the anti-Jewish situation in Germany was a local German question I called attention to the words of Abraham Lincoln. Defenders of slavery urged and excused slavery on the ground that it was local. Lincoln's answer was, "Slavery is local, but freedom is national."

One thing more must be told. Students of the period will recall that one or two days before Boycott Day, April 1, 1933—the day on which the Nazis decreed that an absolute boycott of all Jews was to go into effect—it was reported by cable out of the Reich that a nationwide pogrom was being planned throughout Germany. The pogrom did not take place. The Nazi boycott, of course, was the real beginning of years of Jewish humiliation and agony. But the mass pogrom reportedly scheduled for that day did not come off. A careful study as well as consultation with many German Jews and some non-Jews in the course of the Hitler years served to confirm the rumors of the closing days of March, 1933. It is more than probable that the boycott of April 1 was a mild and belated afterthought and that, in truth, a Teutonic St. Bartholomew's Eve massacre had been planned against the Jews of Germany. But when the Nazi regime considered the strength of the American Jewish Congress indictment uttered by leading American citizens, Catholic as well as Protestant, it took heed of that warning and realized that the Reich would endanger its position in the eyes of the world if it resorted to a Jewish pogrom.

Someday the record may give the answer to this debatable question. I personally satisfied myself on my trip to Europe that summer, which took me to England, France, Czechoslovakia, and Switzerland, and elsewhere.

The European protest movement against Hitler then was undertaken as a result of the inspiration and leadership of the American Jewish Congress. Representatives of the Jewish communities of Poland, Latvia, Czechoslovakia, and Romania told me that they had been in the dark. They did not know what to do. They were waiting for a lead when the cables came from Bernard Deutsch and myself calling for action on March 27, the day we had set for our great protest assembly in New York. Then they felt that they could and must go ahead. They took it for granted that we, far removed from the scene, were sufficiently informed concerning the situation, to know whether it was well for them to strike out.

If my analysis be correct, the American Jewish Congress performed a very great service for German Jewry, for world Jewry, for civilization. In any event, cruel as the first Boycott Day, April 1, 1933, proved to be, it may have been an improvised and belated substitute for something far more bitter and terrible. But the Congress protest was proof that a great people, however awful the threat, would not "take it lying down" and could be trusted to stand on its feet and not crawl on its hands. This word of Josiah Wedgewood, British Labor M.P. and truest of our friends, was an English reminder of the example of Mordecai, who would not bow the head, nor bend the knee before Haman, the Hitler of an earlier Persian day.

In America, we immediately met the counterpart, though happily on a small and individual scale, of both Nazism and timid Jews who, without the excuse of Nazi persecution, lacked self-respect. William Dudley Pelley of the Silver Shirts published in *Liberation:*

> Hitler has a destiny to fulfill. . . . He has already set his hand against the so-called "Lord's Chosen" in Germany. . . . It is the order of things that those wicked and malignant spirits . . . should meet a fearful fate in this closing Cycle of Cosmic Event. That contest is on-the-make and Hitler's job it has been to do the advance work.
>
> But Hitler is not going to finish that work. *The finish of it comes right here in America.*

And a gentleman who carefully described himself in the New York *Post* "As a Hebrew—and as an American whose ancestors have fought in all our wars since that of 1812" (forgetting, if he ever knew, the delightful characterization by the great American humorist who said that those Americans who bragged of their descent often forgot how great the descent had been) fulminated against the American Jewish Congress for daring to hold a mass meeting in protest against Hitler's terror and solemnly announced:

> I predict that even in the Germany of Hitler a patriotic, self-respecting citizen of the Hebrew religion will experience very little difficulty, and will suffer no hardship.

Amidst the early mounting horrors as reported day after day we sought aid from our government. Silence at first both on the part of the American government and the Prime Minister of England filled our cup of woe. We went ahead, pressed forward by the Jewish masses who could not be expected to understand such silence. About mid-April we planned a protest march in New York, on May 10, the day of the ordered burning of Jewish books in Germany. And a great march was held and reported throughout the world. For reasons still inexplicable, the American Red Cross took it upon itself to publicize a statement of the German Red Cross to the effect that: "the reports of atrocities which have been spread abroad for reasons of political propaganda are in no way in accordance with the facts."

Within a few weeks after the mass meeting, members of both the House of Representatives and the Senate voiced their desire to do whatever they could to express America's abhorrence of the conduct of the Nazis.

Day after day and week after week, reliable reports of the breaking of all resistance by the Nazi Brown Shirts came through from many sources. The use of terror had been extended to destroy pacifists, labor leaders, liberals, socialists—in fact any resistance to the Nazi dictatorship. Although, as the *Manchester Guardian* reported on July 21, 1933, the terrorist wave had shattered all actual resistance, the terror had not ceased—but on the contrary had become more universal and more systematic. Priests of the Catholic Church had been arrested and the Protestants were not being spared. The measures against the Jews continued to outstrip in systematic cruelty and planned destruction the terror against other groups. Trade unions were closed to non-Aryans—so that the early prospect for Jewish workers seemed starvation. Clinics managed by Jewish doctors were closed. Farmers and peasants in western Bavaria were prohibited from having any business relations with Jews, under penalty of being officially classified as traitors; Jewish writers were excluded from the Union of Dramatic Writers, thus eliminating their work from the German stage and motion pictures; segregation of Jewish youth in schools, streetcars, and universities was decreed; and sterilization of the unfit was announced—with reports that the unfit would include Jewish children!

That summer (1933) my wife and I went abroad, first to Prague, still the democratic land that Masaryk had re-created, although I saw Hitler youths walking through the streets at night singing their songs of hate. I wanted to go to Germany, but our Ambassador said he would not be responsible for what would happen if I should come and that it might well cause serious complications. We traveled on to the lands surrounding Germany—Austria, Switzerland, and France.

Everywhere I went I visited the asylum or shelters for German Jewish refugees, and through their eyes looked into the depths of hell. When I spoke to one man who became hysterical, I turned to his wife asking if she could not control him so I could understand. She replied, "If you knew what my husband has lived through, what he has seen and heard and experienced—you would not ask that question."

I met an old friend from Munich, who told about Siegel, whose picture had been in the press throughout the world bearing the placard, "I am a Jew. I am a treasonable German." Later he was shot to death at Dachau "trying to escape." My friend, in tears, could only say, "He was a fine, outstanding, honorable member of the Munich bar." The Germans denied that this picture was genuine, said it was nothing but an atrocity fake. But a representative of the *Brooklyn Daily Eagle* told me that he had himself taken the picture from the tower of a Munich church and, when told by a representative of Goebbels that the whole thing was a fake, had the original of the photograph in his pocket!

A physician from Munich and his wife called on me in Paris and said that their little girl of eleven had come from school, her face tear-stained, and asked them: "Is it true that we Jews are all *gemein* [base]? That is what they tell us in school." I learned how the children were compelled to memorize passages which say vile things about the Jews, how they were denied milk and bread when Aryans were fed.

The deepest concern of the Jews in Germany was "our children." Always the greatest joy of Jews was to live with their children. Now, their one hope was to send their children away to safety. Over and over, I heard, "We can endure it, but our children . . ."

I wrote to a friend in July, after having spent days with refugees in London and Paris, that they were living in hell. "I feel this so deeply that if I were to read tomorrow of a pogrom, which may come at any hour, and the murder or suicide of thousands of victims, I could hardly be any sorrier or unhappier than I am over them excepting for the shock and tragedy of their manner of going."

From Zurich, I again begged Ambassador Dodd by telephone to make possible my air flight to Berlin. He was adamant in refusing, insisting that my picture had so often been published in the *Voelkische Beobachter* and in Streicher's *Stuermer* that I might be recognized, particularly because of my unmistakable passport, and give rise to an "unpleasant incident" at a landing place such as Nuremberg.

It was in Germany's neighboring lands that we got our first glimpse of the human desolation that was being wrought by Hitler. In Paris, as well as Prague and Vienna, we met with scores of the earliest homeless refugees, who gathered from time to time amid the necessarily scant hospitality of the hostel, called into being by the French Jews. My wife said at once, "Many of these unhappy beings will soon, they say, come to America. As soon as we return I shall establish a home for refugees, where they may dwell in security and comfort, and thus fit themselves for American life." She was better than her word. Within a few months, three houses of the Jewish Institute of Religion had been refurnished by the Women's Division of the American Jewish Congress under her leadership. Here Mrs. Wise and her associates made homes for eighty to one hundred refugees, young and old, at a time. Some of the most distinguished of the refugees, from 1934 to 1939, lived for a time in these houses, which Mrs. Wise had exquisitely furnished with the help of her friends and comrades. Largely in jest, Professor Einstein, visiting the houses and delighted with their charm and comfort, lamented, "Why cannot I live here? *Ich bin ja auch ein Refugee!*"

I must not omit to tell of a minor victory of the Women's Division of the Congress. At one of their annual luncheons, the speaker was Mayor La Guardia, who, like President Roosevelt, was from the beginning a clear-sighted foe of Nazism. In the course of his luncheon address, the Mayor had made the rather startling suggestion that, after the capture of Hitler, he be brought to this country and exhibited in a cage at the World's Fair, then being held in New York. The Berlin press reported the meeting, stating that "the mad Mayor had made this irresponsible speech before a company of a thousand or twelve hundred loose Jewish women." Despite the idiocy of the remark, the President of the Women's Division of the American Jewish Congress felt justly pained over the insult. In this spirit Mrs. Wise promptly telegraphed to Secretary Hull, insisting that he demand an apology from Germany. The Secretary forwarded the protest to Von Neurath, who promptly tendered an apology for his government, the only occasion, as I recall it, that apology was forthcoming, however grievous the offense committed.

The spirit that moved Mrs. Wise as head of the Women's Division of the congress to act without delay when the honor of Jewish womanhood was assailed led her some years later to act with the same dispatch and dignity when the British government, by its ambassador to Washington, offered her a decoration, the Order of the British Empire, in acknowledgment of the service she and the Congress had rendered British soldiers through the Congress Defense Houses. To a quarter million of men the Congress had offered shelter and hospitality during the war years. She felt so deeply about the conduct of the British mandatory government in Palestine and the grievous wrong it had done to Jewish refugees, many of whom could have been saved by opening the doors of Palestine, that without one moment's delay, she declined the honor, of which she never spoke again.

That summer in addition to meeting with and hearing firsthand accounts of life in Germany from hundreds of refugees, I met with leading statesmen of many lands, conferred with the representatives of Jewish and non-Jewish communities, and studied the activities of various relief agencies. At that early period in the Hitler regime, it still seemed possible that effective action by the League of Nations through a commission and economic pressure by enlightened public opinion, if secured promptly, might bring about the end of the Nazi government and its policy of persecution. And so I strove toward achieving these two objectives, desperately working against time and the unwillingness or inability of statesmen of many lands to see that not to end the Hitler regime would mean war or the destruction of all that civilized men held dear.

In Geneva, the World Jewish Conference was convened on September 5. I introduced and urged the unanimous adoption of a resolution calling for a world Jewish boycott of Germany. The resolution was unanimously adopted. I had been urged to call for such a boycott for many months. While I had believed from the beginning that the boycott was a natural, inevitable weapon in the hands of individuals against the war of extermination launched by the Hitler regime against Jews, I was firmly convinced that a world Jewish boycott could only be declared by a world assembly of Jews.

In answer to a question by the press at that time as to whether this was to be solely a Jewish boycott I answered:

> One of the most grievous disappointments of my life would be the failure of non-Jews, especially of Christian men and women in all lands, to stand by our side and join with us in wielding this weapon of defense against the Third Reich on behalf of the Jewish people. The truth is that tens of thousands of

Christians feel exactly as we do about the crimes planned and perpetrated against the Jews by the Nazi government.

The conference that September decided not only that there must be a continuance and an intensification of the boycott against Germany but that the boycott must be moral as well as political. Even at that time I thought and said that moral and economic boycott ultimately would develop into political action:

> For my part, I cannot believe that liberty-loving countries such as England and France and our own will permanently endure the liberty-destroying, the justice-violating conduct of the Hitlerite Reich toward its own people—

and I added:

> Germany is in truth become a menace to world security and world peace.

A second decision of the World Jewish Conference was that a World Jewish Congress must be held, and it was then scheduled to be convened the following March.

In the months that followed every effort had to be bent toward getting financial help to feed the refugees of Hitler's regime, to move my country, which had been keenly disappointing in its failure thus far to enable German refugees to enter the United States, to strengthen through the World Jewish Congress a self-reliant democratic movement of Jews throughout the world in the face of what seemed relentless destruction, and to help America and other democratic lands to see and understand that their security and peace was in danger. On September 27, I said:

> When I speak of the menace to world security I do not mean that Hitler is going to smash and slash into France tomorrow or next day. He is much too shrewd and careful to do any such thing. The real danger is something much more subtle, much less overt, namely that he will carry the ideal of *Gleichschaltung* one step farther and that means insistence on uniformity. It means the overruling of other racial groups. It means the exercise of ruthless power in a ruthless way. It is all mildly and pleasantly put as *Gleichschaltung* which means little more than agreement or uniformity, but uniformity can be insisted upon only by those who are certain of their own superiority. After uniformity and superiority there will come the inevitable attempt to achieve world domination.

Within three weeks the German Reich had withdrawn from the League of Nations, and in doing so said to those who could hear, "Germany is against the world."

Germany still sought to put the matter as if it were merely a quarrel between Germany and the Jews, as if it were just a disagreement between Herr von Neurath and Sir John Simon, as if it were just a misunderstanding, with Dr. Goebbels on the one hand and Premier Daladier on the other. The truth was that something catastrophic had come upon the life of the world. One of the great, one of the mighty, one of the tremendous historic forces of the world had run amok, had fallen afoul of civilization.

It was only fifteen or sixteen months earlier that the Lausanne agreement had been reached, saying that if France, England, and Italy were lenient toward Germany we, the United States, would scale down the obligations owing to us from the nations to which Germany was the debtor. The world was with Germany then. With incredible naïveté the official organ of the Foreign Office of Berlin asked, "What has happened to change the views of the nations since July?" when Germany was permitted on terms of equality to meet with the nations at the London World Economic Conference, after which it was hoped there would be some abatement of the madness of the Hitler Reich. What happened? Everything happened. The everything was an affront, an absolute challenge to civilization, which civilization would have to meet or else be destroyed. The world was warned, and we Jews were—as we so often have been throughout history—the object lesson, the shock troops of civilization, first under attack. The challenge of each morning and night was how to make the world, our world, understand.

I must have sounded to many like a twentieth-century Cassandra when I spoke after my return from Europe:

> Men and women, remember my prophecy. Let the young people remember my words: you will see what will happen ten and twenty years hence, if this "Aryanism," this *Gleichschaltung,* remains within the Hitler Reich. You cannot have a people uniform, without differences, no variety, no dissent, no heresy, no racial heresy. You cannot have that inside of a nation without that nation finally wrecking itself in the effort to make that race or nation dominant not only inside but outside of the boundaries of that land. When will American civilization challenge Hitlerism?
>
> My answer, the answer not of a Jew but of an American, is: America will and ought to challenge Hitlerism, not with guns, not with arms, not by enmity, but by the voice of the President of the United States. It is a mighty voice, a magic voice, it is the one most potent voice in the whole world. God give it that for the sake of America's soul, that for the sake of civilization, for his own sake, the President's mighty voice may yet be raised in one of the critically decisive hours of human need in human history. Up to this time America has not yet ranged itself alongside of the forces of civilization. It

> cannot, it does not and it will not sympathize with Hitlerism and all that Hitlerism means. Someday, it may be soon, that voice *must* be lifted in no uncertain terms. And after it shall have been, with a new faith, and a new loyalty, we shall thank God for America, our country, and for its leader, our President.

In 1934, I returned to Europe to meet with leaders of Western European lands and to confer again in Geneva with my colleagues on the preparatory body for the World Jewish Congress. Difficult though it was to say certain things to Jews whose lives were in so precarious a state as those in Hitler's Reich, I felt impelled to express two fears: One was that our Jewish brothers in Germany might feel moved or compelled to accept a peace agreement or pact that might mean some slight amelioration or mitigation of their wrongs but that would in effect not alter their intolerable status of second-class citizenship.

There was still something graver to be feared. The Nazi Reich might decide to prevent some of the evil consequence to its regime by such palliative treatment of the Jews as would disarm worldwide Jewish protest. Against that menace to the integrity of Jewish life, we needed to be forewarned and forearmed. Insofar as the Nazi Reich had proclaimed war against civilization, to accept any terms of peace it might specially offer to the Jews would be to side with Hitlerism against civilization, indeed to betray civilization. At Geneva, I said to the World Jewish Conference:

> Our place is indubitably and unalterably in the ranks of those forces of civilization and freedom which cannot exist with Nazism. Grievous fate it is to be among the victims of Nazism without help and without redress. Infinitely more tragic it were to come to an understanding with Nazism. To die at the hands of Nazism is cruel; to survive by its grace were ten thousand times worse. We will survive Nazism unless we commit the inexpiable sin of bartering or trafficking with it in order to save some Jewish victims.
>
> This is not the unheroic or mock-heroic sacrifice of our fellow Jews in Nazi Germany, but rather the refusal to purchase peace and security for some of us at the cost of the honor of us all.

At the beginning of the Hitler regime, the American Jewish Congress had been the only responsible Jewish body in America to call for and support the economic boycott of Germany. It was after, if not because of, our leadership that such mighty voices as those of S. Parkes Cadman, Harry Emerson Fosdick, John Haynes Holmes, Bishop Manning, and Bishop McConnell were raised in America. The aroused Jewish consciousness began the boycott, but the human conscience was now carrying it on. But it is painful to recall that the boycott was unapproved in certain Jewish quarters—and by those same self-appointed Jewish leaders who had urged silence at a time when silence on our part would have resulted in silence on the part of all the forces of civilization.

Thus, for example, as late as February 5, 1935, one of the leaders of the American Jewish Committee, in an interview in the New York *World-Telegram* denounced the boycott movement as "a vicarious sacrifice to one's own emotionalism." "Jews should see to it," he asserted, "that they do not fight Hitler with Hitlerism" because "historically bigotry always begets bigotry." Claiming that the boycott was contrary to the express wish of leading German Jews, he went on to add that the "destructive effects" of the boycott fell "squarely on many Jewish merchants and manufacturers" and that because of the millions of dollars in economic obligations involved in German-American relations, Jews had no right to "disturb the economic and diplomatic relations between America and a country with which America is at peace." The boycott, he concluded "is but the reaction of a small, highly emotionalized minority."

Thus, despite the tragic events within Germany, a Jewish leader was still able to regard firm and unafraid protest against unspeakable injustice as "bigotry" and to dismiss the millions of Jews throughout the world, the distinguished Christian churchmen, the American Federation of Labor, and other groups supporting the boycott as a "highly emotionalized and vocal minority." Nor could he understand that the boycott was not a form of attack but a moral and economic instrument of defense, that it recorded civilization's protest against Nazi Germany. Fortunately, neither the voice of America nor the conscience of the Jews was speaking through one who seemed to suggest that there were no higher obligations than those of the "tens of millions of dollars of German obligations held in America."

Nor was it coincidental that this leader in the same interview denounced the proposal for a World Jewish Congress at which Jews from all lands could meet to take counsel on their common problems as equals. For back of both attitudes, typical at the time of some conservative and wealthy Jews, lay two great unfaiths and distrusts. The first was a fundamental unfaith in the capacity of the Jewish people to manage their own affairs as Jews, an unfaith in the democratic ideal. Only a small number of substantial people, in their view, could guide the affairs of the Jewish people. The second unfaith was in America, and the fear that Americans would be ready to stamp as second-class citizens those Jews who raised their voices in protest and who chose to meet with their fellow Jews of all lands in democratic partnership in the moment of greatest affliction. America and Americans, I have been convinced all my life, respect the Jew who is unafraid and unashamed, who has the power of wrath against injustice, rather than the Jew who is nervous and fearful and who has little faith in the justness of the American people.

In the second half of 1932 the world had seemed to be ready not only for the beginnings of disarmament but for world peace. By March, 1938, the world had seen the mightiest massing of armaments in all the centuries of history. The world had become physically and morally prepared for war again. The world was even then divided into two war camps, led by Germany, Italy, and Japan in one. In the other were England, hesitating France, and possibly America, with an extraordinary passion for isolation and neutrality, which gave maximum help and reinforcement to the Nazi-Fascist world. One country after another had been overwhelmed by Nazi ideology. Treaties had been scrapped or just ignored: Italy in Ethiopia; Japan in China. Undeclared wars had been fought. Continents were being raped. Nazism and international morality had shown themselves to be incompatible. The democratic world was slowly being merged and fused together, alas by its enemies rather than by itself.

It was no accident that the carefully organized arrests of Jews for forced labor, confiscation of Jewish property, the closing of Jewish synagogues, and riots that were so carefully timed and planned as to be clearly government-instituted pogroms should have coincided in May, June, and July of 1938 with the trial mobilization of Hitler's Germany. The handwriting on the wall was made even clearer when the Italian Cabinet on September 1 prohibited Jewish immigration and ordered all foreign Jews and those who had acquired citizenship since January 1, 1919, to leave the country within six months. Other decrees followed. The Hebraic world was, I am not unhappy to recount, denounced as the chief enemy of fascism. And finally in imitation of the hostage system developed by Hitler, Jews throughout the world were told with attempted blackmail that the future of Italian Jews would depend on the future attitude of world Hebraism toward fascist Italy! The axis of death, the destruction of human freedom, and Jewish annihilation had indeed been welded. There could be but one answer to Mussolini as to Hitler:

> Jews in America are unready and unable to meet Mussolini's terms, namely not to oppose fascism as Americans. It is not enough for us to be the

honest supporters of democracy, but we in America need oppose Nazism and Fascism as they oppose and do battle against democracy.

On thing we cannot do for Italian Jews. We will not disavow our democratic faith in order to soften the vigor of the blows which may fall upon them. . . . To the Jew, democracy and all that it means is not a passing type of process of government. Democracy is the political faith of the Jew, and this were true even if it were not bound up with his fate. In an enslaved world, the Jew would not choose to live.

And the final terror against the Jewish people was let loose when a seventeen-year-old grief-crazed Jewish lad named Grynszpan slew a German official in Paris in November, 1938. On the day of the funeral in Düsseldorf, the Nazis took the rabbi of the town and broke his body to pieces and then carried his dead, mangled corpse to his wife, and his wife lost her reason. A thousand men died in Germany who had as much relation to Grynszpan as I. The collective reprisals against the innocent continued. A collective fine equal to virtually all that the German Jews still retained was levied.

The conduct of Hitler's government moved a former president, governors, senators, makers of public opinion, leaders of the Christian churches to speak, and the President of the United States not only spoke but acted in such terms as to make clear that the conduct of Germany placed it, in the eyes of America, beyond the pale of civilization. These were the words of President Roosevelt on November 15, 1938:

The news of the past few days from Germany has deeply shocked public opinion in the United States. Such news from any part of the world would inevitably produce a similar profound reaction among American people in every part of the nation.

I myself could scarcely believe that such things could occur in a twentieth century civilization.

With a view to having a first-hand picture of the situation in Germany I asked the Secretary of State to order our Ambassador in Berlin to return at once for report and consultation.

Six years or nearly six years had passed since the burning of the Reichstag building by the Nazi leaders; four years had passed since the bloodbath or purge of June 30, 1934; three years had passed since the organized and German-directed assassination of Chancellor Dollfuss; three years had passed since the Nuremberg decrees, which took from half a million Jews in Germany their German birthright, as precious to them as my

Americanism is to me; less than three months had passed since the Nazi Reich, with the infinitely tragic concurrence and consent of England and France, had invaded and mutilated one of the dearest hopes of all mankind, Masaryk's and Benes Czechoslovakian Republic.

Some of my people asked at this time why I who had led the protest against Hitler's Germany in 1933, had been silent during these weeks.

> I led the protest in 1933 and ever since. I led the protest and I spoke because the world was largely silent and the American people seemed to be inert and apathetic to and unconscious of what was happening. At last, at long last, America has spoken and the world has spoken, overwhelmed by the barbarism of nationwide reprisals in recent weeks. . . .
>
> How can that Government be expected to keep peace which wages new and savage wars against four hundred thousand because of the act of one youth, which wages new and savage wars against Catholics, Protestants, Jews, against religion, against labor, against liberals? England feels at last after less than two months that it has been tricked, duped insofar as it was led to imagine that peace would ever be the work of them that live by war and for war. . . .
>
> I would be the last person in the world to minimize the act of the President, whose word and deed have been beyond our praise, but in all that has been said and done he has only expressed the heart and voiced the will of the American people.
>
> . . . For the first time in six years the whole American people . . . have recognized in the horrors of suffering inflicted upon the Jews of Germany, an attack upon the sanctity of law and sacredness of justice itself, a violation of the ideals of civilization, a deliberate assault upon the foundations of democracy.

America seemed to stand united behind the President save for some handfuls whose hearts or investments were with the Nazis—save for the deluded who continued to listen Sunday afternoons to Coughlin's voice, though he represented neither America nor the Roman Catholic Church.

One thing more wrote itself out of my heart that day of the November disaster:

> I would say this to the peoples of the world which at last face the monstrous things that have been done in Germany. Had the world felt in March, 1933, as it feels today the awful things of the last five years would never have happened. Ethiopia would still be a free kingdom; Spain would not be devastated by civil war; Czechoslovakia would not be lost to the democracies of civilization; and the Nazi and Fascist regime would not sit supreme upon the ruins of what seemed like yesterday the promise of human civilization.

Late in January, 1939, while again traveling to Europe, mine was the horror of hearing the voice of Hitler calling for the destruction of the Jewish people as warmongers. This hideous experience was a forecast of what I was destined to find throughout the London Conference on Palestine, which I went over to attend. One felt that craven decisions might be made in a world paralyzed by the specter of the dictator countries. Courage seemed to have ceased to rule the hearts of men. Fear had taken its place everywhere.

In those days and after I had a sorry and tragic vindication. Beginning in 1933, I had been warned that I was exaggerating, that things were not so bad as I imagined, that Hitler was just a passing phenomenon and not to be taken too seriously. By 1939 or 1940 the man with whom some Jews and the greater part of the Christian world was ready to compromise and against whom I had lifted my voice and labored with what power I had was become the enemy of mankind.

17. PALESTINE: A NEW JEWISH SOCIETY

Born in Motel, a small shtetl near Pinsk in Russia, Chaim Weizmann (1874–1952) was to become president of the World Zionist Organization (1920–1930, 1935–1946) and the first president of the State of Israel (1948–1952). The "author of a revolution that permanently and deeply altered many human lives," this son of a timber merchant found entrance to a Russian university difficult because of his religion and went to college in Switzerland. Completing his doctorate in chemistry at the University of Freiburg, the young Zionist and chemist accepted a post as reader in chemistry at the University of Manchester, won the gratitude of Great Britain by discovering a process for synthesizing acetone (needed as a base in the explosive cordite) during World War I, and exerted enormous influence upon the men who formed British public opinion (the editors of the Manchester *Guardian* and London *Times* as well as Winston Churchill, Lloyd George, and especially Arthur James Balfour) while arguing for the creation of a Jewish homeland. The beginning of a career dedicated overwhelmingly to Palestine was marked by the Balfour Declaration (1917), but this was to be only the first of many great accomplishments.

Weizmann was able to translate abstractions and doctrines into reality and transform both with his extraordinary tact, charm, humor, and intelligence. His autobiography documents the endless difficulties the Zionist movement faced between 1917 and 1948 and some of its most impressive achievements during this period: vast areas of barren land were brought under cultivation; a modern system of social services was created; political organizations developed; even a university was founded on a bleak hill overlooking the Judean desert. In the following selections Weizmann's own role is clearly delineated, culminating in the spectacular impression he made, late in his life, upon the United Nations Special Committee on Palestine (UNSCOP), the General Assembly of the United Nations, and President Harry S Truman.

Weizmann's autobiography, unusually objective when compared to similar memoirs, was published as *Trial and Error: The Autobiography of Chaim Weizmann* (New York, 1949). Copyright 1949 by The Weizmann Foundation and excerpts used by permission of Harper & Row, Publishers, Inc.

Chaim Weizmann, *Trial and Error*

PALESTINE–EUROPE–AMERICA

Accumulating Difficulties—Obstruction by the Administration—Indifference of Rich Jews—Land Bought in Emek Jezreel—Tension in Palestine —The Tel Hai Tragedy—The Administration Supine—Jerusalem Riots—Jabotinsky Imprisoned—Purpose of the Arab Riots—The San Remo Conference—The Riddle of the Palestine Administration—General Bols's Letter—At San Remo—Balfour Declaration Confirmed—First Large Postwar Zionist Conference—Brandeis Heads American Delegation—Cleavage with the Brandeis Group on Jewish Agency Idea and on Budget—I Am Invited to America—Louis Lipsky—I Become President of the World Zionist Organization.

In those days began to emerge the triple field of force in which I had to move for many years; the Jewish Homeland, British and European politics, American Jewry formed a pattern to which my life had to adapt itself. Jerusalem–London–New York became the focal points: at each point varying fortunes and special complications.

In Palestine I found myself obsessed by the discrepancy between the desirable and the possible. Occasionally the difficulties—political and economic alike—seemed so formidable that I fell a prey to dejection. Then I would go away alone into the hills for a little while, or down to the seashore near Tel Aviv, to talk with some of the older settlers—men like Abraham Shapiro of Petach Tikvah, or Joshua Chankin, or others of their generation. They would tell me of their own early difficulties, their own impressions when they had first come to "this desert," in days when there was not even a Zionist Organization, let alone a Balfour Declaration, when the Turkish blight lay on the land, and a Jew returning to Palestine was looked upon as a sort of religious maniac. They showed me the places that were already cultivated, covered with Jewish orange groves and vineyards: Rehovoth, Rishon-le-Zion, Petach Tikvah: so much had been done with limited means, limited experience, limited manpower, in this country. And then I knew again that Jewish energy, intelligence, and will to sacrifice would eventually triumph over all difficulties.

Abraham Shapiro was in himself a symbol of a whole process of Jewish readaptation. He accompanied me on most of my trips up and down Palestine, partly as guide, partly as guard, and all the while I listened to his epic stories of the old-time colonists. He was a primitive person, spoke better Arabic than Hebrew, and seemed so much a part of the rocks and stony hillsides of the country that it was difficult to believe that he had been born in Lithuania. Here was a man who in his own lifetime had bridged a gap of thousands of years; who, once in Palestine, had shed his Galuth environment like an old coat. There were a few others of his type: the Rosoff family in Petach Tikvah, the Levontins, the Grasovkys, and the Meirowitzes in Rishon. But they were all too few, and the first obvious task was to see to it that their numbers should be increased as fast as possible.

I went back to London in January, 1920, carrying with me the plans which had been prepared by the Jerusalem office—plans of immigration, irrigation, colonization, calling for considerable sums. Little provision was made for land purchase, for we believed, on what seemed sufficient ground, that the Government would shortly place at our disposal stretches of land which were Government property. We were soon to discover that this belief had no basis in fact, and that every dunam of land needed for our colonization work would have to be bought in the open market at fantastic prices which rose ever higher as our work developed. Every improvement we made raised the value of the remaining land in that particular area, and the Arab landowners lost no time in cashing in. We found we had to cover the soil of Palestine with Jewish gold. And that gold, for many, many years, came out of the pockets, not of the Jewish millionaires, but of the poor.

It was an income wholly inadequate for our requirements, but it gave us the opportunity to make our first substantial land purchases, and to take the first tentative steps in organized immigration. Thus, in the summer of 1920, we brought the first Emek Jezreel lands, our one extensive tract up to that date—about eighty thousand dunams (twenty thousand acres). It had formerly belonged to the Sursuk family—typical absentee landlords—and bore only a few half-deserted Arab villages ravaged by malaria. The price we paid was, we then thought, atrociously high, but time has shown it to have been thoroughly justified. We owed it to what was then regarded as the very highhanded action of Mr. Ussishkin, in defiance of the prudent advice of most of his colleagues on the Executive, and particularly of the Americans. I like now to remember that I was among his few supporters in that momentous decision.

I have anticipated a little. My stay in London was a short one; by March, 1920, I was on my way eastward again, this time with my elder boy, Benjamin, who was then twelve. We were to spend the Passover with my mother in Haifa. I might not have returned to Palestine so soon had it not been for a meeting with Lord Allenby in Paris on my westward journey. He was uneasy about the workings of the Zionist Commission, and thought I should be in Jerusalem rather than London.

We arrived to find Herbert Samuel already in Palestine. Allenby and Bols (the latter was then Military Governor of Palestine) had invited him in as adviser to the administration. Everyone was relieved to have Samuel there, for General Allenby's premonition had been only too sound: we all felt that things were not going well, that there was tension in the country. There was a great deal of open agitation in Arab circles, and there was no evidence that local administrators were making any effort to avert trouble; on the contrary, there were members of the official hierarchy who were encouraging the troublemakers. I am not alarmist by nature, and I was inclined at first to be skeptical about the reports. But they persisted, and some of our young people who were close to Arab circles were convinced that "the day" was set for Passover, which that year coincided with both Easter and *Nebi-Musa*—an Arab festival on which the inhabitants of the neighboring villages assemble in Jerusalem to march in procession to the reputed grave of the Prophet Moses on a nearby hill. Galilee, too, was in ferment owing to its nearness to Syria, whence Feisal was being edged out, and where friction between the English and the French was growing daily. Lawless bands prowled and raided on our northern hills, and as is usual in such cases banditry took on an aspect of patriotism. A month before my arrival Joseph Trumpeldor, one of the earliest and greatest of the *chalutz* leaders, had gone up with some companions to the defense of Tel Hai, an infant colony near the Syrian border; and there he and five companions, two of them women, were killed by marauders. The tragedy had plunged the whole *Yishuv* into mourning.

As Passover approached the tension grew more marked, and by that time some of the more friendly of the British officials—for instance Meinertzhagen (now the Palestine administration's political officer)—were apprehensive. Before leaving Jerusalem to spend Passover with my mother, I called on General Allenby, who was then in the city. I found him with General Bols and Herbert Samuel at Government House, still located in the old German hospice on the Mount of Olives. My representations regarding impending trouble made little impression on them. Bols said: "There *can* be no trouble; the town is stiff with troops!" I replied that I had had some experience with the atmosphere which precedes pogroms; I knew also that troops usually proved useless at the last moment, because the whole paroxysm was liable to be over before they could be rushed to the field of action. There would be half an hour or an hour of murder and looting, and by the time the troops got there everything would be "in order" and there would be nothing for them to do but pick up the pieces. However, I could see that I was wasting my breath. I was advised not to worry, and go home to my family for the Passover as arranged. I could feel assured that everything would go off quietly in Jerusalem.

Against my better judgment I went home, though what I could have done after this if I had stayed on in Jerusalem it is difficult to say. Passover in Haifa came and went; and the next morning there was no disturbing news from Jerusalem—no news at all, in fact. I felt uneasy. I tried to telephone, but could get no connection, which naturally increased my anxiety. So I decided—greatly to my mother's disappointment—to go up to Jerusalem and to take Benjy with me. The journey was uneventful as far as Nablus, but there I found a police escort. The Governor of Nablus, who supplied it, dropped a vague hint or two, and I became more and more convinced that "something" really had happened.

Jerusalem, when we got there, looked deserted. A curfew had been imposed, and there was little movement in the streets except for police and military patrols. We made straight for Dr. Eder's flat in the center of the city, and found him deeply disturbed. The story he had to tell was one that has since become all too familiar: Arabs assembling at the Mosque of Omar, listening to speeches of violent incitement, forming a procession fired with fanatic zeal, marching through the streets attacking any Jews they happened to meet. In spite of all the rumors which preceded the attack, the Jews seem to have been caught completely unawares, and practically no resistance was offered. When one small group of young men, under Captain Jabotinsky, had come out to defend their quarter, they had been promptly arrested. The troops had, of course, arrived when all was over, and quiet now reigned in the city. The situation was "well in hand."

In the trials which followed before a military court, Jabotinsky received the savage sentence of fifteen years hard labor. He was later amnestied (by Herbert Samuel when he became High Commissioner), but rejected the amnesty with scorn, because it included Aref el Aref, the main instigator of the pogrom, Amin el Husseini (the notorious grand Mufti of later years), and one or two others of the same type. He insisted on making his appeal, and the sentence was in due course quashed.

The impression made on Benjy by the atmosphere in Jerusalem in the days that followed the pogrom terrified me. He was full of questions to which I had no answers: "How can this happen? Who is guilty? Will they be punished?" I was thankful that we were staying with Eder, where at least the worst of the stories that ran round like wildfire could be kept from him.

All of us felt that this pogrom might have been averted had proper steps been taken in time to check the agitation, had the attitude of the administration been different. The bitterness and incitement had been allowed to grow until they found their natural expression in riot and murder. Philip Graves, no special friend of the Zionist movement, was then in Palestine as *Times* correspondent under Lord Northcliffe; he admitted, in the account he published in 1923, that

> The military, having completed the conquest of Palestine, naturally desired a rest after a long and trying campaign, and therefore took the line of least resistance in dealing with the local situation. They were, moreover, jealous of their own official prerogatives, and strongly objected to the manner in which members and employees of the Zionist Commission too often overstepped their functions and attempted, as the soldiers thought, to dictate to them. . . . But the highly disturbed state of the chief Arab countries . . . and above all, the failure of the British Government to furnish the Chiefs of the Administration in Palestine with any detailed instructions, explain the unwillingness of the soldiers to adopt an "unmistakable and active pro-Zionist attitude.". . . At the same time it must be admitted that, if most of the accusations brought by the Zionists against the Military Administration as a whole were unfounded, there

were cases in which individual officers showed pro-Arab or pan-Arab sympathies. The Arabs, sometimes encouraged, perhaps unwittingly, by such officers, grew more and more petulant.

While suggesting that "the Zionists have made too much of this pogrom," and too little of the difficulties of the military, Graves adds:

> Mistakes were made by some members of the Military Administration. The Chief of Staff to the Chief Military Administrator appears to have left Jerusalem for a trip to Jericho at a moment when crowds were already gathering in ominous fashion near the Jaffa Gate.

It might seem, to a dispassionate British observer, that we were making too much of this pogrom. (Only six Jews were killed, though there were many serious injuries.) But it is almost impossible to convey to the outside world the sense of horror and bewilderment which it aroused in our people, both in Palestine and outside. Pogroms in Russia had excited horror and pity, but little surprise; they were "seasonal disturbances," more or less to be expected round about the Easter and Passover festivals. That such a thing could happen in Palestine, two years after the Balfour Declaration, under British rule ("the town is stiff with troops!") was incomprehensible to the Jews, and dreadful beyond belief. For those whose facile optimism had led them to believe that all political problems were safely out of the way, and that all we had to do was get on with the "practical" work, this was—or should have been—the writing on the wall.

There was, of course, something more to the pogrom than the primitive frenzy of its perpetrators. The instigators, those that had lashed the mobs to blind action, were more farsighted than their illiterate dupes; they knew that within a few weeks there would be held in San Remo, in northern Italy, the Conference of the Allied powers at which the fate of the dismembered Turkish Empire would be considered; they knew that the Balfour Declaration would then come up for inclusion in the disposition of Palestine; from being a statement of policy it would be converted—if Zionist hopes were realized—into the substance of an international agreement. And they hoped by their demonstration of force to prevent this consummation.

I decided that I must return to Europe immediately, to see what could be done. With me traveled Alexander Aaronson (brother of Aaron Aaronson, the discoverer of wild wheat, who had been killed the year before in the London-Paris plane) and Mr. Emanuel Mohl, the representative in Palestine of the American Zionists. We were given a police escort as far as Egypt, and reached Cairo the evening of the same day. We went to the Hotel Continental, where I usually stayed, to discover that a big dance was in progress, and I was painfully surprised to note that a considerable proportion of the guests seemed to be drawn from the Egyptian-Jewish community. A whole world lay between the Jerusalem I had left that morning and the ballroom of the Continental. Disheartened, I went straight to my room and, though the journalists got to work on me soon enough, refused to see anybody. There was only one person I wanted to see, and that was Allenby, and after seeing him I would leave at the earliest possible moment.

I notified Allenby of my presence the next morning, and he invited me to lunch. His first words when we met were: "I'm afraid you're going to say: 'I told you so!' " I answered that I had no intention of saying anything of the sort, but I wanted him to know that we intended to go on with our work, and at a quicker pace than hitherto, because I believed that if we had, say four hundred thousand Jews in Palestine instead of a miserable fifty thousand, such things would be less likely to happen. (Not entirely accurate as prophecy, I fear, but that was how it looked to me at the time.) Allenby asked what he could do. "I suppose you would like us to clear out!" I said: "On the contrary! I very much hope that at San Remo it will at last be definitely decided that the British are to have the Palestine Mandate, and that a more solid regime will then be established. I would like to see a civil administration in Palestine as soon as possible, as I don't think the soldiers understand what are the problems involved, or how to approach them." He pressed his point: "You don't seem to have much faith in the military administration." I said: "That's putting it mildly—in fact, I have none whatsoever! The sooner they leave the better for everyone concerned!"

He took it good-humoredly—one could always talk to Allenby. The subject was dropped and we turned to future plans for immigration, land purchase, and other practical matters. He was skeptical; like most of his officers, he did not really think we could make anything out of this sandy, marshy, derelict country, though he certainly had far more imagination than any of his subordinates. I knew it was no use arguing; only time could show. As I was leaving, he said: "You are going to San Remo; can I do anything for you?" I said I would like a letter from him to Lloyd George, to facilitate my placing our problems before him. He agreed at once—and the letter consisted of two sentences: the first saying that he did *not* share Dr. Weizmann's opinion of his administration, and the second that he did agree with his practical proposals and would be most grateful for anything Mr. Lloyd George could do to further them!

I carried with me another letter—from Colonel Meinertzhagen—describing the pogrom and the period leading up to it, and stressing the blindness (real or willfully induced) of the administration which had refused to see the danger after their attention had been repeatedly called to it.

As we traveled slowly toward Italy I tried to find an answer to a question which was to occupy me for the remainder of my life: Why, from the very word go should we have had to face the hostility, or at best the frosty neutrality of Britain's representatives on the spot? The Home Government at this time was very friendly, even enthusiastic, about the Jewish National Home policy. Enlightened British public opinion regarded the Balfour Declaration—and later the Mandate—as important and creditable achievements of the peace settlement. The "misdemeanors" of which we were later accused, and which were the basis of arguments against us, were still in the future: we had bought no land to speak of, hence no "displaced Arabs" argument; we had brought in few immigrants—hence no "overcrowding" argument—and Palestine was officially described as seriously underpopulated anyhow; nobody had had any experience with us on which to base praise or blame. Why, then, were we damned in advance in the eyes of the official hierarchy? And why was it an almost universal rule that such administrators as came out favorably inclined turned against us in a few months? Why, for that matter, was it later a completely invariable rule that politicians who were enthusiastically for the Jewish Homeland during election forgot about it completely if they were returned to office? I shall have more to say on this point but, to pose the question at its starkest, I shall quote here a letter which General Louis Bols, whom Allenby left behind him as military administrator, wrote to his chief on December 21, 1919:

> Dear General:
>
> I am sending you this by Dr. Weizmann. He has been out here a couple of months and has done much good work in dealing with all matters in a quiet, impartial way. I think there is little doubt that antagonism to Zionism has been reduced by his action, and my view, after a month as Chief Administrator, is that there will be no serious difficulty in introducing a large number of Jews into the country provided it is done without ostentation. There are a few agitators and of course their cry for an undivided Syria will continue.
>
> The country is in need of development quickly in order to make the people content. . . . The moment the Mandate is given we should be ready to produce a big loan, part of which should be subscribed by the inhabitants. I want Sir Herbert Samuel here for advice on this matter. . . .
>
> With such a loan, say ten or twenty millions, I feel certain I can develop the country quickly and make it pay, and gradually the population should

increase from the present 900,000 to 2½ million. There is plenty of room for this. The Jordan Valley should hold a million instead of its present 1,000. . . .

I hope that:

1) You will send Weizmann back soon.

2) You will send Sir H. Samuel for a visit.

3) You will send me a big financial fellow.

4) Consider the plans for a loan.

If this is done I can promise you a country of milk and honey in ten years, and I can promise you will not be bothered by anti-Zion difficulties. . . .

Sincerely yours,
L. J. Bols

It was under General Bols's administration, and in the circumstances already described, that the pogrom took place in Jerusalem less than four months later.

We dawdled northward from Brindisi in constant expectation of finding the line cut after the next station, for the Italian railways were in the throes of a general strike. Eventually we reached Rome, and thence San Remo—tired, grimy, hungry, but generally intact.

In the hall of the Hotel Royal I found Mr. Philip Kerr, then one of Mr. Lloyd George's secretaries; and my mood was such that I started in on him straightaway with congratulations on the first pogrom under the British flag. (Looking back, I am more than a little sorry for Kerr at that moment; he was a good deal taken aback!) I gave him Allenby's letter and asked for an early appointment with the Prime Minister. In a quiet corner of the lounge there sat, while we talked, Sir Herbert Samuel and Mr. Sokolow, both exquisitely groomed, very calm and collected, absolutely undisturbed. I was very conscious of the contrast we presented, in appearance, background, manner, and, above all, frame of mind. So, apparently, was Kerr, my personal friend of many years, for he said, glancing toward them: "When you look a little more like those two, I shall be pleased to fix an appointment for you!" There was much wisdom in that suggestion, though at the time I dismissed it as unwarrantably frivolous.

A week or so passed in San Remo while we waited for the Conference to make up its mind about Palestine. As it was almost the last item on the agenda we had little to do except gaze at the sea and discuss things among ourselves. There was always the uneasy feeling that the recent events in Palestine might bring some revision of policy, but Mr. Balfour assured me that they were regarded as without importance, and would certainly not affect policy, which had been definitely set. I was glad to hear that this view was shared by Lord Curzon, who was known to be no particular friend of ours. One of the first things mooted in those days in the coulisses of the Conference was the suggestion that Herbert Samuel should be our first High Commissioner in Palestine. Samuel himself was willing, Mr. Lloyd George and Mr. Balfour both approved. It was clear that no one had been put off by the incidents in Palestine; the instigators of the pogrom had failed in their main purpose.

The Conference dragged on interminably, and the decision about the Palestine Mandate was not taken until the last few hours. These found me nervously pacing the hall of the Royal Hotel, waiting for the delegates to emerge from the Council chamber. Suddenly I caught sight of Mr. Balfour, waving impatiently to someone in the distance. I went up to him and asked if he was waiting for the delegates. "Oh, no," he answered calmly. "My tennis partners. They're very late!"

At long last the gentlemen came out, and I made for Philip Kerr and the Prime Minister, both of whom proceeded to congratulate me warmly on the result of the meeting: the confirmation of the Balfour Declaration and the decision to give the Mandate to Great Britain. Mr. Lloyd George was particularly kind, telling me that we now had a very great opportunity and must show what good use we could make of it. He said: "You have no time to waste. Today the world is like the Baltic before a frost. For the moment it is still in motion. But if it gets set, you will have to batter your heads against the ice blocks and wait for a second thaw."

Everyone was kind at San Remo, including Lord Curzon, whose attitude I particularly appreciated because I knew him to be far from enthusiastic about the National Home idea. But he was entirely loyal to the policy adopted, and meant to stand by the declaration—as he did, later on, when he became Foreign Secretary.

Even the Arab delegations seemed happy about it all! Anybody entering the dining room of the Royal that evening would have found the Jewish and Arab delegations seated together at a really festive board, congratulating each other under the benevolent paternal gaze of the British delegation at a neighboring table. The only man to ignore the whole business was Philip Sassoon, another of Lloyd George's secretaries—and, as it happens, the only Jewish member of the British delegation.

The violence of the shock which the Jerusalem pogrom had created in the Jewish world, the extent of the fear that a revision of the Palestine policy might ensue, could be gauged from the reaction to the San Remo decision. Representatives of the Genoa Jewish community came over the next day to congratulate us, and we soon learned, by cable and from the press, of the general enthusiasm which the decision aroused everywhere. I was deeply moved when, arriving a few days later at Victoria Station in London, I was met by representatives of the community bearing the Torah—the Scroll of the Law.

To complete the pattern of this chapter, in which I am attempting to indicate the triple field of force which constituted my Zionist work, I shall speak briefly of the first large contact with America, which took place early in July of that year; not, however, in a visit to America—that was to come soon after—but through the arrival in London of a large American delegation to the Zionist Annual Conference. Seven years had passed since the last fully representative gathering of world Zionists—the eleventh Congress, held in 1913. Justice Brandeis headed the American delegation, and there at once became manifest those divergences between the American leaders and ourselves—and within the American delegation, too—of which I have spoken in the last chapter.

With a number of my European colleagues I felt that we should lose no time in approaching the great Jewish organizations which might wish to share in the practical work in Palestine, with a view to the creation of some kind of Jewish council. This was the idea which eventually developed into the Jewish Agency. To the American leaders—for convenience I shall, in this connection, speak hereafter of the Brandeis group—it seemed unnecessary to have any kind of double organization: it was their view that people who wished to cooperate in the work of rebuilding the Jewish National Home could join the Zionist Organization.

This was not merely a difference in formal approach; it represented a real cleavage. The Brandeis group envisaged the Zionist Organization as henceforth a purely economic body. Since, in their view, it had lost its political character by having fulfilled its political function, there was no longer any reason why non-Zionists who were prepared to help in the economic upbuilding of Palestine, but who were not prepared to subscribe to political Zionism, should refuse to become members. But our reason for wishing to keep the Zionist Organization in being as a separate body was precisely the conviction that the political work was far from finished; the Balfour declaration and the San Remo decision were the beginning of a new era in the political struggle, and the Zionist Organization was our instrument of political action. There were numbers of Jewish organizations and individuals which, with all their readiness to lend a hand in the practical work in Palestine, insisted that they would not be implicated in any of our political difficulties. Their attitude might be illogical, but there it was, and it had to be reckoned with. The question was, then, whether a new organization should be formed for the accommodation of the non-Zionists, or whether the Zionist Organization should be completely reorientated, should, in fact, give up completely its political character.

A complicated and sometimes acrimonious discussion developed round this subject; the proposal of the Brandeis group was defeated by a substantial majority.

A second controversial point was the budget. The European group set this at something in the neighborhood of two million pounds a year, to which they had to admit that they themselves could contribute very little. The Americans generally—and not only the Brandeis group—were shocked by this "astronomical" figure, and asserted they could not guarantee more than one hundred thousand pounds a year. Mr. Brandeis contended that this was the utmost that could be got from American Jewry—and this at a time when it was well known that American Jews had acquired and were acquiring considerable wealth.

I found myself explaining that we could not possibly adopt a budget of that order; it was not merely inadequate to the task which faced us, it was derisory: it would damn us in the eyes of friends and enemies alike. I added that if this was all he could find in America, I should have to come over and try for myself.

I doubt if Justice Brandeis ever quite forgave me for that challenge. Eventually the Conference reached agreement with a group of the American delegation—this was the group which was afterward to lead in the struggle against the Brandeis regime—headed by Louis Lipsky, which invited me to come over to America at the earliest opportunity after my return from Palestine, and to see for myself what could and what could not be done.

I found in Lipsky an unusual combination; he was perhaps the leading theoretician among the American Zionists, but he possessed a remarkable understanding of the European movement. Of him, too, I can say that, although for long periods we did not communicate with each other, we almost invariably reached the same conclusions on important problems. During the period of the construction of the Jewish Agency he was under constant attack by the non-Zionists. When they met him, they discovered in him a man of first-rate mind, of charm and integrity. He is still the pillar of Zionism in America, but like myself he is now trying to put some distance between himself and the daily rough and tumble of the movement. His value as an elder statesman will still be great for many years.

To return to the London Conference: toward its close it elected officers to conduct the affairs of the movement until the first postwar Congress should be able to meet; Justice Brandeis became Honorary President, I became President of the Organization, and Mr. Sokolow became chairman of the Executive. Together with the Actions Committee which was then elected, and which met in July, we appointed as departmental heads Mr. Ussishkin, Mr. Julius Simon (representing America), and Mr. Nehemiah de Lieme, of Holland. The Presidium and the departmental heads constituted the Executive.

Thus the movement had once more a constituted, if provisional, governing body, and incidentally I acquired, for the first time, some formal authority. During the greater part of the negotiations in London I had had none whatsoever, though since early in 1917 I had been President of the English Zionist Federation. That, however, was only one of the smaller constituent bodies of the Zionist Congress; its importance had been due only to the fact that it had been at the center of action when the constituted authorities of the movement—those elected by the prewar Congress—could not even be consulted. It will be remembered that we had, in fact, severed all connection with the "Copenhagen Bureau" at an early stage in the war.

One of the highlights of the Conference—and, I must add, one of its few attractive features—was a great public meeting held at the Albert Hall under the chairmanship of Lord Rothschild. This was, I think, the only occasion on which Lord Balfour addressed a great Jewish gathering in England. I dined with him before the meeting at 4 Carlton Gardens, and as we drove from there to Albert Hall, Lord Balfour was struck by the great crowds of Jews making their way to the West End. In his usual vague manner he asked me: "But who *are* all these people?" I reminded him of what I had told him in 1906, that there were Zionist Jews enough to pave the streets of Russia and Poland: "These are a few—a very few—of them!"

When the Conference finally dispersed, my wife and I went for a short rest to Switzerland, returning to London again, via Paris, in the autumn. My thoughts were again turning West, to the American visit which, I was beginning to feel, I had undertaken rather lightheartedly at the Conference. Herbert Samuel's departure for Palestine, as its first High Commissioner, had marked the close of an important chapter in "political Zionism," and opened the door, as we then thought, to a great expansion of Jewish effort in Palestine. But the portent of the Annual Conference remained an ominous cloud on the horizon, and I was haunted by the fear that American Jewry would fail to rise to the occasion.

I felt it best to arm myself, as it were, with another visit to Palestine. This time I went with Sir Alfred Mond. We spent January and part of February touring the country, and Sir Alfred showed himself—hardheaded man of affairs that we all took him to be—profoundly susceptible to the more romantic aspects of the work. I remember still the shock of astonishment which went through me when, as we stood watching a group of *chalutzim* breaking stones for the road between Petach Tikvah and Jaffa, I observed how very close he was to tears. They looked to him, those children of the ghetto, altogether too frail and too studious for the job they had in hand. Perhaps he had just realized that these young men and women were building themselves, as well as the road.

Early in March I was back in London, preparing for my first contact with the New World.

THE WHITE PAPER

Partition torpedoed—The Tripartite Conference, February-March, 1939—The Days of Berchtesgaden and Godesberg—The Coffin Boats on the Mediterranean—The Patria*—Lord Halifax's Astounding Proposal—How the White Paper Was Prepared—The Betrayal of Czechoslovakia—Jan Masaryk's Tragic Visit—Negotiations in Egypt—Last Warning to Chamberlain—His Infatuation with Appeasement—The White Paper Debated in Parliament—The Jews Unanimously Reject the White Paper.*

At the time it issued the Peel Report, in 1937, the British Government began to set up the Woodhead Commission, which was to submit a partition plan. The commission did not proceed to Palestine until April, 1938; and in October of that year it published a report stating that it had no practical partition plan to offer. The following month the Government rejected the idea of partition. It looked as though the commission had been appointed merely to pave the way for a predetermined course of action for which no commission was necessary.

The same may be said of the Tripartite Conference—British, Arabs, Jews—which the Government now proceeded (December, 1938) to call. Just as the Government of that time could and would have done what it did about partition without the gesture of a new commission, so it could and would have done what it did about nullifying the Balfour Declaration without the gesture of the St. James Conference of February–March, 1939. The reader must bear the period in mind: in October, 1938, the Sudetenland had been handed over to Hitler as a result of the Munich Conference; in March, 1939, Hitler annexed the rest of Czechoslovakia; and Mr. Chamberlain still believed, or pretended to believe, that by these concessions he was purchasing "peace in our time." What chance had the Jewish National Home with such a Government, and what likelihood was there that Commissions and Conferences would deflect it from its appeasement course?

Nevertheless the Jews and Arabs were duly invited—Jews representing all sections of opinion, and Arabs representing Palestine and its neighbors, Egypt, Iraq, and so on—and the Conference was opened with much solemnity in St. James's Palace on February 7, 1939. The dignity of the occasion was somewhat marred by the fact that Mr. Chamberlain's address of welcome had to be given twice, once to the Jews and once to the Arabs, since the latter would not sit with the former, and even used different entrances to the palace so as to avoid embarrassing contacts.

The proceedings were usually conducted by Colonial Secretary Malcolm MacDonald, supported by a staff of higher ranking officials of the Foreign and Colonial offices; they were attended from time to time by Foreign Secretary Lord Halifax. Toward the end, for reasons which will appear, they lost any appearance of purpose or intelligibility which may originally have been imparted to them. I did not attend the closing session. But during the Conference I exerted myself—as indeed I have always done—to maintain contacts with the most influential figures in and about the Conference, and with leading personalities generally, among them Lord Halifax, Prime Minister Chamberlain, Colonial Secretary Malcolm MacDonald, and Winston Churchill.

The atmosphere of utter futility which dominated the Conference was, of course, part of the general atmosphere of the time. Those were the days of the Berchtesgaden and Godesberg "conferences." The atmosphere was not peculiar to England; the French were as assiduous in their attendance on Hitler. I remember Léon Blum telling me at that time: "There is a wild hunger for physical safety which paralyzes the power of thought. People are ready to buy the illusion of security at any price, hoping against hope that something will happen to save their countries from invasion." My conversations with Halifax, Chamberlain, Malcolm MacDonald were vitiated from the outset by this frightful mood of frustration and panic. They were determined to placate the Arabs just as they were placating Hitler. That, of course, did not prevent me from carrying on until the last moment—and after.

My personal relations with Lord Halifax were of the best. I had made his acquaintance through an old friend, the late Victor Cazalet, member of Parliament, one of the few members of the House who never failed to speak up in defense of Zionism, and who did whatever he could to keep our case before the public eye. He was, in fact, chairman of the Parliamentary Pro-Palestine Committee. Through Cazalet's willing offices—he was an intimate friend of Halifax—I was able to meet the latter more frequently and a little more informally than might otherwise have been the case. The character of some of these private meetings may be indicated by the two following instances.

Some time before the issuance of the White Paper, when immigration restrictions were already in force, the desperation of the Jews fleeing from the coming destruction began to rise to its climax; the efforts to reach the safety of Palestine led to the tragic phenomenon of the coffin boats, as they were called, crowded and unseaworthy vessels which roamed the Mediterranean in the hope of being able ultimately to discharge their unhappy cargoes of men, women, and children in Palestine. Some sank in the Mediterranean and Black seas. Some reached Palestine either to be turned back or to have their passengers taken off and interned or transshipped to Mauritius.

One of the worst cases—that of the *Patria*—occurred during the war under the Colonial Secretaryship of Lord Lloyd; and on hearing of it I went to him, in despair rather than in hope, to try and persuade him to give permission for the passengers to be landed. I was met with the usual arguments about the law being the law, to which I retorted: "A law is something which must have a moral basis, so that there is an inner compelling force for every citizen to obey. But if the majority of citizens is convinced that the law is merely an infliction, it can only be enforced at the point of the bayonet against the consent of the community."

My arguments were wasted. Lord Lloyd could not agree with me. He said so, and added: "I must tell you that I've blocked all the approaches for you. I know you will go to Churchill and try to get him to overrule me. I have therefore warned the Prime Minister that I will not consent. So please don't try to get at him."

But it seemed that Lord Lloyd had not blocked the approach to the Foreign Office, so I went to see Lord Halifax. Here again I had to rehearse all the arguments about law and ethics and the immorality of the White Paper which was not really a law but a ukase such as might have been issued by a Russian Czar or any other autocrat engaged in the systematic persecution of the Jews. I saw that I was making no dent in Lord Halifax's determination. Finally I said: "Look here, Lord Halifax. I thought that the difference between the Jews and the Christians is that we Jews are supposed to adhere to the letter of the law, whereas you Christians are supposed to temper the letter of the law with a sense of mercy." The words stung him. He got up and said: "All right, Dr. Weizmann, you'd better not continue this conversation. You will hear from me." To my immense relief and joy I heard the next day that he had sent a telegram to Palestine to permit the passengers to land. I met Lord Lloyd soon after, and he said, quite unresentfully: "Well you get past me that time. I thought I'd blocked all the holes, but it seems I'd forgotten Halifax." I was convinced in my heart of hearts that Lloyd was not displeased to have the incident end thus.

An interview of quite another kind with Lord Halifax sticks in my mind. During the St. James Conference he called me in and addressed me thus: "There are moments in the lives of men and of groups when expediency takes precedence over principle. I think that such a moment has arrived now in the life of your movement. Of course I don't know whether you can or will accept my advice, but it would be desirable that you make an announcement of the great principles of the Zionist movement to which you adhere, and at the same time renounce your rights under the Mandate and under the various instruments deriving from it."

At first I did not quite appreciate the full bearing of this proposal. I paused for a few moments, then asked: "Tell me, Lord Halifax, what good would it do you if I were to agree, which in fact I won't and can't? Suppose, for argument's sake, I were to make such an announcement; there could be only one effect, that I would disappear from the ranks of the Zionist leaders, to be replaced by men much more extreme and intransigeant than I am, men who have not been brought up in the tradition I have been privileged to live in for the last forty years. You would achieve nothing except to provoke the Zionist movement to yield to its most extremist elements."

I added: "So much for the movement. And what of myself?" I briefly recounted to him the history of Sabbathai Zevi, who, in the seventeenth century, had been a successful leader of the "Return," who had gathered round him a mass following from all over the world, and who stood at the gates of Constantinople, constituting some sort of menace to the Sultan. The Sultan felt helpless in the presence of this mystical and dangerous assembly, and sent for his Jewish physician, who advised him as follows: "Call in this Jewish leader, and tell him you are prepared to give him Palestine on condition that he embrace Islam." Sabbathai Zevi accepted the proposal and became a Moslem, with the result that his adherents, who counted in the hundreds of thousands, melted away; and of his movement nothing remains except a small group of Turkish Jews who call themselves Dumbies, the descendants of the few apostates who followed Sabbathai Zevi into Mohammedanism. I wound up: "You do not expect me, Lord Halifax, to end my career in the same disgraceful manner." With that we parted.

Lord Halifax was strangely ignorant of what was happening to the Jews of Germany. During the St. James Conference he came up to me and said: "I have just received a letter from a friend in Germany, who describes some terrible things perpetrated by the Nazis in a concentration camp the name of which is not familiar to me," and when he began to grope for the name I realized it was Dachau he was talking about. He said the stories were entirely unbelievable, and if the letter had not been written by a man in whom he had full confidence he would not attach the slightest credence to it. For five or six years now the world had known of the infamous Dachau concentration camp, in which thousands of people had been tortured and maimed and done to death, and the British Foreign Secretary had never heard of the place, and would not believe that such things could go on; only the fortuitous circumstance that he had received the letter from a man in whom he had "full confidence" had arrested his attention. It is difficult to say whether this profound ignorance was typical for the British ruling class, but judging from its behavior at that time it either did not know, or else it did not wish to know because the knowledge was inconvenient, disturbing, and dangerous. Those were Germany's "internal affairs," and they should not be permitted to interfere with friendly relations between two Great Powers.

It was astounding to meet this bland surprise and indifference in high places. When the great burning of the synagogues took place, after the assassination of Vom Rath in Paris, I said to Anthony Eden: "The fire from the synagogues may easily spread from there to Westminster Abbey and the other great English cathedrals. If a government is allowed to destroy a whole community which has committed no crime save that of being a minority and having its own religion, if such a government, in the heart of Europe, is not even rebuked, it means the beginning of anarchy and the destruction of the basis of civilization. The powers which stand looking on without taking any measures to prevent the crime will one day be visited by severe punishment."

I need scarcely add that my words fell on deaf ears. British society was falling all over itself to attend the elegant parties given by Ribbentrop in the German Embassy; it was a sign of social distinction to receive an invitation, and the Jewish blood which stained the hands of the hosts was ignored though it cried out to heaven. I believe that the Duke of Devonshire never accepted any of von Ribbentrop's invitations.

It should be remembered, however, that things were not much better in France, where the walls were being chalked with the slogan *Mieux vaut Hitler que Blum,* though there the relationship with Germany was less amiable than in the case of England. Well, they got their Hitler, and no doubt the taste of it will remain with the French people for a long time. But whether those who used the slogan so widely have been cured of their affection for Hitlerism is much to be doubted.

In those days before the war, our protests, when voiced, were regarded as provocations; our very refusal to subscribe to our own death sentence became a public nuisance, and was taken in bad part. Alternating threats and appeals were addressed to us to acquiesce in the surrender of Palestine. On one occasion Lord Halifax said to me: "You know that we British have always been the friends of the Jews—and the Jews have very few friends in the world today." I need hardly say that this sort of argument had on us the opposite effect of what was intended.

That the tide was running heavily against us was obvious from the beginning of the Conference, but exactly what the Government would do was not so clear at first. In the early days of the Conference we gave a party at our house for all the members as well as the representatives of the Jewish organizations. Lord Halifax, Malcolm MacDonald, and all the high officials accepted. Later the atmosphere was not so cordial. The debates and conversations meandered along, and the Government was reluctant to formulate a program. It limited itself to generalities and bided its time. But the Government had made up its mind. It was only waiting for the most favorable moment for the announcement of its plan.

One day, when the Conference was fairly advanced, we received an invitation to a lunch to be given by His Majesty's Government, and we of course accepted. The lunch was to take place on a Monday. On the Saturday preceding this Monday I received a letter from the Colonial Office, addressed to me obviously by a clerical error—it was apparently meant only for members of the Arab delegation. There, in clear terms, was the outline of what was afterward to be the White Paper, submitted for Arab approval! An Arab State of Palestine in five years; a limited Jewish immigration during these five years, and none thereafter without Arab consent. I could scarcely believe my eyes. We had, indeed, begun to feel that the discussions had become meaningless for us; and after what had happened to Austria and Czechoslovakia nothing should have surprised us. But to see the actual terms, black on white, already prepared and communicated to the Arabs while "negotiations" were proceeding, was utterly baffling.

I happened to remember, when I had finished perusing the extraordinary document, that most of my Zionist friends were at a party being given by Harry Sacher in his home, which was only a few doors from mine. I went over, and we managed to get Lord Reading and Malcolm MacDonald to join us. A heated and extremely unpleasant discussion ensued. We told MacDonald freely what we thought of the document and asked him to cancel our invitations to the luncheon: We would not break bread with a Government which could betray us in this manner. MacDonald was very crestfallen and stammered some ineffective excuses, falling back always on the argument that the document did not represent the final view of His Majesty's Government, that it was only a basis for discussion, that everything could still be changed, that we should not take it so tragically—the usual twaddle. The meeting lasted a long time; its only value, I suppose, was that our delegation was forewarned and the British Government clearly informed of the mood and temper of the Jews. If it was waiting for us to facilitate its publication of the document it was waiting in vain.

After the outbreak of the war I was to learn how elaborately and how far in advance the Government had been preparing the White Paper, and how meaningless the St. James Conference had been. I was in Switzerland on a special mission, and called on the British Minister at Berne, who received me very cordially with the words, "Oh, you're the man I've been wanting to see for quite a time, to get the other side of the story." I asked him to explain and he went on: "I was in on the White Paper. So were most of the Ambassadors and Ministers. Their opinion of it was asked in advance. Well, you know that most Ambassadors and Ministers take on the color of the countries to which they are assigned, and the views we presented were all one-sided. That is why I would like to hear your side of the story." My reply was obvious: "It is too late—and too early—for you to listen to the other side. Had you listened a year ago, the verdict might possibly have been different. Now we are in the midst of the war, and we are trying for the time being to forget the White Paper. Perhaps when the war is over you may still be inclined to listen to the other side."

The disclosure to us of the Government document which was to become the White Paper coincided roughly with Hitler's unopposed and unprotested invasion of Czechoslovakia and the occupation of Prague. I remember that day well, because Jan Masaryk came to dinner with us. Between Masaryk and us there was, until the end, a deep friendship, both on personal and general grounds. There has always been a great affinity between the Masaryks and Zionism—Jan's father, the founder and first President of the Czechoslovak Republic had been a strong supporter of the Balfour Declaration—and now, in the days of the White Paper, the representatives of the Czechoslovak Republic were beginning to be treated by the Great Powers as if they were Jews.

Neither the Jews nor the Czechs will forget the words of Chamberlain on the occasion of Hitler's occupation of the Czech capital. Why should England risk war for the sake of "a far-away country of which we know very little and whose language we don't understand?" Words which were swallowed down by a docile Parliament many members of which must have known very well that the Czech Republic was a great bastion of liberty and democracy, and that its spirit and its institutions had all the meaning in the world for the Western Powers. It was, apart from everything else, a colossal insult to a great people. And I remember reflecting that if this was the way the Czechs were spoken of, what could we Jews expect from a Government of that kind?

When Jan arrived at our house that evening he was almost unrecognizable. The gaiety and high spirits which we always associated with him were gone. His face was the color of parchment, and he looked like an aged and broken man. My wife, my children, and I felt deeply for him—perhaps more than anyone else in London—and without saying too much we tried to make him comfortable. For a while he was silent, then he turned to us and, pointing to the little dog he had brought with him, said: "That's all I have left, and believe me, I am ashamed to look him in the eyes." Once he had broken the silence he went on talking, and what he told us was terrible to listen to. He had had a conversation that morning with the Prime Minister, and had taxed him with the deliberate betrayal of Czechoslovakia. "Mr. Chamberlain sat absolutely unmoved. When I had finished he said: 'Mr. Masaryk, you happen to believe in Dr. Beneš, I happen to trust Herr Hitler.' " There was nothing left for Masaryk but to get up and leave the room.

A great democratic country, a magnificent army, and a superb munition plant had been delivered to the future conqueror of Europe, and a people which had fought valiantly for its freedom was betrayed by the democracies. It was cold comfort to us to reflect that the misfortunes which had befallen Czechoslovakia were in a way more poignant than those we faced—at least for the moment. We could not tell what the future held in store for us; we only knew that we had little to expect in the way of sympathy or action from the Western democracies.

However dark the outlook, however immovable the forces arrayed against us, one had to carry on. We explored the possibility of some sort of understanding with the Arabs. One or two meetings—more or less unofficial—were arranged between us and some members of the Arab delegation. They served no immediate purpose, but they did help to bring about a kind of relationship. Mr. Aly Maher, the Egyptian delegate, was personally friendly. Some of the Iraqi people were inclined to discuss matters with us, and not merely to stare at us as the invaders and prospective destroyers of the Middle East. The most intransigeant among the non-Palestinian Arabs was the Iraqi Premier, Nuri Said Pasha. His attitude was stonily negative, but the probable explanation is illuminating. Iraq is immensely interested in finding an outlet to the Mediterranean; it would therefore look with favor on a greater Syria consisting of Iraq, Syria, Trans-Jordan, and Palestine. Within the framework of such a union Iraq would probably concede the Jewish National Home, with certain limited possibilities of expansion and immigration. Opposition, therefore, to a Jewish National Home, had much more to do with particular Iraqi ambitions than with the rights and wrongs of the Jews and Arabs; but under the circumstances Nuri Said Pasha was adamant.

His colleagues, however, were not so firm in their opposition. Neither did I think the Saudi Arabia delegates entirely inaccessible to reason on our part. It seemed to me that however discouraging the prospect was, it ought to be pursued for whatever it was worth. We left London for Palestine on March 25, and stopped off in Egypt. There Aly Maher, who had arrived before me, arranged a meeting between me and a number of leading Egyptians, among them Mahommed Mahmoud, the Premier. We talked of cooperation between Egypt and the Jews of Palestine, in the industrial and cultural field. The Egyptians were acquainted with and impressed by our progress, and suggested that perhaps in the future they might serve to bridge the gulf between us and the Arabs of Palestine. They assumed that the White Paper (it was of course not yet in existence as such) would be adopted by England, but its effects might be mitigated, perhaps even nullified, if the Jews of Palestine showed themselves ready to cooperate with Egypt.

There was a ray of encouragement in these talks, especially after the dismal atmosphere of the St. James Conference. I felt again, as I have so often before and since, that if the British Government had really applied itself with energy and goodwill to the establishment of good relations between the Jews and the Arabs, much could have been accomplished. But whenever we discussed the problem with the British they found its difficulties insuperable. This was not our impression at all. Of course one had to discount, in these unofficial conversations, both the usual Oriental politeness and the fact that private utterances are somewhat less cautious than official ones.

On my brief visit to Palestine in April, 1939, I was able to confirm at first hand what I already knew from reports—that the Jews would never accept the death sentence contained in the Government proposals. I wrote to many friends in England, Leopold Amery, Archibald Sinclair, Lord Lothian (newly appointed Ambassador to the United States), Sir Warren Fisher, Lord Halifax, among them, to apprise them of this fact. I cabled the Prime Minister:

> Feel it my solemn duty to warn H.M.G. before irrevocable step publication their proposals is taken that this will defeat their object pacification country surrender to demands terrorists will not produce peace but compel Government use force against Jews intensify hatred between Jews and Arabs hand over peaceful Arab population to terrorists and drive Jews who have nothing to lose anywhere to counsels of despair in Palestine. . . . Beg you not underestimate gravity this warning.

It had been my original intention to stay in Palestine for several months—perhaps until the forthcoming Congress which was to be held in Geneva that August. I did not believe that anything more could be done in London at the moment, I was tired out by the physical and nervous strain of the past few weeks, and I felt that it would be a sort of rest to resume my work in Palestine. But my friends insisted that I return to London and make a last-minute effort to convince the Prime Minister in person of the frightful harm which the publication of the White Paper would do to us and to the prestige of England. I was convinced that it was useless, and I told my colleagues so. But still they insisted that the effort be sustained until the last moment.

It was not easy for me to leave my wife in Palestine that spring of 1939. She fortunately did have, for company, Lorna Wingate, staying with us at the house. There was also, as visitor, a young boy of twenty-two by the name of Michael Clark, a charming youngster who was a schoolmate and great friend of my younger son, Michael. Michael Clark had come to Palestine by motorcycle, making his way alone across Europe and Turkey, over the Balkan and the Taurus mountains. With these young people staying at the house in Rehovoth I should have felt more or less easy in mind; but I could not get rid of a feeling of depression when I took my leave. As it turned out, my forebodings were justified. Young Michael had the habit, in spite of the unrest in the country, of traveling about alone on his motorcycle. My wife pleaded with him repeatedly not to expose himself in this reckless fashion, but he gave no heed to her expostulations. Then one day the poor boy was shot from ambush by an Arab near the railway line where it passes through Rehovoth. He was buried in the military cemetery at Ramleh. I was already in England when this happened, and my wife was so shaken by the dreadful incident that I cabled her to come to London by plane. Meanwhile I had the melancholy task of breaking the news to his mother. I met my wife in Paris, and found her shaken and depressed. We had both been deeply attached to Michael.

In spite of the hopelessness of the prospect, I again made arrangements to see Mr. Chamberlain, and again I traveled the *via dolorosa* to Downing Street. I pleaded once more with the Prime Minister to stay his hand and not to publish the White Paper. I said: "That will happen to us which has happened to Austria and Czechoslovakia. It will overwhelm a people which is not a state union, but which nevertheless is playing a great role in the world, and will continue to play one." The Prime Minister of England sat before me like a marble statue; his expressionless eyes were fixed on me, but he said never a word. He had received me, I suppose, because he could not possibly refuse to see someone who, at my age, had made the exhausting flight from Palestine to London just to have a few minutes with him. But I got no response. He was bent on appeasement of the Arabs and nothing could change his course. What he gained by it is now a matter of history: the Raschid Ali revolt in Iraq, the Mufti's services to Hitler, the famous "neutrality" of Egypt, the ill-concealed hostility of practically every Arab country.

Much has been written of Mr. Chamberlain's infatuation with his idea of appeasement, and of his imperviousness to anything which might modify it. I have only one more illustrative incident to add. Some time before the St. James Conference I happened to receive through secret channels an extraordinary German document which I was urgently requested to bring to the attention of the Prime Minister. It had been prepared and forwarded, at the risk of his life, by Herr Gördeler, the mayor of Leipzig, who shortly before the end of the war was implicated in the unsuccessful plot to assassinate Hitler, and executed. The document was a detailed exposé of conditions in Germany, and wound up with an appeal to Mr. Chamberlain not to be bluffed into further concessions when he went to meet Hitler in Godesberg or Munich.

I showed the document to a friend of mine in the Cabinet, and asked him to get Mr. Chamberlain to read it. He failed. I then went to see Sir Warren Fisher, one of the heads of the Civil Service, a close friend of Mr. Chamberlain's, with a room adjacent to his in Downing Street. I showed him the document, and explained that undoubtedly Herr Gördeler had risked his life several times over to accumulate the information it contained. Sir Warren Fisher opened his desk and showed me an exact copy of the document. "I've had this," he said, "for the last ten days, and I've tried and tried again to get Mr. Chamberlain to look at it. It's no use."

The St. James Conference came to its undignified end, the Government proceeded with its preparation of the White Paper, and the time approached for the debate in the House of Commons. We knew that the vote would go against us, such was the temper of the House, which had behind it the record of Vienna and Prague. Our appeals to public opinion were in vain. Shortly after my return from my brief visit to Palestine, I met Winston Churchill, and he told me he would take part in the debate, speaking of course against the proposed White Paper. He suggested that I have lunch with him on the day of the debate. I reported the appointment to my colleagues. They were full of ideas of what Churchill ought to say, and each one told me, "Don't forget this thought," and "Don't forget that thought." I listened respectfully, but was quite certain that a speaker of Mr. Churchill's caliber would have his speech completely mapped out, and that he would not wish to have anyone come along with suggestions an hour or so before it was delivered.

There were present at the lunch, besides Mr. Churchill and myself, Randolph Churchill and Lord Cherwell. I was not mistaken in my assumption. Mr. Churchill was thoroughly prepared. He produced a packet of small cards and read his speech out to us; then he asked me if I had any changes to suggest. I answered that the architecture of the speech was so perfect that there were only one or two small points I might want to alter—but they were so unimportant that I would not bother him with them. As everyone now knows, Mr. Churchill delivered against the White Paper one of the great speeches of his career. The whole debate, indeed, went against the Government. The most important figures in the House attacked the White Paper; and I remember particularly Mr. Herbert Morrison shaking a finger in the direction of Malcolm MacDonald, and reminding him of the days when he was a Socialist; declaring, further, that if a Socialist Government should come into power, it would not consider itself bound by the terms of the White Paper. This last statement, delivered with much emphasis, was loudly applauded by the Labor benches.

The Government answer, delivered by Mr. MacDonald, was a clever piece of sophistry which could carry conviction only to those who were ignorant of the details of the problem. As for those with whom the question of conviction was secondary in that time of panic, nothing that was said mattered. But it is worth recording that even in that atmosphere the Government victory was extremely narrow. There were two hundred sixty-eight votes in favor, one hundred seventy-nine against, with one hundred ten abstaining. As a rule the Government obtained over four hundred votes for its measures. As I left the House with my friends I could not help overhearing the remarks of several members, to the effect that the Jews had been given a very raw deal.

One consolation emerged for us in those days: the firmness and unanimity of the Jewish delegation. There were represented on it all the major Jewish communities of the world, and every variety of opinion from the stalwart and extremist Zionism of Menachem Ussishkin to the cautious and conciliatory philanthropic outlook of Lords Bearsted and Reading. At a meeting in the offices of the Zionist Organization the question was put to the formal vote whether the White Paper could be considered as forming a basis for discussion. The unanimous decision, without a single abstention, was in the negative.

F. The Holocaust

18. THE REFUGEES

On January 30, 1933, Adolf Hitler and the Nazi party came into power in Germany. Hitler's views and programs, including his rabid anti-Semitism, had been widely publicized in *Mein Kampf* and through the political activities of his party. Any misguided hopes that the responsibilities of public office would moderate Nazi extremism quickly dissipated. The major institutions of German democracy were suppressed, and all of German society was soon controlled by Hitler and his party.

Anti-Semitism was a preoccupation of the newly constituted authorities. On April 1, 1933, a boycott of Jewish businesses was called; on April 4, 1933, Jews were barred from the civil services; on September 15, 1935, Jews were disqualified from German citizenship; on November 10, 1938, a wave of governmentally instigated assaults on synagogues and Jewish establishments was unleashed; immediately thereafter a fine of one billion marks was levied on German Jewry for its alleged crimes.

By the mid-1930s, numerous Jews had begun to flee the new Germany. In a certain sense, many of those who suffered most in these early years were ultimately the most fortunate—their dislocation forced them out of Germany in time to avoid total destruction. Many of these refugees were distinguished men of science and the arts, who were cordially welcomed in the democracies of Western Europe and the Americas. For lesser lights, however, the process of relocation was an arduous one. The great earlier haven for oppressed Jews, the United States of America, had drastically reduced its immigration quotas; the new refuge that the Jews had hoped to create in Palestine was in the process of being strangled by the British mandatory powers; the rest of the Western nations were disinterested at best.

As the refugee problem increased in intensity, the facilities of the League of Nations and the private relief organizations proved less and less effective. In 1938 Franklin Roosevelt, President of the United States, called an international conference to deal with the issue. Conceived in a spirit of humane concern, the Évian Conference foundered on the shoals of political intrigue and deep-seated suspicions. While the disappointing efforts of the thirty-two delegations gathered at Évian have often been analyzed, they are depicted most poignantly in the fictionalized account of the German novelist Hans Habe. Centering on a bizarre mission undertaken by a famous Viennese physician, Habe views from Dr. Benda's perspective the political machinations and the underlying inhumanity which eventually destroyed this last effort to aid Germany's refugees. By the following year, the war had begun and the refugee problem had given way to Hitler's Final Solution.

Hans Habe's moving novel was translated into English as *The Mission* (New York, 1966). The following excerpt is reprinted by permission of Coward, McCann & Geoghegan, Inc. from *The Mission* by Hans Habe. English translation copyright © 1966 by Coward-McCann, Inc.

Hans Habe, *The Mission*

The Évian Conference was opened on Wednesday the 6th of July, 1938, at four in the afternoon in the so-called Grand Salon of the Hôtel Royal.

The thirty-two delegations—consisting of about two hundred people including attachés, advisers, experts, and secretaries—had already been in conference the whole morning. The discussions took place in the delegates' apartments, in the lounges, and in the gardens of the hotel. Most of the delegates preferred the summer park on whose beautifully kept lawns tables, chairs, and sunshades had been picturesquely arranged. The park and hotel lie only about three hundred yards above Evian, but the hill falls so steeply down to the little spa that the park, framed in thick clumps of flowers and beds of blossoming roses, forms a terrace with an uninterrupted view of Lake Geneva, the city of Lausanne and the mountains of Vaud. The hotel, whose semicircular wooden balconies are reminiscent of the artistic Spanish bird cages of the seventeenth century, has something of the lavish elegance of the turn of the century about it, a grace that contains nostalgia and a feeling of farewell and combines elements of grandeur with a conquering bad taste.

As is almost always the case with international conferences, these morning consultations were concerned primarily with questions of procedure, which can always give the practiced observer an indication of the future course of the conference.

Two groups had already crystallized during the morning hours: those who thought the Conference might create a commission, an office, perhaps a permanent organization to devote itself to the problems of the refugees within the League of Nations, housed nearby; and a second that was in favor of establishing a new and independent committee concerned solely with refugee questions. Naturally the High Commissioner for Refugees and the General Secretary of the venerable Nansen Office were present. The latter especially, who was at the same time the chief delegate from Norway, threw himself ardently behind the move to create a department within the League of Nations, since he feared that the setting up of an entirely new and independent commission would lead to confusing demarcation difficulties, the division or diminution of his own budget, and of course also a certain competition with his time-honored office. Even on the first day, however, it became clear that, although he was vigorously supported by the British, he was on the losing side, because the United States, which did not belong to the League of Nations, was strongly opposed to any incorporation within the hypertrophied body in Geneva.

Another subject was thornier and had to be handled with the greatest diplomatic tact. The refugees from Germany and Austria who had already managed to cross the frontier had their own representative bodies, associations, and aid committees, more or less recognized by some governments, and these had sent delegates to Évian. One of them, Artur Rosenberg by name, but in no way related to the Third Reich's racial ideologist of the same name, had requested that his and other associations should be admitted to the Conference, which after all, so he argued, was there to discuss the refugees from National Socialist barbarity. A splendid unanimity, perhaps promising agreement later over other, more important matters, prevailed among participants in the Conference that sunny morning. The intervention of refugees in the Conference was to be prevented from the outset, and this for many, well-considered reasons. For one thing, remarked the Swiss delegate, the chief of his country's political police, the admission of emigrants would unnecessarily antagonize the German Reich; second, Paraguay's envoy convincingly argued, it would be impossible to admit one association without likewise accepting other, more or less private committees. But the American Ambassador settled the question. He possessed certain information, he said, indicating that Germany had permitted individual Jews to come to Évian; if they were allowed to take part in the discussion it would be impossible to prevent Berlin, either directly or via the Gestapo, from being informed of the progress of the Conference at an unsuitable juncture. By midday Professor von Benda, who also spent his time in the Hôtel Royal, where he made the acquaintance of Artur Rosenberg, had learned that, like many other people, he was welcome in the lobbies, lounges, and gardens of the fine hotel, but could only observe the actual deliberations of the Conference from outside.

This prohibition, issued with absolute politeness and without personal animosity, applied, of course, only to the secret sessions. When the Conference was meeting in public, entry to the Grand Salon, provided there were sufficient seats, was not forbidden to the Jewish representatives any more than it was to the wives of the delegates, the notables of the town, and finally to the international press, which included the representative of the *Völkischer Beobachter* and similarly interested newspapers. Whether there would be any public sesssions at all, apart from the opening and closing ceremony, appeared doubtful, since complete agreement over this procedural question had already been obtained that morning. If the Conference was to proceed without complaint, if the delegates were to speak with uninhibited frankness and the possible impression of a division of opinion was to be avoided as far as the outside world was concerned, the Conference must meet behind closed doors.

The solemn opening of the Conference took place punctually at four in the afternoon. In the center of the room stood a horseshoe-shaped conference table covered with green baize at which the chief delegates—three ambassadors, thirteen envoys, three ministers, and thirteen other high diplomats, all in black—had taken their seats, while their assistants occupied the two rows of chairs immediately behind them. Three further rows had been reserved for the audience. Here, in the last row, Heinrich von Benda had been given a seat between an old lady and a Hungarian journalist.

The hall was high, but only of medium size, a lounge that was certainly not intended for such a serious, one might almost say macabre, occasion. The light walls, decorated in both the classicist and the secessionist style, were topped by a fresco ceiling on which stood the proud initials of the hotel framed by lacelike scrolls; the healing springs, parks, and promenades of the town of Évian-les-Bains were also depicted, half realistically, half idealized, leaving one with the impression of being in an emporium rather than a conference hall.

The session was opened by the French Ambassador as the representative of the host country. Immediately after him the Ambassador rose and extolled the humanitarian aims that had moved the President of the United States to call the Conference. America, he said, had already raised the quota for German and Austrian immigrants to 27,370 persons per annum; his government was certain that it would meet with understanding and sympathy among all the participating states. "I need not emphasize," said the Ambassador, "that the discrimination against minorities, the pressure that is being brought to bear upon them, and the disregard of elementary human rights contradict those principles which we have come to regard as the standards of our civilization. We have heard from time to time of the disastrous consequences of the flooding of the international markets with certain goods which is known as 'dumping.' How much more disastrous, gentlemen, must it be if there is an involuntary and chaotic 'dumping' of large numbers of unfortunate human beings."

A cold shudder ran down the spine of Heinrich von Benda in the last row of seats. The American President's special envoy was speaking words founded upon noble intentions, but was he not also speaking of the persecuted as though they were merchandise, was not he too comparing them with the cheap and superfluous objects that some countries, particularly those of the Far East, had been pouring out on the markets of recent years?

The American Ambassador's speech was greeted with polite cheers; now the United Kingdom representative rose to speak. His lordship, member of the House of Lords and Chancellor of the Duchy of Lancaster, was a man who, whatever figures were contained in his coat of arms, could very well stand as an image of Britain. His lean figure, strongly marked cheekbones with the hollow cheeks, the protruding upper lip with two large incisors, the reddish-blond, thin hair surrounding a high forehead, betrayed the Englishman even at a distance, while his careful enunciation, his shy and at the same time unconstrained gestures, the cut of his double-breasted suit, and his college tie indicated a family of high lineage.

The chief British delegate extolled the humanitarian aims that had moved the President of the United States to call the Conference. It had always been a British tradition, he said, to offer asylum to those persecuted for religious or racial reasons. On the other hand, he went on, he must point out that the United Kingdom was not "a country of immigration." "Britain is a highly industrialized country, densely populated, and at present engaged in a difficult fight against unemployment." The same applied, if to a lesser degree, to Britain's overseas possessions. At the same time they were certainly in a position to take a limited number of refugees, more particularly young people willing to take part in the process of industrialization. Whether the Conference could begin work with good prospects of success depended primarily upon the refugees' country of origin—he avoided using the word Germany. "No country," declared his lordship, weighing his words and carefully stressing certain of them, "can be expected to take people who have been robbed of their means of existence before even embarking on their emigration. Nor can private associations be expected to replace those means of which the emigrants have been deprived in their country of origin." The resettlement of refugees, he concluded, had a chance of success only if the refugees were permitted to bring their goods and chattels with them.

It was fortunate, thought Professor von Benda, that he was forbidden to make his voice heard at this meeting. If he had been allowed to speak, how could he have resisted the temptation of asking his lordship on this very first day, at this solemn hour, whether the refugees from the Spanish Inquisition, the Protestants of Flanders and Brabant, the Huguenots, the aristocrats fleeing from Robespierre's guillotine, and Kosciusko and Mazzini and Kossuth, who died in exile, had been allowed to bring their "goods and chattels" with them, whether a regime that set out to carry off women and murder children did not naturally also rob "minorities" of their "means of existence," whether one could really expect furniture vans to cross the snow-covered Swiss Alps, that had become the grave of so many refugees, whether a human being was only worth as much as the money he carried in his bag.

Meanwhile the French Ambassador had begun to speak, this time in his capacity as representative of the Republic—a pale, thin man who possessed a fine intellectual's head, strikingly beautiful hands, and the noble diplomatic language belonging to the nation of Talleyrand. His Excellency extolled the humanitarian aims that had moved the President of the United States to call the Conference, but he was manifestly the realist among the representatives of the Great Powers, because he immediately began to quote figures—France had already taken in 200,000 refugees and she was a country with forty million inhabitants for whom a total of three million foreigners represented even without this an almost insoluble problem. With an elegance to which the clumsier representatives of the Anglo-Saxon nations could not aspire, he did what they, if far less skillfully, had also done—he threw the ball into the court of the other participants in the Conference. He pointed out what services immigrants and also refugees had rendered the younger states of the world, the two Americas and especially Australia, so that the countries of these continents would doubtless welcome the refugees with open arms.

After the American Ambassador had been unanimously elected chairman, the Conference declared its wish to get down to the real work, and since diplomatic work is best carried out *in camera caritatis,* the public was asked to leave the hall. The Professor left the Grand Salon with the other nonparticipants.

Heinrich von Benda had the feeling, as he entered the crowded lobby, that the American Ambassador was gazing after him. He was not suffering from an illusion. The conversation he had had with the Professor the previous evening had not left the Ambassador's mind. He had informed the President, in a coded cablegram, of the Reich Government's strange, suspiciously indirect proposal, but he expected no answer to his report; he had to deal on his own with the problem that had arisen so surprisingly. To the Ambassador, who had long experience with diplomatic conferences, this was above all a question of procedure. The general assembly would very soon break up into committees and subcommittees, and this was a good thing, because the more people spoke the less they said. The important thing now—during the night the Ambassador had considered various possibilities—was to persuade the Conference to elect a committee empowered to negotiate with the Germans, or the "country of origin." Once such a committee had been formed responsibility would no longer rest exclusively on his, the Ambassador's shoulders; then the committee could hear Professor von Benda and, who knows, receive the German Reich's proposal. The Ambassador looked around—old stale diplomats, young ambitious diplomats, fair Anglo-Saxons, dark Latin Americans, overbred aristocrats, and broad-shouldered Socialists; which of these, the Ambassador asked himself, was best fitted to act as chairman of the committee, to whom could he skillfully, with extreme caution and without betraying his true purposes, pass the ball?

Now the Conference was in "secret" session, and the Australian delegate, his country's Minister of Trade and Customs, had asked to speak. Certainly, he began, the honorable representative of the République Française had rightly spoken of the blessings brought to the distant continent of Australia by immigration, but he had overlooked the fact that it was the British immigration that had so admirably contributed to Australia's standing and prosperity. "Up to now," he cried, "we in Australia have had no racial problem, and we do not wish to create one now."

A racial problem? The American Ambassador made no reply, but it seemed to him at that moment that he had little reason to be glad about his flattering election to the chair. The old man from Vienna, who had sat facing him yesterday evening and was now no doubt waiting outside the curtained glass doors for the result—what would the Professor have thought if he could have heard the Australian's speech? To the Minister sent by Australia—the Minister for Trade and Customs; why just this one?—the Jews were a "race"; he used the same vocabulary in which other words also appeared—foreigner, intruder, subhuman on one page, blood, soil, Aryanism, master race on the other—the Jews were a race and probably political refugees were a race by themselves, a foreign race, to which belonged all those who did not correspond to his own conception of nation, state, and government. Poor old man, thought the old man in the chairman's chair, but he did not consider it appropriate to intervene, at least not at such an early stage.

His British lordship expressed his gratitude for the uplifting words in which his Australian colleague had described British immigration into Australia. He himself wished first to clarify a matter of principle. When the American President called the Conference, he must certainly have had in mind more than the problem of asylum. "First things first" was an old and well-tried English principle; it would be best to deal first with the emigrants who had already succeeded in escaping. A not inconsiderable proportion of the refugees had left their country of origin illegally; these emigrants were now in foreign countries without money or papers, a regrettable state of affairs which little could now be done to remedy, but which contained within it a further danger. Others might learn from the bad example and place the countries of asylum in "an embarrassing situation." Before starting to encourage emigration or immigration it must be unequivocally stated that the emigration and immigration must take place according to the correct forms; asylum could be afforded only to those who did not prove themselves from the outset unworthy of asylum by disregarding frontier, passport, and immigration regulations.

Applause from several quarters. No one could read behind the stony mien of the chairman. He had long since realized that high politics, or what people understood by high politics, had entered Évian. The loyalty of the colonies and dominions was not as solid as was pretended in London. But Évian was a sidetrack, and it didn't cost the colonies and dominions much, cost them at most the lives of a few million Jews, to demonstrate their solidarity with the mother country, just as it didn't cost England much to hold back the troublesome stream of foreigners from the countries of the Crown. On the Ambassador's desk lay a memorandum from the Jewish Agency for Palestine stating that the number of Jews in the Holy Land had risen between 1918 and 1937 from 60,000 to 416,000, that the country of the Jews was entirely capable, if given support in solving its irrigation problem, of taking in 240,000 Jews at once and another half million in the course of time. The simplest solution, certainly, but also the most complicated. A million Jews in Palestine—that would mean for England, at war with the Jews of Palestine who were demanding independence, a suicidal import of potential enemies. Was there not a proverb that said that only the stupidest calves choose their own butcher? That very morning the New York *Times* had reported a bomb attack in Haifa under the headline TWENTY-THREE DEAD IN ISRAEL UPRISING—twenty-three dead and also a British soldier had been injured. To be sure, Jewish intellectuals in Berlin, merchants in Frankfurt, artisans in Vienna, Jewish women and children in other parts of Europe had little to do with those Maccabees who had grown out of the meager soil of Palestine—but at this point the problem became so complex that one dared not think about it, let alone attack it. Who were they, these Jews? Were they symbols of intolerant persecution, the believers of a religious community, European minorities, American citizens, a nation in Palestine, disillusioned German patriots, the salt of the earth, human beings like any others, or, who knows, members of a particular race of which the Australian Minister for Trade and Customs had spoken?

In the meantime the Ambassador had almost automatically called upon the Haitian envoy to speak, the only Negro at the Conference table, a corpulent man with a shiny bald patch and a brilliant white waistcoat, his country's commercial attaché in Paris who had been given the title of envoy extraordinary and minister plenipotentiary especially for Évian.

If the Conference was to be crowned with success, as all *"hommes de bonne volonté"*—he spoke in French—wished with all their hearts, then they must come to terms with certain realities.

The gentlemen around the green table nodded their agreement, because nothing arouses more unanimous agreement at international conferences than the commonplace to which no objection can be raised and which everyone can interpret in his own way.

The realities, the corpulent man continued, demanded honest collaboration with Germany—he said *"l'Allemagne,"* not *"pays d'origine."* Germany was a state in which the rule of law prevailed. The Conference would be ill advised to act as though the Jews of Germany and what used to be Austria were actually in danger of their lives. On the other hand, for reasons which it was unnecessary to go into here, they were in danger of having to forfeit their material possessions, but precisely this might be prevented if a sensible agreement were reached with Germany. The Jews of the German Reich were reputed to possess two hundred million dollars, a considerable sum, certain German sources even put it at seven hundred to eight hundred million. If they could take this with them, their welcome would be ensured. Moreover there was a further consideration which he could not honestly conceal from the Conference. He might be considered to speak for most of the small Latin American republics when he pointed out the important, continually increasing and fruitful commercial relations between these countries and Germany. It was scarcely in the interest of the great wealthy states to delay or prevent such a healthy development through precipitate steps defamatory to the German Reich. It was true that Germany had refused the invitation to Évian, but it was a matter for the Conference, he said, to set up a committee to investigate German intentions and, if it proved possible, to maintain contact with Berlin. Here, he concluded, he was making a concrete proposal on which he asked the Conference—he bowed to the chairman—to vote.

Now it was up to the American Ambassador to proceed tactically, that is to say with tact. Earlier than he had expected, the demand for the establishment of a committee to negotiate with Germany had been made even if not by the right man and not for the right purpose. His eye fell on the delegate from Colombia, who was sitting only a few chairs away from him. In reality this was not the chief delegate from the republic on the River Magdalena; he had fallen ill and his place had been taken by the government's legal adviser, a university professor from Bogotá. Why hadn't the Ambassador thought of him straightaway? The little bald-headed professor was known throughout the diplomatic world for his acute commentary on international law and for his contribution to the legal structure of the League of Nations; he was an authority; he was a liberal thinker and on top of that—a gleam of light at last—a Latin American, so that he would enjoy the confidence of no less than nineteen Latin American delegations.

The Ambassador seized his chance. Whether they wished to act upon the suggestions of the honorable representative of Haiti in their entirety or only in part, he said, there could be no doubt that a committee must be set up to sound out German intentions—only the full assembly of the Conference would have the right to negotiate directly with Germany. He seconded the proposal, put it to a vote and at the same time, although this was not necessarily part of his function, he proposed that the honorable delegate of the Republic of Colombia should be elected chairman of the new committee. Speed was essential and if the chairman were elected now he could suggest the other members of his committee to the plenary session tomorrow morning. With this vote—without doubt an excellent result for this first afternoon—he, the chairman, would like to adjourn the meeting until tomorrow. "It is getting close to eight, gentlemen, and the stomachs of diplomats speak no less loudly than any other stomachs."

A *bon mot* that neatly concluded the first day's work—but the Ambassador wasn't hungry. After the vote and as he made his way laboriously to the elevator between the waiting journalists, who bombarded him with questions, he managed things so as to be standing beside the delegate from Colombia. He invited him to dine with him in his private suite.

There he informed him of the strange affair which he called the "Benda Mission."

19. THE GHETTOS

As early as September, 1939, Reinhard Heydrich ordered all the Jews of Poland to move into the large Polish cities; subsequently the Jews of Warsaw, Lodz, Lublin, and Cracow were to be quarantined off from the rest of the Polish population, tightly packed in slum areas, and slowly suffocated from lack of adequate jobs, food, and sanitation. A Jewish Council *(Judenrat)* was established in each of the major ghettos, and it was the task of this bureaucracy to execute all the Nazi economic, political, religious, and social instructions. These decisions included who should live (temporarily) and who should die.

By the late summer of 1940, the Germans moved to isolate the Warsaw ghetto totally, beginning with an eight-foot-high fence around the Jewish quarter and permanently sealing it on November 15, 1940. The Jewish section, about one hundred square blocks, contained 240,000 Jews in September, 360,000 Jews by November, and upward of 470,000 Jews by the summer of 1941. As the ghetto was encircled with walls, no Jew was permitted to remain outside. There were no exceptions; even converted Jews with Aryan spouses were separated from their mates and forced into the confines of the ghetto. Astonishingly, as disease and starvation increased (the average food ration was 800 calories per day), rich Jewish cultural expressions (drama, lectures, seminars, concerts) multiplied. It was not until the spring and summer of 1942 that the numbers and the programs were significantly reduced, as the Nazis began to empty Warsaw and move toward the Final Solution.

Emmanuel Ringelblum, the author of the *Notes from the Warsaw Ghetto,* was born in 1900. A historian, he received his Ph.D. from the University of Warsaw and specialized in medieval Polish Jewry. Refusing to leave his teaching and philanthropic work when the Nazis invaded Poland, he remained in Warsaw and began his *Notes* (January, 1940) shortly after Warsaw fell to the Germans. A leader of the Jewish resistance, which culminated in April–May, 1943, with the Warsaw ghetto uprising, Ringelblum was executed in Warsaw in 1944 by the Nazis. He buried his *Notes* in a rubberized can which was not found until after the war. The selection from his *Notes* provides impressionistic sketches of the sealing off of the Warsaw ghetto from the outside world and the struggle for existence which continued inside the inferno. The second selection, taken from Tovia Bozhikowski's *In Fire and Blood,* gives us a firsthand depiction of the courage, the bloodiness, and the ultimate repression of the famed Warsaw ghetto revolt.

19a. Emmanuel Ringelblum, *Notes from the Warsaw Ghetto*

November 8, 1940

My dear:

There's been the growth of a strong sense of historical consciousness recently. We tie in fact after fact from our daily experience with the events of history. We are returning to the Middle Ages.—Spoke to a Jewish scholar. The Jews created another world for themselves in the past, living in it forgot the troubles around them, allowed no one from the outside to come in. As for parallels: The present expulsion is one of the worst in Jewish history, because in the past there were always cities of refuge. Someone said to me: "It's bad to read Jewish history, because you see that the good years were few and far between. There were always troubles and pogroms." A memento left over from history is this plague of informers we are suffering from so badly. Take the incident of Sachsenhaus who was supported for three months in the apartment of a Jewish communal figure, Nergep. Imbibed their culture and from being a decent human being became a slippery one. The Sachsenhaus incident reminds you of the proverb: "You beat my Jew, and I'll beat your Jew."

Often, police chiefs appear at the office of the Jewish Council and demand money for Jewish workers. The "amulet" on the door stating that everything must go through Leist has been of no avail.—People think nothing of having their things taken away, because they have faith in better times coming. Their only hope is to survive the present.—The fact that the Jews have many artisans evokes the amazement of the Others.—The ragmen in the Lodz Ghetto, as well as the scrap collectors, live outside the Ghetto. They have the right to travel by train. The janitors are exploiting the situation of the last few days and the setting up of the Ghetto in Warsaw. They have become the middlemen for apartments. They are doing business in produce.—The increase in typhus a result of the growing density of the Jewish population.—Customary thing in official documents, the appelation "Jude," occasionally "Herr," but very seldom.—I marvel at the pious Jews who sacrifice themselves by wearing beards and the traditional frock coats. They are subjected to physical abuse.—Saw traces in the Jewish Council office of Advocate Popower's blood. It was he who issued the verdict against Sachsenhaus for requisitioning a Jewish apartment. Sachsenhaus made a speech to the Others about the necessity of introducing order in the Jewish Council. Recently the number of typhus cases has increased (35). Heard about someone who moved seven times because the Ghetto boundaries kept shifting. Another person, four times—turned out of Hoza Street, Freta Street, 68 Grzybowska Street, and another place.—The long wall at Wielopole Street looks like a prison wall.—It has been taking an hour and more to get to the office lately. You have to wait at the courtyard gate a long time before the danger of seizure is past. When people are seized for forced work on Leszno Street, it is known immediately at Muranowska Street.—Heard from someone that there was nothing to eat in the Lodz Ghetto, so that a man who was very rich a short time ago asked a friend for the potato leavings.—A waiter in the Lodz self-maintenance kitchen called Kaminski used to be a well-known manufacturer.

Today, the 8th of November, rumors again that the Ghetto would be postponed until April.—At Falenti Street Jews who are exempt from forced labor because of their age or occupation are ordered to exchange shoes or other articles of clothing with those who remain behind. In the same place they ordered a young man with a beard to announce to all the Jewish work gangs that he was twenty years old, and then to scream *"Ohne Beruf"—"No Occupation"*—louder and louder. Finally, a Jew had to shave the young man's beard off.—Every German institution has its Jew, who is well treated though other Jews are mistreated. For example, there's a man they call "Moses" in the Dinance Park garages. He has been able to get a number of Jews exempted from work.

Today the Jewish Council received a written notice that the Jews must move out by the 15th of November. This puts an end to all the rumors about the postponing or enlarging of the Ghetto. There's a growing fear of the prospect of a closed Ghetto, especially since the Polish police were said to have been ordered out of the Ghetto today.—Everyone who can is hoarding as much as possible.—The commandant of the Falenti work camp takes produce from the peasants "for my Jews."

A police chief came to the apartment of a Jewish family, wanted to take some things away. The woman cried that she was a widow with a child. The chief said he'd take nothing if she could guess which one of his eyes was the artificial one. She guessed the left eye. She was asked how she knew. "Because that one," she answered, "has a human look."

There was said to have been an announcement over the loudspeaker yesterday that it was forbidden to speak of the "Jewish Ghetto"; the proper term was "Jewish quarter," like the German and Polish quarters.—Today a Jewish tailor on Orla Street had goods taken away from him. There was a Jew in the crowd who ripped the collars off fur coats and hid them in his breast.—PCH ("Pay Conductory Half") is what they call the Jewish streetcars nowadays; they're half empty. A Jew was ordered to take off his fur coat. He answered: "I'd gladly give it to you, but I've just come out of the hospital. I had the typhus." That scared Them off.—Heard that some 200 persons have died of natural causes or been killed in the work camps: In Belzec alone 80 people have died of dysentery, and an equal number have been killed at work.

The news that apartments are to be requisitioned has started people looking for cheap boarders, to fill up the apartments.—Those who turn informer get 10 percent of the spoils. Four of them accompanied a police chief (who happened to be an honest man) to a Jewish business on Nalewki Street. They grabbed linen and other things, which they stuck into their trousers, and came out bulging like bears.—*Heute Tag Ohne Ausweisen*—"No Work Certificates Today." The joke is that that means They're seizing people for work today even if they have certificates exempting them. That's what some of the press gangers say.—Often, when Jews salute the Others, They gesture "It isn't necessary." Most of Them pass by as though the salute had nothing to do with them. The worst thing is when two or three Jews come along in a group, and only one of them salutes. Very often courteous Germans reply to the salute.

The Ghetto is much more painful now than it was in the Middle Ages, because we that were so high and mighty are now fallen so low. The appeal to develop high standards in the Ghetto: to work for leveling of, for example, taxes on silk, clothing, weddings; for mutual-aid institutions, for a rich community life.—Walls are being put up around the Ghetto at a feverish pace. It's hard to walk from Leszno Street to Grzybowska Street. The crowds on Solna and Ciepla Streets, making it impossible to get through.

November 19, 1940

My dear:

The Saturday the Ghetto was introduced (16th of November) was terrible. People in the street didn't know it was to be a closed Ghetto, so it came like a thunderbolt. Details of German, Polish, and Jewish guards stood at every street corner searching passersby to decide whether or not they had the right to pass. Jewish women found the markets outside the Ghetto closed to them. There was an immediate shortage of bread and other produce. There's been a real orgy of high prices ever since. There are long queues in front of every food store, and everything is being bought up. Many items have suddenly disappeared from the shops.—There's no connection between Twarda and Leszno Streets. You have to go by way of Zelazna Street.—Jewish businesses in the Aryan part of the city have been shut tight, to prevent pilfering.—Neither Saturday nor Sunday did the Jewish doctors get passes. The Jewish Council levies a tax of five zlotys per pass.—Saturday Jewish workers were not allowed to leave the city on their outside work details. On the first day after the Ghetto was closed, many Christians brought bread for their Jewish acquaintances and friends. This was a mass phenomenon. Meanwhile, Christian friends are helping Jews bring produce into the Ghetto.

At the corner of Chlodna and Zelazna Streets, those who are slow to take their hats off to Germans are forced to do calisthenics using paving stones or tiles as weights. Elderly Jews, too, are ordered to do push-ups. They tear paper up small, scatter the pieces in the mud, and order people to pick them up, beating them as they stoop over. In the Polish quarter Jews are ordered to lie on the ground and They walk over them. On Leszno Street a soldier came through in a wagon and stopped to beat a Jewish pedestrian. Ordered him to lie down in the mud and kiss the pavement.—A wave of evil rolled over the whole city, as if in response to a nod from above. At the same time there are still official optimists who believe that there will be no Ghetto, or it will not be a closed one.—The Jewish Law and Order Service (which appeared on the 16th of November) was ordered to dance on one foot around a group of Jews performing calisthenics in the street. The Jewish Council is said to be preparing a plan for a post office, food-supply service, and Jewish currency.—Because of the closing of the Ghetto and the feverish buying up of everything, all the Jewish streets are full of people milling about. It's simply impossible to pass through. Pedestrians overflow the sidewalk, spill over on the street.—Friday night, Jews were arrested in Praga and driven by car to Muranowska and other streets in the Ghetto, and there deposited. They spent the night on the stoops and in the courtyard gateways. Took nothing with them except hand baggage.—Saturday saw groups of Jews being driven from Praga into the Ghetto. Under guard they were settled down in houses and schools, dance halls, etc. The Jewish Council is requisitioning single rooms for them from Jews who have large apartments.—A scene: At the corner of Chlodna and Zelazna Streets, a Jewish family says its farewells to a Polish one. They kiss, shake hands, invite one another to "come visit us next week."—At the end of Tlomackie Place and Bielanska Street—the borderline between the Ghetto and the Other Side—stand a long line of streetcars being searched for Jews trying to smuggle themselves out of the Ghetto. Everybody is ordered out of the streetcar and their papers examined. It looks like a border point between two countries. Sometimes a streetcar stands there for as long as ten–fifteen minutes.—"*Greco banditto, toto ferditto, popo babitto,* Benito." A telegram from Mussolini to Hitler after the Greeks had defeated the Italian army.—Was told about a group of workers from a work camp. Shadows of human beings, shoeless, feet wrapped in rags.—The furniture requisitioned from Jewish apartments is taken to the Splendide movie house (the Sphinx), and can be bought back there a little at a time. *Our brethren the children of Israel* are helpful in this business.—The revolting informing on Muni. —One of the sad developments of the resettlement has been the large number of beggars that have turned up (Jews from the suburbs).—A groups of Jewish workers together with their foreman had to do calisthenics at the corner of Leszno and Zelazna Streets.—The doctors who rode the streetcar to the hospital at Czista Street on Sunday were taken off the car and made to do calisthenics for an hour. An elderly Jew passed the guards on Twarda Street and did not—for reasons of piety—take off his hat in salute although the Jewish guards warned him. So They tortured him a long time. An hour later, he acted the same way. "They can go to hell."

Many Jews make their living outside the Ghetto, and now they're cut off from it. Firms that are administered by the city commissariat, it is said, will have to move to the Other Side—i.e., the Jews who make part of their livng out of these firms will lose that part, too.—It is said that the Ghetto will be half open until the 25th of November, afterward. . . .

A big man came to Adam, kissed him, cried, and said that he did not agree with the idea of having a Ghetto. People are paying 2,500 zlotys moving money for the administration that handles the Jewish houses; the same amount for concessions in monopoly items. There's also talk in the courtyards about having all the neighbors in the courtyard cook collectively, because of the shortage of wood and coal. The same thing happened in Lodz, where as early as the third day [after the Ghetto was introduced] they even had a common pot to brew coffee in.—Heard today how King Chaim Rumkowski rooted out the bribe-takers from the Law and Order Service men [Jewish police] of his Lodz Ghetto. Went into the room and tore badges off the first ten Law and Order men he saw, saying he didn't have time to investigate. The resettlement was handled very well in Lodz. They had German guards to help them in cases where Christians put up opposition. The first night of the Lodz resettlement there were 7 deaths, the second night 70, and the third night 133. A total of 300 were killed.

A Christian was killed today, the 19th of November, for throwing a sack of bread over the Wall.—The rabbi of Wengrow was stabbed last year. The blood flowed from his wound, but he kept working for four hours until he fainted.—Many Jews of means who until now never gave a groschen for relief have suddenly begun to give large sums to the Self-Aid Society, so that it can purchase produce for the winter for the poor people in the courtyards. The Ghetto game is continuing. It is said that the electricity has been turned off in the Lodz Ghetto. Jews have to sit in the dark there. The rumor has spread that electricity will cost four times as much for Jews as for Christians. One of those good ideas of ours that the Nazis are happy to adopt!

December 10, 1940

Today, in the morning, at the corner of Chlodna and Zelazna Streets, sacks of bread, fats, etc., were taken away from Jews because a Polish guard insisted they had been smuggled in. Later, Jewish guards came and proved that the Jews had been walking through Jewish streets all the way, so the bread was distributed among the poor.—The Jewish Hospital will be evacuated by April.—There are 750 Jewish doctors in Warsaw.—The dollar is up again, to 108. This is explainable by two facts. First, the populace is buying merchandise, feeling that money is valueless now; and second, the Others are supposed to be buying dollars in large amounts.—It is said that four Germans were killed on the Other Side, which explains why a few streets have been cut off.—The Wall, to the people on the Other Side, is a symbol of the Jewish Council's graft. That is what the Christian and Jewish health officials say when they arrive with their steam baths for disinfection and want graft themselves.—Yesterday, a soldier sprang out of a passing automobile and hit a boy on the head with an iron bar. The boy died.—There was a massacre on Grzybowska Street yesterday. Some of the Others got drunk and beat and injured dozens of Jewish passersby. The estimate is 100 wounded, one boy killed.—A great many dispatches are arriving from Oswiecim with news of the deaths of inmates. People are forced to exercise under showers every day for three hours there; this produces inflammation of the lung and death follows. Postcards have been received describing the difficult situation there, the writers wishing themselves dead.

Heard an interesting interpretation of the new mode in high shoes. The power and bearing of the Others is impressive. People are trying to rise above the general mass of mankind and make an impression wearing the same high shoes as the Others.—Juvenile delinquents ride around town beating innocent Jewish passersby with their whips.—The dollar has gone up to more than 100 for soft (paper) currency; 115 for hard (gold); bread is 3.50 zlotys a kilo, potatoes 5–6 zlotys.—The Jewish Council is setting up a transfer office. For 150,000 zlotys they remodel a house so that the windows facing the Ghetto are screened off.

December 15, 1940

My dear:

During the last few days, Jewish stores on the Other Side were opened up. It turns out they are empty. One can guess that the storekeepers were themselves the "thieves."—Jewish artisans will be able to transport their tools and family mementoes from the Other Side into the Ghetto. But not their merchandise.—Today I was at a concert in the Judaic Library. Jewish artists appeared and sang in Yiddish for the first time. The program was entirely in Yiddish. Perhaps this is the beginning of a return to Yiddish.—It is said that the priest who came to the Ghetto Sunday to preach to the converts was not allowed to pass through the gate. Some were converted as long as forty to sixty years ago, and now they must suffer the Jewish exile in the Ghetto. Some of them have had to separate from their Aryan wives, who have remained behind on the Other Side.—A man came along with a pass. The watchmen on Grzybowska Street took him into the guard room, tortured him there for two hours, forcing him to drink urine, have sex relations with a Gentile woman. They beat him over the head, then cleaned the wounds with a broom. The next day, they treated him humanely, gave him food and drink, took him to his destination, on the way saying that Jews are people, too.—The Jewish Council proposed thirty-odd names of possible commissars to the authorities for their approval.—They struck out twenty, and proposed replacements. The Others gave swindlers jobs at 3,000 zlotys per job.

There are some honest people among "the Thirteen" gang.—This reminds us that Adam Czerniakow was informed on some time ago. Our "fine fellows" tell the Germans: "We'll locate the rich Jews' money. Then we can split it." "The Thirteen" are on the same tack. They're supported by the S.S. and want to become a second Council and look after the Jews—and themselves, too, incidentally. They have some shady characters there.—The Council has taken over the administration of Jewish houses. It is said that people who refused to pay rent will have to live in barracks.—Heard this joke: Someone comes to a fortune-teller in a chauffeur's uniform and asks to have his fortune told. He is told: "You'll run out of gasoline, your axle will break, and your driver's license will be taken away."—Yesterday, there was a big to-do at the Council. They divided the administrative jobs amongst their own. Kaminar gave his daughters the biggest houses, such as 28, 32, and 34 Swientojerska Street, and the like.—A well-dressed man approached the corner of Leszno and Zelazna wearing a derby. He wouldn't take it off and was beaten. The hat was thrown on the ground, but he wouldn't stoop to pick it up.—An original way of smuggling into the Ghetto. Two trucks stand on either side of the boundary line near the market; a Jewish truck with empty milk cans and an Aryan truck with full cans. After a while, when both guards are busy, the cans are switched and the trucks drive off.

Today, the 17th of December, it is bitter cold: 14 degrees (Centigrade), and no coal to be had. Coal costs 1,000 zlotys per ton. The game of taking bread from Jews at the Leszno-Zelazna corner and throwing it over the Wall to Christians is continuing. Smuggling is persisting for the time being. The base of operations is said to be located in the night spot used by the courtyards in Leszno Street. The Poles have access from one side; the Jews from the other. German police chiefs execute the transactions. The last few days, a large amount of wheat grain has been imported, to be ground in the Ghetto mills.—Yesterday the rabbi of Praga was badly beaten, because, though he did take his hat off, he left the skull cap on underneath it.—The transport firm of Hartwig is doing wonderful business. They take finished merchandise out of the Ghetto and carry raw material in.—The difference in the price of coal—inside and outside the Ghetto—is very great: Here, it costs more than 1,000 zlotys per ton; there, 400 zlotys. Saw someone from Ger. He'll tell nothing about what happened to him, but he's lost 24 kilos (from 82 down to 58). "People live here, people live there; they die there, too. There are some ninety such places in the country. Jews are separated from the rest."—This is all he would say. It is said that it will be possible to leave [the Ger Ghetto]; only relatives will have to pay 700 dollars first.—For 300 zlotys, you can rent a truck and have as much merchandise as you want brought in [to the Warsaw Ghetto].

August 26, 1941

There is a marked, remarkable indifference to death, which no longer impresses. One walks past corpses with indifference. It is rare for anyone to visit the hospital to inquire after a relative. Nor is there much interest in the dead at the graveyard.

Next to hunger, typhus is the question that is most generally absorbing for the Jewish populace. It has become the burning question of the hour. The graph line of typhus cases keeps climbing. For example, now, the middle of August, there are some six or seven thousand patients in [private] apartments, and about nine hundred in hospitals.

The disproportion between the number of patients at home and those treated in hospitals is to be explained by the fact that the hospitals have, for a thousand reasons, lost their therapeutic character. They have become "places of execution," as Dr. Milajkowski, director of the Ghetto Health Department, expressed it. The patients die from hunger in the hospital, because they get nothing to eat but a little soup and some other minor nourishment. The patients don't die from typhus, really, but because of their weakened condition. Typhus is particularly dangerous for the so-called "better class of people," who can't resist it and die—while the common people, though more poorly nourished, survive. Some 8 percent of the patients die. The phenomenon of high mortality among the professional class was also true during the First World War, especially in Russia, Serbia, etc. Actually, the professionals do everything to avoid the lice. Some of them smear oil and naphtha on their bodies, others carry [vials of] foul-smelling sabidilla around with them to drive off the lice. But the lice are omnipresent. They literally fly through the air, and it is almost impossible to avoid them. The so-called "disinfection columns" sent out by the Jewish Council health office actually spread lice. The same is true of the health-department doctors, who are fearfully corrupt. The "disinfection columns" extort money from the rich, whom they exempt from disinfection. The doctors cooperate. The disinfection steam bath organizations sell bath certificates, so that those who need to be disinfected buy the certificates and do not bathe. The sulphur used in the disinfection is so weak that the lice survive, so that the whole antiepidemic operation is, in fact, a swindle, perpetrated chiefly by the doctors and the "sanitation columns."—Inoculation against typhus is very expensive and [consequently] available only to a few. An injection costs 400–500 zlotys for two people. However, the rumor is spreading that Professor Hirszfeld has been placed at the head of the antiepidemic campaign.—Every house is supposed to have its own shower and disinfector. The House Committees are supposed to see to it. Equally ineffective is the quarantine, after which one comes back even lousier than before. The disinfectors have an effectiveness of 60 percent; 40 percent of those treated remain lousy. In all, 300 of the 1,400 houses in the Ghetto have suffered from typhus, i.e., some 150,000 people have had to take disinfection steam baths. But they've stopped closing the gates [to prevent epidemic], because it would have been necessary to keep all the houses closed, and the baths are in no position to bathe so many persons. It would be necessary to bathe 8,000 people a day, and only 2,000 can be handled. The figure 8,000 applies when there are about forty typhus cases a day. But, as the number of cases has gone up to seventy or eighty, it would seem that some 16,000 persons ought to be bathed daily. Typhus has latterly been spreading very fast among the personnel of the community organizations, particularly among the staff of the refugee centers, the community center workers, the help in the public kitchens, etc.—Recently, houses where there are cases of typhus are closed for one day, to allow all those whose apartments are dirty to go to the baths. Those who live in the apartment with a case of typhus have to go to the quarantine. But this happens very rarely, because they all run away, taking their things and the lice with them. In my house [at 18 Leszno Street] there was a typhus case. The residents of the house took all the invalid's identification papers away from him, put him in a ricksha, and bought off a Polish policeman. The patient pretended to be unconscious. He died in the hospital, and the house avoided disinfection. Taking all this into consideration, the prospects for the winter, when the epidemic will truly spread, are perilous indeed. The doctors calculate that every fifth Jew will be sick with typhus in the winter. Consequently, persistent rumors have spread about the possible resettlement [deportation] of the Jews from Warsaw. This is said to be considered as one possible way of removing the peril of typhus.—Doctors who illegally attend thousands of patients at home are doing wonderful business. They limit the number of home visits they make each day.—The problem of [disposing of] corpses is a pressing one in the houses of the poor. Not having the money to bury their dead, the poor often throw the corpses in the street. Some houses shut their gates and refuse to permit tenants [with a corpse at home] to leave until they have had the body buried. On the other hand, the police district chiefs, not wanting to bother with the formalities connected with [disposing of] corpses, simply throw the bodies from one streetcar to the next. The bodies are buried in mass graves at the graveyard, where there are tremendously high sand mounds in the old section. On hot summer days, the stench from these mass graves is so strong you have to hold your nose when you pass. It seems the graves were dug too shallow, and that is what is responsible for the smell.—The undertakers, particularly the brothers Pinkiert, are doing exceptionally good business; some of the undertakers have special carts for individual houses, which give them business every day. Corpses are carried. . . .*

August 30—Tragedy in Osowa, near Chelm, where there is a voluntary work camp. There were a few cases of typhus. The S.S. men took over, ordered the Jewish workers (around fifty of them) to line up. Five men dug a trench grave behind the lineup, another five were machine-gunned [and fell into the trench], then still another five dug and were machine-gunned, etc. Finally only five or six men were left of the whole camp—the Jewish policeman, the cook, the council representative. A terrible warning that if the epidemic doesn't subside. . . . Curiously enough, the typhus cases recovered and came here to the Ghetto from the hospital.

* Manuscript breaks off.

Characteristically, there has been but one case of murder in the Ghetto.

May 8, 1942

The period ending that fateful Friday, April 18, may be termed "the period of legal conspiracy." All the political parties in the Ghetto conducted activities that were practically semilegal. Political publications sprouted like mushrooms after rain. If *you* publish your paper once a month, *I'll* publish mine twice a month; if *you* print twice a month, *I'll* print weekly; it finally reached the point where the bulletin of one of the parties was appearing twice a week. These publications were distributed openly, "in full view of the people and the congregation." The political leaflets and communiqués used to be read in offices, factories, and similar public places.

The various parties used to hold their meetings practically in the open in public halls. They even had big public celebrations. At one such meeting, a speaker addressing an audience of 150 preached active resistance. I was myself present at a celebration along with 500 young people who all belonged to the same party. The names of the authors of the anonymous articles that appeared in the party newspapers were common knowledge.

We had even begun to debate and insult one another, as in the good old prewar days. We imagined that anything went. Even such illegal Polish publications as *Barykada Wolnosci* [*Barricade of Freedom*] used to be printed and distributed in the Ghetto. (I haven't checked this fact.) Everybody imagined that the Germans were indifferent to what the Jews were thinking and doing in their Ghetto. We thought that all that the Germans were concerned about was ferreting out Jewish merchandise, money, currency —that they were uninterested in intellectual matters. We turned out to be sadly mistaken. That bloody Friday, when the publishers and distributors of illegal publications were executed, proved that our political constellation is not a subject of indifference to Them, particularly when it has some connection with what is happening in the Polish, non-Jewish part of Warsaw.

The Jewish Council people have tried to exploit the bloody Friday for their own purposes: to repress completely the social and political life of the Ghetto. First they spread the rumor that Friday's massacre was attributable to the illegal publications. And then they warned the people of the Ghetto that if these [illegal publications] were to be repeated, the fate of Lublin would be visited on Warsaw—i.e., the deportation of the Jewish population. The only question that rises in one's mind is: Why were there similar massacres (courtyard executions by gunfire) in Radom and other places where there were no illegal publications? One body of opinion would have it that Friday's massacre has "rehabilitated" the Ghetto [morally]. This is the first time that Jewish blood has been spilled for reasons of political—not purely personal—activity.

Bloody Friday has had strong repercussions. The illegal press has stopped publishing. There has been a significant weakening of political activity. The interest in social undertakings has slackened. It was a hard blow to people's spirits; half the city spends the night away from home these days. Anyone who had anything at all to do with any kind of community work is terrified. Since the slaughter was the result of tattling by Jewish informers (apparently, from the Kohn and Heller firm), people tremble to speak a word. The English communiqués, which used to be so widely disseminated (some people actually made a living out of them!), have ceased appearing. However, since people are hungry for every tidbit of news, lies are fabricated out of whole cloth. Every day we have another batch of lies. After Friday's slaughter, a crew of swindlers turned up who persuaded people to part with money for the privilege of having their names removed from new lists of those doomed to slaughter. The example of Blajman, who during the weeks before the slaughter was blackmailed for 5,000 zlotys ransom money, has made people mortally fearful of blackmailers. But gradually, little by little, people are beginning to straighten up again. The only thing is that what used to be a kind of "legitimate" conspiracy is now being transformed into the real thing and is going deep underground.

The Pawia Street prison has become a center of persecution, outside as well as in. Inside, the prisoners are tortured ceaselessly—a new prison guard has taken over recently. But whether the guard be old or new, prisoners are tortured. The Pawia Street prison has become the point of departure for Oswiecim. Also, a number of people have been taken from the prison and shot outside, right in the street. Lately, the prison has also become a source of misery for those on the outside—for its neighbors and those who pass by on either side of Pawia Street. The neighbors have had to cover their windows with thick black paper or black wooden slats. Night and day, windows have to be closed.

The Jewish Gestapoists are now busy looking for an alibi. They are desperately trying to look good, so as to prove that they, at any rate, are real Jews, true Jews with a sense of public interest. Gancwajch, e.g., is turning into a regular Maecenas, supporting Jewish literature, art, theater. He arranges "receptions" for Jewish writers and artists, where there is plenty of food—nowadays the important thing. A short time ago he threw an all-night party at the El Dorado night spot. . . . The party was opened with the dedication of an ambulance, named Miriam (after Gancwajch's wife at home). Gancwajch's business interests are flourishing. He has the administration of 100 buildings, which brings him in a pretty penny. Beside, he issues thirty certificates a month, at the rate of several thousand zlotys per certificate; he's also a partner in various businesses. In a word, he's thriving. Gancwajch's function in the Gestapo is not completely clear. But one thing is certain: He gets nothing for nothing. He has to pay for every favor. To help them meet their Passover needs, Gancwajch sent the Jewish writers 6,000 zlotys.

One can judge the depths of poverty in the Ghetto from the fact that there are houses where everything has been sold—even pillowcases and sheets, so that people are sleeping right on the feathers of their pillows and beds. You come across beggars who are covered all over with feathers. These have sunk below the threshold of hope.

Death lurks in every chink, every little crack. There have been cases of everyone living in an apartment being fearfully tortured because someone opened a shutter. One of the tortures is to have the culprit strip naked and then roll down a pile of coke. The pain is excruciating, and every part of the body bleeds. Besides, every now and then, Jews who just happen to be passing by the Pawia Street prison are seized, tortured, and beaten. The Germans driving prisoners in trucks to the Pawia Street prison beat the passersby on the street mercilessly. The Gestapo agent sitting in the back of the car leans out the window, reaches along the narrow Karmelicka Street, and slashes at passersby with a long, lead-tipped stick. He overturns rickshas, and beats the ricksha drivers. At sight of the truck, people run into the nearest courtyard to hide. Often the Gestapo agents shoot. Many a man has been killed or wounded by one of these wild street shootings, which have become the thing since the 18th of April, bloody Friday.

The heroic girls, Chajke and Frumke—they are a theme that calls for the pen of a great writer. Boldly they travel back and forth through the cities and towns of Poland. They carry "Aryan" papers identifying them as Poles or Ukrainians. One of them even wears a cross, which she never parts with except when in the Ghetto. They are in mortal danger every day. They rely entirely on their "Aryan" faces and on the peasant kerchiefs that cover their heads. Without a murmur, without a second's hesitation, they accept and carry out the most dangerous missions. Is someone needed to travel to Vilna, Bialystok, Lemberg, Kowel, Lublin, Czestochowa, or Radom to smuggle in contraband such as illegal publications, goods, money? The girls volunteer as though it were the most natural thing in the world. Are there comrades who have to be rescued from Vilna, Lublin, or some other city?—They undertake the mission. Nothing stands in their way, nothing deters them. Is it necessary to become friendly with engineers of German trains, so as to be able to travel beyond the frontiers of the Government General of Poland, where people can move about with special papers? They are the ones to do it, simply, without fuss, as though it was their profession. They have traveled from city to city, to places no delegate or Jewish institution had ever reached, such as Wolhynia, Lithuania. They were the first to bring back the tidings about the tragedy of Vilna. They were the first to offer words of encouragement and moral support to the surviving remnant of that city. How many times have they looked death in the eyes? How many times have they been arrested and searched? Fortune has smiled on them. They are, in the classic idiom, "emissaries of the community to whom no harm can come." With what simplicity and modesty have they reported what they accomplished on their journeys, on the trains bearing Polish Christians who have been pressed to work in Germany! The story of the Jewish woman will be a glorious page in the history of Jewry during the present war. And the Chajkes and Frumkes will be the leading figures in this story. For these girls are indefatigable. Just back from Czestochowa, where they imported contraband, in a few hours they'll be on the move again. And they're off without a moment's hesitation, without a minute of rest.

May 22, 1942

Friday, the whole police force was called out. There was a big disturbance in the street. Some people were talking loudly about an imminent resettlement of the old, the sick, the unemployed. Others said that people were being impressed for the camps. It turned out that what was happening was that people with specialties were being impressed for the work camps. Specialists such as locksmiths, rug-weavers, and the like were picked up at their addresses. If the person in question was not at home, his father was taken, or the nearest of kin at home at the time. Those picked up were sent to Zembrow. The misfortune is that many of those who declared themselves to be specialists during the registration are not such in reality; they purported to be craftsmen rather than figure as unemployed. Friday's pickup is said to be the beginning of a big operation, the aim being to pull the Jewish populace into the factories where Poles have been working until now. If this turns out to be true, the Warsaw Ghetto can be saved for the time being.

"Jews won't work." That's what the German newspapers say. As an illustration of the contrary, I offer the following scene: 103 Plaza Zelazna is the place where those who work for the Germans outside the Ghetto change shifts. A truck arrives, and Jews throw themselves at it from all sides. They climb all over it. The soldiers can't handle the mob. They beat at those nearest with their rifles, but it does not good; the mob won't retreat. They want to get up into the truck at any cost, and there are many more than the outside work can use. The soldiers shoot in the air—but that does no good, either; the mob won't leave. Finally, the driver backs up, the mob disperses, but not before one person is badly injured. That, finally, restores order. But why do they mob the truck? The answer is simple. People working outside the Ghetto are given two good soups and half a kilo of bread a day. That's the reason for the mob.

19b. Tovia Bozhikowski, *In Fire and Blood*

Monday, April 19, was the day before Passover, and the first day of spring. Sunshine penetrated even to the cheerless corners of the [Warsaw] ghetto, but with the last trace of winter the last hope of the Jews had also disappeared. Those who had remained at their battle stations all night were annoyed by the beauty of the day, for it is hard to accept death in the sunshine of spring.

As members of *Dror,* we were stationed at Nalevskes 33. I stood on the balcony of a building on Nalevskes-Genshe with several friends, where we could watch the German troops who stole into the ghetto. Since early dawn long lines of Germans had been marching—infantry, cavalry, motorized units, regular soldiers, S.S. troops, and Ukrainians.

I wondered what we could do against such might, with only pistols and rifles. But we refused to admit the approaching defeat.

By 6:00 A.M. the ghetto was surrounded. The first German detachment advanced toward Nalevskes. As it neared the crossroads of Nalevskes-Genshe-Franciskaner we opened fire with guns, grenades, and small home-made bombs.

Our bombs and grenades exploded over their heads as they returned our fire. They were excellent targets in the open square, while we were concealed in the buildings. They left many dead and wounded. The alert, confident attitude of our men was impressive. The youthful Jacob shot his pistol continuously, while Abraham Dreyer and Moshe Rubin commanded from windows. Zachariash, *Dror* commander, moved among the men, building their courage. Liaison officers scurried between positions with messages. The battle went on for two hours.

Rivka, an observer, watched the enemy retreat. There were no more Germans on the front street. Zachariash returned beaming from his survey of the battlefield; forty dead and wounded Germans were left behind, but we suffered no losses.

But even in our satisfaction we realized we would eventually be crushed. It was, though, a triumph to gladden the hearts of men who were about to die.

Quite a while passed without a sign of returning German troops. We discussed the battle, and some of us slept, our fingers firmly on our guns. Then our observers reported German tanks on the Maranovski side and German troops crawling along the Genshe walls.

Zachariash had hardly ordered battle readiness when heavy cannonading began. The Germans had set up a barricade on the corner of Genshe and Franciskaner and attacked from its shelter. We shot only on target, for bullets were dear.

During a lull we ascertained dozens of German casualties. Our formations remained intact. We threw a flaming jar of gasoline on their barricades. They replied with incendiary bombs, and we decided to pull back.

Our way led through attics, the avenues of communication in the ghetto. We learned that Genshe 6, which was to be our second position, was surrounded. Our Nalevskes 33 position was flaming. We were cut off. The floors beneath our feet were beginning to burn and the smoke was suffocating.

We had sent out a patrol earlier to find an escape route, but they had not yet returned. The Germans had begun to reach the roofs. We fired at them, and Moshe hit one. The others ran off. We stripped the dead German of his weapons, conscious that we would pay for this with out lives but determined to take as many Germans as we could with us.

Our patrol finally returned and led us back. We continued operations from Kozie 4.

On Wednesday, April 20, I was stationed on Mila 29 under Berel Broida. With me were men who had fought on Zamenhofa Street. For the first time since the fighting began I learned what had happened on other fronts.

After their defeat at Nalevskes-Zamenhofa the Germans no longer approached the ghetto with pomp. Now they moved cautiously, one by one, seeking shelter behind buildings. They massed their strength against our forces concentrated at 28, 32, 38, and 50 Zamenhofa. Our defense was coordinated among groups from *Dror, Hashomer Hatzair,* P.P.R., and Bund. We let the first German troops pass into the ghetto and met them with a hail of bullets and grenades at Zamenhofa and Mila. We surrounded them, and soon the street was littered with German dead.

For the first time since the occupation we watched Germans run in panic. We had suffered one casualty, Yechiel of *'Shomer Hatzair.*

The Germans then tried new tactics. They burned everything in sight. The ghetto was in flames, and the fires spread to the basements, which sheltered many Jews in hiding. Those who were not burned died of bullet wounds. Our people's panic and confusion was overwhelming. We wept not for those who had died but for those who yet lived.

We should have adjusted our strategy to their new methods, but instead of mass resistance we organized isolated, sporadic attacks on German patrols and small units. We attacked at night, when the ghetto was comparatively free of large German detachments. Our losses were heavy, but our spirit remained high.

In the dark, the Germans wore rubber-soled boots to muffle their steps. We wrapped our shoes in rags and were able to sneak up on them. As the German offensive progressed our condition deteriorated. It was impossible to breathe in the cellars, under burning houses. People ran from one refuge to another, but the fire was everywhere. There were often a hundred Jews in cellars which could accommodate ten. A deep fear contributed to our physical and moral decline, fear the Germans would soon locate the *"Malinas."* The cries of infants often put the Germans on the trail of the hidden ones.

On April 24 we were evacuated to a new fighting position at Mila 9. The transfer, under Lutek Rothblatt of Akiva and Pavel of P.P.R., was accomplished in perfect order. At Mila 9 was now concentrated the meager remaining fighters—2,000 men.

We spent the night in the open, waiting for the German assault. We were divided into several groups, guarding the various entrances to the street. Suddenly reports came of Germans at Kozie 24, and we sent more men there. After a brief exchange of shooting several Germans fell and the others set fire to the entire street. It spread to Mila 9. Thousands ran in panic to nearby homes, but there were flames everywhere.

Eight of us gathered to lay plans in one of the burning homes. We knew we could not hold out for long, and decided to send a patrol of four men to the Aryan side to organize an escape route for the others.

At dawn the next day, Sunday, April 25, Haliner and Yeshya of *'Shomer Hatzair,* Dorca of P.P.R., and I set out for the sewerage system. I cannot forget those first moments as we waded into the canal. Hundreds of Jews stood in the filthy, putrid water, doubled up in despair as their little ones lay unconscious at their feet.

We edged our way amid dead and dying. It took us six hours to reach the Aryan side. But at the exit was a booth filled with German guards and Polish police. The police caught the fleeing Haliner and Dorca and turned them over to the Germans. Jeremiah was caught as his foot touched the soil, and shot as he tried to escape. As I stuck out my head a policeman began firing. Luckily, he missed and I ducked back into the canal. I was the only one to return to the ghetto.

I found my unit battling at Kozie 3. We killed six Germans. We fought through the night at Mila 5 and 17, amidst fire, bullets, and exploding mines.

On the nights of May 7 and 8 a few of us tried the canal again. This time we headed for Smotcha Street, but at the exit were again met with shooting and had to turn back. On the way back we had to pass the corner of Walynska and Zamenhofa. We stopped, and Mordecai of *'Shomer Hatzair* went ahead to ascertain the situation. He signaled us to follow, but the minute we entered Zamenhofa shots rang out. We scattered, tossing hand grenades as we ran. The fighting lasted an hour, and a few Germans died. Seven men succeeded in breaking through to Mila 18, but four of them were seriously wounded. Myself, Mordecai, and Israel Canal were cut off from the others. The Germans pursued us until 6 A.M.

After twenty hours of roaming amid ruin and devastation we managed to reach Mila 18. There was not a living being there.

The Germans had apparently made a concentrated attack on these last positions a few hours before our arrival. Rather than surrender, the last of our comrades had committed suicide. The sight broke us completely.

We roamed together through the burned-out streets, over corpses and shattered homes.

That night I joined another group looking for a canal exit on Franciskaner 22 and Nalevskes 37. This time we had better luck. After much wandering we met Kozhik, who headed several emissaries from the Aryan side. They had been searching for us for more than a week. P.P.R. had readied a place for us on the Aryan side.

We returned to the ghetto for our comrades. After forty-eight hours of wandering through the canals, forty of us reached the Aryan side on May 10. From there we were taken by truck to the nearest forest. Had we made contact earlier, the tragedy of Mila 18 would never have happened.

20. THE FINAL SOLUTION

The Nazi plans for the extermination of European Jewry evolved in stages from open-air killings to gas chambers. The first phase was initiated in the summer of 1941, when the Germans invaded Russia. The S.S. forces *(Einsatzgruppen)*, organized into small mobile units at each occupied military front and accorded excellent cooperation by the regular army, machine-gunned to death and then buried thousands of Jews at a time in White Russia, the Ukraine, and Latvia. The sheer horror and depravity of these massacres is captured in the testimony of Mrs. Rivka Yosselevscka, given almost twenty years after the fact at the trial of Adolf Eichmann.

The second phase of European Jewry's annihilation was referred to by the Germans as the Final Solution. Although this program developed slowly from 1939 through 1942, by early 1942 Reinhard Heydrich, chief of the Gestapo and the Reich Main Security Office, was able to reveal it in some detail to his top staff members. The Wannsee Conference, at which the Final Solution was unveiled, marks a decisive turning point in the history of European Jewry. Soon extermination camps were established throughout Poland (Kulmhof, Belzec, Sobibor, Maydanek, Treblinka, Auschwitz), camps whose gas chambers liquidated some three million European Jews in less than three years. The second and third selections describe these camps, first from the perspective of the Jews entering their gates and then from the view of the outside Gentile observers. "The sweetish odor," "a strong smell of something burning," and "smoke rising from the camp" are mute testimony to the destruction of innumerable lives.

All of the following selections are taken from Raul Hilberg, *Documents of Destruction,* copyright 1971 by Raul Hilberg. Used by permission of the publisher, Franklin Watts, Inc.

20a. Rivka Yosselevscka, "Testimony at the Eichmann Trial"

[The witness was born in Zagrodski, a town containing some five hundred Jewish families, in the Pinsk district. Her father, owner of a leather goods shop, was considered a notable there. Mrs. Yosselevscka was married in 1934, and when the Germans arrived she had one child. The events she describes took place in mid-August, 1942.]

Attorney General: Do you remember the Sabbath at the beginning of the Hebrew month of Elul, 1942?

A. I remember that day very well. Jews were not allowed to go to pray, yet they would risk their lives and go into a cellar in the ghetto . . . the only Jews left in the ghetto would endanger their very lives to go into the cellar to pray—very early, before dawn. On that night, there was too much commotion in the ghetto. There was always noise in the ghetto. Germans would be coming in and leaving the ghetto during all hours of the night. But the commotion and noise on that night was not customary, and we felt something in the air.

We did not let our father go into the cellar to hold prayers, but he did not listen to us. He did go down to pray, into the cellar. We saw that the place was full of Germans. They surrounded the ghetto. We went down and asked—there were some of the police that we knew—and we asked what was going on. Why so many Germans in the ghetto?

Presiding Judge: Who were these policemen?

Witness: White Russians. The policemen were White Russians—those we asked. And we asked—why so many Germans in the ghetto? They told us that there was a partisan woman trying to get into the ghetto and mix with us. A group of partisans, and if they succeed in mixing amongst us, they hope not to be caught. This was not true. Our father came up from the cellar, after his prayer. He could not speak to us. He only wished us "a good month." This was the first day of the month. I remember very well—this was the first day of the month of Elul—the month of prayer and before the Jewish New Year. We were told to leave the houses—to take with us only the children.

We were always used to leave the ghetto at short order, because very often they would take us all out for a roll call. Then we would all appear. But we felt and realized that this was not an ordinary roll call, but something very special. As if the Angel of Death was in charge. The place was swarming with Germans. Some four to five Germans to every Jew.

Attorney General: Then all of you were driven out, and were taken to this square—weren't you?

Witness: No, we were left standing in the ghetto. They began saying that he who wishes to save his life could do so with money, jewels, and valuable things. This would be ransom, and he would be spared. Thus we were held until the late afternoon, before evening came.

Presiding Judge: And did the Jews hand over jewels and so on?

Witness: We did not. We had nothing to hand over. They already took all we had before.

Presiding Judge: I see.

Attorney General: Yes. And what happened toward sunrise?

Witness, Yosselevscka: And thus the children screamed. They wanted food, water. This was not the first time. But we took nothing with us. We had no food and no water, and we did not know the reason. The children were hungry and thirsty. We were held this way for twenty-four hours while they were searching the houses all the time—searching for valuables.

In the meantime, the gates of the ghetto were opened. A large truck appeared and all of us were put onto the truck—either thrown, or went up himself.

Attorney General: Did they count the Jews?

A. Yes—they were counted. They entered the ghetto again, and searched for every missing person. We were tortured until late in the evening.

Q. Now—they filled up this truck. And what happened to the people for whom there was no room in the truck?

A. Those for whom there was no room in the truck were ordered to run after the truck.

Q. And you ran with your daughter?

A. I had my daughter in my arms and ran after the truck. There were mothers who had two or three children and held them in their arms—running after the truck. We ran all the way. There were those who fell—we were not allowed to help them rise. They were shot—right there—wherever they fell. All my family was amongst them. When we all reached the destination, the people from the truck were already down and they were undressed—all lined up. All my family was there—undressed, lined up. The people from the truck, those who arrived before us.

Q. Where was that?

A. This was some three kilometers from our village—the marketplace.* There was a kind of hillock. At the foot of this little hill, there was a dugout. We were ordered to stand at the top of the hillock and the four devils shot us—each one of us separately.

Q. Now these four—to what German unit did they belong?

A. They were S.S. men—the four of them. They were armed to the teeth. They were real messengers of the Devil and the Angel of Death.

Q. Please go on—what did you see?

A. When I came up to the place—we saw people naked lined up. But we were still hoping that this was only torture. Maybe there is Hope—hope of living. One could not leave the line, but I wished to see—what are they doing on the hillock? Is there anyone down below? I turned my head and saw that some three or four rows were already killed—on the ground. There were some twelve people amongst the dead. I also want to mention that my child said while we were lined up in the Ghetto, she said, "Mother, why did you make me wear the Shabbat dress; we are being taken to be shot"; and when we stood near the dugout, near the grave, she said, "Mother, why are we waiting, let us run!" Some of the young people tried to run, but they were caught immediately, and they were shot right there. It was difficult to hold on to the children. We took all children not ours, and we carried—we were anxious to get it all over—the suffering of the children was difficult; we all trudged along to come nearer to the place and to come nearer to the end of the torture of the children. The children were taking leave of their parents and parents of their elder people.

Presiding Judge: How did you survive through all this?

Attorney General: She will relate it.

Presiding Judge: Please will you direct the Witness.

Witness: We were driven; we were already undressed; the clothes were removed and taken away; our father did not want to undress; he remained in his underwear. We were driven up to the grave, this shallow. . . .

Attorney General: And these garments were torn off his body, weren't they?

A. When it came to our turn, our father was beaten. We prayed, we

* Interpreter's comment: The Prosecution corrects that the witness did not say the "marketplace," but the witness said "to the place."

begged with my father to undress, but he would not undress, he wanted to keep his underclothes. He did not want to stand naked.

Q: And then they tore them off?

A: Then they tore off the clothing off the old man and he was shot. I saw it with my own eyes. And then they took my mother, and she said, let us go before her; but they caught mother and shot her too; and then there was my grandmother, my father's mother, standing there; she was eighty years old and she had two children in her arms. And then there was my father's sister. She also had children in her arms and she was shot on the spot with the babies in her arms.

Q: And finally it was your turn.

A: And finally my turn came. There was my younger sister, and she wanted to leave; she prayed with the Germans; she asked to run, naked; she went up to the Germans with one of her friends; they were embracing each other; and she asked to be spared, standing there naked. He looked into her eyes and shot the two of them. They fell together in their embrace, the two young girls, my sister and her young friend. Then my second sister was shot and then my turn did come.

Q: Were you asked anything?

A.: We turned toward the grave and then he turned around and asked "Whom shall I shoot first?" We were already facing the grave. The German asked "Who do you want me to shoot first?" I did not answer. I felt him take the child from my arms. The child cried out and was shot immediately. And then he aimed at me. First he held on to my hair and turned my head around; I stayed standing; I heard a shot, but I continued to stand and then he turned my head again and he aimed the revolver at me and ordered me to watch and then turned my head around and shot at me. Then I fell to the ground into the pit amongst the bodies; but I felt nothing. The moment I did feel I felt a sort of heaviness and then I thought maybe I am not alive anymore, but I feel something after I died. I thought I was dead, that this was the feeling which comes after death. Then I felt that I was choking; people falling over me. I tried to move and felt that I was alive and that I could rise. I was strangling. I heard the shots and I was praying for another bullet to put an end to my suffering, but I continued to move about. I felt that I was choking, strangling, but I tried to save myself, to find some air to breathe, and then I felt that I was climbing toward the top of the grave above the bodies. I rose, and I felt bodies pulling at me with their hands, biting at my legs, pulling me down, down. And yet with my last strength I came up on top of the grave, and when I did I did not know the place, so many bodies were lying all over, dead people; I wanted to see the end of this stretch of dead bodies but I could not. It was impossible. They were lying, all dying; suffering; not all of them dead, but in their last sufferings; naked; shot, but not dead. Children crying "Mother," "Father"; I could not stand on my feet.

Presiding Judge: Were the Germans still around?

Witness: No, the Germans were gone. There was nobody there. No one standing up.

Attorney General: And you were undressed and covered with blood?

Witness: I was naked, covered with blood, dirty from the other bodies, with the excrement from other bodies which was poured onto me.

Q.: What did you have in your head?

A.: When I was shot I was wounded in the head.

Q.: Was it in the back of the head?

A.: I have a scar to this day from the shot by the Germans; and yet, somehow I did come out of the grave. This was something I thought I would never live to recount. I was searching among the dead for my little girl, and I cried for her—Merkele was her name—Merkele! There were children crying "Mother!" "Father!"—but they were all smeared with blood and one could not recognize the children. I cried for my daughter. From afar I saw two women standing. I went up to them. They did not know me, I did not know them, and then I said who I was, and then they said, "So you survived." And there was another woman crying "Pull me out from amongst the corpses, I am alive, help!" We are thinking how could we escape from the place. The cries of the woman, "Help, pull me out from the corpses!" We pulled her out. Her name was Mikla Rosenberg. We removed the corpses and the dying people who held on to her and continued to bite. She asked us to take her out, to free her, but we did not have the strength.

Attorney General: It is very difficult to relate, I am sure, it is difficult to listen to, but we must proceed. Please tell us now: after that you hid?

A.: And thus we were there all night, fighting for our lives, listening to the cries and the screams and all of a sudden we saw Germans, mounted Germans. We did not notice them coming in because of the screamings and the shoutings from the bodies around us.

Q.: And then they rounded up the children and the others who had got out of the pit and shot them again?

A.: The Germans ordered that all the corpses be heaped together into one big heap and with shovels they were heaped together, all the corpses, amongst them many still alive, children running about the place. I saw them. I saw the children. They were running after me, hanging on to me. Then I sat down in the field and remained sitting with the children around me. The children who got up from the heap of corpses.

Q.: Then the Germans came again and rounded up the children?

Witness Rivka Yosselevscka: Then Germans came and were going around the place. We were ordered to collect all the children, but they did not approach me, and I sat there watching how they collected the children. They gave a few shots and the children were dead. They did not need many shots. The children were almost dead, and this Rosenberg woman pleaded with the Germans to be spared, but they shot her.

Attorney General: Mrs. Yosselevscka, after they left the place you went right next to the grave, didn't you?

A.: They all left—the Germans and the non-Jews from around the place. They removed the machine guns and they took the trucks. I saw that they all left, and the four of us, we went onto the grave, praying to fall into the grave, even alive, envying those who were dead already and thinking what to do now. I was praying for death to come. I was praying for the grave to be opened and to swallow me alive. Blood was spurting from the grave in many places, like a well of water, and whenever I pass a spring now, I remember the blood which spurted from the ground, from that grave. I was digging with my fingernails, trying to join the dead in that grave. I dug with my fingernails, but the grave would not open. I did not have enough strength. I cried out to my mother, to my father, "Why did they not kill me? What was my sin? I have no one to go to. I saw them all being killed. Why was I spared? Why was I not killed?"

And I remained there, stretched out on the grave, three days and three nights.

Q.: And then a shepherd went by?

A.: I saw no one. I heard no one. Not a farmer passed by. After three days, shepherds drove their herd onto the field, and they began throwing stones at me, but I did not move. At night, the herds were taken back and during the day they threw stones believing that either it was a dead woman or a mad woman. They wanted me to rise, to answer. But I did not move. The shepherds were throwing stones at me until I had to leave the place.

Q.: And then a farmer went by, and he took pity on you.

A.: I hid near the grave. A farmer passed by, after a number of weeks.

Q.: He took pity on you, he fed you, and he helped you join a group of

Jews in the forest, and you spent the time until the summer of '44 with this group, until the Soviets came.

A.: I was with them until the very end.

Q.: And now you are married and you have two children?

A.: Yes.

20b. Viktor Emil Frankl, *From Death Camp to Existentialism*

When one examines the vast amount of material which has been amassed as the result of many prisoners' observations and experiences, three phases of the inmate's mental reactions to camp life become apparent: the period following his admission; the period when he is well entrenched in camp routine; and the period following his release and liberation.

The symptom that characterizes the first phase is shock. Under certain conditions shock may even precede the prisoner's formal admission to the camp. I shall give as an example the circumstances of my own admission.

Fifteen hundred persons had been traveling by train for several days and nights: there were eighty people in each coach. All had to lie on top of their luggage, the few remnants of their personal possessions. The carriages were so full that only the top parts of the windows were free to let in the gray of dawn. Everyone expected the train to head for some munitions factory, in which we would be employed as forced labor. We did not know whether we were still in Silesia or already in Poland. The engine's whistle had an uncanny sound, like a cry for help sent out in commiseration for the unhappy load which it was destined to lead into perdition. Then the train shunted, obviously nearing a main station. Suddenly a cry broke from the ranks of the anxious passengers, "There is a sign, Auschwitz!" Everyone's heart missed a beat at that moment. Auschwitz—the very name stood for all that was horrible: gas chambers, crematoriums, massacres. Slowly, almost hesitatingly, the train moved on as if it wanted to spare its passengers the dreadful realization as long as possible: Auschwitz!

With the progressive dawn, the outlines of an immense camp became visible: long stretches of several rows of barbed wire fences; watchtowers;

searchlights; and long columns of ragged human figures, gray in the grayness of dawn, trekking along the straight desolate roads, to what destination we did not know. There were isolated shouts and whistles of command. We did not know their meaning. My imagination led me to see gallows with people dangling on them. I was horrified, but this was just as well, because step by step we had to become accustomed to a terrible and immense horror.

Eventually we moved into the station. The initial silence was interrupted by shouted commands. We were to hear those rough, shrill tones from then on, over and over again in all the camps. Their sound was almost like the last cry of a victim, and yet there was a difference. It had a rasping hoarseness, as if it came from the throat of a man who had to keep shouting like that, a man who was being murdered again and again. The carriage doors were flung open and a small detachment of prisoners stormed inside. They wore striped uniforms, their heads were shaved, but they looked well fed. They spoke in every possible European tongue, and all with a certain amount of humor, which sounded grotesque under the circumstances. Like a drowning man clutching a straw, my inborn optimism (which has often controlled my feelings even in the most desperate situations) clung to this thought: These prisoners look quite well, they seem to be in good spirits and even laugh. Who knows? I might manage to share their favorable position.

In psychiatry there is a certain condition known as "delusion of reprieve." The condemned man, immediately before his execution, gets the illusion that he might be reprieved at the very last minute. We, too, clung to shreds of hope and believed to the last moment that it would not be so bad. Just the sight of the red cheeks and round faces of those prisoners was a great encouragement. Little did we know then that they formed a specially chosen elite, who for years had been the receiving squad for new transports as they rolled into the station day after day. They took charge of the new arrivals and their luggage, including scarce items and smuggled jewelry. Auschwitz must have been a strange spot in this Europe of the last years of the war. There must have been unique treasures of gold and silver, platinum and diamonds, not only in the huge storehouses but also in the hands of the S.S.

Fifteen hundred captives were cooped up in a shed built to accommodate probably two hundred at the most. We were cold and hungry and there was not enough room for everyone to squat on the bare ground, let alone to lie down. One five-ounce piece of bread was our only food in four days. Yet I heard the senior prisoners in charge of the shed bargain with one member of the receiving party about a tie-pin made of platinum and diamonds. Most of the profits would eventually be traded for liquor—schnapps. I do not remember anymore just how many thousands of marks were needed to purchase the quantity of schnapps required for a "gay evening," but I do know that those long-term prisoners needed schnapps. Under such conditions, who could blame them for trying to dope themselves? There was another group of prisoners who got liquor supplied in almost unlimited quantities by the S.S.: these were the men who were employed in the gas chambers and crematoriums, and who knew very well that one day they would be relieved by a new shift of men, and that they would have to leave their enforced role of executioner and become victims themselves.

Nearly everyone in our transport lived under the illusion that he would be reprieved, that everything would yet be well. We did not realize the meaning behind the scene that was to follow presently. We were told to leave our luggage in the train and to fall into two lines—women on one side, men on the other—in order to file past a senior S.S. officer. Surprisingly enough, I had the courage to hide my haversack under my coat. My line filed past the officer, man by man. I realized that it would be dangerous if the officer spotted my bag. He would at least knock me down; I knew that from previous experience. Instinctively, I straightened on approaching the officer, so that he would not notice my heavy load. Then I was face to face with him. He was a tall man who looked slim and fit in his spotless uniform. What a contrast to us, who were untidy and grimy after our long journey! He had assumed an attitude of careless ease, supporting his right elbow with his left hand. His right hand was lifted, and with the forefinger of that hand he pointed very leisurely to the right or to the left. None of us had the slightest idea of the sinister meaning behind that little movement of a man's finger, pointing now to the right and now to the left, but far more frequently to the left.

It was my turn. Somebody whispered to me that to be sent to the right side would mean work, the way to the left being for the sick and those incapable of work, who would be sent to a special camp. I just waited for things to take their course, the first of many such times to come. My haversack weighed me down a bit to the left, but I made an effort to walk upright. The S.S. man looked me over, appeared to hesitate, then put both his hands on my shoulders. I tried very hard to look smart, and he turned my shoulders very slowly until I faced right, and I moved over to that side.

The significance of the finger game was explained to us in the evening. It was the first selection, the first verdict made on our existence or nonexistence. For the great majority of our transport, about 90 percent, it meant death. Their sentence was carried out within the next few hours. Those who were sent to the left were marched from the station straight to the crematorium. This building, as I was told by someone who worked there, had the word "bath" written over its doors in several European languages. On entering, each prisoner was handed a piece of soap, and then—but mercifully I do not need to describe the events which followed. Many accounts have been written about this horror.

We who were saved, the minority of our transport, found out the truth in the evening. I inquired from prisoners who had been there for some time where my colleague and friend P——— had been sent.

"Was he sent to the left side?"

"Yes," I replied.

"Then you can see him there," I was told.

"Where?" A hand pointed to the chimney a few hundred yards off, which was sending a column of flame up into the gray sky of Poland. It dissolved into a sinister cloud of smoke.

"That's where your friend is, floating up to Heaven," was the answer. But I still did not understand until the truth was explained to me in plain words.

But I am telling things out of their turn. From a psychological point of view, we had a long, long way in front of us from the break of that dawn at the station until our first night's rest at the camp.

Escorted by S.S. guards with loaded guns, we were made to run from the station, past electrically charged barbed wire, through the camp, to the cleansing station; for those of us who had passed the first selection, this was a real bath. Again our illusion of reprieve found confirmation. The S.S. men seemed almost charming. Soon we found out their reason. They were nice to us as long as they saw watches on our wrists and could persuade us in well-meaning tones to hand them over. Would we not have to hand over all our possessions anyway, and why should not that relatively nice person have the watch? Maybe one day he would do one a good turn.

We waited in a shed which seemed to be the anteroom to our disinfecting chamber. S.S. men appeared and spread out blankets into which we had to throw all our possessions, all our watches and jewelry. There were still naïve prisoners among us who asked, to the amusement of the more seasoned ones who were there as helpers, if they could not keep a wedding ring, a medal, or a good-luck piece. No one could yet grasp the fact that everything would be taken away.

I tried to take one of the old prisoners into my confidence. Approaching him furtively, I pointed to the roll of paper in the inner pocket of my coat and said, "Look, this is the manuscript of a scientific book. I know what you will say, that I should be grateful to escape with my life, that that should be all I can expect of fate. But I cannot help myself. I must keep this manuscript at all costs; it contains my life's work. Do you understand that?"

Yes, he was beginning to understand. A grin spread slowly over his face, first piteous, then more amused, mocking, insulting, until he bellowed one word at me in answer to my question, a word that was ever present in the vocabulary of the camp inmates: "Shit!" At that moment I saw the plain truth and did what marked the culminating point of the first phase of my psychological reaction: I struck out my whole former life.

20c. "Notes on Belzec"

1. NOTES BY A GERMAN NONCOMMISSIONED OFFICER [WILHELM CORNIDES] OF AUGUST 31, 1942

Rawa Ruska (Galicia) German House, August 31, 1942, 2:30 P.M.

At 10 minutes past noon I saw a transport train run into the station. On the roof and running boards sat guards with rifles. One could see from a distance that the cars were jammed full of people. I turned and walked along the whole train: it consisted of thirty-eight cattle cars and one passenger car. In each of the cars there were at least sixty Jews (in the case of enlisted men's or prisoner transports these wagons would hold forty men; however, the benches had been removed and one could see that those who were locked in here had to stand pressed together). Some of the doors were opened a crack, the windows crisscrossed with barbed wire. Among the locked-in people there were a few men and most of those were old; everything else was women, girls, and children. Many children crowded at the windows and the narrow door openings. The youngest were surely not more than two years old. As soon as the train halted, the Jews attempted to pass out bottles in order to get water. The train, however, was surrounded by S.S. guards, so that no one could come near. At that moment a train arrived from the direction of Jaroslav; the travelers streamed toward the exit without bothering about the transport. A few Jews who were busy loading a car for the Armed Forces waved their caps to the locked-in people. I talked to a policeman on duty at the railway station. Upon my question as to where the Jews actually came from, he answered: "Those are probably the last ones from Lvov. That has been going on now for five weeks uninterruptedly. In Jaroslav they let remain only eight, no one know why." I asked: "How far are they going?" Then he said: "To Belzec." "And then?" "Poison." I asked: "Gas?" He shrugged his shoulders. Then he said only: "At the beginning they always shot them, I believe."

Here in the German House I just talked with two soldiers from frontline prisoner-of-war camp 325. They said that these transports had lately passed through every day, mostly at night. Yesterday a seventy-car one is supposed to have gone through.

In the train from Rawa Ruska to Cholm, 5:30 P.M.

When we boarded at 4:40 P.M. an empty transport had just arrived. I walked along the train twice and counted fifty-six cars. On the doors had been written in chalk: 60, 70, once 90, occasionally 40—obviously the number of Jews that were carried inside. In my compartment I spoke with a railway policeman's wife who is currently visiting her husband here. She says these transports are now passing through daily, sometimes also with German Jews. Yesterday six children's bodies were found along the track. The woman thinks that the Jews themselves had killed these children—but they must have succumbed during the trip. The railway policeman who comes along as train escort joined us in our compartment. He confirmed the woman's statements about the children's bodies which were found along the track yesterday. I asked: "Do the Jews know then what is happening with them?" The woman answered: "Those who come from far won't know anything, but here in the vicinity they know already. They attempt to run away then, if they notice that someone is coming for them. So, for example, most recently in Cholm where three were shot on the way through the city." "In the railway documents these trains run under the name of resettlement transports," remarked the railway policeman. Then he said that after Heydrich ["Protector" of Bohemia-Moravia] was murdered, several transports with Czechs passed through. Camp Belzec is supposed to be located right on the railway line and the woman promised to show it to me when we pass it.

5:40 P.M. Short stop. Opposite us another transport. I talk to the policemen who ride on the passenger car in front. I ask: "Going back home to the Reich?" Grinning, one of them says: "You know where we come from, don't you? Well, for us the work does not cease." Then the transport train continued—the cars were empty and swept clean; there were thirty-five. In all probability that was the train I saw at 1 P.M. on the station in Rawa Ruska.

6:20 P.M. We passed camp Belzec. Before then, we traveled for some time through a tall pine forest. When the woman called, "Now it comes," one could see a high hedge of fir trees. A strong sweetish odor could be made out distinctly. "But they are stinking already," says the woman. "Oh nonsense, that is only the gas," the railway policeman said laughing. Meanwhile—we had gone on about 200 yards—the sweetish odor was transformed into a strong smell of something burning. "That is from the crematory," says the policeman. A short distance farther the fence stopped. In front of it, one could see a guardhouse with an S.S. post. A double track led into the camp. One track branched off from the main line, the other ran over a turntable from the camp to a row of sheds about 250 yards away. A freight car happened to stand on the table. Several Jews were busy turning the disk. S.S. guards, rifle under the arm, stood by. One of the sheds was open; one could distinctly see that it was filled with bundles of clothes to the ceiling. As we went on, I looked back one more time. The fence was too high to see anything at all. The woman says that sometimes, while going by, one can see smoke rising from the camp, but I could notice nothing of the sort. My estimate is that the camp measures about 800 by 400 yards.

2. ADDITIONAL EYEWITNESS REPORTS

a) A railway policeman at the switchyards in Rzeszow told me the following on August 30, 1942. "In Rzeszow a marble plaque with golden letters will be erected on September 1, because then the city will be free of Jews. The transports with the Jews pass almost daily through the switchyards, are dispatched immediately on their way, and return swept clean, most often in the same evening. In [from] Jaroslav six thousand Jews were recently killed in one day."

b) An engineer told the following in the evening of August 30, 1942, in the German House of Rawa Ruska: "Jews, who for the most part have now been transported away, were employed next to Poles and prisoners-of-war in the work on the drill field which is being built here. The productivity of these construction crews (among them also women) was on the average 30 percent of what would have been achieved by German workers. To be sure, these people received from us only bread—the rest they had to provide themselves. In Lvov recently I have accidentally seen a loading of such a transport. The cars stood at the front of a slope. How these people were driven down by the S.S., sometimes with sticks and horsewhips, and how they were pushed into the cars, that was a sight I won't forget for the rest of my life."

As he told this story the man had tears in his eyes. He was about twenty-six and wore the party emblem. A Sudeten German peasant official, who sat at the same table, remarked on that: "Recently a drunken S.S. man sat in our canteen and he was bawling like a child. He said that he was on duty in Belzec and if that was going to go on for another fourteen days he will kill himself because he can't stand it anymore."

c) A policeman told the following in the beer hall in Cholm on September 1, 1942: "The policemen who escorted the Jewish trains are not allowed in the camp. The only ones who get in are the S.S. and the Ukrainian Special Service (a police formation of Ukrainian volunteers). But these people are doing a good business over there. Recently a Ukrainian visited us, and he had a whole stack of money in notes, and watches and gold and all kinds of things. They find all of that when they put together the clothing and load it." Upon the question as to how these Jews were actually being killed, the policeman answered: "They are told that they must get rid of their lice, and then they must take off their clothes, and then they come into a room, where first off they get a hot blast of air which is already mixed with a small dose of gas. That is enough to make them unconscious. The rest comes after. And then they are burned immediately."

In answer to the question why this whole action is being undertaken in the first place, the policeman said: "Up to now the Jews have been employed as auxiliaries everywhere by the S.S., the Armed Forces, and so on. Naturally they snapped up quite a bit of information and they pass on everything to the Russians. That's why they must go. And then they are also responsible here for the entire black market and driving up prices. When the Jews are gone, one will be able to put into effect reasonable prices again."

Note: Rawa Ruska is located about fifty miles northwest of Lvov. Belzec is located on the Lvov-Cholm railway line, about twenty-five miles northwest of Rawa Ruska.

G. Postwar Turmoil

21. *THE STATE OF ISRAEL*

Out of the suffering of the Holocaust came a renewed sense of the urgency of the Zionist program. Broad segments of world Jewry committed themselves to the establishment of a Jewish state, in order to foreclose the possibility of future calamities. At the same time, concern with the immediate plight of uprooted refugees, unwilling to remain in Europe and unwelcome in many other quarters, moved Jews and non-Jews alike to appeal to the British mandatory authorities to ease their immigration restrictions. Buffeted by international pressures and by a rising tide of violence in Palestine, England admitted failure and turned the problem over to the newly created United Nations. On November 29, 1947, the world organization accepted the majority report of the United Nations Special Committee on Palestine (UNSCOP) and stipulated partition of the strife-torn area into an Arab and a Jewish state. On May 14, 1948, a few hours before the British mandate was to expire, David Ben-Gurion rose in a crowded hall in Tel Aviv to proclaim the establishment of "a Jewish State in the land of Israel—the State of Israel."

Israel's first Prime Minister, David Ben-Gurion (1886–1973), was born David Gryn in Plonsk, a market town in northern Poland, then under Russian rule. Migrating to Palestine in 1906 and working as a farm laborer and then a journalist, Ben-Gurion, as General-Secretary of the Histadrut (Confederation of Labor) in the 1920s, was able to coalesce various political factions together with the Histadrut into Mapai (the Worker's United Party)—the faction that led Israel's governments during every one of its first twenty-five years. The de facto leader of Palestinian Jewry through the 1930s and 1940s, Ben-Gurion's reflections of that momentous May day provide a revealing survey of the critical years prior to Israel's emergence as a state (selection 20a).

The state that was called into being in May, 1948, was immediately attacked by its Arab neighbors and had to wage war in order to substantiate its claims to existence. During the entire first quarter-century of its history, Israel has never been free of the threat of renewed warfare, a threat that materialized in 1956, 1967, and 1973. While directing a major share of her resources and energies toward military preparedness, the fledgling state has faced other problems as well, particularly the economic and social stresses related to the absorption of large numbers of immigrants. During the first two and a half decades of its existence, rapid strides have also been made toward the development of a modern, technologically advanced society, with a rich culture all its own. In our second selection, based on a series of interviews with young Israelis, we sense the overwhelming concern with military security, the recurring problems of immigrant absorption, strong pride in Israel's achievements, frustration at the inability to do more, and serious questioning as to the ultimate goals of the new state.

The first selection is taken from *Ben-Gurion Looks Back,* edited by Moshe Pearlman (New York, 1965). Reprinted by permission of Simon and Schuster, Inc. Copyright © 1965 by Moshe Pearlman and David Ben-Gurion. The second comes from *The New Israelis,* by David Schoenbrun with Robert and Lucy Szekely. Copyright © 1973 by David Schoenbrun. Reprinted by permission of Atheneum Publishers, Inc.

21a. *Ben-Gurion Looks Back*

REFLECTIONS ON INDEPENDENCE DAY

Moshe Pearlman. Ben-Gurion, your greatest moment must have been your declaration of Israel's independence on the 14th of May, 1948, and I don't suppose there is anything about that day you can ever forget. What were your thoughts at this historic ceremony?

Ben-Gurion. I do not know that I can recapture all the thoughts that crowded into my mind on that occasion, but I can remember the core of my thinking, for it was something I had dreamed of and fought for the whole of my life, as had most of the Jews in Israel and many many Jews outside: I thought, now at last we are responsible for our own destiny. It is ours to shape. We had been a minority element in scores of lands for almost two thousand years, our fate determined by others. Sometimes, and in some lands, we enjoyed kind treatment, there was tolerance and the opportunity to develop. At other times, we were restricted, hounded, persecuted, murdered. We had just lost six million of our people, slaughtered by the Nazis. For centuries we had been like flowers in a wood, some plucked by friendly hands, given water and nurtured, others trampled underfoot and crushed. At no time could we be ourselves, enjoy independence, with the freedom to live a normal national life on our own soil, making our own decisions affecting our destiny. Now the hour had struck. We were independent once again. These reflections were uppermost in my mind.

Coupled with them was the knowledge that while I was reading the Declaration of Independence the armies of the neighboring Arab States were massing on our borders ready to march across.

When, some hours later, I went to inspect the damage done by the Egyptian bombing which marked the opening of the Arab war on the new State, I remember thinking that if we were now responsible for our destiny, the rational question might well be whether in a few days or a few weeks we would have a destiny to shape. For we had no planes to match their planes, no artillery, no tanks. Yet none of us at the time had any doubt about the outcome.

A few days earlier, I had received an urgent message from General George Marshall. He was United States Secretary of State at the time, and he urged me desperately not to go ahead with my declared intention of proclaiming independence. I had had similar messages from several other governments and distinguished individuals, some friends, some not so friendly. Marshall was a friend, a true friend, and he tried to discourage me not because he was opposed to a Jewish State but because he thought we would be quickly destroyed by the overwhelmingly superior forces of the Arab States. He thought they would attack us if we declared our statehood, and our small, poorly armed forces would be overrun. He begged me to wait for a more favorable political climate and in the meantime international arrangements might be made whereby the United Nations Partition Resolution could be implemented in some form.

Here, then, was the counsel of a friend and the military appreciation of our situation by one of the world's outstanding soldiers. On the face of it, such advice was not to be dismissed lightly. Yet it could not deflect us from our chosen course. For Marshall could not know what we knew—what we felt in our very bones: that this was our historic hour; if we did not live up to it, through fear or weakness of spirit, it might be generations or even centuries before our people were given another historic opportunity—if indeed we would be alive as a national group. However grave might be the repercussions of the decision to declare our independence, I knew that the future would be infinitely worse for my people if we did not do so. We decided to go ahead and proclaim our independence as planned. Let me add that there was absolute unanimity among all my colleagues in the thirteen-member National Administration [the body which became the Provisional Government of Israel the moment the Proclamation had been read and signed].

I remember that these thoughts were in my mind when, on my way home from the late afternoon Independence ceremony, I watched the people dancing in the streets, celebrating the historic act to which we had all put our hand. I did not dance with them, though I felt with them the emotion of the moment. It was something to see—the sheer joy in their faces, the light in their eyes, the exuberance of their movements, all caught in a surge of ecstasy. They were right to dance, I thought, even though I was all too aware—as many of the dancers must have been aware—of the dangers that faced us and the sacrifice we would suffer in defending the statehood we had just gained.

It had been the same, I reflected, some five and a half months earlier when the United Nations passed their Partition resolution calling for the end of the Mandate over Palestine and the establishment of independent Arab and Jewish States. I was asleep when that U.N. decision came through, on the 29th of November, 1947, because of the time difference between New York and Jerusalem, and I was awakened to be given the news. I was in Kalia at the time, on the northern edge of the Dead Sea, where I had gone to rest. Next day I returned to Jerusalem to find the streets alive with rejoicing and celebration. I rejoiced too, but I was much concerned with the morrow; the attacks did in fact come the next day.

As a matter of fact, on the night of Independence I was also awakened—twice. The first time was to hear the news of President Truman's declaration recognizing the new State of Israel. The second was to be persuaded to make an Independence broadcast to the world—it was about four o'clock in the morning, so that with the time difference it reached New York listeners in the evening. While I was broadcasting, listeners heard the crump of bombs landing near the improvised Tel Aviv studio from an Egyptian bomber.

As soon as I had finished my broadcast, I went to inspect the bomb damage, and the plea and warning of General Marshall came back to me. Would he prove right? I did not think so, though I knew his fears were well grounded. I knew equally well in my heart that no one outside Israel could possibly feel as we did, that we *had* to seize the historic moment and that despite the odds we would win. It is probably Clausewitz who talked of the conflict of wills in warfare: the stronger of the two wills wins. I knew, with Marshall, that we would be vastly outnumbered, and that we would face an enormous superiority of arms. But I also knew, what Marshall did not know, that our will would prove stronger—not because we were more militaristic than the Arabs but because we would be fighting for a cause and also because defeat for us would mean national destruction. For the armies of the neighboring Arab States, it was largely a battle for spoils. Failure for them would not mean the loss of their countries, nor an end to their existence as national entities.

It is also true, as Marshall indicated, that we had only a partisan force to fling against the regular armies of the Arab States. These armies, fully fledged military machines, had been trained for the kind of warfare that would soon be upon us. They were equipped with the standard weapons appropriate to a regular army, and were organized in the standard formations suitable for large-scale warfare—corps, divisions, brigades. We had the Haganah, an underground defense force with all the limitations of a force that had had to train and operate in secrecy and conceal its weapons from the Mandatory authorities—no heavy weapons, small formations, an emphasis on local defense, much of it static. As a matter of fact it was only two months earlier, in March, 1948, that for the first time we had undertaken engagements in which we committed a force as large as a brigade—and a very small brigade at that.

But I had read my Washington, as Marshall had also certainly done, though no doubt with different eyes. What struck me so deeply was the nature of Washington's army—they were underfed, underarmed, with no proper clothing and meager transport. They could have been called a rabble. Yet they had the stronger will—and they were victorious. I don't say there is not a limit to the odds that can be faced and overcome. I do say, however, that the will of a people and the spirit and morale of its army are immeasurably powerful factors in war and can be decisive. I knew they would be decisive in our war of independence.

In the event, General Marshall proved to be right in his reading of his intelligence reports: the Arab armies *did* attack soon after I had finished reading the Independence Scroll; they *did* march across our frontiers; and they *did* outnumber us very heavily in men and arms. He was wrong in his prediction of the outcome. (So were many other military experts, including Britain's Field Marshal Montgomery who, someone told me, had uttered the thought that "the Arabs would hit Israel for six!") I do not blame Marshall for being mistaken—he was pleased, by the way, to have been proved wrong—for he could not have known our people as we know ourselves. He could not have known of what our people would be capable when roused to a supreme effort—as they were by the threat of destruction.

Another figure springs to mind as I talk of "threat of destruction" and of people "roused to a supreme effort"—Winston Churchill. And something I witnessed in London not long after he became Prime Minister may well have had a bearing on my decision to go ahead with the Declaration of Independence.

I had flown to England by a circuitous route in the early summer of 1940, leaving Haifa on the 25th of April and reaching London on the 1st of May—some three weeks after Germany invaded Norway and Denmark, nine days before she entered Holland and Belgium, nine days before Churchill replaced Neville Chamberlain as Prime Minister. I was Chairman of the Jewish Agency for Palestine at the time, and I had come to England to try to persuade the British Government to authorize the establishment of a Jewish army and to get it to utilize Palestine as a supply base for the forces in the Middle East by developing her industry and agriculture. I was also anxious to secure a change in the Mandatory Administration, particularly the replacement of the High Commissioner, Sir Harold McMichael. Because of my position I had been granted the appropriate military priority for a seat in the plane, even though both the Palestine Administration and the Colonial Office were vehemently opposed to the Jewish Army project and to developing Palestine as a supply base. They were highly reluctant to do anything which they thought would strengthen the Jewish position in Palestine, even though it would at the same time be promoting the Allied war effort. They had even refused recruitment to the forces of Palestinian Jews who had rushed to join up as soon as war broke out, and only at the insistence of short-staffed local British military commanders did they finally agree to accept them—but even then only at the same rate as Arabs volunteered. Since there was almost no Arab volunteering, this proviso soon had to go by the board, and Palestinian Jews were accepted into British regiments; but under political pressure, many of them at first were kept on noncombatant duties.

We felt that we had the right to fight, and we had the same right as other nations to fight under our own banner as part of the Allied Forces—particularly as Hitler had singled us out for special treatment and had declared war on us long before he had attacked anyone else. Soon after the outbreak of war we had urged the acceptance of a Jewish fighting formation.

In London, Weizmann [Dr. Chaim Weizmann, later to become Israel's first President] had been most active, seeing members of the government, army generals, members of Parliament, newspaper editors, exhorting, entreating, begging them to accept our help. But the British Government showed no disposition to do so. I resolved to add my voice to the efforts of my London colleagues. There were a few members of the government who were friendly and sympathetic to our cause, the most outstanding being Churchill. But there was strong opposition from the very ministerial colleagues who were directly responsible for Palestinian affairs, notably Malcolm MacDonald, who was Colonial Secretary under Chamberlain, and Lord Lloyd, who replaced him when Churchill became Prime Minister. (Though let me say right away that, unlike Malcolm MacDonald, Lloyd was a sincere and honest man who spoke his mind straightforwardly, and I always respected him even though he was an anti-Zionist.) Though Churchill was the kind of man who could have pushed through policy despite opposition, particularly after he became Prime Minister, it was perhaps understandable that our affairs were not at the top of his list of urgent priorities. The project was shelved for the time being, and Palestinian Jewish volunteers continued to serve in British regiments—they were now allowed in combat units. Only in 1944 was our proposal finally approved, though in limited form, and the Jewish Brigade Group was set up. Credit for this must go largely to Weizmann and Moshe Sharett.

But this is not the story I wanted to tell you. This is just the background to my presence in London in 1940. It is what I witnessed there at the time that I recalled some eight years later on the eve of our independence. What I witnessed was the Battle of Britain, the battle that turned the tide, the battle of "the few against the many." It climaxed several terrible months, perhaps the most terrible and the greatest months in Britain's history, when she stood alone, after the fall of Norway, Denmark, Holland, Belgium, and France, with Italy linked to Germany, the United States neutral, German submarines taking a savage toll of British shipping and invasion expected daily. Then came the nightly attacks by the Luftwaffe, with their massive destruction and dreadful casualties to the British people. I saw the nightly trek to the shelters at the sound of the siren, and was impressed by the orderly and cheerful manner in which the people behaved. I sometimes saw them when they emerged after the long night to find their homes in ruins. I saw them go about their business during the day as if the nightly horror did not exist, and proceed without panic to the shelters when there were daylight raids. I heard the defiant tones of Churchill on the radio, and I saw defiance growing daily in the expressions and actions of the people. "We can take it" was their slogan at the time, though any rational analysis of the respective strength of Germany and Britain would have shown that they did not have a chance. Few of them could have told you how they would win, but they were utterly certain that they would.

I was enormously impressed by the spirit of this people who faced such odds with such confidence. My faith in human capacity has always been strong, and what I witnessed then reinforced it.

As a matter of fact, I wrote something of this in a letter home to my colleagues at the time—on the 21st of August, 1940: "Last week was the turning point in the war. . . . Hitler suffered his greatest defeat. . . . Since the 8th of August, more than 700 German aircraft have been destroyed. . . . The danger is not yet past. Churchill realizes this better than most. In his great speech yesterday, he did not gloss over the difficulties. . . . The general spirit of confidence is based on the will and capacity to fight. . . . This has been an extraordinary example of HOW IMPORTANT IS MORAL FORCE IN THE BALANCE OF MILITARY POWER. ENGLAND'S VICTORY THIS WEEK IS PRIMARILY A VICTORY OF COURAGE AND SELF-CONFIDENCE. IT WAS THE HEROIC VICTORY OF A FREE PEOPLE DETERMINED TO REMAIN FREE AT ALL COSTS."

In Tel Aviv in May, 1948—Jerusalem was then under siege and isolated—as I pondered the dangers of an independence declaration and the odds against us, I recalled the men and women of London during the blitz. And I said to myself: "I have seen what a people is capable of achieving in the hour of supreme trial. I have seen their spirit touched by nobility. This is what man can do. This is what the Jewish people can do."

We went ahead.

Of course my faith in my own people in Israel was not a blind faith. The story of the few against the many was the story of our lives. I knew what they could do because I had seen what they had accomplished in Palestine against adversity. I had seen it almost from the moment I had stepped off the ship at Jaffa as a young man of nineteen in the summer of 1906 after a two week's voyage—steerage—aboard a Russian freighter.

I had seen young intellectuals, who had forsaken the material comforts of middle-class life in Eastern Europe and who had never done a day's work with their hands, now laboring in the resistant fields of the land they sought to rebuild, back-breaking work from dawn to dusk under the hot Middle Eastern sun, with precious little nourishment that could be secured from the pittance they were paid. And they stuck it out, year in year out. I had seen some of them braving the heat and humidity of swamps which they cleared for cultivation, and braving disease which took its vicious toll. Yet they stood their ground and did not desert the swamps for healthier climes. I had seen them beat off attacks by Arab marauders. I had seen the rise of the kibbutzim, seen young Jewish men and women respond to the challenge of pioneering and not be put off by hardship. Later, during the organized nationwide Arab onslaughts on the Jewish community, I had seen how my people reacted to physical danger; and when the Mandatory Administration tried to curb our development, I had seen how they reacted to political danger. The story of Haganah, the story of "illegal" immigration, the story of the creation of farm settlements in isolated areas, all accomplished under conditions of adversity, of constant physical danger and rigorous administrative restrictions, showed courage, ingenuity, and a sense of purpose. I do not say that other peoples would not have displayed the same qualities under these circumstances, given the same historic background. I say only that my people did. And this knowledge was part of me, pervading my mind at all times, and especially in moments of major decision. I said that the British experience of 1940 had made an impact on me, and I had remembered it in 1948 on the eve of our independence. Coupled with my knowledge of what my own people had done, it enabled me to make one of the greatest decisions in my life with comparative ease—that is, with a minimum of doubt and a maximum of confidence.

21b. David Schoenbrun, *The New Israelis*

Philippe Rosenau is preparing his doctorate in mathematics at Tel Aviv University. His wife is finishing her B.A. degree. They have been married for six months, hope to start raising a family when they finish their studies and get teaching appointments.

"I vote Herut [rightist party]. I believe in the strongest defense of Israel. We should waste no time arguing about the justification for our being in

Palestine. That is a trap for endless discussion, without point. We are here. The U.N. itself agreed on the partition of Palestine. There is nothing to discuss.

"For Jews, there is only one question. Do we have the right to live? There is only one answer. Yes, we do. So let's get on with it.

"Never in history has a people been so generous, so open to brotherhood as we Jews. We want to live in peace with our neighbors. We open our doors to our brothers and sisters of the world.

"America vaunts itself as the country welcoming immigrants, offering a new life, free of religious persecution. But that was in the past. Today America has quotas on immigration. I do not say this in criticism. Let America do what it thinks best for itself. But do not tell us what to do.

"No, no Americans have the right to say that we must let the Arabs come back, unless they are ready to return their own lands to the Indians. Are the Russians ready to return the huge hunk of Poland the Russian bear bit off in World War II? Will the East Germans take back the refugees they expelled? Who are they to give us lessons?

"There are almost half a million Arabs living in Israel quite freely. Myself, I think they ought to leave, for, as free as they are, they are a small minority of Moslems among the Jews. I do not want to live like that; that is why I'm glad my parents brought me here as a boy from Poland, where Jews could not live a decent life in freedom. If the Arabs want to stay, let them stay. But I think everyone is happier living among his own. If the Palestinians had their own country, they could spend their energies building for themselves instead of the stupidity of trying to drive us out.

"I understand that the Arabs living today look upon us as invaders of Arab Palestine. Historically they are wrong; Palestine is not exclusively Arab. But from their viewpoint, yes, I know how they feel. But we Jews must stand together for our own rights. When they see it is hopeless, when they have a state of their own, then there will be hope of peace. Not before. And, alas, not soon.

"American immigrants do not come here looking for freedom; they have freedom in America. They come either out of frustration with American life or looking for some kind of ideal society in Israel. These are the wrong reasons. They should come only because they want to live as a majority among their fellow Jews; then they would not be so disillusioned.

"One day, I hope that Israel will have such a society that it will attract people who are not persecuted but are idealists. We are not there yet. But, remember, our government is only just going to celebrate our twenty-fifth anniversary. That's a very short time and I think we have done fabulously well so fast."

Philippe listened to our question and replied, "No, of course I am not satisfied. I know there have been failures. Our government calls itself socialist but it has failed to solve elementary social problems, even educational problems. Take the Afro-Asian slum of Hatikva, here in Tel Aviv. Why, we should pay double the salary for a teacher in Hatikva as against the rich districts of Tel Aviv. We should attract the best teachers to the disadvantaged children. Instead, the children with the best-educated parents, who help them at home, get the best teachers in school.

"The pretension of equality is at the root of our social problem. Everyone may be equal under the law, but not in social and psychological terms. We should recognize the difference between equality in theory and equality in practice, between de facto and de jure freedoms. That's our problem. I think many other countries, even the freest, have the same problem."

Yitzhak was born in Israel and his parents were born in Palestine, a family of old settlers. His father works in the post office. He is taking his degree in economics at Tel Aviv University. He is twenty-four.

"Maybe it's because we came a long time ago, but I do not believe in Zionism. Zion exists and we have a tremendous job to make our Jewish state strong and viable. Waves of immigration are very troublesome, costly, a great burden now. This sounds selfish, but nothing is more important now than strengthening the state.

"The Arabs get more help than Israel. They get help from Russia and the United States both. They get help and arms from the French. They have oil billions. The U.N. is pro-Arab and anti-Israel. We have had some help from America and American Jews, for which we are grateful—vital help. But we have had to do most of the work and fighting ourselves against terrible odds.

"I vote for the Gahal party. I think we should keep most of the territories, keep the Arab guns as far away as possible.

"Yes, there are classes here that are disadvantaged but also there is great social mobility. They should study and work harder instead of complaining and looking for handouts. Like some of the new immigrants, too.

"No, I don't oppose the program of *aliya;* I support immigration, but at slower rates and with less special privileges."

Esther, at twenty-five, is a dental student. She came to Israel from

Casablanca when she was seventeen. Her French is better than her Hebrew. She is a militant in the Civil Rights Movement for Sephardim.

"Our system here in Israel makes no allowance for Oriental culture. It is all European-based. Perhaps that is necessary to some extent, for European culture is more modern, but it is overemphasized and not enough allowance is made for cultural lag and cultural shock, affecting more than half the population, which is of Afro-Asian origin.

"Since so many Afro-Asian Jews are dark-skinned, while Europeans are lighter-skinned, we begin to see an outline of racial distinction coincidental with class and cultural distinctions. The government denies this. My fellow students deny this, but it is the simple truth. Look around you; you will see how they cluster in groups, how they segregate.

"Yes, true, it works both ways, the Sephardim also tend to segregate themselves, but mainly because they have not had the special training they need.

"No, that's all that interests me. I care nothing about politics itself. No, no, the civil rights movement and my dental studies—that's already a lot."

Beni was born in a Nazi camp. Somehow his parents survived, kept him alive, and brought him, as a baby, to Israel in 1948.

His father had been a farm manager in Galicia, in Poland. His mother ran a grocery store. They both work now for a grocer. Beni is in the army but taking courses for his degree in history.

"I finished my army service but signed up for another three years because the army is financing my education. Without the army, I would not have an education; that is, a university education. It is wonderful what they do for us.

"Of course I'm a student. Why do you ask? Oh, being in the army does not stop me being a student. They help me study. Not a student like normal students? I guess not, if you mean doing nothing but going to class. But you know many young Israelis do not only go to class. We are not professional students.

"I am religious. I go by the Bible, for religion and for history. I hope to teach classical Jewish history.

"I vote Gahal. Many of my friends do. Maybe next time I'll vote Avoda, a government party. One has to be realistic, support the government, push it in the direction one wants. We cannot afford a severe split. We must be united.

"Golda does a good job. She's a juggler. Keeps all the balls in the air, lets nothing fall.

"What we need most is an unequivocal guarantee from America that you will not let Israel go down. We'll do the rest.

"Israel may be in the Middle East, but our future is with the West."

Iliezer, twenty-two, is taking his degree in law. He is an Israeli, born and bred, third generation of his family born in Palestine, then Israel.

"You want to know what we're really like? We're what you call 'square' in America, and we don't think it is an insult.

"The American kids, they'd die if they thought they were square. Nonconformism is the new American conformism. They make me sick.

"I've smoked hash. Don't like it. Don't like whisky, either. Awful taste. I know there's a lot that's wrong, but I can get along. I can make my way. If everybody did the same, we'd be all right."

We sat in the garden, in the cool of evening, in the graceful home of Amnon Rubenstein, Dean of the Law School of Tel Aviv University. His handsome brunette wife, Rowena, had made a fruit punch and was suggesting a "spike" of vodka. It was too hot a day for any alcohol, so we gratefully filled up on the punch alone as we told of our experiences in Jerusalem.

Dean Rubenstein, a fit-looking man in his early forties, is a well-known columnist and television commentator, a cultured, witty, well-informed man about Israel.

"Well," he said, "as so often is true in a discussion of that kind, they all were right and all were wrong. Foreign criticism is very helpful but, as is natural, is always resented. That's why Ari said, 'Why don't you make a sacrifice, a contribution before you shoot off?' But, it's good for us to listen to new immigrants. That is how our society will continue to improve itself.

"Among youth, they can work it out. But it gets more passionate between the youth and their parents, the youth and the government. There is certainly a generation gap here in Israel. It is composed of many factors.

"Peace and war, this is the major issue. Those who must do the fighting should be listened to, and I agree that our government has, in many sectors, a hard line. But Ari is right when he says that the new immigrants, particularly from America, carry a special chip on their shoulders—a kind of passionate attachment to their own alienation.

"We don't have that kind of alienation here—not at all. Maybe our biggest danger is the opposite. You will surely find a good deal of conformism amongst Israeli youth. The majority is more like your own 'silent majority' than like the S.D.S."

Rowena Rubenstein came back to the garden carrying a platter with a big pitcher and tall frosted glasses. It was one of the few Israeli specialties we loved; most of the time they served salted nuts, cheese crackers—everything to make you thirsty and hold the water until you felt you would burst of bloat. This was iced coffee, filled with balls of ice cream, a joy in summertime Tel Aviv.

"My students are, to a degree you do not have in the States, career-oriented, serious, pragmatic, and, to put it bluntly, very square," said Dean Rubenstein.

"It is not easy for progressive Americans to relate to them. They are intelligent, excellent students, mature, and hardworking. But they are not sufficiently curious intellectually. They are not trained for free discussion and argument as they are in American universities. Sometimes you look at them and see row after row of inkwells that you are pouring facts into and that they pour back into exams. That is not very inspiring for a good teacher. It's our own fault. We ought to make changes in the early educational process."

The dean thought a moment and ate some ice cream.

"We have had a turbulent history. We have lived with crisis. It is inevitable, I guess, that a new generation comes along that wants normalcy. That could be healthy, but on one condition. It's something that worries me. If they are pragmatic, that's one thing. But if they are indifferent, that's something else. I'm not yet sure where the majority is going, to a cool intellectual, responsible politics—fine!—or to a material acquisition of goods and comforts, leaving the affairs of state to others, in search of the middle-class bourgeois life for itself; then, not so fine. In fact, that would be tragic.

"I cannot agree with the student who said, 'If Israel is going to be just another state, then to hell with it.' After all, this is my country, how can I say the hell with it? But there is something very important in the thought that Israel must not be 'just another state.' No, it must not be and it is not.

"I hope the young generation will not forget the origins of this country. We do not ask them all to be Chaim Weizmann, Golda Meir, or Moshe Dayan. They don't want to be heroes. Fine! We have enough heroes. But Israel is a hope, a promise, an example, and it would be tragic to lose this. I do not think we will."

We asked to meet a student leader at Tel Aviv University and were told to start with Yoel. The friends who recommended Yoel had a suppressed smile but would not explain why. We discovered why when we met him.

Yoel has dark brown hair, a thick beard, is very fat, active, noisy—the type known as "irrepressible." He is twenty-seven years old, getting on a bit to be a student leader, even in Israel where students are older.

Yoel is a student organizer. When we asked what he organized he said, "Well, everything, but my main concern is organizing immigration of students to Israel and caring for new immigrants when they come here."

We were surprised. This was not exactly what we thought student organizers did. Later we met many other student activists, concerned about politics, social affairs, course orientation, college reform, the kind of issues that motivate student activists in other countries, although not in the same numbers or with anything like the passions on campuses in the Western world. Israeli students are very different from their counterparts elsewhere.

Yoel began by giving us a dissertation on Israel's right to be in Palestine. We told him we had gone into that thoroughly on other levels and wanted most to hear from him, as a student leader, the principal interests and concerns of Israeli students.

"We are most concerned about our borders; that is, how to get peace on our borders. Everyone will tell you peace is the first concern. But there are many arguments on how to achieve it and what our borders should be. I think, and the majority of students here think, that we must keep Jerusalem and the Golan Heights and maybe a strong defensive position in the Sinai, in face of Egypt, but all the rest should go back.

"There are almost a million Arabs on the West Bank. If we hold it, annex it, what kind of a state will Israel be, part Jewish, part Arab? No, that is not possible. Also, we are not colonialists, not imperialists. We must not rule over Arabs. Not on the West Bank, not in Gaza. On the other hand, the Arabs must agree to let Jews live in ancient Jewish settlements. Why should the Jews not live in Hebron, a historic Jewish city? Do the Christians and Arabs not live in Nazareth, in freedom under Israel? We should place tough conditions on freedom for Jews if we give back Arab lands.

"We favor the creation of a Palestinian state for the Arabs of Palestine, just as we have a Jewish state. But on condition that they don't use their territory to make war upon us. That is the main problem involved in return of territories, which is a major step toward peace. How to be sure that the Arabs won't use returned territories as a launching ramp for war—that is the question, the big question. I don't know the answer."

Yoel scratched his stomach, hitched up his trousers, frowned. An idea was gestating and troubling him.

"Frankly, we need a new 'cultural revolution,' something like the fervor of 1948. Our rich citizens should open their arms and purses for the immigrants and take a big load off the state budget, so that the state could do more for old immigrants, thus ending the rivalry and jealousy between the old immigrants, the Afro-Asians, living in bad conditions, and the new immigrants from Russia, who get good new accommodations."

We kept trying to steer this student leader to talk to us about student affairs.

"You want to know about our students. Well, the truth is they are not very idealistic. Partly it is our educational system, which teaches us that Israel is a great country, our leaders miracle-workers—as they are—and that we are right about everything. This tends to make us self-satisfied, even arrogant.

"Since we are a great country, why should we not have a great life for ourselves, make a lot of money, and so forth? Perhaps, too, the pendulum had to swing from our idealistic parents to a more pragmatic generation. Interested only in ourselves, I admit.

"You know, I organized a big public meeting between American students here and Israeli students. There are twelve thousand registered Israeli students at Tel Aviv University. Only four showed up for the meeting. The Americans were very disappointed and hurt.

"I went around and saw my fellow students the next day to find out what had happened. They told me they all supported *aliya,* immigration, particularly of Americans, but they had too much to do—their studies, part-time jobs—and had no time for meetings. That's true, you know; a lot of the students have to work, and the school study schedules are heavy. It's hard to organize student activities here. And then the students are older, and don't care much about student activities. In truth, they are not students; they are men and women getting a degree."

Yoel frowned again; he was unhappy all through the interview, not with us, not with our questions, but with the answers that the truth obliged him to make.

"You know, there's a lot of bullshit along with the truth. I was a student, I worked part-time. I had a tough schedule, but I found time to concern myself with general activities. I'm only twenty-seven, so I'm part of the young generation, but I must say that those five years younger than myself are already different from me. I think the young generation, below twenty-five, looks like a selfish one, without social conscience. I don't like it, I fear it; it's not good for Israel. It's not very Jewish. They're a new kind of Israeli, these kids, a new kind of Jew. They worry me.

"They all worry me—the Ashkenazim, who don't care about anything but getting ahead for themselves, and the Black Panthers, who make me sick imitating the Black Power rebels in America. That makes no sense at all. The two extremes are bad: pragmatists without social concern and rebels without a true cause. Oh, sure, the Panthers and other disadvantaged Israelis have a real grievance, but a grievance is not a cause.

"What's the difference? Well, a grievance is tactical. I mean, things are not being done efficiently, so complain. Okay. But a cause is strategic; it grows out of a bad social policy, a bad philosophy. That's not the case in Israel. Our social philosophy is good, but not always carried out as well as possible. The Black Panthers don't make this distinction."

Yoel turned to his friend Michael Kleiner to ask what he thought. Michael is the grandson of the owner of the Rowal cafés of Tel Aviv, a rich leading family of Israel.

"I think we have talked ourselves into believing we are 'super-Jews,' " said Michael.

"In 1948, our parents created this state against all odds, against the whole world. Besides, Jews have played an extraordinary role in world history, well beyond our numbers. Moses, Jesus, Spinoza, Marx, Einstein, Freud—the greatest thinkers of history. Jews are rarely average; we are either very good or very bad, very idealistic or not at all. We are a unique people, a chosen people, chosen for exemplary fortune or misfortune. Maybe now, at last, we will become ordinary people. Is that good or bad? I really don't know."

Michael's intervention recalled to mind a story told us by Walter Eytan when he was Israeli Ambassador to Paris.

One day, his French driver asked him, "Your Excellency, how many of you are there in the world?"

"You mean Israelis?" asked Eytan.

"No, I mean Jews," said the Frenchman. "How many Jews are there?"

"Well, we do not have a precise census, but something around thirteen and a half million," Eytan replied.

"Ah," said the Frenchman. "Now, Monsieur l'Ambassadeur, can you tell me how many Chinese there are?"

"Oh, about seven hundred and fifty million."

"C'est remarquable! Seven hundred and fifty million Chinese and only thirteen and a half million Jews. How come I never meet any Chinese?"

It is true that one meets many Jews and few Chinese around the world. It is true that Jews have had an impact on world history and still have an impact on world affairs out of all proportion to the numbers of Jews in the world or the numbers of Israelis, one thousandth of the world's population. Sometimes the Jews change the world, as with Einstein. Sometimes they are the victims of a world shock, as in the tragic murder of the Israelis at the height of the XXth Olympiad in Munich in September, 1972.

One cannot truly say that the Jews chose their fate, their geniuses, their tragedies. Only the most religious can believe they were chosen. Whatever the truth, their fate has been and is out of all proportion to their numbers.

Would they willingly choose to lose their genius if it meant losing their tragedy?

To judge from the attitudes of the new Israelis, the new Jews of Israel, one is tempted to say yes. Young Israelis certainly do not seek an exemplary role in the world, even in Israel itself. If this tendency is confirmed by the years ahead, then we may be living on the threshold of a complete change in Jewish life and in the Jewish role in the world.

We want to emphasize the words "if" and "may be," for it is too early in the evolution of the new generation to make definitive statements, but, as conscientious reporters, we feel it is legitimate to mention the existence of this new, startlingly different tendency.

That we found strong evidence of this tendency in the general population of the young is one thing; that it also evidenced itself so sharply among the college and university students, the elite, the future intellectual leaders, is even more persuasive.

22. *SOVIET JEWRY*

Since 1967, dramatic expressions of national consciousness and militant assertions of national rights on the part of Soviet Jews have surprised observers both within and without the Soviet Union. This national consciousness is not a thing of the immediate past but of longer duration, having as its stimuli the Holocaust, the influx of a large number of nationally conscious and even militant Jews *(zapadniki)* from the territories annexed by the Soviet Union in the wake of World War II, the establishment of the State of

Israel in 1948, Soviet anti-Semitism, and the Arab-Israeli wars of 1967 and 1973. It gained strength from the relative success of active dissent movements in the Soviet Union in the late 1960s, and soon began to acquire a dynamic of its own. Abraham Shifrin, sentenced to death as a spy for Israel in 1953 and released in 1962 after his sentence was commuted, testifies to some of the events that demonstrate the incipient growth of Jewish national consciousness in the Soviet Union: Golda Meir's visit to Moscow in 1948, Geula Gil's concert in Moscow in 1966, and the Six Day War (selection 22a).

One of the significant events in this struggle between Soviet repression and Jewish expression of identity was the Leningrad "hijack" trial and sentences in 1970. The "Leningrad 11" (nine of whom were Jews) were arrested at the Leningrad Airport on June 15, 1970, at 8:00 A.M., while walking from the terminal to an airplane, and accused of plotting to seize a plane to fly to Israel. The arrest was followed by the detention of more than forty Jews at homes, work, and vacation spots (some as far away as Odessa and Kishinev by 9:00 A.M.). Most of those seized were persons under suspicion for their involvement in the Hebrew and Jewish cultural renaissance, or as a result of their stated desire for emigration to Israel. All articles of Israeli or Jewish interest found during the searches were confiscated and many of the detained were subsequently arrested—apparently to frighten Soviet Jews and repress their recent interest in *aliyah* and Jewish cultural activity.

A transcript of the trial is printed below (selection 22b). The "Leningrad 11" were charged with crimes that included "betrayal of the fatherland," anti-Soviet agitation and propaganda, participation in anti-Soviet organization, and misappropriation of state or public property. The trial was twice postponed—reportedly because of difficulties in obtaining satisfactory confessions of guilt—for Soviet trials are the final act of a process in which guilt is taken for granted and demonstrated.

Two of the defendants, Mark Dimshitz and Eduard Kuznetsov, were at first sentenced to death for their uncommitted "crime." The others were sentenced (December 24, 1970) to long terms at hard labor. Under pressure of worldwide public protests (a group of noted non-Jewish jurists in the United States and Europe, having offered to defend the "11," called the arrests "one of the most shocking episodes in our time"), the Soviet court commuted Dimshitz and Kuznetsov's sentences to fifteen years at hard labor.

The testimonies below, reprinted with permission from *Midstream* (February, 1971), demonstrate the tragic plight of Jews in the Soviet Union who wish to articulate their national consciousness or to emigrate.

22a. "The Case of Abraham Shifrin"

"I was tried by a court-martial consisting of three officers," [Shifrin] says. "There were no witnesses. They accused me of committing treason for Israel. Nobody gave any evidence—I had refused to confess. They stripped me of my medals, reduced me to the ranks, and condemned me to death."

What medals and decorations had he earned in World War II?

"They were nothing; everybody got them. I had the orders of the People's Army and the Red Flag. We had a joke in Russia at one time, when shoes were in very short supply—a girl asked a man on the telephone whom she was going to meet for the first time how she could identify him; he said that he would be wearing new shoes and no medals."

He has just said that he refused to confess—was he tortured in an attempt to extract a confession from him? What techniques do the Russians use to get those crazy confessions of incredible crimes that seem to have been invented by deranged thriller writers?

"In my case, they never beat me. But they kept me in a cell that was ten centimeters deep in mud. I had no mattress, no blanket. I got one cup of water and three hundred grams of bread a day. Every day they told me to confess. This went on for twenty-nine days. Then they interrogated me for one month under strong arc lights without a moment's sleep. There was a group of ten interrogators, who worked in relays, some questioning while others slept. Sometimes I fell asleep in the chair while they questioned me; they would jab me with their fingers and say, 'Wake up, don't sleep,' but still I slept.

"One man they beat, they beat him for three months. In the end he said he would confess anything they liked. Was he a spy? Yes, he was a spy, they should write down whatever they wanted. For whom was he a spy? Whoever they said, they should just write it down, he would sign. No, that wasn't good enough, he must tell them, it was not for them to tell him. So he said he was a spy for Guatemala. He got twenty-five years.

"One man in our camp was a deaf mute; he got twenty-five years because he made a derisive gesture when he walked past a banner glorifying socialism in Russia. I'll tell you a strange thing; we had two Eskimos in the camp. They told us that they had seen a strange sort of whale, which they attacked with their harpoons; suddenly the whale opened up and swallowed them. It was a U-boat and they were given twenty-five years as terrorists—they had never seen a building or an automobile in their lives, let alone a U-boat."

Shifrin was in camps in Irkutsk, Kazakhstan, Potsma, together with many other people. In every camp there were from ten to thirty Jews, convicted of spying for Israel. He escaped seven times, but was recaptured on every occasion, though during some of these escapes his comrades got away.

Suddenly he was released, on condition that he could never return to Moscow, where he was born. So he went to Odessa. On five occasions he applied for a visa to emigrate to Israel; every time he was turned down. He applied again, and was turned down. He applied again, and was turned down once more, but a few days later he received a telephone call from the authorities: "We'll give you a visa provided you leave Russia forever in ten days." "Ten days? I'll be out in three," he answered.

He still does not know what suddenly made the Russians change their minds.

In his case he was an openly avowed Zionist. Did other Jews, who were not Zionists, suffer from open anti-Semitism? The Russians claim that it is outlawed.

"Of course they suffered. Jews couldn't get into universities, they could not get good jobs. If a man with a Jewish name or a Jewish nose applied for a job, he was told that there was no vacancy. If he went around the corner and telephoned again, giving a Russian name, he was told that there was a job going."

He is an older man who remembered his Judaism; the amazing thing is that a third generation of Jews, born and bred since the Bolshevik Revolution, raised under the banner of the hammer and sickle, ignorant of the Jewish religion and the Hebrew language, should still remember Zion.

"It is a miracle, nothing less than a miracle. When I was a child, I was a member of a Russian pioneer scout movement. To have a Bible in the home was a crime. Imagine how much more remote are the young people in their teens and twenties—yet they are all, all of them, Zionists. It is wonderful, it is like the coming of the Messiah. If somebody had told me in Irkutsk that I would live to see the young Jews defying the Russian Government and demanding visas to Israel I would never have believed it."

What brought about the miracle? The Six Day War?

"The Six Day War made a great deal of difference, but it began before the war. I was present when the Jews of Moscow met Golda in 1948—today I met her for a second time. There is a Russian proverb that if two good things happen, a third will—I am waiting for the third happening.

"In 1966, Geula Gil came to sing in Russia. She was wonderful. Every Russian Jew treasures a picture of her and a record of her concert in Moscow, if he can get these things. I gave mine to a friend. When she came on the stage, an Israeli girl, and sang songs about Israel, it gave us strength and hope. I shouted to her to sing the Palmach song, and she did. Everyone stood up and sang the chorus. For the Russian Jews Geula became like a banner. I think she is the finest Israeli singer.

"Then came the Six Day War. It was a revelation to us. Our youth really understood that our strength lay in the strength of Israel to survive, that our salvation lay in Israel. Only through courage and casting out fear can the Jews go on living. This was the message of the Six Day War, and from that time on we have gone without fear. That is why Jews write letters abroad saying they want to leave for Israel, they give their names and addresses, they defy the Russian Government. Hundreds of Jews, thousands of them, have the courage now to tell the Russian Government: 'This is not my country, this is not my culture. My land is Israel, my future is Israel. Let me go.' I don't think anyone in the West can begin to understand what courage is needed to defy the Russian Government in this way. But they are not afraid. If I have a message to send to the Jews of the world from the Western Wall it is this: 'Don't you be afraid for the Russian Jews, since they are not afraid for themselves. Stand up and tell the truth, struggle with all your might.' "

Does he think that protests and demonstrations in Jerusalem and New York will worry people like Kosygin? Are we not like gnats trying to worry a bear?

"If the whole world takes up these protests, it will worry the Russians. But even more important is that the message will reach the Jews of Russia; they will know that they are not alone, that there is light at the end of the tunnel of darkness. They are heroes, but they must never be left to feel that nobody knows and nobody cares about their heroism. So I say to Jews everywhere, 'Write letters, don't be afraid—they are not afraid.' Show them that you are with them, heart and soul, this is more important than material aid.

"The Russians will give in—they will have to let the Jews go. We have seen many miracles; we will see this too."

22b. "Statements of the Leningrad 11"

DIMSHITZ, M. Y.—FORTY-THREE YEARS OLD

Obviously, every criminal considers his punishment too severe. And yet I want to express my opinion concerning the proposed punishment. I consider the request of the state prosecutor excessively cruel. The prosecutor often used the word "if." The citizen prosecutor, I think, exhausted the whole supply of the most terrible assumptions. If we had landed in Finland and had been extradited, then . . . ? If there were passengers . . . ? I know well what struggle is. You need such severe punishment as a lesson to others. I myself suggested the first variation [of the hijack plan], but we also abandoned it ourselves. Citizen public prosecutor spoke for the pilots. It is unfortunate, that those from the personnel department to whom I unsuccessfully applied for work were not sitting beside him [during the trial]. They may have been able to stop me until the fall of 1969—after that only the organs of the KGB were able to stop me. We, the group of defendants, are people of varied character. Many of us met on the final day. It is gratifying that we did not lose human countenance even here, and we did not start biting each other, like spiders in a jar. I thank the authorities for humaneness shown to my wife and daughter. I ask the court to treat me justly and humanely also.

ZALMANSON, SILVA—TWENTY-SEVEN YEARS OLD

I can't pull myself together . . . I am stunned by the prison terms demanded for us by the prosecutor. Now the prosecutor has recommended that heads roll because of something that was not completed. If the court agrees, then such wonderful people as Dimshitz and Kuznetsov will perish. I think that Soviet law should not regard a person's intention to live in another country as treason, and am convinced that, according to law, those who illegally trample our right to live where we please should be brought to trial. Let the court at least take into account the fact that if we had been allowed to leave, there would have been no "criminal conspiracy," which caused us so much and caused even more suffering for our relatives. Israel is a country to which we Jews are bound spiritually and historically. I hope that the government of the USSR will soon decide this question positively. We will never abandon the dream of being reunited with our ancient homeland. Some of us didn't believe that this venture would succeed, or believed very little. At the Finland Station [in Leningrad] we had already noticed that we were being trailed. But obviously we couldn't go back . . . go back to the past, to regret, and provisional living from suitcases. Our dream to live in Israel was incomparable to our fear of the suffering that could be caused us. Our departure would have harmed no one. I wanted to live with my family there and to work. I wouldn't have become involved in politics. All my interest in politics consisted of the simple wish to leave [the USSR]. Even now I don't doubt for a minute that some time I will leave anyway and will live in Israel. I will never abandon this dream sanctified by two thousand years of hope. Next year in Jerusalem! And now I repeat: If I forget Thee, O Jerusalem, may my right arm wither.

MENDELEVITCH, YOSIF—TWENTY-THREE YEARS OLD

I want to tell you once more that I recognize my actions aimed at the seizure of an airplane and the violation of the border of the USSR to be criminal. But my guilt also lies in the fact that I allowed myself to be indiscriminate in the selection of the means with which to realize my dream. This half a year [of preventive detention] taught me that emotions must be subordinate to reason. I understand that I must accept my punishment, and call upon the court to show magnanimity to my comrades.

KUZNETSOV, EDUARD SAMUILOVITCH–THIRTY-ONE YEARS OLD

The State Prosecutor assumed that once abroad I would begin to engage in activities hostile to the Soviet Union. He bases this assumption on my allegedly anti-Soviet beliefs, which I, however, expressed to no one. I did not intend to cause damage to the Soviet Union. All I wanted was to live in Israel. I did not consider a possible request for political asylum to be a hostile political act. The indictment is misleading on this point. I didn't express the desire to hold a press conference anywhere and I didn't discuss this question with anybody. Apart from other reasons for the absence of such intentions, I say only that my characteristic ironic frame of mind safely guarded me against making any political appearances. I sincerely regret that I consented to take part in this affair, and I consider myself only partially guilty according to Article 72 in connection with Articles 64-A of the Criminal Code of the RSFSR. I beg the court to show lenience toward my wife Silva Zalmanson. I beg for justice for myself also. You live only once.

ZALMANSON, ISRAIL–TWENTY-ONE YEARS OLD

The only thing that impelled me to this was the desire to live and work in the State of Israel—my spiritual homeland. This wish has become the goal of my life; during the interrogation I understood the mistakenness of my act. I want to assure you that henceforth no circumstances will compel me to break the law.

MURZHENKO, ALEXEI–TWENTY-EIGHT YEARS OLD, UKRAINIAN

Before I speak of myself, I beg the court for leniency on behalf of Kuznetsov and Dimshitz. I am in complete agreement with my lawyer. The prosecutor asserts that I am anti-Soviet and that I took part in this action for this reason. Due to my first conviction, the prosecutor concludes that I am anti-Soviet. But this is not true. The reason for my first conviction was the totally unsettled state of my life. But my participation in this endeavor was the result of my inexperience in life. My life has consisted of eight years at the Suvorov Academy, six years in labor camps for political prisoners, and only two years of freedom. Living in a remote corner I didn't have the opportunity to apply my knowledge and had to bury it. You are deciding my fate, my life. The fourteen years of imprisonment requested by the prosecutor, signify that I am considered incorrigible and am given up as lost. I have never followed criminal goals. I beg the court to sentence me to a term which would leave me some hope for happiness, for my future and that of my family.

FEDOROV, YURI PAVLOVITCH—? YEARS OLD, RUSSIAN

Pondering what we have done, I have become convinced that we had but one goal—to leave the USSR. No one had the goal to harm the USSR. I believe that we took every measure to insure the safety of the pilots. I plead guilty only to the attempt to violate the border of the USSR and I am ready to bear the responsibility for this, but I do not feel guilty as a matter of conscience—I have done nothing [wrong]. The prosecutor has not been stingy with the sentences, but is he aware what even three years in a labor camp mean? The speech of the public prosecutor was directed against the seizure of the plane, and one can agree with this speech. As far as the revolver is concerned, it was taken along, in case the Finland variation was put into effect. I parted with my anti-Soviet beliefs while still in the labor camp. In planning the seizure of the airplane, we did not suspect that some of us would be more guilty than others. Everyone did what he could. And suddenly it turned out that Dimshitz and Kuznetsov were more guilty in the whole affair. Dimshitz has at least planned to pilot the plane, but I can't understand why Kuznetsov was suddenly found more guilty than the rest. As far as the possible consequences [of the attempt] are concerned, I can say that since the action did not materialize, it is not worth guessing how it might have turned out. I beg the court to show mercy toward . . . I [unclear] . . . on my part [in the action] but Murzhenko was lured into it by me even against [unclear].

ALTMAN, ANATOLI

Citizen judges, I appeal to you to spare the lives of Kuznetsov and Dimshitz and to allot the minimal punishment to the only woman among us, Silva Zalmanson. I express deep regret; I am sincerely sorry that my comrades and I ended up on this [defendants'] bench. I hope that the court will find it possible not to punish us too severely. It is not possible for me to escape punishment for participation in the crime, but one circumstance amazes me; the fact of the matter is that in 1969 I applied for an emigration permit to Israel, that is to change my homeland. At that time my wish resulted only in scorn toward me, and now in a trial. My amazement is not frivolous, because we are dealing with isolation, deprivation of freedom, and the suffering of our loved ones. I was born during the Soviet era and have spent my whole life in the Soviet state. I haven't had time to fully comprehend the class essence of Zionism, but I am well aware that peoples and countries experience varying political conditions at various times and do not become better or worse because of this. Today, as my fate is being decided, I feel both wonderful and grieved; I am hopeful that peace will come to Israel. To you, my land, I this day send these wishes. Sholom Aleykhem. Peace to you, Land of Israel.

KNOKH, ARIE (LEIB)—TWENTY-FIVE YEARS OLD

Citizen judges. I beg you to show mercy to my two comrades and leniency to the only woman among us. I can only repeat that my actions were not directed against the national security of the USSR. My only goal was to live in the State of Israel, which I have long considered my homeland, a land where my people emerged as a nation, where the Jewish state and Jewish culture existed and are now developing, where my native language is spoken, where my relatives and loved ones live. I have no anti-Soviet views. Two witnesses incorrectly interpreted my views. Apparently they live in those regions of the USSR where Jews do not apply to the OVIR. And both of them told the court that I didn't touch upon the essence of the socialist system. My only goal is to live in Israel, the true homeland of Jews.

23. *JEWISH LIFE IN AMERICA*

There is considerable sociological literature on the influence of the suburban milieu on religious practices, but there are few reliable studies documenting the texture of Jewish suburban life. The few popular studies available have suggested high intermarriage rates, low ritual observance, high rates of nonaffiliation, and high proportions of those without Jewish education. The appearance of the Lakeville study in 1967 offered the first serious opportunity to document the content and quality of suburban Jewish life in the United States.

"Lakeville" is a suburb of a Midwest city where one third of the 25,000 inhabitants are Jews. Although there are some first- and second-generation families, the community consists primarily of third- and fourth-generation Jews. There is little doubt that Lakeville is most of American Jewry in the 1960s and 1970s, and thus the interest in the relationship that the authors find between suburbanization and Jewish identification.

Judaism, for the Jews of Lakeville, is defined in moralistic rather than sacramental terms in the respondents' thought (a "good Jew" is one who leads an ethical and moral life), but is expressed by such involvement as Jewish education for their children, synagogue affiliation, support of Jewish causes, a concern with issues of Jewish survival, and developing social relationships with fellow Jews and Jewesses. Lakeville's Jews also reveal an interesting contrast: a general decline in ritual along with a clear tendency toward increased Jewish education for the youth and heightened observance of selected religious ceremonies.

Thus the suburbanization of American Jewry has proven to belie a simple comprehension. On the one hand Jews have become thoroughly acculturated to the American middle-class way of life while, concomitantly, there seems to be an intensified identification with Jewish education, culture, religion, and organizational life. As the contemporary community abandons traditional patterns, it develops new forms of identity. Some of these new forms are carefully analyzed in the following selection from Chapter 3 of Marshall Sklare and Joseph Greenblum's *Jewish Identity on the Suburban Frontier: A Study of Group Survival in the Open Society* (New York, 1967),

Marshall Sklare and Joseph Greenblum, *Jewish Identity on the Suburban Frontier*

MITZVOT IN THE LAKEVILLE HOME

Given our objective of analyzing religious practice, we could study observance of the mitzvot by our respondents in a variety of settings: their synagogues, their places of business, the meetings of their Jewish organizations, or their homes. The home is by far the best starting point. Unlike the Jewish organization, where directives from the national office may influence local practice, what the family does is formulated and instituted by a group of intimates. Unlike a synagogue, where procedures are necessarily a compromise between contending conceptions (or where someone may attend a religious service to be "seen" or because one has been invited by a relative or friend), religious practice in the home is a more nearly perfect reflection of individual conviction and desire. And unlike the house of worship, where practice may be influenced by a religious specialist, the home has no professionals.

The unique importance of the home for our analysis is also connected with the secularism that characterizes the general society. Observance of Jewish sacramentalism is rendered difficult by such secularism, especially for those who desire to participate in the general society. But even if there is no such impetus, a prescriptive approach to observance is rendered difficult. As we have seen, in medieval days economic relationships between Jew and Gentile made it difficult to observe the old norms. In our day, the problem is compounded: the very practice of business has become strongly secularized. One aspect of this change is commented on in the other volume: that business is routinely conducted in social settings, or that there is at least the attempt to diminish social distance in the pursuit of occupational objectives.

The aspect of this sociability which is of particular interest to us is the serving of food. The business lunch, the dinner at the club, the banquet of the trade or professional association, all mean that, unless the individual has a very firm commitment to the practice of kashrut and is willing to be excluded from the prevailing sociability pattern, he will violate the dietary laws in the course of his occupational activities. But the individual who has some commitment to the dietary laws may continue to observe them in his home, for there sacred values can be implemented without modifying expected occupational routines. Because it is by definition the most personal of all institutional settings, at least theoretically the home can remain a fortress of sacramentalism, even if surrounded by a highly securlarized society.

The further fact is that if any one institutional setting is the focus of Jewish sacramentalism, it is the home. Since Judaism constitutes a way of life, it must by definition center in the home. There the individual's earliest Jewish experiences take place; there he spends much of his time, in spite of the fact that under modern conditions occupational duties are performed almost entirely outside his domicile. For the traditional Jew the synagogue is, in a sense, merely the lengthened shadow of his home, rather than the central institution of cultic worship.

Because of these reasons for concentrating on religious practice in the Lakeville home, we presented our respondents with a list of eleven observances and asked, "Which of the following observances are practiced more or less regularly in your home?" To establish changing levels and patterns, we also inquired into which of the rituals were practiced in their parental home when the parents "were about your present age." The list is as follows:

Bacon or ham never served.
Kosher meat bought regularly.
Kosher the meat.
Special dinner on Friday night.
Lighting of candles on Friday night.
Kiddush on Friday night.
No smoking allowed in house on Sabbath.
Seder on Passover.
Bread not eaten in home on Passover.
Either or both parents fast on Yom Kippur.
Candles lit on Hanukkah.

This list is, of course, merely a selection from a vast number of regulations constituting the "prepared table" of Jewish sacramentalism. It emphasizes the observance of holidays and festivals, particularly (1) the Sabbath, (2) the High Holidays, (3) Passover, and (4) Hanukkah. In addition to whatever dietary regulations are observed in connection with these occasions, it includes some items on the general observance of kashrut. Furthermore, all the items represent only primary aspects of religious practice rather than finer points of observance. For example, the one on Passover dietary observance concerns whether or not bread is eaten in the home; it does not inquire into the extent to which the home is freed of chametz.

We find that of the eleven practices, the mean number observed is 2.8. Some 19 percent of the respondents observe none of the rituals, while only 10 percent observe seven or more. The largest group of respondents observe only one or two rituals. The conclusion to be drawn is that religious practice in most of the homes is at a very low level and that observance of the traditional sacramental pattern by the Lakeville Jew is minimal.

In their deviation from tradition, our respondents are not merely following the pattern of observance which they knew as children, for they were reared in homes where a considerably higher level of observance was practiced. In contrast to their 2.8 observances, the mean number of rituals followed in their parental homes is 5.2. Inasmuch as a total of 41 percent of the older generation practiced seven or more rituals, many of our respondents were raised in homes which by present Lakeville standards are quite observant. On the other hand, in only a relatively small group of homes was there really a prescriptive orientation, for only 14 percent of the parents observed all eleven rituals.

Since we do not have information about the ritualistic orientation of grandparents and great-grandparents, we cannot say exactly at what point modernism made its initial inroads. Thus we do not know when observance became more personalistic than prescriptive, but it is apparent that our respondents have merely continued a process initiated by prior generations. They may be said to exemplify an intensified personalism, rather than a break from prescriptivism to personalism.

Given the contrast between the 2.8 mean of Lakeville and the 5.2 mean of the older generation, the question arises as to whether our respondents constitute the last generation in which the Jewish home has any recognizable religious character. Based on the fact that nonobservance has not grown (whereas 21 percent of the older generation abstained from any ritualistic observance, only 19 percent of the present generation does so), we have no grounds for projecting such a trend. Rather, our data suggest the possibility of the stabilization of religious practice, of course at very minimal levels. We shall have more to say about this at a later point, where we consider the influence of generational status on religious observance.

Since parents and children differ, we must ask which rituals have survived and which have withered away. We see that the ritual most frequently observed by our respondents is the lighting of candles on Hanukkah, a mitzvah observed in 68 percent of the homes. One other ritual is practiced by a majority: the holding of a Seder on Passover in 60 percent of the homes.

In contrast to Hanukkah and Passover, the Sabbath is marked by only a minority. While according to Jewish tradition observance of the Sabbath is of cardinal importance, in only 32 percent of the homes are the Sabbath candles lit. Other Sabbath rituals are observed by a smaller group.

Dietary observance is maintained in but a few Lakeville homes. The most minimal observance—that of abstaining from serving pork products—is practiced by 9 percent. While dietary observance per se is highly exceptional, when a dietary observance is connected with a holiday or festival—as, for example, refraining from eating bread in the home on Passover or fasting on Yom Kippur—it is observed more widely than the daily dietary laws. The lack of appeal of the dietary laws can be understood by contrasting the 32 percent in whose home the candles are lit on Friday nights, the 30 percent who have a special meal, and the 16 percent who make the benediction over the wine (Kiddush) with the 5 percent who purchase and serve kosher meat at the Sabbath meal.

Turning to parents, we find that not only were Hanukkah and Passover celebrated in a majority of their homes but the Sabbath was observed in some form in one half of their homes, and some of the daily dietary laws were followed in almost half of their homes. In contrast to the present generation, where a special dinner on Friday is observed much more frequently than is the serving of kosher meat, almost as many parents observed the latter as the former. In any case, the greatest differences between the generations are in daily dietary observances such as the purchase of kosher meat: 46 percent of the older generation did this, in contrast to 5 percent of the younger generation. But even dietary observances connected with holidays or festivals were observed more frequently by the older generation: considerably more parents than children fasted on Yom Kippur or refrained from eating bread on Passover.

Our respondents in Lakeville thus demonstrate a declining sacramentalism when their religious observance is contrasted with that of their parents. It is notable that, in spite of this shift, observance of the Seder and of the lighting of the Hanukkah candles remains relatively stable. In fact, the lighting of candles on Hanukkah has increased somewhat in the present generation; it is the single religious practice that registers any gain. Paradoxically, this ceremony does not bulk large according to traditional norms.

The prominence of Hanukkah, however, is not entirely the work of our respondents, for the trend is evident even among the parents, where observance of Hanukkah is exceeded only by that of Passover. And in the parental generation, fasting on such a preeminent occasion as Yom Kippur is no more frequent than lighting the candles on Hannukkah.

The trend that we have noticed toward declining sacramentalism needs to be supplemented by a comparison of the two generations at similar levels of observance. We have selected four such levels: 1, 2–4, 5–7, and 8–10 observances. Bearing in mind that parents average 5.2 rituals and our respondents 2.8, the present analysis will enable us to determine whether there has occurred any change in the pattern of observance of specific rituals between the two generations with the same level of observance.

The results indicate that the younger generation exhibits greater consensus in terms of the rituals they observe. Thus, whatever customs each of the two generations emphasizes, except at the 8–10 level more of the younger generation practice their high-priority customs than did the older generation. In essence, the parents observed a diversified ritual pattern, while the younger generation observes a specialized pattern.

Turning to specifics, we find that the younger generation tends toward (1) increased emphasis on Hanukkah, (2) increased emphasis on the Passover Seder, (3) maintenance or even increased observance of some Sabbath ritual, and (4) sharply decreased observance of the dietary laws. Reviewing these trends in greater detail, we find that there is:

1. *Increased emphasis on Hanukkah.* Among the younger generation, the lighting of the menorah ranks either first or second at all levels of observance, but among the older generation other holidays received greater emphasis. The contrast between the generations is sharpest at lower observance levels. Thus, 89 percent of the younger generation who observe only 2 to 4 rituals celebrate Hanukkah, compared to 50 percent of the older generation. Furthermore, in marked contrast to the older generation, the majority of our respondents who practice only a single ritual rely on Hanukkah.

2. *Increased emphasis on the Passover Seder.* With the exception of those who observe only one ceremony, the predominance of Hanukkah among our respondents does not mean less emphasis on the holding of a Seder. Even at the 2–4 observances level, 85 percent of the present generation celebrate Passover by participating in a Seder.

3. *Maintenance or even increased observance of some Sabbath ritual.* With the exception of the single-observance family, at all levels the younger generation observe Sabbath rituals as frequently as did their parents. Some-

times they even exceed them. The recitation of the Kiddush was not stressed among the older generation; it is recited in 50 to 80 percent of the more observant younger homes in contrast to only 14 to 54 percent of parental homes. In more observant younger homes, the lighting of the Sabbath candles and a special Friday night dinner are also widely observed. The tendency to Sabbath observance among that minority of the younger generation who are at the higher levels of observance does not extend, however, to the prohibition against the lighting of a fire; only among those at the very highest observance level is a home encountered where smoking is avoided on the Sabbath.

4. *Uniform decline in observance of dietary laws.* Whatever the level of observance, fewer of the younger generation observe the dietary laws. The kashrut situation is most apparent at higher observance levels. For example, at the 5–7 observances level, 50 percent recite the kiddush on Friday evening, but only 5 percent buy kosher meat. In the parental generation, this relationship is reversed: some 44 percent bought kosher meat, but only 14 percent recited the kiddush.

Of these four trends, perhaps the most notable one is Sabbath observance. On an overall basis, fewer of the younger generation observe any Sabbath ritual than did their parents, but those younger people who are at the higher levels of religiosity continue to remember the Sabbath. Their Sabbath observance is, of course, not fully traditional; practically no one refrains from lighting a fire. But on the other hand, the pattern of the older settlers in Lakeville—who neglected such rituals and, as we shall see, were even willing to observe Sunday as their Sabbath—has not prevailed. True, very few of those who perform Sabbath rituals are the offspring of these first families. Nevertheless, it may be considered remarkable that there is a group of residents who continue with these rituals. They persist in their remembrance of the Jewish Sabbath despite the fact that the Sabbath is not part of Lakeville's mode of living. After sunset on Friday, life in the community goes on as usual.

To the traditional Jew, a home where the burning lights of the Sabbath candles are on display while kashrut is neglected constitutes an anomaly. But to the Lakeville Jew who remembers the Sabbath, it is the "Kitchen Judaism" of his parents or grandparents which is the anomaly. Whatever the effect of the disintegration of kashrut observance on the ultimate destiny of the Judaism practiced by our respondents and their descendants, the proclivity of the more observant to mark the arrival of Queen Sabbath is notable. . . .

SYNAGOGUE ATTENDANCE

Since some 19 percent of our respondents observe no rituals in their home and another 37 percent observe only one or two practices, we must conclude that the majority of Jewish homes in Lakeville lack a distinctive religious character. If the Jewish home is not a fortress of sacredness in a secular society, the possibility exists that the focus of sacramentalism has shifted to the synagogue and that this is now the prime sanctuary of Jewish faith and future. If this is, indeed, the case, it indicates the high acculturation of our respondents and their adherence to the prevailing pattern of American religiosity—a pattern in which religious activities are centered in an institution specifically dedicated to religious ends, which in turn is surrounded by other institutions dedicated to secular ends. If this shift has, in fact, taken place, it should be evidenced by a high degree of membership in congregations and by a higher level of attendance at synagogue services than of home observance. As we shall see in Chapter 5, the first qualification is fulfilled, for the majority of the Jews of Lakeville belong to a synagogue. Our present interest is the extent of attendance at religious services.

In inquiring about attendance, we did not ask about daily services; we were aware that such services are held in only one of the synagogues in the community and that this synagogue finds difficulty in gathering the quorum necessary for public worship. Thus the most frequently conducted service about which we asked was that held on the Sabbath. Additionally we asked about the Festivals—specifically about attendance at the services held during Sukkot—and also about attendance at the High Holiday services of Rosh Hashanah and Yom Kippur. An index of synagogue attendance was constructed, with zero representing those who never attend and 9 representing those who have attended High Holiday and Sukkot services for each of the past three years and a Sabbath service every week, or almost every week, during the past year.

Only 3 percent of our respondents, we find, are in the highest category, and only an additional 10 percent are in the next-highest category. Thus a total of 13 percent may be considered as regular worshipers by Lakeville standards: generally they attend High Holiday services each year, they come to Festival services occasionally or regularly, and they attend Sabbath services at least twice a month. The majority of our respondents—74 percent—are irregular worshipers: they are located in the 1–2 group (generally those who attend High Holiday services in some years but not others, or who attend regularly on Yom Kippur), the 3–4 group (generally those who attend High Holiday services regularly and Sabbath services a few times each year), and the 5-6 group (generally those who attend High Holiday services regularly, Festival services occasionally, and Sabbath services either monthly or a few times each year). Almost half of the 74 percent group are located in the 3-4 category. Finally, there are the nonattenders: the 13 percent who never come to any service.

How does this picture of synagogue attendance compare with what we already know about home observance? Any such comparison has an element of arbitrariness, but it is evident that a greater number of respondents abstain from home observance than absent themselves from synagogue attendance. There is a relationship between home and synagogue, where we find that more than half (59 percent) of those who do not perform any rituals in their home *do* attend religious services on occasion. In the majority of cases, such attendance is confined to the High Holidays. Further, many of those whose home observance is minimal attain more than a minimal level of synagogue attendance.

To be sure, there are also cases where home observance exceeds synagogue attendance. But those whose synagogue attendance exceeds their home observance are more numerous. It is this group which engages our attention, since their pattern indicates the impact of a pervasive acculturation and represents a decisive break with the Jewish sacramentalism of old. The most striking example of such a break is the type of Lakeville woman who joins the congregation for Sabbath worship but does not perform the mandatory ritual of lighting the Sabbath candles in her home. According to Jewish tradition, such behavior is anomalous. It would seem that her sacramental pattern has been influenced by the environment, with its stress on public worship, for instead of observing one of the three mandatory "womanly" mitzvot, this woman performs an act which is optional for her sex: that of attending a religious service.

In regard to generational differences, we see that our respondents participate in public worship considerably less frequently than did their parents. This decline does not result from a growth in nonattendance but rather is a consequence of the diminishing number of regular worshipers: while 37 percent of the parents attended services regularly (scoring 7–8 and 9), only 13 percent of our respondents do so. The contrast between the generations is not so sharp as we noticed in respect to home observance, but it still constitutes a decline of sizable magnitude.

When we analyze the particular religious services that appeal to Lakeville Jews, we see nothing like the emergence in the synagogue of anything which resembles Hanukkah in the home, that is, an occasion of minor significance which has been escalated into major significance. While the older generation exceeds the younger in High Holiday attendance, these services still outrank all others by a wide margin. Thus more than seven out of ten of our respondents attend services on both Rosh Hashanah and Yom Kippur every year or almost every year.

The relatively high level of attendance at High Holiday services suggests the unique character and appeal of Rosh Hashanah and Yom Kippur as well as the operation of one of our criteria for ritual retention: the annual and the infrequently performed ritual. It appears that the criteria are operative both in synagogue attendance and in home observance, for despite the fact that according to traditional norms attendance at weekly Sabbath services is of crucial significance (observance of the Sabbath is no less important than observance of the High Holidays), only 5 percent of our male respondents attend services each week. Of course, just as with home observances, the break with prescriptive Judaism occurred two or more generations ago: only 29 percent of the fathers of our men respondents attended Sabbath services each week. In the parental generation, 39 percent abstained from all Sabbath worship. Thus the pattern was either regular attendance or nonattendance. Among the Lakeville generation, however, sporadic attendance, as distinct from regular attendance, is encountered more frequently.

If the preeminence of the Sabbath as an occasion for synagogue attendance has declined, it is the Festival services which have suffered the greatest attrition; since 72 percent of the Jews of Lakeville never come to these services, nonattendance is the dominant pattern. The contrast between the generations is strong: while 46 percent of the parents attended these services at least fairly regularly, only 18 percent of our respondents do so. In sum, the Jews of Lakeville retain the High Holidays as a major event in the Jewish calendar, they attend Sabbath services very irregularly, and they ignore the Festivals as occasions for public worship.

Can we say, then, that Lakeville Judaism is a synagogue Judaism rather than a home Judaism? Not entirely; but the trend in this direction is unmistakable. There is the fact that some of those who observe little or no ritual in their homes attend religious services. There is the additional fact that while the Jewish home in Lakeville is ritualistically very weak, the synagogue is strong and growing stronger. True, it must struggle to attract worshipers; its religious services do not draw the majority of the Jews of Lakeville on a daily, weekly, or even monthly basis. Nevertheless, the synagogue as an institution prospers. We are certainly justified in saying that the growing strength of the Lakeville synagogue does not derive from the Jewishness of the Lakeville home; if it were dependent on that home, synagogue attendance would be at a considerably lower level than it is at present.

The changing relationship between home and synagogue sets the stage for the development of a new pattern: home observance as derivative from synagogue involvement. Rather than conceiving of the synagogue as an extension of the home, those in Lakeville who seek to arrest the decline in observance think in terms of remaking the home through the influence of the synagogue. They feel that the synagogue is the only place where the new Jew will learn how to be a Jew—the only place where he can be impressed with the importance of conducting a Jewish home, inspired to observe rituals which he presently neglects, and instructed in their performance. However, even the rabbis and the synagogue leaders of Lakeville do not seek to return to the old ritualism, with its tendency to encompass all of life within the realm of the sacred. Rather they seek to narrow the wide chasm between the synagogue and the Jewishly denuded home of Lakeville. . . .

GENERATION

Much recent writing in the field of the sociology of religion proceeds on the assumption that the main determinant of religiosity is generational status, rather than parental patterns or the influence of the life cycle. As exemplified by Will Herberg, this approach stresses that the second generation deviates maximally from the religious pattern of the first generation, while the third generation experiences a "return." The second generation attempts to evade the traditions of its immigrant parents, but the third is attracted to that which the second attempted to reject. The second generation, dissociating itself from the heritage of its immigrant past, concentrates on seeking acceptance and status in the larger society and in doing so refuses to embrace traditions dear to the parents. The third generation, however, feeling greater security because of its acculturation, seeks a more particularistic group identity and social location within the structure of American religious pluralism. It is attracted to the religious—if not the ethnic—heritage of its grandparents.

Since our respondents are not representative of Jews in the nation at large, we are not in a position to settle definitely the dispute about the effect of generational status. Our effort will rather be to discover whether, within the context and the limits of the religious pattern of our respondents, each generation in Lakeville evidences a distinctive response. The case for the existence of such a response seems plausible, for each generation has a particular status in American society and a different level of acculturation. Furthermore, since social change has been so rapid, each generation is distinctive in that the religious legacy it inherits differs both in size and kind from that received by prior generations.

Our procedure for studying generational differences is to analyze the religious observance of our respondents against the background of what prevailed in the parental home. As a consequence, we are able to compare the religious observances not only of respondents who happen to belong to different generations but also of each such generation and its parents. Most sociologists who have studied the religious influence of generational position have not presented family-linked statistics. Because we gathered data on religious observance of the parents as well as of our respondents themselves, we do not have to treat our first-generation interviewees as if they were the parents of our second-generation respondents, or the latter as if they were the parents of the third-generation respondents.

In order to eliminate any religious influences which derive from differing social and cultural heritages rather than from generational status, we shall follow the procedure of controlling for descent. This control is based on the assumption that the generational concept is meaningful only if it involves a comparison between groups who are fairly homogeneous. The contrasts in the social characteristics of our descent groups, even in the third generation, suggest that those descended from German and East European Jews have different personal histories and inherit different social and religious legacies. Furthermore, German-origin Jews are overrepresented in the more advanced generations and underrepresented in the less advanced generations. As a consequence, were all our respondents of the same generation considered as a single unit, rather than divided into three descent groups, some important differences may be obscured.

It will be recalled that our respondents are at a level of religious observance much inferior to the one occupied by their parents: their mean of home observance is 2.8, compared to 5.2 for their parents; their mean score on synagogue attendance is 3.7, compared to 5.0 for their parents. In the level of religious observance achieved by each Lakeville generation against the base line of the observance level of their parents, we find, of course, that first-generation Lakeville respondents of East European descent were exposed to by far the most traditional pattern of observance: their parents practiced an average of 9.2 out of a possible 11 home rituals and had an average score for synagogue attendance of 6.8 out of a possible 9. The respondents, however, observe only 4.1 home rituals and score only 4.4 on synagogue attendance. Thus, instead of the observant newcomer pictured by the generational school of thought, the Lakeville immigrant is a highly acculturated individual.

While the differences between first-generation East Europeans and their parents are the largest of all, the gap between second-generation East Europeans and their parents is also considerable. Since the second-generation East Europeans are numerically the most prominent, their response is of special significance. Among those of German and mixed descent, the gap between the least advanced generation (the second generation) and their parents is also sizable. Furthermore, each successive generation in each descent group is reared in an increasingly more restricted pattern of home observance and synagogue attendance. Nevertheless, we find that while each generation in Lakeville almost always follows an observance pattern more limited than the one in which it was reared, the deviations from the parental pattern among the more advanced generations are generally not as sizable as among the less advanced generations. For example, while differences between second-generation respondents of East European descent and their parents are wide, the gap is much reduced in the case of the third generation of the same descent group and their parents.

The smaller deviations from the parental pattern by the more advanced generations in Lakeville suggest, then, that generational status *does* have an influence on religious performance. Indeed, if the performance of each generation were solely responsive to the base line established by the parents, second-generation respondents of East European descent should exhibit a much higher level of religious observance than they actually do. Instead of occupying substantially the same level of home observance and synagogue attendance as their third-generation contemporaries, they should exceed them. Or looked at from a different perspective, the third generation should occupy a much lower level of religious observance than they actually do. A similar logic would apply to the third generation of German descent, compared to their fourth-generation contemporaries, and to similar generations among those of mixed descent. However, with the possible exception of the latter, the religious observance of the most advanced generations is no less than that of their contemporaries in the preceding generation. Whether expressed in mean figures or in proportions at given observance levels, both home rituals and synagogue attendance are found to be either at about the same level or at a higher level. *In the more advanced generations, then, the trend toward declining religious observance is halted. Within each descent group the overall trend is for stabilization to set in.*

We reason that among second-generation East Europeans the orientation to the parents' religious way of life is more ambivalent than that of their third-generation contemporaries and that this greater ambivalence holds true for third-generation Germans, as compared with their fourth-generation contemporaries. We see that while the less advanced generation is subject to stronger childhood religious influences than the more advanced generation, it pulls away from them more sharply. This greater deviation seems to be due to the influence of generational position. Such a negative pull appears to reflect the cleavage that occurs when parents, particularly of an early generation, follow a traditional pattern of religious observance. The more advanced generation, exposed to a less demanding religious regimen, narrows the gap between itself and its parents. In extreme instances of religious neglect, it may even exceed its parents.

While the family-linked generational comparisons tell us part of the story, the effect of generational status becomes even clearer when the influence of disparate patterns of religious rearing is controlled. For example, third-generation East Europeans were reared in less observant homes than second-generation East Europeans, but there is considerable overlap of the childhood observance patterns of the two generations. If our data are so arranged that each generation is given an equal religious start, we shall be in a better position to gauge the effect of generational status on religious performance independent of the influence of the parental pattern.

We note that third-generation East Europeans exceed their second-generation contemporaries who had a similar childhood exposure to religious observances. This superiority is consistent, whatever the level of observance which prevailed in the home of the respondents' parents. For example, among those reared in highly observant homes, over eight out of ten of the third generation preserve three or more home observances; only two thirds of their second-generation contemporaries do so. Among those reared in minimally or unobservant homes, only three in ten of the second generation observe a similar number of rituals, compared to almost half of the third generation. Furthermore, fourth-generation respondents of German descent are more observant even when they share with the prior generations the same low level of religious exposure.

Among those with minimal religious rearing, the higher level of observance achieved by more advanced generations applies both to home practices and synagogue attendance. But those from more traditional parental homes do not achieve a substantially higher level of synagogue attendance. This suggests that when the East European immigrant parents are observant, the changes initiated by the second generation result in a less radical reduction in synagogue attendance than in home observance. This reflects the trend to a synagogue-centered Judaism, with which we are already familiar.

We find that among those whose East European parents were moderately or highly observant, the decrease in home observance—but not synagogue attendance—of the second generation is more extreme than that of the third generation. It is also significant that among those with little or no religious rearing, both Germans and East Europeans of more advanced generations have a consistently greater increase over their parents' level of both home and synagogue observance than is true for less advanced generations.

This effect persists despite the fact that the more advanced generations are younger and therefore have a higher proportion of families in the earlier, and thus in the least observant, phases of the life cycle. We find, in fact, that in each phase of the life cycle more advanced generations exceed less advanced generations. This difference is maximized when religious rearing is also controlled. Among respondents of East European origin who have had similar levels of childhood religious exposure and are in the early-school or peak-school phases of the life cycle, the third generation shows a consistently higher level of home observance and synagogue attendance than the second generation. Furthermore, the decline of the third generation from high or moderate parental observance levels is not so steep as that of the second, while its increase over minimal or nonobservant parental levels is greater.

In sum, generational position has dynamic religious effects. With descent, parents' observance level, and life cycle controlled, a persuasive case can be made for the influence of generational status. Admittedly, the picture is sharper with our respondents than it would be for others. Since Lakeville residents have risen so far, have acculturated so fast, and have done so in an era of particularly rapid social change, we should expect them to maximize any generational effect: the world of most Lakeville sons is quite different from that of their fathers. The picture of stabilization and increased observance that emerges would be described by some—in our opinion, inaccurately—as a "return" to religious observance.

In any case, the picture is quite remarkable in one respect: the more advanced generations maintain a higher observance level, despite the fact that their educational achievement is considerable. If we make the assumption that general education contributed to the ambivalence of the second-generation East Europeans toward their parents' religious heritage, it is apparent that it did not produce a similar result in the religious life of the third generation. The formal education of the second generation may have provided them with ideological support for their rejection or radical modification of the "foreign" elements in the religious system of their immigrant parents. For the third generation, general learning no longer presented such a stark constrast with the more acculturated religious pattern of *their* parents.

BIBLIOGRAPHY

A. THE ONSET OF CHANGE

Primary Sources

Bauer, Bruno. *The Jewish Problem.* Cincinnati, 1958.

Glatzer, Nahum N., ed. *The Dynamics of Emancipation.* Boston, 1965.

Grégoire, Henri. *An Essay on the Physical, Moral, and Political Reformation of the Jews.* London, 1791.

Hess, Moses. *Rome and Jerusalem.* New York, 1918.

Lessing, Gotthold. *Nathan the Wise.* New York, 1955.

Mahler, Raphael, ed. *Jewish Emancipation.* New York, 1941.

Marx, Karl. *On the Jewish Question.* Cincinnati, 1958.

Maslin, Simeon, ed. *Selected Documents of Napoleonic Jewry.* Cincinnati, 1957.

Voltaire. *Philosophical Dictionary.* London, 1961.

Secondary Readings

Adler, H. G. *The Jews in Germany from the Enlightenment to National Socialism.* Notre Dame, 1969.

Bamberger, Fritz. "Zunz's Conception of History." *Proceedings of the American Academy for Jewish Research* XI (1941): 1–25.

Baron, Salo. "The Impact of the Revolution of 1848 on Jewish Emancipation." *Jewish Social Studies* XI (July, 1949): 195–248.

———. "Modern Capitalism and Jewish Fate." *The Menorah Journal,* XXX (July, 1942): 116–138.

Barzilay, Isaac E. "Moses Mendelssohn (1729–1786): A Study in Ideas and Attitudes." *Jewish Quarterly Review* LII (October, 1961): 175–186.

Hertzberg, Arthur. *The French Enlightenment and the Jews.* New York, 1968.

Katz, Jacob. *Emancipation and Assimilation.* London, 1972.

———. *Out of the Ghetto.* Cambridge, Mass., 1973.

Kober, Adolph. "The French Revolution and the Jews in Germany." *Jewish Social Studies* XVII (October, 1945). 291–322.

———. "Jews in the Revolution of 1848 in Germany." *Jewish Social Studies* X (April, 1948): 135–164.

Lipman, V. D., ed. *Three Centuries of Anglo-Jewish History.* Cambridge, 1961.

Mahler, Raphael. *A History of Modern Jewry.* New York, 1971.

Necheles, Ruth. "The Abbé Grégoire and the Jews." *Jewish Social Studies* XXXIII (April–July, 1971): 120–140.

Posener, S. "The Immediate Economic and Social Effects of the Emancipation of the Jews in France." *Jewish Social Studies* I (1939): 271–326.

Roth, Cecil. *A History of the Jews in England.* 3d ed. Oxford, 1964.

B. DISEQUILIBRIUM AND THE JEWISH RESPONSE

Primary Sources

Bieber, Hugo, ed. *Heinrich Heine: A Biographical Anthology.* Philadelphia, 1956.

Freehof, Solomon. *Reform Jewish Practice and Its Rabbinic Background.* New York, 1963.

Graetz, Heinrich. *A History of the Jews.* 5 vols. Philadelphia, 1891–1898.

Heine, Heinrich. *The Rabbi of Bacherach.* Berlin, 1937.

Hirsch, Samson R. *Nineteen Letters of Ben Uziel.* New York, 1942.

Mendelssohn, Moses. *Jerusalem.* Edited by Alfred Jospe. New York, 1969.

Plaut, W. Gunther, ed. *The Growth of Reform Judaism.* New York, 1968.

———, ed. *The Rise of Reform Judaism.* New York, 1963.

Wise, Isaac M. *Reminiscences.* Cincinnati, 1901.

Wolf, Immanuel. "On the Concept of a Science of Judaism." *Year Book of the Leo Baeck Institute* II (1957): 194–204.

Secondary Readings

Altmann, Alexander. *Moses Mendelssohn.* University, Ala., 1973.

———, ed. *Studies in Nineteenth Century Jewish Intellectual History.* Cambridge, Mass., 1964.

Baron, Salo. *History and Jewish Historians.* Philadelphia, 1964.

Barzilay, Isaac. *Shlomo Yehudah Rappoport and His Contemporaries.* Jerusalem, 1969.

Kupferberg, Herbert. *The Mendelssohns.* New York, 1972.

Liptzin, Solomon. *Germany's Stepchildren.* Philadelphia, 1944.

Marcus, Jacob. *Israel Jacobson.* Cincinnati, 1972.

Meyer, Michael A., ed. *Ideas of Jewish History.* New York, 1974.

———. *The Origins of the Modern Jew.* Detroit, 1967.

Morton, Frederick. *The Rothschilds.* New York, 1962.

Petuchowski, Jakob. *Prayerbook Reform in Europe.* New York, 1968.

Philipson, David. *The Reform Movement in Judaism.* New York, 1907.

Raisin, Jacob. "The Reform Movement before Geiger." *Yearbook of the Central Conference of American Rabbis* XXI (1911): 97 ff.

Reissner, H. G. "Rebellious Dilemma." *Year Book of the Leo Baeck Institute* II (1957): 179–193.

Rotenstreich, Nathan. *Tradition and Reality.* New York, 1972.

Schechter, Solomon. "Abraham Geiger." *Studies in Judaism.* 3d series. Philadelphia, 1924.

———. "Nachman Krochmal and the 'Perplexities of the Times.'" *Studies in Judaism.* 1st series. Philadelphia, 1911.

Wallach, Luitpold. *Liberty and Letters.* London, 1959.

Wiener, Max. *Abraham Geiger and Liberal Judaism.* Philadelphia, 1962.

———. "Abraham Geiger and the Science of Judaism." *Judaism* II:1 (January, 1953): 41–48.

C. THE NEW ANTI-SEMITISM

Primary Sources

Dreyfus, Alfred, and Dreyfus, Pierre. *The Dreyfus Case.* New Haven, Conn., 1937.

Herzl, Theodore. *Complete Diaries.* New York, 1960.

———. *The Jewish State.* New York, 1917.

———. *Old New Land.* New York, 1941.

Lazare, Bernard. *Antisemitism: Its History and Causes.* London, 1967.

Paléologue, Georges Maurice. *An Intimate Journal of the Dreyfus Case.* New York, 1957.

Snyder, Louis, ed. *The Dreyfus Case.* New Brunswick, N.J., 1973.

Secondary Readings

Arendt, Hannah. *The Origins of Totalitarianism.* New York, 1951.

Bein, Alex. *Theodore Herzl.* Philadelphia, 1941.

Bernstein, Herman. *The Truth about "The Protocols of Zion."* New York, 1935.

Byrnes, Robert. *Antisemitism in Modern France.* New Brunswick, N.J., 1950.

Chamberlain, Houston S. *Foundations of the Nineteenth Century.* New York, 1914, 1968.

Chapman, Guy. *The Dreyfus Trials.* New York, 1972.

Cohn, Norman. *Warrant for Genocide.* New York, 1967.

Halasz, Nicholas. *Captain Dreyfus.* New York, 1955.

Johnson, Douglas. *France and the Dreyfus Affair.* London, 1966.
Lewis, David. *Prisoners of Honor.* New York, 1973.
Marrus, Michael. *The Politics of Assimilation.* Oxford, 1971.
Massing, Paul. *Rehearsal for Destruction.* New York, 1949.
Meyer, Michael. "Great Debate on Antisemitism." *Year Book of the Leo Baeck Institute* XI (1966): 137–170.
Pulzer, Peter. *The Rise of Political Anti-Semitism in Germany and Austria.* New York, 1964.
Schorsch, Ismar. *Jewish Reactions to German Anti-Semitism 1870–1914.* New York, 1972.
Tal, Uriel. "Religious and Anti-Religious Roots of Modern Anti-Semitism." *Leo Baeck Institute Lecture.* New York, 1971.

D. THE SLUMBERING GIANT: EASTERN EUROPEAN JEWRY

Primary Sources

Adler, Cyrus. *The Voice of America on Kishineff.* Philadelphia, 1904.
Ahad Ha-am. *Basic Writings.* Edited by Hans Kohn. New York, 1962.
Antin, Mary. *The Promised Land.* Boston, 1912.
Borochov, Ber. *Nationalism and the Class Struggle: A Marxian Approach to the Jewish Problem.* Edited by Moshe Cohen. New York, 1937.
Cohen, Morris Raphael. *A Dreamer's Journey.* Boston, 1949.
Davitt, Michael. *Within the Pale.* New York, 1903.
Dawidowicz, Lucy, ed. *The Golden Tradition.* Boston, 1967.
Hapgood, Hutchins. *The Spirit of the Ghetto.* New York, 1902.
Hertzberg, Arthur, ed. *The Zionist Idea.* New York, 1959.
Hindus, Milton, ed. *The Old East Side.* Philadelphia, 1969.
Levin, Shmarya. *Forward from Exile.* Philadelphia, 1967.
Netanyahu, Benjamin, ed. *Road to Freedom: Writings and Addresses by Leo Pinsker.* New York, 1944.
Schoener, Allon, ed. *The Lower East Side: Portal to American Life 1870–1925.* New York, 1967.
Shazar, Zalman. *Morning Stars.* Philadelphia, 1967.
Simon, Leon, ed. *Selected Essays of Ahad Ha-am.* Philadelphia, 1912.
Singer, Isaac B. *In My Father's Court.* New York, 1966.
Singer, Israel J. *Of a World That Is No More.* New York, 1970.
Waife-Goldberg, Marie. *My Father, Sholom Aleichem.* New York, 1968.
Waxman, Mordechai, ed. *Tradition and Change.* New York, 1958.
Weizmann, Chaim. *Trial and Error.* New York, 1949.
Weizmann, Vera. *The Impossible Takes Longer.* New York, 1967.

Secondary Readings

Adler, Cyrus. *Jacob H. Schiff.* 2 vols. New York, 1928.

Baron, Salo. *The Russian Jew under Tsars and Soviets.* New York, 1964.

Bentwich, Norman. *Solomon Schechter.* Philadelphia, 1938.

Bookbinder, Hyman H. *To Promote the General Welfare: The Story of the Amalgamated Clothing Workers.* New York, 1950.

Cohen, Naomi. *A Dual Heritage.* Philadelphia, 1969.

———. *Not Free to Desist: A History of the American Jewish Committee 1906-1966.* Philadelphia, 1972.

Davis, Moshe. *The Emergence of Conservative Judaism.* Philadelphia, 1963.

Dubnow, Simon. *History of the Jews in Russia and Poland.* 3 vols. Philadelphia, 1916–1920.

Epstein, Melech. *Jewish Labor in the United States of America.* New York, 1969.

———. *Profiles of Eleven.* Detroit, 1965.

Fishman, Judah L. *The Mizrahi Movement.* New York, 1928.

"From Kishineff to Bialystok." *American Jewish Year Book* 5667 (1906–1907): 34–89.

Frumkin, Jacob, et al. *Russian Jewry (1860–1917).* New York, 1966.

Gartner, Lloyd. *The Jewish Immigrant in England 1870–1914.* London, 1960.

Glazer, Nathan. *American Judaism.* Chicago, 1957.

Goren, Arthur. *New York Jews and the Quest for Community.* New York, 1970.

Halpern, Ben. *The Idea of the Jewish State.* 2d ed. Cambridge, Mass., 1969.

Herberg, Will. "The Jewish Labor Movement in the United States." *American Jewish Year Book* LIII (1952): 3–74.

Higham, John. *Strangers in the Land.* New Brunswick, N.J., 1955.

Laquer, Walter. *A History of Zionism.* New York, 1972.

Manners, Ande. *Poor Cousins.* New York, 1972.

Mendelsohn, Ezra. *Class Struggle in the Pale.* Cambridge, Mass., 1970.

Pinson, Koppel. "Arkady Kremer, Vladimir Medem, and the Ideology of the Jewish Bund." *Jewish Social Studies* VII (July, 1945): 233–264.

Rischin, Moses. *The Promised City: New York's Jews 1870–1914.* Cambridge, Mass., 1962.

Samuel, Maurice. *Blood Accusation.* Philadelphia, 1966.

———. *Prince of the Ghetto.* New York, 1948.

———. *The World of Sholom Aleichem.* New York, 1943.

Sanders, Ronald. *The Downtown Jews.* New York, 1969.

Shapiro, Yonathan. *Leadership of the American Zionist Organization 1897–1930.* Urbana, Ill., 1971.

Simon, Leon. *Ahad Ha-am.* Philadelphia, 1960.

Sokolow, Nahum. *History of Zionism.* 2 vols. London, 1919.

Taylor, Philip. *The Distant Magnet: European Emigration to the U.S.A.* New York, 1971.

Tcherikower, Elias. "Jewish Immigrants to the United States 1881–1900." *Y.I.V.O. Annual of Jewish Social Science* VI (1951): 157–176.

Tobias, Henry. *The Jewish Bund in Russia.* Stanford, 1972.

Urofsky, Melvin I., and Levy, David, eds. *Letters of Louis D. Brandeis. Vol. 2 1907–1912, People's Lawyer.* Albany, 1972.

Wischnitzer, Mark. *To Dwell in Safety*. Philadelphia, 1949.

Zborowski, Mark, and Herzog, Elizabeth. *Life Is with People.* New York, 1952.

Fiction

Agnon, S. Y. *The Bridal Canopy.* Garden City, N.Y., 1937.

Angoff, Charles. *Journey to the Dawn.* New York, 1951.

Brudno, Ezra. *The Fugitive.* New York, 1904.

Cahan, Abraham. *The Rise of David Levinsky.* New York, 1966.

———. *Yekl and the Imported Bridegroom.* New York, 1970.

Howe, Irving, and Greenberg, Eliezer, eds. *A Treasury of Yiddish Stories.* New York, 1954.

Malamud, Bernard. *The Fixer.* New York, 1966.

Nyburg, Sidney. *Chosen People.* Philadelphia, 1917.

Rosten, Leo. *The Education of Hyman Kaplan.* New York, 1937.

Sholom Aleichem. *The Adventures of Menachem-Mendel.* New York, 1969.

———. *The Great Fair.* New York, 1955.

Singer, Isaac B. *The Estate.* New York, 1969

———. *The Family Moskat.* New York, 1950.

———. *The Magician of Lublin.* New York, 1966.

Singer, Israel J. *The Brothers Ashkenazi.* New York, 1936.

Tobenkin, Elias. *Witte Arrives.* New York, 1916.

Yezierska, Anzia. *Hungry Hearts.* Boston, 1920.

Films

Act One

The Dybbuk

Fiddler on the Roof

The Fixer

Green Fields

Meerle Efros

Storm of Strangers

E. WORLD WAR I AND ITS AFTERMATH

Primary Sources

Adler, Cyrus. *I Have Considered the Years.* Philadelphia, 1941.
Babel, Natalie, ed. *Isaac Babel: The Lonely Years 1925–1939.* New York, 1964.
Begin, Menachem. *The Revolt.* New York, 1951.
Ben Gurion, David. *Israel: A Personal History.* New York, 1971.
——. *Letters to Paula.* Pittsburgh, 1972.
——. *Rebirth and Destiny of Israel.* New York, 1954.
Buber, Martin. *At the Turning.* New York, 1952.
——. *Moses.* Oxford, 1946.
——. *On Judaism.* Edited by Nahum Glatzer. New York, 1967.
——. *The Prophetic Faith.* New York, 1949.
Committee of Jewish Delegations. *The Pogroms in the Ukraine under the Ukrainian Governments 1917–1920.* London, 1927.
Ehrenburg, Ilya. *Memoirs: 1921–1941.* Cleveland, 1963.
Heifetz, E. *The Slaughter of the Jews in the Ukraine in 1919.* New York, 1921.
Laqueur, Walter, ed. *The Israel-Arab Reader.* New York, 1969.
Mandelstam, Nadezhda. *Hope against Hope.* New York, 1970.
Reznikoff, Charles, ed. *Louis Marshall: Champion of Liberty.* Philadelphia, 1957.
Rosenzweig, Franz. *The Star of Redemption.* New York, 1970.
Ruppin, Arthur. *Building Israel.* New York, 1949.
——. *Memoirs, Diaries, Letters.* London, 1971.
Samuel, Edwin. *A Lifetime in Jerusalem.* London, 1970.
Voss, Carl, ed. *Stephen S. Wise: Servant of the People.* Philadelphia, 1969.
Weinryb, Bernard. *Jewish Emancipation under Attack.* New York, 1942.
Weizmann, Chaim. *Letters and Papers.* 2 vols. Oxford, 1969, 1971.

Secondary Readings

Adler, Selig. "The Palestine Question in the Wilson Era." *Jewish Social Studies* X (1948): 303–334.
Baron, Salo. *The Russian Jew under Tsars and Soviets.* New York, 1964.
Bar-Zohar, Michel. *Ben Gurion: The Armed Prophet.* Englewood Cliffs, N.J., 1967.
Berlin, Isaiah. *Chaim Weizmann.* New York, 1958.
Cang, Joel. "The Opposition Parties in Poland and Their Attitude toward the Jews and the Jewish Problem." *Jewish Social Studies* I (1939): 241–256.
Choseed, B. "Jews in Soviet Literature." *Through the Glass of Soviet Literature.* Edited by Ernest J. Simmons. New York, 1953.

Gitelman, Zvi. *Jewish Nationality and Soviet Politics.* Princeton, N.J., 1972.
Glatzer, Nahum. *Franz Rosenzweig.* New York, 1953.
Hallett, R. W. *Isaac Babel.* Letchworth, England, 1972.
Hurewitz, Jacob. *The Struggle for Palestine.* New York, 1950.
Janowsky, Oscar. *People at Bay: The Jewish Problem in East Central Europe.* New York, 1938.
Johnpoll, Bernard. *The Politics of Futility.* Ithaca, N.Y., 1967.
Kochan, Lionel. *The Jews in Soviet Russia Since 1917.* London, 1970.
Lenin, V. I. *Lenin on the Jewish Question.* Edited by Alexander Trachtenberg. New York, 1936.
Leschnitzer, Adolph. *The Magic Background of Anti-Semitism.* New York, 1956.
Mahler, Raphael. "Jews in Public Service and the Liberal Professions in Poland 1918–1939." *Jewish Social Studies* VI (1944): 291–350.
Meyer, Peter, et al. *The Jews in the Soviet Satellites.* Syracuse, N.Y., 1953.
Mosse, George. *Germans and Jews.* New York, 1970.
Nevins, Allan. *Herbert H. Lehman.* New York, 1963.
Niewyk, Donald. *Socialist, Anti-Semite, and Jew.* Baton Rouge, La., 1971.
Rosenstock, Morton. *Louis Marshall: Defender of the Faith.* Detroit, 1966.
St. John, Robert. *Ben Gurion.* Garden City, N.Y., 1959.
Schechtman, Joseph. *The Vladimir Jabotinsky Story.* 2 vols. New York, 1956, 1961.
Schleunes, Karl. *The Twisted Road to Auschwitz.* Urbana, Ill., 1970.
Schoenbaum, David. *Hitler's Social Revolution.* Garden City, N.Y., 1966.
Scholnick, Myron. "The New Deal and Anti-Semitism in America." Ph.D. dissertation, University of Maryland, 1971.
Schwarz, Solomon. *The Jews in the Soviet Union.* Syracuse, N.Y., 1951.
Shapiro, Yonathan. *Leadership of the American Zionist Organization 1897–1930.* Urbana, Ill., 1971.
Stein, Leonard. *The Balfour Declaration.* London, 1961.
———. *Weizmann and England.* London, 1964.
Stern, Fritz. *The Politics of Cultural Despair.* Garden City, N.Y., 1965.
Teller, Judd. *Strangers and Natives.* New York, 1968.
Weinreich, Max. *Hitler's Professors.* New York, 1946.
Weisgal, Meyer, and Carmichael, Joel, eds. *Chaim Weizmann: A Biography by Several Hands.* New York, 1963.
Wyman, David. *Paper Walls: America and the Refugee Crisis 1938–1941.* Amherst, Mass., 1969.
Zebel, Sydney. *Balfour.* Cambridge, Mass., 1973.

Fiction

Babel, Isaac. *Collected Stories.* New York, 1960.
———. *Red Cavalry.* New York, 1929.

———. *You Must Know Everything*. New York, 1969.
Brenner, Yosef Haim. *Breakdown and Bereavement.* Philadelphia, 1971.
Feuchtwanger, Lion. *The Oppermanns*. New York, 1934.
Fuchs, Daniel. *The Williamsburg Trilogy*. New York, 1972.
Gold, Michael. *Jews without Money*. New York, 1930.
Levin, Myer. *The Settlers*. New York, 1972.
———. *Yehuda*. New York, 1931.
Lewisohn, Ludwig. *The Island Within*. New York, 1928.
———. *Israel*. New York, 1925.
Roth, Henry. *Call It Sleep*. New York, 1934.
Shulberg, Budd. *What Makes Sammy Run?* New York, 1941.
Singer, Israel J. *East of Eden*. New York, 1939.

Films

Gentlemen's Agreement
The Golden Age of Second Avenue
The Great Dictator
The Last Chapter
Mein Kampf
The Song and the Silence
The Three-Penny Opera

F. THE HOLOCAUST

Primary Sources

Berg, Mary. *Warsaw Ghetto: A Diary*. New York, 1945.
Fermi, Laura. *Illustrious Immigrants: The Intellectual Migration from Europe 1930–1941*. Chicago, 1968.
Frank, Anne. *The Diary of Anne Frank.* Garden City, N.Y., 1959.
Friedlander, Albert, ed. *Out of the Whirlwind*. New York, 1968.
Glatstein, Jacob, et al. *Anthology of Holocaust Literature*. Philadelphia, 1969.
Goebbels, Joseph. *Diaries 1942–1943*. Edited by L. P. Lochner. New York, 1948.
Hilberg, Raul, ed. *Documents of Destruction*. Chicago, 1971.
Hitler, Adolf. *Hitler's Secret Conversations 1941–1944*. Edited by H. R. Trevor-Roper. New York, 1953.
Kaplan, Chaim. *Scroll of Agony*. New York, 1965.
Korman, Gerd, ed. *Hunter and Hunted*. New York, 1973.
Rudashevski, I. *Diary of the Vilna Ghetto*. New York, 1973.
Senesh, Hannah. *Hannah Senesh, Her Life and Diary*. New York, 1972.

Wiesel, Elie. *One Generation After.* New York, 1970.
Wiesenthal, Simon. *The Murderers among Us.* New York, 1967.

Secondary Readings

Arendt, Hannah. *Eichmann in Jerusalem.* New York, 1964.
Bauer, Yehuda. *They Chose Life.* New York, 1973.
Bloom, Solomon F. "Dictator of the Lodz Ghetto." *Commentary* VII:2 (February, 1949): 111–122.
Braham, Randolph. *The Destruction of Hungarian Jewry.* 2 vols. New York, 1963.
Feingold, Henry. *The Politics of Rescue.* New Brunswick, N.J., 1970.
Friedlander, Albert. *Leo Baeck: Teacher of Theresienstadt.* London, 1973.
Friedlander, Saul. *Pius XII and the Third Reich.* New York, 1966.
Friedman, Philip. "Jewish Resistance." *Yad Vashem Studies* II (1958): 113–131.
———. *Their Brothers' Keepers.* New York, 1957.
Hilberg, Raul. *The Destruction of the European Jews.* Chicago, 1961.
Lapide, Pinchas. *Three Popes and the Jews.* New York, 1967.
Lewy, Guenther. *The Catholic Church and Nazi Germany.* New York, 1964.
Morse, Arthur. *While Six Million Died.* New York, 1968.
Poliakov, Leon. *Harvest of Hate.* Syracuse, N.Y., 1954.
Presser, Jacob. *The Destruction of the Dutch Jews.* New York, 1969.
Reitlinger, Gerald. *The Final Solution.* New York, 1953.
Robinson, Jacob. *And the Crooked Shall Be Made Straight.* Philadelphia, 1965.
Stone, I. F. *Underground to Palestine.* New York, 1946.
Suhl, Yuri. *They Fought Back.* New York, 1967.
Trunk, Isaiah. *Judenrat.* New York, 1972.
Tushnet, L. *Pavement of Hell: Three Leaders of the Judenrat.* New York, 1972.
Yahil, Lena. *The Rescue of Danish Jewry.* Philadelphia, 1969.

Fiction

Amichai, Yehuda. *Not of This Time, Not of This Place.* New York, 1968.
Arnold, Eliot. *A Night of Watching.* New York, 1967.
Donat, Alexander. *The Holocaust Kingdom.* New York, 1965.
Elman, Richard M. *The 28th Day of Elul.* New York, 1967.
Forsyth, Frederick. *The Odessa File.* New York, 1972.
Hersey, John. *The Wall.* New York, 1950.
Hochhuth, Rolf. *The Deputy.* New York, 1963.
Kuznetsov, Anatoly. *Babi Yar.* New York, 1967.
Levin, Meyer. *The Fanatic.* New York, 1964.
———. *The Stronghold.* New York, 1965.
Lewis, Robert. *Michel, Michel.* New York, 1967.

Opatoshu, Joseph. *A Day in Regensburg*. Philadelphia, 1968.
Presser, Jacob. *Breaking Point.* Cleveland, 1958.
Schwarz-Bart, André. *The Last of the Just.* New York, 1961.
Steiner, Jean-François. *Treblinka.* New York, 1967.
Uris, Leon. *Mila 18.* Garden City, N.Y., 1961.
———. *Q B VII.* New York, 1970.
Wells, Leon. *The Janowska Road.* London, 1966.
Wiesel, Elie. *Dawn.* New York, 1962.
———. *The Gates of the Forest.* New York, 1966.
———. *Night.* New York, 1960.
———. *The Oath.* New York, 1973.

Films

Border Street
Denmark '43
The Fifth Horseman Is Fear
The Garden of the Finzi-Continis
Hitler's Executioners
I Never Saw Another Butterfly
In the Beginning: The Warsaw Ghetto
Line of Demarcation
Nuit et Brouillard
The Pawnbroker
The Shop on Main Street
Sighet, Sighet
The Sorrow and the Pity
Transport from Paradise
The Warsaw Ghetto
The Witnesses

G. POSTWAR TURMOIL

Primary Sources

American Jewish Year Book.
Ben-Gurion, David. *My Talks with Arab Leaders.* New York, 1973.
Commentary.
Dayan, Moshe. *Diary of the Sinai Campaign.* London, 1966.
Eban, Abba. *Voice of Israel.* New York, 1957.

Goldmann, Nahum. *Sixty Years of Jewish Life.* New York, 1969.
Jacobs, Paul. *Is Curly Jewish?* New York, 1973.
Karsov, Nina, and Szechter, Szymon. *In the Name of Tomorrow.* New York, 1970.
Memmi, Albert. *Portrait of a Jew.* New York, 1971.
Midstream.
Nissenson, Hugh. *Notes from the Frontier.* New York, 1968.
Podhoretz. Norman. *Making It.* New York, 1967.
Response.
Shapira, Avraham, ed. *The Seventh Day.* New York, 1970.
Slanska, Josefa. *Report on My Husband.* New York, 1969.
Sleeper, James, and Mintz, Alan, eds. *The New Jews.* New York, 1971.
Wiesel, Elie. *The Jews of Silence.* New York, 1966.

Secondary Readings

Alter, Robert. *After the Tradition.* New York, 1969.
Eliav, Arie. *Between Hammer and Sickle.* Philadelphia, 1967.
Bar-Zohar, Michael. *Ben Gurion: The Armed Prophet.* Englewood Cliffs, N.J., 1967.
———. *Spies in the Promised Land.* Boston, 1972.
Bauer, Yehuda. *Flight and Rescue: Brichah.* New York, 1970.
———. *From Diplomacy to Resistance.* Philadelphia, 1970.
Curtis, Michael, and Chertoff, Mordechai, eds. *Israel: Social Structure and Change.* New Brunswick, N.J., 1973.
Draper, Theodore. *Israel and World Politics.* New York, 1968.
Elon, Amos. *The Israelis.* New York, 1971.
Forster, Arnold, and Epstein, Benjamin. *The New Anti-Semitism.* New York, 1974.
Gilboa, Yehoshua. *The Black Years of Soviet Jewry.* Boston, 1971.
Glock, Charles, and Stark, Rodney. *Christian Beliefs and Anti-Semitism.* New York, 1966.
Glock, Charles, et al. *The Apathetic Majority.* New York, 1966.
Goldstein, Sidney, and Goldscheider, Calvin. *Jewish Americans.* Englewood Cliffs, N.J., 1968.
Herman, Simon. *Israelis and Jews.* Philadelphia, 1971.
Janowsky, Oscar, ed. *The American Jew: A Reappraisal.* Philadelphia, 1965.
Kochan, Lionel. *The Jews in Soviet Russia Since 1917.* London, 1970.
Korey, William. *The Soviet Cage.* New York, 1973.
Kramer, Judith, and Leventman, Seymour. *Children of the Gilded Ghetto.* Hamden, Conn., 1961.
Kurzman, Dan. *Genesis 1948.* New York, 1970.
Lapierre, Dominique, and Collins, Larry. *O Jerusalem!* London, 1972.
Laqueur, Walter. *The Road to War.* Baltimore, 1970.
Lendvai, Paul. *Antisemitism without Jews.* Garden City, N.Y., 1971.

Liebman, Charles. *The Ambivalent American Jew.* Philadelphia, 1973.
Lissak, M. *Social Mobility in Israeli Society.* Jerusalem, 1969.
Meyer, Peter, et al. *The Jews in the Soviet Satellites.* Syracuse, N.Y., 1953.
Neusner, Jacob. *American Judaism.* Englewood Cliffs, N.J., 1972.
Porter, Jack, and Dreier, Peter, eds. *Jewish Radicalism.* New York, 1973.
Prittie, Terence. *Eshkol.* New York, 1969.
Rabinowitz, Dorothy. *The Other Jews.* New York, 1972.
Rose, Peter. *The Ghetto and Beyond.* New York, 1969.
Rosenberg, Louise. *Jews in the Soviet Union: Bibliography.* New York, 1971.
St. John, Robert. *Ben Gurion.* Garden City, N.Y., 1959.
———. *Eban.* Garden City, N.Y., 1972.
Schmelz, Oskar. *Jewish Population Studies 1961–1968.* Jerusalem, 1970.
Sidorsky, David, ed. *The Future of the Jewish Community in America.* New York, 1973.
Sklare, Marshall. *America's Jews.* New York, 1971.
Slater, Leonard. *The Pledge.* New York, 1970.
Spiro, Melford. *Kibbutz.* Cambridge, Mass., 1956.
Stember, Charles. *Jews in the Mind of America.* New York, 1966
Syrkin, Marie. *Golda Meir.* New York, 1969.
Teveth, Shabtai. *Moshe Dayan.* Boston, 1973.
Weinstein, Jacob J. *Solomon Goldman: A Rabbi's Rabbi.* New York, 1973.

Fiction

Bellow, Saul. *Herzog.* New York, 1964.
Blocker, Joel, ed. *Israeli Stories.* New York, 1962.
Kahn, S. J., ed. *A Whole Loaf.* Tel Aviv, 1957.
Kaniuk, Yoram. *Himmo King of Jerusalem.* New York, 1969.
Malamud, Bernard. *The Assistant.* New York, 1957.
Megged, Aharon. *Living on the Dead.* New York, 1970.
Michener, James. *The Source.* New York, 1965.
Oz, Amos, *Elsewhere, Perhaps.* New York, 1973.
———. *My Michael.* New York, 1972.
Peneuel, S. Y., and Ukhmani, A., eds. *Hebrew Short Stories.* Tel Aviv, 1965.
Potok, Chaim. *The Chosen.* New York, 1967.
———. *My Name Is Asher Lev.* Greenwich, Conn., 1973.
Roth, Philip. *Goodbye, Columbus.* Boston, 1959.
Uris, Leon. *Exodus.* Garden City, N.Y., 1958.
Wiesel, Elie. *A Beggar in Jerusalem.* New York, 1970.
Yizhar, S. *The Midnight Convoy.* Jerusalem, 1969.

Films

Cast a Giant Shadow
Ervinka
Exodus
Goodbye, Columbus
The Hasidim
The House on Chelouche Street
Kazablan
Kibbutz Daphna
Shalosh Means Three
Siege
A Wall in Jerusalem

INDEX

N.B. This index includes primarily persons, places, organizations, and events related to the modern period only.